LIFE OF JOHN RANDOLPH.

VOL. I.

ENGRAVED BY J. SARTAIN.

JOHN RANDOLPH.

THE LIFE

OF

JOHN RANDOLPH

OF ROANOKE.

BY

HUGH A. GARLAND.

VOL. I.

NEW-YORK:
D. APPLETON & COMPANY, 200 BROADWAY.
PHILADELPHIA:
GEO. S. APPLETON, 164 CHESNUT-STREET.
M.DCCC.LI.

PREFACE.

The author of this book has had, perhaps, as good an opportunity as any other man, who was not a contemporary and intimate friend, to form a just estimate of Mr. Randolph's character, and also to collect valuable and copious materials for his biography. He was educated in Mr. Randolph's district, was familiar with all the local associations of that devoted son of the Old Dominion, often saw him among his beloved constituents, and heard him under most favorable circumstances both on the hustings and in the Virginia Convention. The writer was then but a youth, full of all the eager interest and curiosity that would naturally be excited by so extraordinary a man. Since Mr. Randolph's death, it has been his good fortune to have been thrown into the circle of his most intimate and confidential friends, some of whom the writer feels justified in saying he also may claim as his friends. While the thought of writing a life of Mr. Randolph is of recent date, the character of the man and the incidents of his life have been for many years the subject of interest and of inquiry, which were abundantly gratified by those who knew him and delighted to discourse on the peculiarities and eccentricities of their departed friend.

Some ten or twelve years before his death, Mr. Randolph

made a will liberating his slaves; a short time before his decease, while under the influence of utter debility and disease, he made various and conflicting dispositions of his property. Here, of course, was a fruitful theme for the Courts. Was Mr. Randolph capable of making a will in the latter part of his life? was the subject of inquiry. Nearly every body who had known him, or who had had any dealings with him, from the earliest period, were summoned to give testimony. Many interesting and important facts, that would properly find a place in his biography, were elicited on that occasion. The whole testimony was taken down by an accurate stenographer, and the most important parts afterwards were written out in full. These valuable materials were placed in the hands of the writer of this memoir. In 1845, the whole subject again underwent a thorough investigation before the Circuit Court of Petersburg, many additional witnesses were summoned, and much new and important information elicited. The writer was a personal attendant on that Court during the trial.

To Mrs. Elizabeth Bryan, who is the niece of Mr. Randolph, and to Mr. Bryan himself, who is the son of his earliest friend, we are indebted for the interesting correspondence to be found in the first volume of this work. To Mrs. Dudley, Judge Beverly Tucker, the Hon. John Taliaferro, and Governor Tazewell, who were the youthful companions and schoolmates of Mr. Randolph, we are indebted for the incidents of his early life. By far the most interesting and important part of the work is the copious and unreserved correspondence of Mr. Randolph with the late and much lamented Francis S. Key, Esq., of Washington, and Dr. John Brockenbrough, of Virginia. This latter gentleman was, *par excellence,* the friend of his bosom. Not a thought or a feeling was concealed from him, and from 1811 to May, 17, 1833 ,but a few days before his death, Mr. Randolph wrote constantly, many times daily, to this invaluable friend. The entire correspondence is now in the hands of the writer. Without these materials and this unreserved confidence on the part of one who most valued the reputation of his departed friend, the author would never have undertaken the difficult task of writing the life of John Randolph. Very many of the letters have been inserted in their proper places—and many of the facts and incidents interwoven into the narrative, were obtained from others which have been suppressed—the author's chief study has been to use discreetly the unbounded confidence that was reposed in his prudence and judgment. It would be almost impossible to enumerate all the persons to whom we are indebted for many of the incidents narrated in this biography; every body knows something of the extraordinary man who is the subject of it; but we have given each one, we trust, credit for his contribution in its proper place. Many of the anecdotes and witticisms commonly attributed to Mr. Randolph are not found in this work, because there is no authority for them. "All the bastard wit of the country," said he to a friend, "has been fathered on me."

As to the *printed sources* of information connected with Mr. Randolph's public career, besides a valuable collection of pamphlets obtained from the estate of the late John Clopton, the author has had free access to the library of Congress, which, having been collected by Mr. Jefferson, is very copious on all subjects connected with the history and politics of the country. Besides these, Mr. Ritchie was so kind as to lend the only full file of the Enquirer in his possession. The reader needs not to be informed that the Richmond Enquirer contains a full chronicle of every thing that has been said and done in Virginia, worthy of being recorded in history, from 1804 to the present time.

Such were the materials in possession of the author. The difficulty was not to obtain—but to sift, digest, and arrange the abundant treasures in his possession. The book was commenced when the author had leisure to write to his satisfaction; it has been finished in the intervals of a laborious profession, and he feels that there are many defects which more time and leisure would have enabled him to correct. Many of the chapters were written under feelings of depression and anxiety while that dread pestilence, the cholera, had overshadowed with gloom and made desolate our devoted city. Whatever may be the defects of the book, however, the reader may be assured that nothing will be found in it that the author has not good reason to believe is true.

H. A. GARLAND.

SAINT LOUIS, August, 1850.

CONTENTS OF VOL. I.

PAGE

CHAPTER XXXVI.

CHAPTER XXXVII.

CHAPTER I.

BIRTHPLACE.

Cawsons, situated on a commanding promontory, near the mouth of Appomatox river, was the family seat of Colonel Theodorick Bland, Senior, of Prince George. After winding amidst its woody islands, around the base of this hill, the river spreads out into a wide bay; and, together with the James, into which it empties, makes towards the north and east a magnificent water prospect, embracing in one view Shirley, the seat of the Carters, Bermuda Hundred, with its harbor and ships, City Point, and other places of less note. In the midst of this commanding scene, the old mansion-house reared its ample proportions, and, with its offices and extended wings, was not an unworthy representative of the baronial days in which it was built—when Virginia cavaliers, under the title of gentlemen, with their broad domain of virgin soil, and long retinue of servants, lived in a style of elegance and profusion, not inferior to the barons of England, and dispensed a hospitality which more than half a century of subdivision, exhaustion, and decay, has not entirely effaced from the memory of their impoverished descendants.

At Cawsons, scarcely a vestige now remains of former magnificence. The old mansion was burnt down many years ago. Here and there a solitary out-dwelling, which escaped the conflagration, like the old servants of a decayed family, seem to speak in melancholy pride of those days, when it was their glory to stand in the shadow of loftier walls, and reflect back their loud revelry, when

> "The misletoe hung in the castle hall,
> The holly branch shone on the old oak wall;
> And the baron's retainers were blithe and gay,
> And keeping their Christmas holiday."

The serpentine paths, the broad avenues, and smooth gravel, the mounds, the green turf, and the shrubbery of extended pleasure-grounds, are all mingled with the vulgar sod. The noble outlines of nature are still there; but the handiwork of man has disappeared.

In a letter to his friend, F. S. Key, dated March 20, 1814, John Randolph says:—"A few days ago I returned from a visit to my birthplace, the seat of my ancestors on one side—the spot where my dear and honored mother was given in marriage, and where I was ushered in this world of woe. The sight of the broad waters seemed to renovate me. I was tossed in a boat, during a row of three miles across James river, and sprinkled with the spray that dashed over her. The days of my boyhood seemed to be renewed; but at the end of my journey I found desolation and stillness as of death—the fires of hospitality long since quenched; the parish church, associated with my earliest and tenderest recollections, tumbling to pieces; not more from natural decay than sacrilegious violence! What a spectacle does our lower country present! Deserted and dismantled country-houses, once the seats of cheerfulness and plenty, and the temples of the Most High ruinous and desolate, 'frowning in portentous silence upon the land.' The very mansions of the dead have not escaped violation. Shattered fragments of armorial bearings, and epitaphs on scattered stone, attest the piety and vanity of the past, and the brutality of the present age."

Colonel Bland was an active promoter of the Revolution. When Lord Dunmore, in the spring of 1775, under instructions from England, undertook to disarm the people, by secretly withdrawing the muskets and powder from the Magazine in Williamsburg, Colonel Bland was among the first to rouse the country to resistance. As munitions of war were scarce, he, his son Theodorick Bland, Jun., and his son-in-law, John Randolph, father of the late John of Roanoke, sold forty negroes, and with the money purchased powder for the use of the colony. Endowed with an ample fortune and a manly character, having been for a series of years in succession lieutenant of the county of Prince George, clerk of the court, and representative in the House of Burgesses, he possessed a commanding influence among the people. His house was the centre of a wide circle of friends and relations, who had pledged their lives, fortunes, and sacred honor, to the cause of independence. Though they did not rise to be master-spirits in that eventful struggle, the Blands, the Banisters, the Bollings, and the Eatons, were inferior to none in zeal, devotion, and heroic sacrifice.

The political spirit of the times may be inferred from the following incident:—The old man growing weary of a solitary life of widowhood, was advised by his son to look for a matrimonial connection in a certain quarter. After spying out the land, he wrote to his son: "Our politics differed so much that we parted by mutual consent;" and in allusion to his own choice, he says: "the person I have thought of, is a lady of great goodness, sensible, and a true whig."

Among those who frequented Cawsons at this time, and partook of its welcome and generous hospitality, and shared with its inmates a proud defiance of the encroachments of England, was a young foreigner—though he can scarcely be called a foreigner who speaks our own mother tongue, and was bred up almost in sight of the American shores.

St. George Tucker was born of respectable parents in the island of Bermuda, where he commenced the study of law, but came to Virginia, before the Revolution, in order to complete his academic exercises in William and Mary College. His urbanity, social disposition, and literary attainments, introduced him into the best company and fashionable circles of the city. His general good conduct and deportment procured him the favor of most of the distinguished gentlemen of that place. When he had completed his college courses, he resumed the study of law, and settled permanently in Williamsburg; but, on the breaking out of the disturbances with Great Britain, he took part with his adopted country, laid aside his legal pursuits, and engaged in other occupations. It doubtless was his intention to have served in the tented field; but what he might have done in the way of military achievement, is left only to conjecture. That he might have rivalled Kosciusko, or Pulaski, or De Kalb, he afterwards gave ample proof on the field of Guilford; but the glittering butterfly of military glory was destined to fade before the more substantial charms of female beauty.

Though Cawsons was a pleasant place, its chief magic lay in the Colonel's youngest daughter, Mrs. Frances Randolph, who, in her "unhappy widowhood," (to use her own expressive language,) had for the most part forsaken her own solitary home, and sought society and consolation beneath her father's roof. Mrs. Randolph was possessed of high mental qualities and extraordinary beauty. Though one might suppose she was endowed with little personal attraction, from an expression of her brother, Colonel Theodorick Bland, Jun., who was accustomed to call her, "my tawny sister." But tradition, confirmed by the portraits extant, speaks in admiration of her uncommon charms. The high, expanded forehead; smooth, arched brow, and brilliant dark eyes; the well-defined nose, and full, round, laughing lips, pregnant with wit and mirthfulness; the tall figure and expanded chest; the dark hair, winding in massy folds around the neck and bosom; an open, cheerful countenance—all suffused with that deep, rich, oriental tint that never fades—made her the most beautiful, sprightly, and attractive woman of her age.

Though clad in widow's garments, and on her brow lay a pensive stillness, as of one dreaming, she was yet young and beautiful. By her side, or on her knee, as inseparable as her own shadow, was a child—her youngest child—a little boy, her favorite John, the very image of his mother. In his dark eyes were reflected the sadness of her own soul; on his orphan brow was imprinted a kiss, that ever and anon a tear washed away. So much of subdued loveliness could not fail to win the sympathy of old and young, and to call forth sighs of pity and regret.

St. George Tucker, the first time he beheld the mother and her child, was filled with that mingled sentiment which more agitates the soul, and takes deeper hold on the affections, than any single passion. He soon found himself an ardent lover at the feet of the charming widow. A wife at sixteen, she was not long to be persuaded at six-and-twenty to abandon her unhappy widowhood. In an old family Prayer Book, in her own handwriting, is found the following record:

The unhappy widowhood of Frances Randolph commenced on the 28th day of Oct., in the year 1775.

John Randolph and Frances Bland were married the 9th of March, 1769.

Richard Randolph, their first son, was born the 9th of March, 1770.

Theodorick Bland Randolph, their second son, was born the 22d of January, 1771.

John Randolph, their third son, was born the 2d of June, 1773.

Jane Randolph, their first daughter, was born Nov. 10th, 1774, and died on the 26th of Nov., 1774.

The following additions to the above record is found in the handwriting of the late John Randolph of Roanoke:

John Randolph, Junior, fourth son of Richard Randolph, of Curles, in the County of Henrico, was born on the 29th of June, 1742, O. S.,—answering to the 10th of July, N. S.

Frances Bland, fifth and youngest daughter of Theodorick Bland, of Cawsons, in the county of Prince George, was born on the 24th of Sept., 1752, N. S.

John Randolph, Esq., died at Matoax, on the 28th of October, 1775; and on the 23d of Sept., 1778, his widow married St. George Tucker, of Bermuda.

CHAPTER II.

MATOAX—GENEALOGY.

MATOAX, the residence of John and Frances Randolph during his life, of Mrs. Randolph in her widowhood, and of herself and Mr. Tucker, her second husband, till the time of her death, was situated on Appomatox, about two miles above Petersburg, on the opposite side; midway the falls, and on a high bluff, commanding a wide prospect of the surrounding country. At the time Mr. Tucker was introduced there by his elegant and accomplished bride, it was the centre of a populous, wealthy, and fashionable neighborhood. To say nothing of the town, there were Battersea, Mayfield, Burlington, Mansfield, Olive Hill, Violet Hill, Roslin, all on the same river; many in sight, and none more than two miles distant. These were the residences of gentlemen of ample fortunes, liberal education, polished manners, refined hospitality, and devoted patriotism. They have all since passed into other hands; some have gone down entirely; and the wild pine and the broom sedge have made such steady encroachments, that a wilderness has grown up in the place of fruitful fields, and more wild deer can be caught within a circuit of ten miles around the second most populous city in the State, than in a similar space in the prairies of the West. A statue of Niobe, in her own capitol—of Niobe weeping for her children—would be no unfit emblem of Old Virginia; her sons gone, her hearths cold, her fields desolate.

The mansion house at Matoax, like that at Cawsons, was burnt down many years ago. Nothing now remains but a heap of ruins. When we visited the spot, the factory boys, with their hounds, were chasing the hares over those solitary hills where once the proud sons of a proud race pursued the same light-footed game. A high hill to the eastward of that on which the mansion was, and separated from it by a deep ravine, is crowned by a thick cluster of oaks and other trees. At the foot, and under the shadow of those trees, are two graves, covered with simple marble slabs, level with the earth,—containing the following inscriptions:

Johannes Randolph, Arm:
Ob. xxviii. Octo,
MDCCLXXV,
Æt. xxxiv.
Non opibus urna, nec mens
virtutibus absit.

(*Translated.*)

John Randolph, Esq., died Oct. 28th, 1775, aged 34. Let not a tomb be wanting to his ashes, nor memory to his virtues.

I. H. S.
Francescæ Tucker Blandæ,
Conjugio
Sti Georgii Tucker.
Quis desiderio sit modus?
Obiit xviii. Januarii,
MDCCLXXXVIII,
Æt. xxxvi.

(*Translated.*)

Jesus, Saviour of mankind.
When shall we cease to mourn for Frances Bland Tucker, wife of St. George Tucker? She died 18th January, 1788, aged 36.

The father and the mother of the late John Randolph of Roanoke! It was his wish to be buried by their side. In a letter dated London, Dec. 19, 1830, he says: "I have personally but one wish; it is to be buried by the side of my honored parents at old Matoax, and I have taken measures to effectuate it. It is not long since this desire sprung up in my heart, where all else is withered, hard and dry."

Matoax was a part of the vast inheritance which descended from Richard Randolph of Curles, to his four sons, Richard, Brett, Ryland, and John.

His will is still extant, and bears date about the time of the birth of his youngest son, John, and a short time before his own death, 1742. It makes disposition of not less than forty thousand acres of the choicest lands on the James, Appomatox, and Roanoke rivers. Most of this vast estate was accumulated by his own "industry and economy," as we learn from a monument erected to his memory at Turkey Island by his third son, Ryland. To his daughters—Mary, who married Archibald Cary, of Ampthill; Jane, who married Anthony Walke, of Princess Anne; and Elizabeth, who married Richard Kidder Meade—he left only personal property. All the lands were divided among the four sons. Those on Appomatox fell to John; those on Roanoke, jointly to John and Ryland. Ryland died without heir, and his portion descended to his brother; so that John, at the time of his death in 1775, was possessed of large and valuable estates on Appomatox and Roanoke.

Richard Randolph of Curles, was the fourth son of Col. Wm. Randolph, of Warwickshire, England, who was the first of the name that emigrated to Virginia, and settled at Turkey Island. He died April 11th, 1711. That he was of Warwickshire, we learn from a monument at Turkey Island; but the late John Randolph, who took great pride in searching into the genealogy of his family, says that he was of Yorkshire. Between the researches of the Hon. John, and the monument at Turkey Island, we leave the reader to judge. William Randolph was the father of seven sons and two daughters, who became the progenitors of a widespread and numerous race, embracing the most wealthy families, and many of the most distinguished names in Virginia history.

We will not cumber our pages with their complicated and unintelligible genealogy. In the course of our narrative, we shall give such portions as may become necessary for its elucidation. At present, we are only concerned with Richard Randolph of Curles, the fourth son. He married Jane Bolling, who was the daughter of John Bolling, who was the son of Robert Bolling and Jane Rolfe his wife, who was the granddaughter of Pocahontas, the beautiful Indian princess, daughter of Powhatan, whose pathetic story is so well known.

The portrait of Mrs. Randolph (Jane Bolling) is still extant. A more marked and commanding countenance is rarely to be met with. A perfect contrast to the luxurious ease, graceful manners, fluent and courtly conversation, betrayed by the full round face, ruddy complexion, low projecting eyes, smooth brow, and the delicate person and features of her husband. If the portrait be true to nature, none of the Indian complexion can be traced in her countenance. Her erect and firm position, and square broad shoulders, are the only indications of Indian descent. The face is decidedly handsome; while the lofty, expanded, and well marked forehead, the great breadth between the eyes, the firm distended nostril, compressed lips, and steady eye, display an intellect, a firmness, and moral qualities, truly heroic and commanding. Worthy descendant of the daughter of Powhatan.

Placing the two portraits side by side, one cannot fail to trace in the general contour of countenance, and cranial development, a striking resemblance between this lady and her grandson, the late John Randolph of Roanoke.

CHAPTER III.

CHILDHOOD.

A WISE poet and philosopher has said, "The child is father of the man," and that our days are "Bound each to each in natural piety." Who has not felt the force of this truth, so beautifully expressed? Who is not conscious that his personal identity cannot be measured by time—that he is the same to-day he was yesterday, and as far back as memory can reach? Though covered with years and busied with graver trifles, who does not feel that he is the same being that once gambolled on the plain with his school-fellows, and sought childish sports with cheerful heart by flood and field? Life is a continuous growth. The outspreading oak that shades the venerable old man at its root, is but the gradual development of the little nut that lay concealed in the acorn, which in his childhood he carelessly planted there. Had it been planted in a more genial soil, it might have attained a prouder growth. In a Siberian clime it would have been stunted and mean. Circumstances, therefore, do not make, but they develope the man. To know one thoroughly as he is; why he is thus and not otherwise; the man he is and not another; we must go back to his childhood. We must go to the salient point, to take the scope and direction of his character. We must see him surrounded by the circumstances that gave the first impulse; the influences that first stamped their impress on the plastic clay; we must know by what scenes he was surrounded; was he reared by the mountain-side, the running stream, or on the ocean's shore? was he in daily converse with the tamer scenes of nature, or with the grand, or the beautiful? what sort of people were his father and mother, his brothers and sisters, his playmates, and the men and women that went in and out before him? what books lay in his way? what lessons were taught him, not in the school-house, but the nursery, and by the domestic fireside? what were the traditions, opinions, passions, prejudices, that constituted a part of his heritage far more important than lands or merchandise?

Could we but know these things about the heroes, the statesmen, the orators and the poets, who excite our wonder and admiration, and have stamped the impress of their character not only on their own age, but on the world's history, how different would be our judgment in regard to them! We behold the outside alone; we are only made acquainted with the histrionic, the acted part of their life. What we see is but a masquerade, a succession of magnified and illuminated faces passing before the disk of a magic lantern. What we wish to see and long to know is far otherwise. Each, like Mephistopheles, has caught up some garment best suited to his nature or his purpose, and strives to *personate* (*persona* originally meant an actor's *mask*), to seem what he is not. Could we but draw aside the coverings by which they strive to conceal their motives, how many a sigh should we hear escape from heroic bosoms; how many a wail from the proud and silent spirit! The wounded pride of authorship gave birth to Manfred and Don Juan. The want of bread has caused many a swanlike strain to pour from the lips of the famishing author. More than one Helen or Cleopatra has set the heroes of the world in motion. Pericles governed Athens, his wife Pericles; the son the mother—the schoolmaster the son, and he in his turn—but where would this end? Oh the subtlety and complexity of human motives!

And yet without some tolerable insight into these, history is but an empty cloud-castle, built of mist, and shadow, and sunbeams. There are two kinds of history—the outward acted history, which is false, and the inner, secret history of causes and influences; this alone is true and worth knowing, and without it we know nothing; it matters not how learned we may be in facts and dates. It is said that Dr. Johnson would insult any man who began to talk to him about the Punic wars. What does the wise man care to know about battles or the marching and counter-marching of a multitude with swords, and battle-axes in their hands. He wants to know the condition and circumstances of the people that made war necessary; the train of secret causes that brought it on; the master-spirits that controlled it, and the motives that influenced them. He is not dazzled by the helmet or the martial dress, but lends a willing ear to the murmurings of the mad Achilles in his tent, for it is there, in those breathings of discontent, in those outpourings of a genuine living man, that he hopes to find some glimmering of the truth. A little insight into the private life of the humblest Roman would be worth all we know of the Punic wars, its galleys, and battles of Cannæ. A mere narrative of events abstracted from the man who wrought them, is like the human body when the life has gone out of it—cold, stiff, and cumbrous. All true history consists in biography. And there can be no biography where the author does not forget the hero, and write of the man. It is not a history of the Revolution that we want, but the Life of Washington. Under the influence of these opinions, we have commenced the task of writing the Life of John Randolph.

John Randolph was born at Cawsons, the second day of June, 1773. The fiery star was in the ascendant at his birth, and pursued him through life; both as a destroying element, and a subtle Promethean flame consuming the soul. It is a remarkable coincidence, that his birthplace, the cherished home of his childhood, and the house in which he spent the first fifteen years of his manhood, Cawsons, Matoax, and Bizzarre, were all in succession destroyed by fire.

Shortly after the destruction of Bizzarre, which was complete—involving his books and papers—he was asked by a friend why he did not write something to leave behind him. "Too late, sir, too late," was the reply; "all I ever wrote perished in the flames; it is too late to restore it now." He felt himself to be a child of destiny; he had a work given him to do, but some cross fate prevented; he failed to fulfil his destiny, and was wretched. "My whole name and race," he has been known to say, "lie under a curse. I am sure I feel the curse cleaving to me." He was not two years and a half old when his father died. What could he know of death? He only grieved in sympathy with his mother's tears. It was not till long after, that he learned the value of the treasure that lay buried beneath the marble slab on the hill under the old oak tree.

Much of the time of her "unhappy widowhood" was spent by Mrs. Randolph at Cawsons. Here the little John was always a welcome guest. He was a great favorite with the whole household, especially with his grandfather and his cousin Anna Eaton, about ten years older than himself, now the venerable Mrs. Anna Bland Dudley, of Franklin, Tennessee. He was so delicate, reserved, and beautiful, that he attracted the notice of all who frequented the house. His skin was as soft and delicate as a female. "There is no accounting for thinness of skins in different animals, human or brute," says he in a letter dated January 31, 1826. "Mine I believe to be more tender than many infants of a month old. Indeed, I have remarked in myself, from my earliest recollection, a delicacy or effeminacy of complexion, that, but for a spice of the devil in my temper, would have consigned me to the distaff or the needle." A spice of the devil in his temper! Well might he say that. Before he was four years old, Mrs. Dudley has known him to swoon away in a fit of passion, and with difficulty could be restored: an evidence of the extreme delicacy of his constitution, and the uncontrollable ardor of a temper that required a stronger frame to repress and restrain it. Notwithstanding his excitable nature, he was always devoted to his mother; would hang fondly about her neck, and could only be soothed by her caresses. Of her Mrs. Dudley thus speaks:—"She was a woman, not only of superior personal attractions, but excelled all others of her day in strength of intellect, for which she was so justly celebrated." This excellent and highly gifted lady trained up her child in the way he should go. He was allowed to come in contact with nothing low, vulgar or mean. Mrs. Dudley,

Governor Tazewell, and the Hon. John Talliaferro, who remember him well in childhood, speak with admiration of his moral purity, and entire exemption from all vicious habits. His mother early taught him to read, and impressed on his mind the best lessons. She was a member of the Church of England, a faith from which her son never long departed. On her bended knees, with him by her side, she repeated day after day the prayers and collects of that admirable litany, which were never effaced from his tenacious memory. Often through life has he been known, in mental agony, to ejaculate them with an earnestness that called forth tears from all who heard him.

"When I could first remember," says he to a friend, "I slept in the same bed with my widowed mother—each night, before putting me to bed, I repeated on my knees before her the Lord's Prayer and the Apostle's Creed—each morning kneeling in the bed I put up my little hands in prayer in the same form. Years have since passed away; I have been a skeptic, a professed scoffer, glorying in my infidelity, and vain of the ingenuity with which I could defend it. Prayer never crossed my mind, but in scorn. I am now conscious that the lessons above mentioned, taught me by my dear and revered mother, are of more value to me than all that I have learned from my preceptors and compeers. On Sunday I said my catechism, a great part of which at the distance of thirty-five years I can yet repeat."

CHAPTER IV.

FAMILY CIRCLE.

In the autumn of 1778, the family circle at Matoax consisted of Mr. and Mrs. Tucker, and her three sons, Richard, Theodorick, and John Randolph. Richard was in his ninth year, Theodorick was nearly eight, and John was in the sixth year of his age. They were all sprightly and interesting boys; and cheerfulness was once more restored to this happy family. A more amiable and exemplary step-father than Mr. Tucker could not be found. This trait in his character was proverbial among his acquaintance every where. "I remember to have heard a brother of mine," says the late Daniel Call, "who married a niece of Mrs. Randolph of Curles, and was thus occasionally thrown into circles, where he sometimes met the Matoax family, once say, that 'Mr. Tucker must be the best father-in-law in the world, or his step-children would not be so fond of him.'" Up to this time the boys had never been to school. All of their instruction had been received at the hands of their mother. Mr. Tucker now undertook their education. But it cannot be supposed that he devoted himself to school-keeping with the rigid discipline of a pedagogue. The life of ease and elegance which he is known to have lived, amidst literary pursuits to which he was devoted, and in the society of wealthy and fashionable neighbors, of which he and his accomplished lady were the chief ornament, would not justify such a conclusion. His leisure was given to their instruction; and he at all times took a lively interest in their improvement. In his letters to Colonel Bland, Jr., who was stationed with a regiment at Charlottesville to guard the captured troops of Burgoyne's army, he often mentions them, and always with great solicitude. In one dated Matoax, July 20, 1779, not ten months after his connection with the family, he writes:—"What you wrote about Bob (Robert Banister, a cousin, then with his uncle, Colonel Bland) has inspired the boys with the spirit of emulation, which I hope will be productive of some benefit to them. I find he serves as a very good spur to them when they are growing a little negligent. Two of them appear to be blessed with excellent capacities, but I confess I am afraid that the genius of your namesake (Theodorick), though possessed of great quickness and acuteness in many respects, does not lie in the literary line. * * * * I shall continue to give them all the assistance that leisure will permit."

John was too young and too delicate to be confined. We may imagine also that, with so indulgent a teacher and so amiable a man, having a spice of the devil withal in his own temper, he could not have learnt much. He was not boisterous, nor inclined to the athletic out-door sports of which boys are so fond. He sought amusements within. When any of the boys and girls from the neighborhood came to Matoax, he introduced the play of "Ladies and Gentlemen," in which each one personated some known or imagined character, male or female, and acted as they supposed such persons would under similar circumstances have acted. He was decidedly of a dramatic turn. And his ardent temper and oriental imagination, precociously developed, invested with an earnestness and a reality all the sports and pastimes of his childhood. But he was not idle.

There was a certain closet to which he stole away and secreted himself whenever he could. It was not redolent—that closet—of cakes or the perfume of sweetmeats, but the odor of books,—of old musty tomes arranged along its shelves. With a mysterious awe,—as if about to commune with mighty spirits and beings of another world, as he really was—would he close the door upon himself, and devour, with "more eagerness than gingerbread," the contents of those old volumes. His mind, young as he was, craved after ethereal food, and there he found the richest repast.

The first book that fell in his way was Voltaire's History of Charles XII. of Sweden. An admirable writer on education has said, that "whatever the young have to read ought to be *objective*, clear, simple, and precise; ought to be the thing itself, and not roundabout dialogues about the thing." No book could fill this description more completely than the above-mentioned History—full of stirring incidents, with a style of simple narrative as rapid and perspicuous as that master of style could make it. How his young heart must have burned within him as he pursued the eventful career of the bold, reckless and indomitable Charles! Feeling the impulses of a kindred spirit, his sympathy must have been intense for the wild, stout-hearted Scandinavian. The next book he read was the Spectator; but only the narrative and dramatic parts as we might suppose. The young mind can only be interested in things, objects, and not in roundabout dialogues about things. He delighted in Humphrey Clinker—Reynard the Fox came next; then Tales of the Genii and Arabian Nights. What a field of delight was opened here—what a world of glory in those old tales of wonder, the genuine poetry for children! The Arabian Nights and Shakspeare were his idols. He had read Goldsmith's Roman History, and an old History of Braddock's War. When not eight years old, he used to sing an old ballad of his defeat:

"On the sixth day of July, in the year sixty-five,
At two in the morning did our forces arrive;
When the French and the Indians in ambush did lay,
And there was great slaughter of our forces that day."

But the "Thousand and One Tales" and Shakspeare were his idols! All others were in a sense shallow and limited—had bounds that could be measured—but these were fathomless, boundless; opening up to the rapt vision a world of enchantment, ever varying, ever new. He was a poet, a born poet, *nascitur non fit.* He did not write poetry; but he spoke it, he felt it, he lived it. His whole life was a poem, of the genuine epic sort; sad, mournful, true. "For poetry," says he, "I have had a decided taste from my childhood; this taste I have sedulously cultivated." Let that old closet tell! Only think of the boy who had read the books we have cited, and Don Quixotte, Gil Blas, Quintus Curtius, Plutarch, Pope's Homer, Robinson Crusoe, Gulliver, Tom Jones, Orlando Furioso, and Thomson's Seasons, before he was eleven years of age!

For more than two years the old closet was to that young genius the cave of Aladdin; and those old tomes the magic lamp by whose aid he could summon to his presence the giants and the genii, the dwarfs and the fairies, the Calibans and the Mirandas, and all the wonderful creations of fancy and imagination. With the clear, open sense and loving heart of childhood, he devoured those narrations and tales, which as he grew up became the themes of reflection, the objects of his aptest illustrations, and the sources whence he drew his lessons of profoundest wisdom. What a force of illustration, and even of argument, is found in his beautiful allusions to the marriage of Sinbad the Sailor to the corpse of his wife; the Old Man of the Sea; and the Vision of Alnascar! As to Shakspeare, he was so thoroughly imbued with his spirit, his own genius so akin to the Avon bard, that he thought and spoke as Shakspeare in his station would have thought and spoken.

He lamented in after life his rambling way of reading. But it could not have been otherwise. He belonged to the *irritabile genus* —was a born poet, and could not brook the restraint or the gin-horse routine of a grammar school. "I have been all my life," says he, "the creature of impulse, the sport of chance, the victim of my own uncontrolled and uncontrollable sensations; of a poetic temperament. I admire and pity all who possess this temperament." Poor fellow! What could mother or step-father do with such a thin-skinned, sensitive, impulsive, imaginative boy? With his fits of passion and swooning, what could they do? Nature is her own best guide. Develope nature according to her own instincts, and the best has been done that the case will admit of. So thought the kind parents of this delicate boy. They put no restraint upon him. Gentleness and tender care followed all his footsteps. He was suffered to roam freely over the hills and by the waterfalls of Appomatox. The quiet sport of angling was his chief source of amusement. When tired, he stole away into the closet, and none took heed of him. In this happy, ever-remembered dream of childhood, two years and a half passed away. Christmas, in the year seventeen hundred and eighty, was destined to be the last Christmas he would ever spend at Matoax as his home—as his home and dwelling-place.

CHAPTER V.

FLIGHT FROM MATOAX.

The new year seventeen hundred and eighty-one commenced with the invasion of Virginia by the traitor Arnold. He had been intrusted with an expedition to that province, not with the hope of conquest, or with the expectation of achieving any important military enterprise, but solely for the purpose of plunder and devastation. What the proud soldier scorned to do was fit work for the betrayer of his country. The name of Arnold, before it became a by-word of reproach, was a sound of terror, not to armed men, but to defenceless women and children. The fame of his rapine and murder in his native State had preceded his arrival in Virginia. On the 3d of January, it was rumored at Matoax that the enemy were coming up James river, and that they were destined for Petersburg or Richmond. Mrs. Tucker had then been but five days mother to her last child, the present eminent jurist, Judge Henry St. George Tucker, of the University. "The first time I ever saw that gentleman," said John Randolph once in a speech, "we were trying to get out of the way of the British." The enemy that night landed at Hood's, of which being apprised early next morning, and hearing that they had marched as far as Bland's Ordinary, in their way to Petersburg, Mr. Tucker came to the conclusion, whatever might be the consequence, to remove his family out of the way of danger, if possible. Hasty preparations were ordered for their immediate departure. What bustle and confusion that frosty morning reigned through the halls at Matoax—each hurrying into trunks or boxes, or loaded wagons, such articles as to them seemed most valuable, heaping imprecations at the same time on that new name of dread, Benedict Arnold. Whether John stole into the old closet for the last time, and took out such volumes as pleased him, we are not informed. Early next morning, the 5th of January, Syphax drove off with the mother and her child; Essex and the boys brought up the rear; and in a few hours Matoax, solitary and alone, with all its effects, was abandoned to its fate. Mrs. Tucker met with a most kind and hospitable reception at the house of Mr. Ben. Ward, Jun'r, at Wintopoke: an ominous name in conjunction with that of John Randolph. It was the daughter of this gentleman to whom in after years he became so much attached. The unsmooth current of their loves (as all true love is) greatly affected his sensitive nature, and had no little influence on the most important events of his life. Those children, when they first met together around the fireside at Wintopoke, and joined in the innocent plays of childhood, how unconscious were they of the deep drama of life in which they were destined to play so sad a part! After recruiting her health and strength a few days, which had been somewhat impaired by fatigue and hurry of spirits, Mrs. Tucker pursued her journey to Bizarre, a large and valuable estate on both sides of the Appomatox, where she and the boys were destined to spend alone the remainder of this stirring and eventful year. So soon as his family were in a place of safety, Mr. Tucker hastened back to the scene of action to assist old Col. Bland in his escape, and to secure such property, belonging to himself and friends, as had not been destroyed by the enemy. This done, he threw himself at the head of the Chesterfield regiment of militia and joined General Greene, then manœuvring before Cornwallis's army on the borders of North Carolina and Virginia. He was at the battle of Guilford, which took place the 8th of March, where he behaved very gallantly. When Gen. Greene marched into South Carolina after this engagement, he returned to Virginia, spent a few weeks with his family at

Bizarre, then joined General La Fayette, with whom he continued till the capture of Cornwallis, the 19th of October, at Yorktown.

Notwithstanding his active participation in the military operations of that period, his solicitude for the education of the boys was unabated. From Bizarre, May the 23d, he wrote to Colonel Bland: "Lose no opportunity of procuring a tutor for the boys, for the exigency is greater than you can imagine." Again, from Richmond, July 17th, he writes on the same subject; and then from Williamsburg, amidst the active preparations for that great event which was to end the war, and secure the independence of the country. In a letter dated Williamsburg, Sept. 21st, he says: "The boys are still without, and more than ever in want, of a tutor. Walker Maury has written to me lately, and given me such a plan of his school, that unless you procure a tutor before Christmas, I would at all events advise sending them to him immediately after. I know his worth; I know that his abilities are equal to the task; and I know that his assiduity will be equally directed to improve their morals and their understandings, as their manners. With this prospect, I would not advise the providing any but a man of superior talents as a private tutor." The year '81 was full of stirring life to the men, but of idleness to the boys; yet we are not to suppose that because the young Randolphs had not the benefit of a tutor to teach them the Latin and Greek languages, they were entirely destitute of instruction: with such a mother as they were blessed, they could not grow up in vice or idleness. Her sprightly wit, sound judgment, good temper, and pious example, impressed their character more favorably than all the learning of the schools. Her precepts were law to their plastic minds; and they ever afterwards retained a lively recollection of their wisdom and truth. When riding over the vast Roanoke estates one day, she took John up behind her, and, waving her hand over the broad acres spread before them, she said: "Johnny, all this land belongs to you and your brother Theodorick; it is your father's inheritance. When you get to be a man you must not sell your land; it is the first step to ruin for a boy to part with his father's home: be sure to keep it as long as you live. Keep your land and your land will keep you." In relating this anecdote, Mr. Randolph said it made such an impression on his mind that it governed his future life. He was confident it saved him from many errors. He never did part from his father's home. His attachment to the soil, the old English law of inheritance, and a landed aristocracy (we have no other word to express our meaning), constituted the most remarkable trait in his character. The Virginia law of descents, framed by Pendleton, Wythe, and Jefferson, never found favor in his eyes. While descanting on its evils, he has been heard to say, "Well might old George Mason exclaim, that the authors of that law never had a son!" In a letter addressed to a friend at a very late period of life, he says: "The old families of Virginia will form connections with low people, and sink into the mass of overseers' sons and daughters; and this is the legitimate, nay, inevitable conclusion to which Mr. Jefferson and his levelling system has brought us. They know better in New-York, and they feel the good effects of not disturbing the rights of property. The patroon is as secure in his rents as any man in the community. The great manor of Philipsburg was scandalously confiscated, and the Livingstons have lost their influence by subdivision. Every now and then our old acquaintance, Burr, finds out some flaw in the titles of the usurpers, and a fine estate is restored to its legitimate owners." In this passage the reader will find "the key words," to use his own expression, that decipher every thing in the character of John Randolph.

The subdivision or alienation of his father's inheritance was a subject he could not contemplate. Like Logan, he was alone—all alone—and no one of his father's house after him to inherit his father's home; hence the apparent inconsistency in the disposition of his estates, the facility with which he made and unmade wills—in short, the monomania with which he was charged on the subject of property.

CHAPTER VI.

AT SCHOOL.

After Christmas the boys were sent to Walker Maury's school in Orange county. Before he was nine years of age, John was separated from the brooding watchfulness of a devoted mother, and exposed to the dangers, evil examples, and vices of a public school. Tender and delicate as a female, he was forced out on the society of ruder boys, to endure or to resist as he might their kicks, cuffs, and bruises. Early did he begin among his equals to learn that personal merit is of more avail than birth or riches; and that truth, fortitude, and courage, are more to be valued than much learning.

At the school in Orange, the young Randolphs remained until about the middle of October, 1782, when it was broken up, and Mr. Maury removed to the city of Williamsburg.

He had been invited to that place to establish a Grammar School as an appendage to William and Mary College, in which there was no professorship of Humanity existing at that time. The school was regulated most judiciously; and was soon attended by more pupils than any other Grammar School that had been before established or has since existed in Virginia. More than one hundred, at one time, were in attendance, including boys from every State in the Union, from Georgia to Maryland, both inclusive. Such a number of pupils made it necessary that they should be divided into classes. The greater proportion of these classes were consigned to assistants, of whom there were four. Soon after Mr. Maury was established in Williamsburg, the young Randolphs followed him there, and again became members of his school. Richard, the eldest, was placed in the second class, under the immediate direction of Mr. Maury himself. Theodorick and John were placed in the fourth class, which was the head class assigned to the superintendence of the chief usher, a Mr. Elliot. When the class was so augmented, it was reading, and had nearly finished, Eutropius. One of the books then used by a classmate, with a class-roll written on the fly-leaf, is still extant. In a short time after the young Randolphs joined it, the class had made such progress that it was transferred from the usher's department to that of the principal. It then became the third class. While John Randolph continued a member of it, which was more than a year, it was engaged in reading Sallust and Virgil, and had made some progress in learning the Greek and French languages, and the elements of Geometry. Though he complained of having learned but little at this school, his attainments for the short time he was connected with it must have been very considerable. While there he learned to repeat the Westminster Greek Grammar by heart, as he could the alphabet.

It was around the base of Lord Bottetourt's statue, in the old Capitol, the great clock, now removed to the church in Williamsburg, vibrating overhead, that he committed his lessons to memory. His attainment in Latin also must have been considerable. The boys were in the habit of acting plays in the original language from Plautus and Terrence. He was always selected to perform the female parts. His feminine appearance, and the "spice of the devil in his temper," rendered him peculiarly fitted for that purpose, and his performance was admirable. One who remembers his personal appearance at that time, in speaking of him, lifted up both hands, and exclaimed, "he was the most beautiful boy I ever beheld!" He was, indeed, the admiration of all who saw him, was a great favorite with the ladies, but his proud temper and reserved manners prevented him from forming any intimate associations with his school-fellows. Though a promiscuous intercourse was repugnant to his feelings, no one was capable of appreciating true merit, and of forming closer, more unreserved, warmer, and lasting attachments than John Randolph. Shunning vulgar society and repelling familiarity, he was the more open and devoted to those who were honored with his friendship. He had a natural instinct for discovering character; and was remarkable in earliest youth for his discernment and scrutiny into motives.

Among the hundreds of boys with whom he came in daily contact, he associated with, and formed an attachment to, one class-mate alone. That class-mate was Littleton Waller Tazewell. With a genius as brilliant as his own, a heart as warm, and a person as prepossessing, young Tazewell was worthy of the distinction. A mutual respect and friendship grew up between them, which lasted to the end of Mr. Randolph's life; and the recollection of which is still warmly preserved by the noble survivor. In a manner peculiar to John Randolph, this early attachment was often called to remembrance, and cherished. Near forty years afterwards, when he had heard a lady sing some Scotch airs, he wrote to a friend: "Among others she sang 'There's nae luck aboot the house' very well, and 'Auld Lang Syne.' When she came to the lines:

'We twa ha'e paidlet in the burn,
Frae morning sun till dine,'

I cast my mind's eye around for such a "trusty feese," and could light only on Tazewell (who, God be praised, is here), and you may judge how we met."

In the spring of 1784, after he had been in Williamsburg a little more than one year, John Randolph was taken away from school. His parents went on a visit to Mr. Tucker's friends in the island of Bermuda, and as John's health was very delicate, they took him along with them. When about to take his leave, he proposed to young Tazewell that they should exchange class-books, that each might have some testimonial of their mutual friendship and of its origin.

They accordingly exchanged Sallusts. Not many years since, while he was in Norfolk, preparing to depart on his mission to Russia, he showed Mr. Tazewell the identical Sallust he (Tazewell) had given him. On the fly-leaf of the book he had written, at the time he received it, how, when, and from whom he had acquired it. To this he had added this hexameter: "Cœlum non animum mutant qui transmare currunt."

He continued abroad more than eighteen months, and not having the advantage of daily recitation, the Greek language, which he had begun so successfully to acquire in his promenades around Lord Bottetourt's statue, was entirely effaced from his memory; and he barely kept alive the more extensive knowledge he had acquired of the Latin. Though these newly acquired elements of learning were readily abandoned, and easily effaced, pursuits more genial to his taste were followed with unabated vigor. Poetry continued to be the charm of his life. While abroad, he read Chatterton and Rowley, and Young and Gay. Percy's Reliques and Chaucer then became his great favorites. On his return to Virginia, in the latter part of 1785, we do not learn that he returned to Walker Mauray's school in Williamsburg; on the contrary, we presume he did not, for he then would have formed an acquaintance in early youth with John Brockenbrough, the most intimate friend of his after life.

The letter from which the above paragraph was taken continues in this wise: "During the time that Dr. Brockenbrough was at Walter Mauray's school (from the spring of 1784, to the end of 1785), I was in Bermuda; and (although he was well acquainted with both my brothers) our acquaintance did not begin until nearly twenty years afterwards. Do you know that I am childish enough to regret this very sensibly? for, although I cannot detract from the esteem or regard in which I hold him, or lessen the value I set upon his friendship, yet, had I known him then, I think I should enjoy 'Auld Lang Syne' more, when I hear it sung, or hum it to myself, as I often do."

How he spent the next twelve or eighteen months after his return from Bermuda, we have not been able to learn. When we see him again it is at Princeton College, in the autumn of 1787. The manner in which he spent his time there and at Columbia College, New-York, shall be given in his own words.

"My mother once expressed a wish to me, that I might one day or other be as great a speaker as Jerman Baker or Edmund Randolph! That gave the bent to my disposition. At Princeton College, where I spent a few months (1787), the prize of elocution was borne away by mouthers and ranters. I never would speak if I could possibly avoid it, and when I could not, repeated, without gesture, the shortest piece that I had committed to memory. I remember some verses from Pope, and the first anonymous letter from Newberg, made up the sum and substance of my spoutings, and I can yet repeat much of the first epistle (to Lord Chatham) of the former, and a good deal of the latter. I was then as conscious of my superiority over my competitors in delivery and elocution, as I am now that they are sunk in oblivion; and I despised the award and the umpires in the bottom of my heart. I believe that there is nowhere such foul play as among professors and schoolmasters; more especially if they are priests. I have had a contempt for college honors ever since.

My mother's death drew me from Princeton, (where I had been

forced to be idle, being put into a noisy wretched grammar school for Dr. Witherspoon's emolument: I was ten times a better scholar than the master of it,) and in June, 1788, I was sent to Columbia College, New-York; just then having completed my fifteenth year. Never did higher literary ambition burn in human bosom. Columbia College, New-York, was just rising out of chaos; but there was an Irishman named Cochran, who was our humanity professor.

I now (July, 1788) mastered the Eaton grammar, and gave Cochran, who was a scholar, "and a ripe and good one," a half-joe, out of my own pocket, for months, to give me private lessons. We read Demosthenes together, and I used to cry for indignation at the success of Philip's arts and arms over the liberties of Greece. But some disgust induced my master to remove to Nova Scotia, where a professor's chair was offered him, about three months after I became his pupil. Next to the loss of my mother, and my being sent to Walker Mauray's school (and one other that I shall not name), this was the greatest misfortune of my life.

"Unhappily, my poor brother Theodorick, who was two years older than myself, had a strong aversion to books and a decided taste for pleasure. Often when I had retreated from him and his convivial associates to my little study, has he forced the lock, taken away my book, and rendered further prosecution of my purpose impossible. From that time forward I began to neglect study (Cochran left no one but Dr. Johnson, the president, of any capacity behind him, and he was in the Senate of the United States from March, 1789), read only the trash of the circulating library, and never have read since, except for amusement, unless for a few weeks at Williamsburg at the close of 1793; and all my dear mother's fond anticipations and all my own noble and generous aspirations have been quenched; and if not entirely—if a single spark or languid flame yet burns—it is owing to my accidental election to Congress five and twenty years ago."

He was recalled from Princeton by the death of his mother, That sad event took place the 18th of January, 1788. She was but thirty-six years old when she died. Cut off in the bloom of youth and beauty, he ever retained a most vivid and impassioned remembrance of her person, her charms, and her virtues. He always kept her portrait hanging before him in his chamber. Though he was not yet fifteen years old, the loss to him was irreparable. She knew him; she knew the delicacy of his frame, the tenderness of his heart, the irritability of his temper; and she alone could sympathize with him. Many years after this event—the day after his duel with Mr. Clay—while reflecting on the narrow escape he had made with his life, and the professions of men who disappear in such an hour of trial, his mind naturally reverted to his dear mother, who understood and never forsook him; he wrote thus to a friend: "I am a fatalist. I am all but friendless. Only one human being ever knew me. *She* only knew me." That human being was his mother! The loss to him was irreparable; nor did he ever cease to mourn over it. Rarely did he come to Petersburg or its vicinity, that he did not visit old Matoax, in its wasted solitude, and shed tears over the grave of those honored parents, by whose side it was the last wish of his heart to be buried.

The spring of the year 1788 was spent in Virginia. It does not appear that he was engaged in any regular course of study. Much of his time, as was his custom whenever he could, was devoted to friendship. He spent several weeks of this vacation with young Tazewell, at his father's house, in Williamsburg. While there, he discoursed at large on the various incidents he had met with while abroad in Bermuda, and at college in Princeton, thus early displaying that faculty of observation and fluent narrative that in after years rendered his conversation so brilliant and captivating. After his departure on the present occasion, he commenced a correspondence, which, with short intervals, was kept up through life. Such was Mr. Tazewell's reputation for profound learning on all subjects touching the laws and the Constitution of the country, that Mr. Randolph consulted him on every important occasion as it arose in Congress. Often in one line would he propound an inquiry that cost his friend weeks of investigation to answer. His own early letters displayed an inquiring mind far beyond his years. In his first letter, written on his arrival in New-York (June, 1788), he stated that alien duties had been exacted by the custom-house there, not only upon the vessel in which he had taken his passage, which was owned in Virginia, but upon the passengers on board of her, all of whom were natives of Virginia. This statement was accompanied by many reflections, designed to show the impolicy of such exactions on the part of New-York, and the ill effects that would result from persisting in such a course. This incident took place before the adoption of the present Constitution of the United States, and when the subject of it was just fifteen years old. It is mentioned merely to show "the precocious proclivity" of John Randolph to the investigation of political subjects.

Another letter addressed to the same friend, was confined to an account of the first inauguration of General Washington as President of the United States, which took place the 30th of April, 1789, in the city of New-York. John Randolph was an eye-witness of the scene. His letter contained a narrative of many minute but very interesting incidents that do not appear in any of our public records or histories. This narrative, being written at the moment such incidents occurred, by an ingenuous youth, an eye-witness of the events, had an air of freshness and truthfulness about it that was most captivating. As the letter related to nothing but matters of general interest, young Tazewell showed it to his father, who was so much pleased with it, that shortly afterwards he requested his son to read it to a party of friends who were dining with him. The late Colonel James Innis, the attorney-general, was one of the party. He was considered, at that time, the most eloquent speaker, and the best belles-lettres scholar in Virginia. Colonel Innis was so much pleased with the letter, that he took it from the hands of the owner, and read it over and over again, pronouncing it to be a model of such writing, and recommended to the young man to preserve it, and study its style.

CHAPTER VII.

THE CONSTITUTION IN ITS CHRYSALIS STATE.

No man with a growing intellect was ever content with his early education. The boy turns a contemptuous look on the swaddlings of infancy. The wisest instruction is so inadequate to the wants of the human mind, that when one grows up to manhood he looks back with mortification on the dark gropings of youthful ignorance, and with disgust on the time and effort wasted in pursuing barren paths, where experience taught him no truth could be found. John Randolph was not singular in lamenting that he had disappointed the fond anticipations of his friends, and mourning that "all his noble and generous aspirations had been quenched." Had Theodorick and his noisy companions left the ambitious student alone to his books and his closet, we should still have heard the same complaint. No attainment can satisfy the aspirations of genius. But it is true he was not without just cause of discontent. His frequent changes of school, not less than five times in as many years; the long interruptions thereby occasioned—by his travels abroad, the death of his mother, and the daily vexations of ill health and of noisy companions, with whom he was compelled to associate—rendered it impossible for him to give that continuous and ardent devotion to study which is indispensable to mental discipline, and the acquisition of learning. In disgust he gave up the effort, and abandoned himself to the loose habit of promiscuous reading. His classical studies, so often interrupted, were finally closed before he was sixteen years of age. "I am an ignorant man, sir!" though sounding like sarcasm from his lips, was uttered with sincerity. Though the broad foundation of solid learning was wanting to him, his active and inquiring mind was scarcely conscious of the deficiency. Nature had designed him for a statesman; he was eminently a practical man, and drew his lessons of wisdom from experience and observation. He was, while yet a youth, in daily intercourse with statesmen and men of learning. He enjoyed great and rare opportunities for acquiring information on those subjects towards which his mind had "a precocious proclivity." Practical politics, and the science of government, were the daily themes of the statesmen with whom he associated. He was a constant attendant on the sittings of the first Congress. He was in Federal Hall, the 4th of March, 1789, when only thirteen members of the new Congress under our present Constitution appeared and took their seats. Two only presented themselves from the south side of the Potomac; Alexander White, from Virginia, and Thomas Tudor Tucker, from South Carolina. Mr. Tucker was the brother of St. George Tucker, the father-in-law of John Randolph. The 14th of March, Richard Bland Lee, a cousin of John Randolph, Mr. Madison, and John Page, from Virginia, entered the hall, and cheered the hearts of those who had assembled from day to day for more than a week without a quorum, and were beginning to despond and doubt lest this new government might prove a failure. The 30th of March, Col. Theodorick Bland, the uncle of John Randolph, made his appearance. It was not till the 1st of April, nearly a month after the time appointed by the Constitution, that a quorum was obtained, and the House organized for business. Such was the feeble and doubtful infancy of this great and growing Republic. "I was at Federal Hall," said Randolph once in a speech to his constituents; "I saw Washington, but could not hear him take the oath to support the Federal Constitution. The Constitution was in its chrysalis state. I saw what Washington did not see; but two other men in Virginia saw it—George Mason and Patrick Henry—*the poison under its wings.*" That this was no vain boasting in a boy of sixteen, the reader will soon see.

The arduous and responsible task of organizing a new government devolved on the first Congress. In that body were a number of men who preferred the Old Confederation, with some modifications to give it energy; and were strenuously opposed to a strong centralizing system, such as they apprehended the new government to be. They, therefore, looked with watchfulness and jealousy on every step that was taken in its organization. The most prominent among those who thus early opposed the assumptions of federal power, were Theodorick Bland and Thomas Tudor Tucker, the two uncles of John Randolph. Col. Bland was a great admirer and follower of Patrick Henry. He was a member of the Convention that met, June, 1788, in Richmond, to ratify the new Constitution. It is well known that Patrick Henry opposed the ratification with all his eloquence. The very day in which he shook the capitol with a power not inferior to that with which he set the ball of Revolution in motion, Col. Bland, writing to a friend, says: "I see my country on the point of embarking and launching into a troubled ocean, without chart or compass, to direct her; one half of her crew hoisting sail for the land of *energy*, and the other looking with a longing aspect on the shore of *liberty*." After declaring that the Convention which framed the Constitution had transcended its powers, Patrick Henry exclaimed: 'It is most clearly a consolidated government. I need not take much pains to show that the principles of this system are extremely pernicious, impolitic, and dangerous. We have no detail of those great considerations which, in my opinion, ought to have abounded before we should recur to a government of this kind. Here is a revolution as radical as that which separated us from Great Britain. It is as radical, if in this transition our rights and privileges are endangered, and the sovereignty of the States be relinquished: and cannot we plainly see that this is actually the case? Is this tame relinquishment of rights worthy of freemen? Is it worthy of that manly fortitude that ought to characterize republicans? The Confederation—this same despised government—merits, in my opinion, the highest encomium: it carried us through a long and dangerous war; it rendered us victorious in that bloody conflict with a powerful nation; it has secured us a territory greater than any European monarch possesses: and shall a government which has been thus strong and vigorous, be accused of imbecility, and abandoned for want of energy? Consider what you are about to do before you part with this government." "It is now confessed that the new government is national. There is not a single federal feature in it. It has been alleged within these walls, during the debates, to be national and federal, as it suited the arguments of gentlemen. But now when we have the definition of it, it is purely national. The honorable member was pleased to say, that the sword and purse included every thing of consequence. And shall we trust them out of our hands without checks and barriers? The sword and purse are essentially necessary for the government. Every essential requisite must be in Congress. Where are the purse and sword of Virginia? They must go to Congress. What is become of your country? The Virginian government is but a name. We should be thought unwise indeed to keep two hundred legislators in Virginia, when the government is, in fact, gone to Philadelphia, or New-York. We are as a State to form no part of the government. Where are your checks? The most essential objects of government are to be administered by Congress. How then can the State governments be any check upon them? If we are to be a republican government, it will be consolidated, not confederated. This is not imaginary; it is a formidable reality. If consolidation proves to be as mischievous to this country as it has been to other countries, what will the poor inhabitants of this country do? This government will operate like an ambuscade. It will destroy the State governments, and swallow the liberties of the people, without giving them previous notice. If gentlemen are willing to run the hazard, let them run it; but I shall exculpate myself by my opposition, and monitory warnings, within these walls. Another gentleman tells us that no inconvenience will result from the exercise of the power of taxation by the general government. A change of government will not pay money. If from the probable amount of the import, you take the enormous and extravagant expenses, which will certainly attend the support of this great consolidated government, I believe you will find no reduction of the public burdens by this new system. The splendid maintenance of the President, and of the members of both Houses; and the salaries and fees for the swarm of officers and dependents on the Government, will cost this continent immense sums. After satisfying their uncontrolled demands, what can be left for the States? Not a sufficiency even to defray the expense of their internal administration. They must, therefore, glide imperceptibly and gradually out of existence. This, Sir, must naturally terminate in a consolidation. If this will do for other people, it will never do for me. I never will give up that darling word *requisition;* my country may give it up; a majority may wrest it from me; but I never will give it up till my grave. The power of direct taxation was called by the honorable gentleman the soul of the government: another gentleman called it the lungs of the government. We all agree that it is the most important part of the body politic. If the power of raising money be necessary for the general government, it is no less so for the States. Must I give my soul—my lungs to Congress? Congress must have our souls; the State must have our souls. These two co-ordinate, interfering, unlimited powers of harassing the community are unexampled; it is unprecedented in history; they are the visionary projects of modern politicians. Tell me not of imaginary means, but of reality: this political solecism will never tend to the benefit of the community. It will be as oppressive in practice as it is absurd in theory. If you part from this, which the honorable gentleman tells you is the soul of Congress, you will be inevitably ruined. I tell you they shall not have the soul of Virginia."

After speaking of the "awful squinting towards monarchy" in the executive; and of the great powers conferred on the judiciary, Mr. Henry concluded in one of those bursts of rapt eloquence, which can only be compared to the eloquence of Demosthenes, when on a similar occasion—in a last appeal to his countrymen to defend themselves against the invasion of Philip—he called on the spirits of the mighty dead, those who fell at Thermopylæ, at Salamis, and at Marathon, to rise and protect their country against the arts and arms of the Macedonian Tyrant.

"The gentleman, tells you," said Mr. Henry, "of important blessings which he imagines will result to us, and to mankind in general, from the adoption of this system. I see the awful immensity of the dangers with which it is pregnant. I see it,—I feel it. I see beings of a far higher order anxious concerning our decision. When I see beyond the horizon that bounds human eyes, and look at the final consummation of all human things, and see those intelligent beings which inhabit the ethereal mansions, reviewing the political divisions and revolutions which in the progress of time will happen in America, and the consequent happiness or misery of mankind, I am led to believe, that much of the account, on one side or the other, will depend on what we now decide. Our own happiness alone is not affected by the event. All nations are interested in the determination. We have it in our power to secure the happiness of one half of the human race. Its adoption may involve the misery of the other hemispheres."

When the vote was about to be taken on the ratification, Patrick Henry, seconded by Theodorick Bland, moved a resolution, "That previous to the ratification of the new constitution of government recommended by the late Federal Convention, a declaration of rights asserting and securing from encroachment the great principles of civil and religious liberty, and the inalienable rights of the people, together with amendments to the most exceptionable parts of the said constitution of government, ought to be referred by this convention to the other States in the American confederacy for their consideration." This resolution was lost by a majority of *eight votes*. Many who voted for it were members of the first Congress; and some of them were among the most influential and distinguished men in Virginia. William Cabell, Samuel Jordan Cabell, Benjamin Harrison, John Tyler, father of the late President, Isaac Coles, Stephen Thompson Mason, Abraham Twigg, Patrick Henry, Theodorick Bland, William Grayson, James Monroe, and George Mason. These same persons voted against the adoption of the Constitution, which was only carried by a majority of *ten*. So great was the impression made on the public mind by the arguments in the Convention against the evil tendencies of the Constitution, that a majority of the Virginia Legislature that met the ensuing October, to appoint senators, and pass laws for electing members of Congress, was decidedly anti-federal; that is, opposed to the Constitution, as it came from the hands of its framers, without important modifications. Patrick Henry was the master spirit of that assembly. He was offered a seat in the Senate of the United States; but he declined it, as he had previously declined a seat in the Federal Convention. Through his influence the appointment of senator was conferred on William Grayson, and on Richard Henry Lee.

Mr. Grayson distinguished himself in the Virginia Convention by a very elaborate analysis of the new Constitution, pointing out its defects, and illustrating by history its dangerous tendencies He gave utterance to a prediction, which many believe has been in the daily process of fulfilment from that time to the present moment. "But my greatest objection is," says he, speaking of the Constitution, "that it will, in its operation, be found unequal, grievous, and oppressive. If it have any efficacy at all, it must be by a faction—a faction of one part of the Union against the other. There is a great difference of circumstances between the States. The interest of the carrying States (since manufacturing States) is strikingly different from that of the producing States. I mean not to give offence to any part of America, but mankind are governed by interest. The carrying States will assuredly unite, and our situation will then be wretched indeed. Every measure will have for its object their particular interest. Let ill-fated Ireland be ever present to our view. I hope that my fears are groundless, but I believe it as I do my creed, that this government will operate as a faction of seven States to oppress the rest of the Union. But it may be said, that we are represented, and cannot therefore be injured—a poor representation it will be! The British would have been glad to take America into the Union like the Scotch, by giving us a small representation. The Irish might be indulged with the same favor by asking for it. (As they have done, and with what result?) Will that lessen our misfortunes? A small representation gives a pretence to injure and destroy. But, sir, the Scotch Union is introduced by an honorable gentleman as an argument in favor of adoption. Would he wish his country to be on the same foundation with Scotland? They have but 45 members in the House of Commons, and 16 in the House of Lords. They go up regularly in order to be bribed. The smallness of their number puts it out of their power to carry any measure. And this unhappy nation exhibits the only instance, perhaps, in the world, where corruption becomes a virtue. I devoutly pray, that this description of Scotland may not be picturesque of the Southern States, in three years from this time."

The other senator from Virginia was Richard Henry Lee. He stood by Patrick Henry from the commencement of our revolutionary struggles to their end. He was one of the first delegates to the first Congress. His name appears on almost all the important committees of that body. He was selected by the Virginia delegation to move the declaration of independence. For his patriotism, statesmanship, and oratory, he was regarded as the Cicero of his age. His classical and chaste elocution possessed a tone of depth and inspiration that charmed his auditory. While his great compatriot poured down upon agitated assemblies a cataract of mingled passion and logic, he awakened the attention, captivated the heart, and convinced the understanding of his hearers by a regulated flow of harmonious language, generous sentiment, and lucid argument. "In his personal character, he was just, benevolent, and high-spirited, domestic in his tastes, and too proud to be ambitious of popularity." This distinguished patriot and statesman was strenuously opposed to the Constitution as it came from the hands of its framers. He was a member of Congress to whom it was referred, and by whom it was expected to be recommended to their respective States. "When the plan of a Constitution," says Mr. Madison, "proposed by the Convention came before Congress for their sanction, a very serious effort was made by Richard Henry Lee to embarrass it. It was first contended that Congress could not properly give any positive countenance to a measure which had for its object the subversion of the Constitution under which they acted. This ground of attack failing, he then urged the expediency of sending out the plan with amendments, and proposed a number of them corresponding with the objections of Col. Mason."

He then addressed a letter to Governor Edmund Randolph, of Virginia, who as a member of the Convention had refused to sign the Constitution. After giving his objections in detail, he says: "You are, therefore, sir, well warranted in saying, either a monarchy or aristocracy will be generated—perhaps the most grievous system of government will arise. It cannot be denied with truth, that this new Constitution is, in its first principles, highly and dangerously oligarchic; and it is a point agreed, that a government of the few, is, of all governments, the worst."

"The only check to be found in favor of the democratic principle, in this system, is the House of Representatives; which, I believe, may justly be called a mere shred or rag of representation; it being obvious to the least examination, that smallness of number, and great comparative disparity of power, render that house of little effect to promote good, or restrain bad government. But what is the power given to this ill-constructed body? To judge of what may be for the general welfare, seems a power coextensive with every possible object of human legislation." Such were the first senators from Virginia, and of a like complexion were a majority of those returned to the House of Representatives. For devoting himself so ardently to the election of men known to be hostile to the Constitution as it stood, Mr. Henry was charged with a design of subverting that which he could not prevent. It is said that his avowed attachment to the confederation was mere hypocrisy; that he secretly rejoiced in its imbecility, and did not desire a union of the States under any form of government. He was attacked in a most virulent and personal manner by a writer who signed himself Decius. He charged Mr. Henry with a design of forming Virginia and North Carolina into one republic, and placing himself at the head as their dictator. "Were I to draw the picture of a tyrant for this country," says Decius, "it should be very different from that which some others have sketched out. He should be a man in every instance calculated to soothe and not to threaten the populace; possessing a humiliating and not an arrogant turn; affecting an entire ignorance and poorness of capacity, and not assuming the superiorities of the illumined; a man whose capacity should be calculated to insinuate itself into the good esteem of others by degrees, and not to surprise them into a compliance on a sudden · whose plainness of manners and meanness of address first should move our compassion, steal upon our hearts, betray our judgments, and finally run away with the whole of the human composition."

This description of the demagogue winning his way by affected humility and low cunning to the supreme command, was intended to be applied to Mr. Henry. Many of his own expressions are used in drawing the portrait, but no man less deserved the epithet of ambitious. There can be no doubt that he delighted to sway the passions of the multitude, and to influence the decision of legislative bodies by the powers of his eloquence; but that his ambition extended to the acquisition of supreme executive command, there is not the slightest ground of suspicion.

The virulence with which he was assailed must be attributed to the high party excitement of the times, which indiscriminately assaulted the most spotless characters, and paid no respect to exalted services or venerable age.

CHAPTER VIII.

GEORGE MASON.

George Mason was a wise man. He was at once the Solon and the Cato, the lawgiver and the stern patriot of the age in which he lived. At a period when republics were to be founded, and constitutions of government ordained for growing empires, he was the first to define and to guard with watchful care the rights of the people—to prescribe limitations to the different departments of government, and to place restrictions on their exercise of power. The Bill of Rights, and the Constitution of Virginia, are lasting monuments to his memory. One sentence of the former contains more wisdom and concentration of thought, than all former writings on the subject of government. The sentence is this; "that no man or set of men is entitled to exclusive or separate emoluments, or privileges from the community, but in consideration of public services; which, not being descendible, neither ought the offices of magistrate, legislator. or judge, to be hereditary." Here is a volume of truth and wisdom, says an eminent writer, a lesson for the study of nations, embodied in a single sentence, and expressed in the plainest language. If a deluge of despotism were to overspread the world, and destroy those institutions under which freedom is yet protected, sweeping into oblivion every vestige of their remembrance among men, could this single sentence of Mason be preserved, it would be sufficient to rekindle the flame of liberty, and to revive the race of freemen. Though Mr. Mason did not object to a union of the States for their mutual defence and welfare, he yet regarded the commonwealth of Virginia as his country, and her government as the only one that could guarantee his rights or protect his interests. So far back as 1783, Mr. Madison, speaking of him, says, "his heterodoxy lay chiefly in being too little impressed with the necessity or the proper means of preserving the confederacy." Virginia was a great empire within herself, and had every thing to sacrifice in surrendering her sovereignty to a central government. On the independence of the States also rested his only hope of preserving the liberties of the people. He entered the Federal Convention, therefore, in 1787, with a stern resolution never to surrender the sovereignty of the States. Others, on the contrary, could conceive of no other plan but a consolidated government, by which the States should be reduced from political societies to mere municipal corporations. The middle ground of compromise had not yet been thought of. Mr. Madison had but a dim perception of its possibility. Even he was for a strong government. In a letter addressed to Edmund Randolph, dated New-York, April 8th, 1787, he says: "I hold it for a fundamental point, that an individual independence of the States is utterly irreconcilable with the idea of an aggregate sovereignty. I think, at the same time, that a consolidation of the States into one simple republic, is not less unattainable than it would be inexpedient. Let it be tried, then, whether any middle ground can be taken." To the untiring exertions of Mr. Madison, both in the Federal Convention and in the Convention of Virginia, are we indebted for the existence of the Constitution. But to Colonel Mason are we indebted for the only democratic and federal features it contains. But for Madison we should have been without a government; but for Mason, that government would have crushed the States, and swallowed up the liberties of the people. To Mason are we indebted for the popular election of members of the House of Representatives, the election of senators by the State Legislatures, and the equal representation of the States in the Senate. In the first, there is some guarantee for the rights of the people; in the second, some protection to the sovereignty and independence of the States. So important were Mr. Mason's services, that we must detain the reader by a few quotations from his speeches to establish his claim to the high distinction here awarded him. When the question of electing members to the House of Representatives by the State Legislatures instead of the people, was before the Convention, Mr. Mason said: "Under the existing Confederacy Congress represent the *States*, and not the *people* of the States; their acts operate on the *States*, and not on the *individuals*. The case will be changed in the new plan of government. The people will be represented; they ought therefore to choose the representatives. Much," he said, "had been alleged against democratic elections. He admitted that much might be said; but it was to be considered that no government was free from imperfections and evils, and that improper elections, in many instances, were inseparable from republican governments. But compare these with the advantage of this form, in favor of the rights of the people, in favor of human nature!" Mr. Mason urged the necessity of retaining the election by the people. "Whatever inconvenience may attend the democratic principle, it must actuate one part of the government. It is the only security for the rights of the people."

When the organization of the Senate was under consideration, Mr. Mason said, "he never would agree to abolish the State Governments, or render them absolutely insignificant. They were as necessary as the General Government, and he would be equally careful to preserve them. He was aware of the difficulty of drawing the line between them, but hoped it was not insurmountable. It has been argued on all hands, that an efficient government is necessary; that to render it such, it ought to have the faculty of self-defence; that to render its different branches effectual, each of them ought to have the same power of self-defence. He did not wonder that such an argument should have prevailed on these points. He only wondered that there should be any disagreement about the necessity of allowing the State governments the same self-defence. If they are to be preserved, as he conceived to be essential, they certainly ought to have this power; and the only mode left of giving it to them, was by allowing them to appoint the second branch of the National Legislature." Dr. Johnson said: "The controversy must be endless while gentlemen differ in the grounds of their arguments; those on one side considering the States as districts of people composing one political society; those on the other, considering them as so many political societies. The fact is, that the States do exist as political societies, and a government is to be formed for them in their political capacity, as well as for the individuals composing them. Does it not seem to follow, that if the States, as such, are to exist, they must be armed with some power of self-defence? *This is the idea of Colonel Mason, who appears to have looked to the bottom of this matter.* Besides the aristocratic and other interests, which ought to have the means of defending themselves, the States have their interests as such, and are equally entitled to like means. On the whole he thought, that, as in some respects the States are to be considered in their political capacity, and in others as districts of individual citizens, the two ideas embraced on different sides, instead of being opposed to each other, ought to be combined; that in *one* branch the *people* ought to be represented, in the *other* the *States.*"

Notwithstanding Col. Mason labored to modify the Constitution through its various stages, as much as he could in favor of liberty and the independence of the States, he finally voted against it. His objections were radical, extending to every department of government. He objected to the unlimited powers of taxation, conferred on a House of Representatives, which was but the shadow of representation, and could never inspire confidence in the people. He objected to the marriage, as he called it, between the President and the Senate, and the extraordinary powers conferred on the latter. He insisted that they would destroy any balance in the government, and would enable the President and the Senate, by mutually supporting and aiding each other, to accomplish what usurpations they please upon the rights and liberties of the people. He objected to the judiciary of the United States being so constructed and extended as to absorb and destroy the judiciaries of the several States, thereby rendering the administration of laws tedious, intricate, expensive, and unattainable by a great part of the community. He objected to the

Executive because the President of the United States has no constitutional counsel (a thing unknown in any safe and regular government); he will therefore be unsupported by proper information and advice; and will generally be directed by minions and favorites—or he will become a tool to the Senate—or a council of state will grow out of the principal officers of the great departments—the worst and most dangerous of all ingredients for such a council in a free country; for they may be induced to join in any dangerous and oppressive measures to shelter themselves, and prevent an inquiry into their own misconduct in office.

In a word, said Col. Mason, the Confederation is converted to one general consolidated government, which, from my best judgment of it, is one of the worst curses that can possibly befall a nation.

Such was George Mason—the champion of the States, and the author of the doctrine of State Rights. Many of the prophecies of this profound statesman are recorded in the fulfilments of history—many of the ill forebodings of the inspired orator are daily shaping themselves into sad realities. To the indomitable courage, Roman energy, and inspiring eloquence of Mason and of Henry, we are as much indebted for our independence, as to the sword of the warrior. To their wisdom and sagacity we owe the preservation and the future safety of the ship of state, which, without their forewarning, would have long since been dashed to pieces against the rocks and the quicksands that lay concealed in its pathway. While the eyes of many good and wise men were dazzled with the strength and briliancy of the young eagle, now pluming himself for a bold and arduous flight, they with keener vision saw the *poison under his wing*, and sought to extract it, lest, in his high career, he might shed pestilence and death on the country which it was his destiny to overshadow and protect.

CHAPTER IX.

EARLY POLITICAL ASSOCIATES.

In the foregoing chapters we may have gone more into detail, and dwelt more on collateral subjects than might appear consistent with a work of this kind. But it was necessary to give the reader a clue to the political opinions of John Randolph. No one can fail to ponder over those chapters, and study the character of those men we have briefly attempted to portray, and do justice to the subject of this memoir. He was bred up in the school of Mason and of Henry. His father-in-law, his uncles, his brother, and all with whom he associated, imbibed the sentiments of those great statesmen, shared their devotion to the principles and the independence of the Commonwealth of Virginia, and participated in all their objections to the new government. Randolph, as we have seen, was a constant attendant on the debates of the first Congress, which had devolved on it the delicate task of organizing the government, and setting its wheels in motion. A majority of the members in that body, from Virginia, belonged to the political school of Mason and of Henry. They owed their appointment to the influence of those men and the alarms excited in the public mind by their predictions. Many of them were the blood relations of John Randolph, and all of them his intimate friends. With these he associated. For the sage delights to take ingenuous youth by the hand, and address to his attentive ear words of truth and of wisdom. When Richard Henry Lee, and Grayson, and Bland, and Tucker, and Page, were seated around the domestic fireside, holding free and familiar discourse on those great questions involved in founding a Republic, we may well conceive that their young friend and kinsman was a welcome and an attentive listener to those high themes, teaching

> "What makes a nation happy and keeps it so,
> What ruins kingdoms and lays cities flat."

We may well conceive how his bosom dilated, and his eye kindled with unwonted fire, as they narrated the great battle of giants in the Convention, told of the many-sided wisdom of George Mason, who in majestic unaffected style better taught the solid rules of civil government than all the oratory of Greece and Rome, and spoke of the deep-toned awful eloquence of Patrick Henry, which rivalled the thunders that rolled over their heads, as he uttered his words of warning. From these familiar communings he daily repaired to Federal Hall, there to hang upon the bar of the House of Representatives, and with keen vision see enacted before him the fulfilment of the statesman's prophecy.

The great subject of taxation was the first to attract his attention. No sooner had Congress been organized, than they commenced, as he conceived, the work of oppression. The unlimited powers conferred on Congress to tax the people, excited the alarm of those who looked to the independence of the States as the only protection to liberty. They sought a modification of this power in the Convention. Failing there, they asked an amendment of the Constitution. But all their efforts to place restrictions on this all-absorbing power of government, were unavailing. The first exercise of it justified, in their opinion, the worst suspicions which had been excited as to its dangerous and oppressive tendency. They declared that no duty or tax had been imposed, that did not operate as a bounty to one section and a burden on another. While the import and tonnage bills were under discussion, Mr. Smith of South Carolina said, "that the States which adopted the Constitution, expected its administration would be conducted with a favorable hand. The manufacturing States wished the encouragement of manufactures; the maritime States the encouragement of ship building, and the agricultural States the encouragement of agriculture. Let us view the progress we have made in accommodating their interests :—We have laid heavy duties upon foreign goods to encourage domestic manufactures; we are now about to lay a tonnage duty, for the encouragement of commerce; but has any one step been taken to encourage the agricultural States? So far from it, that all that has been done operates against their interest: every duty we have laid will be heavily felt by South Carolina, while nothing has been done to assist or even encourage her or her agriculture." Mr. Tucker said: "I am opposed to high duties, because they tend to the oppression of certain citizens and States, in order to promote the benefit of other States and other classes of citizens." Mr. Bland laid it down as an incontrovertible truth, "that the agricultural interest is the permanent interest of this country, and therefore ought not to be sacrificed to any other." Mr. Jackson of Georgia, who had accustomed himself, as he said, to a blunt integrity of speech, that attested his sincerity, exclaimed: "They call to my mind a passage of Scripture, where a king, by the advice of inexperienced counsellors, declared to his people, 'my father did laden you with a heavy yoke, but I will add to your burdens.'" Follow those men through all their legislative career and it will be found, though history has given them little credit for it, that they steadily pursued one object as their polar star—resistance to the encroachments of power, and protection to the rights of the people.

The awful squinting towards monarchy which Henry saw in the Executive, made them particularly jealous of that department of government, and caused them to oppose every measure that might tend to increase its power or patronage. On the much mooted question, for example, of removal from office, they insisted that the Senate should be associated with the President. Mr. Bland was the first to give expression to opinions which have since been so often repeated, and the policy of which is still a question. He thought the power given by the Constitution to the Senate, respecting the appointments to office, would be rendered almost nugatory if the President had the power of removal. He thought it consistent with the nature of things, that the power which appointed, should remove; and would not object to a declaration in the resolution, that the President shall remove from office by and with the advice and consent of the Senate.

The bill to establish the Treasury Department contained a clause making it the duty of the Secretary, "to digest and report plans for the improvement and management of the revenue and for the support of public credit."

Mr. Page moved to strike out these words, observing, that to permit the Secretary to go farther than to prepare estimates, would be a dangerous innovation on the constitutional privilege of that house. It would create an undue influence within those walls, because members might be led by the deference commonly paid to men of abilities, who gave an opinion in a case they have thoroughly considered, to support the plan of the minister even against their own judgment. Nor would the mischief stop there. A precedent would be established, which might be extended until ministers of the government should be admitted on that floor, to explain and support the plans they had digested and reported, thereby laying a foundation for an aristocracy or a detestable monarchy.

Mr. Tucker seconded the motion of Mr. Page. He hoped the house was not already weary of executing and sustaining the powers vested in them by the Constitution; and yet the adoption of this clause would argue that they thought themselves less adequate than an individual to determine what burdens their constituents were able to bear. This was not answering the high expectations that had been formed of their exertions for the general good, or of their vigilance in guarding their own and the people's rights.

But nothing could equal the ferment and disquietude occasioned throughout the country by the proposition which came from the Senate, to confer titles on the President and other officers of government. The committee of the Senate reported, that it was proper to style the President *his highness the President of the United States of America, and Protector of their liberties.* In some of the newspapers the President was called *his highness the President General.* Some even went farther, and declared that as he represented the *majesty of the people,* he might even be styled "*His Majesty,*" without reasonable offence to republican ears. The Senate was denominated *most honorable,* and the same epithet was applied to the members of that body. For instance, it was published that *the most honorable* Rufus King and *the most honorable* Philip Schuyler were appointed senators. And when Mrs. Washington came to New-York, she was accompanied by the "lady of the most honorable Robert Morris." The representatives, and even the secretaries of the executive departments were favored with no higher title than honorable. This habit of conferring titles and drawing distinctions between the different departments of government, and extending those titles and distinctions to persons no way connected with the government, had become very common, and would unquestionably have grown into something worse, but for the debates called forth in the House of Representatives, and the indignation shown by the leading members of that body against such proceedings. "What, sir," said Mr. Tucker, "is the intention of this business? Will it not alarm our fellow-citizens? will it not give them just cause of alarm? Will they not say, that they have been deceived by the Convention that framed the Constitution? That it has been contrived with a view to lead them on by degrees to that kind of government which they have thrown off with abhorrence? Shall we not justify the fears of those who are opposed to the Constitution, because they considered it as insidious and hostile to the liberties of the people?"

"Titles, sir," said Mr. Page, "may do harm and have done harm. If we contend now for a right to confer titles, I apprehend the time will come when we shall form a reservoir for honor, and make our President the fountain of it. In such case may not titles do an injury to the Union? They have been the occasion of an eternal faction in the kingdom we were formerly connected with, and may beget like inquietude in America; for I contend, if you give the title, you must follow it with the robe and the diadem, and then the principles of your government are subverted."

Such were the men with whom John Randolph daily associated, such were the high-toned principles of liberty he was daily accustomed to hear. It was not from the reading of books in his closet, nor from second-hand that he acquired his knowledge of politics, and that extensive acquaintance with the leading characters of the country for which he was so remarkable, but from familiar intercourse with the statesmen and sages who laid the foundations of the government, and commenced the first superstructure of laws and precedents to serve as guides and examples to the statesmen who should come after them.

It was the fortune of this young man to behold the Government in its feeble beginnings, like the simple shepherds on the snowy Vesolo, gazing in the overshadowed fountain of the Po with his scanty waters.

Mirando al fonte ombroso
Il Po con pochi umori.

It was his destiny also never to lose sight of it, but to follow it through near half a century of various fortune, now enfeebled by war and faction, now strengthened and enlarged by new States and new powers. How like the Po! he receives as a sovereign the Adda and the Tessino in his course, how ample he hastens on to the sea, how he foams, how mighty his voice, and to him the crown is assigned.

Che 'l Adda, che 'l Tessino
Soverchia in suo cammimo,
Che ampio al Mar' s'affretta
Che si spuma, e si suona,
Che gli si da corona!

CHAPTER X.

THOMAS JEFFERSON.

In the winter of the year 1790–1, Philadelphia had again become, as in times of the old Continental Congress, the great centre of attraction. By a recent Act it had been made the seat of the Federal Government for *ten* years. The national legislature, adjourning the 12th of August in New-York, were to assemble the first Monday in December in the new Capitol. The papers and officers of all the Executive Departments were removed thither early in October, under the conduct of Col. Hamilton, the Secretary of the Treasury. The President returning from Mount Vernon about the 1st of December, took up his lodgings in a house belonging to Robert Morris, which had been hired and fitted up for the purpose. And Tuesday, the 7th of December, the 3d session of the 1st Congress was organized in the new Court House of the city, which had been tendered to the government by the town authorities. We find also our young friend, in this general removal, transferred to the city of Philadelphia. He took up his residence at No. 154 Arch-street, where he continued with short intervals, till the spring of 1794, when he returned to Virginia.

He was attached to the family of Edmund Randolph, the Attorney General of the United States—the same person his mother pointed him to as the model of an orator, worthy of his imitation. Edmund Randolph was a kinsman in the collateral line. He was the son of John Randolph, the King's Attorney General about the time of the Revolution.

"Mr. Randolph," says Wirt, "was, in person and manners, among the most elegant gentlemen in the colony, and in his profession one of the most splendid ornaments of the bar." He was the son of Sir John (Knight), who was the son of William of Turkey Island, the great American progenitor of the family. Edmund Randolph inherited many of the accomplishments of his father. But he was more showy than solid. He was also of a vacillating character; voting against the Constitution, then violent in its favor; striving at first to steer above the influence of party, he was at length ingulfed and swept away by its current. "Friend Edmund," said John Randolph years afterwards, "was like the aspen, like the chameleon, ever trembling, ever changing." We may, therefore, suppose that his influence over the mind and character of his pupil was not so great as that of another kinsman who was also a member of General Washington's Cabinet. We allude to Thomas Jefferson, the first cousin of John Randolph's father, and the intimate friend of his youth.

Mr. Jefferson had been abroad some years as Minister to France. Returning on a visit to America, he was invited by General Washington to take charge of the State Department. The invitation was accepted, and he was no soonor installed in office in the spring of 1790, than he became the head and leader of the Republican State-Rights Party, then struggling into existence. Is was not the exalted station alone, but other circumstances that forced him into this unenviable and critical position. The author of the doctrine of State Rights and its eloquent defender, George Mason, and Patrick Henry, were both in retirement. The latter had been offered a seat in the Senate at its organization, but declined. It was tendered to him the second time, on the death of Col. Grayson; he again declined on the ground that he was *too old to fall into those awkward imitations which have now become fashionable*, spoken in allusion to the levees of Mrs. Washington, and the etiquette observed in presentations at the Executive Mansion.

Richard Henry Lee was still in the Senate. He was the gentleman, the scholar, and the orator, but his thoughts ran too much in the smooth channel of established forms, his oratory too elaborate and polished, his disposition too indolent and unambitious to make him the fit leader of a party just coming into existence in a new era, with new thoughts, new principles, and an untried experiment before them. Thomas Jefferson was the man. The qualities of his mind, his education and previous course of life, fitted him to be the bold and intrepid pioneer of that untried course the people had entered upon.

His mind, not of the Platonic cast, was eminently perceptive. The abstract had no charms for him—the spiritual no existence. Devoted to the natural sciences, his metaphysics savored of materialism. Locke's Philosophy of the Senses bounded his conceptions of the human understanding. And the French Disciples, who pursued the doctrines of their master, to the legitimate consequence of sensualism and infidelity, were his chief authorities on all questions of morality and religion.

He was a bold, free thinker, bound to no school. "I never submitted the whole system of my opinions," says he, "to the creed of any party of men whatever, in religion, in philosophy, in politics, or in any thing else."

He was born in a country in the vigor of its youth, untrammelled by habit, and new in all its social relations. He was a child of the Revolution. His ardent temper was kindled by its stormy passions, and his bold intellect grasped the master idea of that great popular movement, which was unfettered freedom to mind, body, and estate. By him the law of primogeniture was destroyed in Virginia, religious freedom established, and universal liberty and equality proclaimed in the Declaration of Independence.

His ruling desire to strike the padlock from the mind, and the fetter from the limbs of mankind, was rather strengthened than abated by his long residence abroad under a despotic government. Being a man of letters and of taste, he was in intimate association with the great writers and master spirits that set the ball of the French Revolution in motion. In boldness and freedom of discussion they surpassed even himself. Speaking of them he says, "the writers of this country (France) now taking the field freely, and unrestrained, or rather revolted by prejudice, will rouse us all from the errors in which we have been hitherto rocked."

A witness of the assembling of the States General, May, 1789, he rejoiced in the downfall of the worn-out French monarchy, of which that was the signal; and was the friend and adviser of those who sought to rebuild on its ruins a freer government, with broader and deeper foundations. He heard the rights of man, the origin of government, the abuses and limitations of power, more freely discussed in the cafés and saloons of Paris than in the court-yards of Virginia.

When the usages and precedents of past times, and of other governments, were scornfully rejected, he saw our own proceedings pointed to as a model, and regarded with an authority like that of the Bible, *open to explanation, but not to question.*

Coming from those scenes of enthusiasm in which he so warmly participated; coming from a land where old prejudices and long established abuses were vanishing away; where the titles of feudalism and the privileges of despotism had been swept away in a night, and a great nation was rejoicing in the dawn of a new era of freedom; he expressed himself astonished to find his own government, which was regarded by others as a model and an example, possessed with a spirit that seemed to him so anti-republican.

This false direction of the government he mainly attributed to the financial schemes of Alexander Hamilton, Secretary of the Treasury.

It is well known that Hamilton advised a Constitution far different from the one adopted. His was a plan of consolidation, with a strong infusion of the aristocratic principle. Having experienced the imbecility of the Confederation, he did not believe the new government practicable. Without a successful example in history, he did not believe in the capacity of the people for self-government. Judging of mankind by the oppressed and degraded specimens of the army and of the Old Country, he did not duly appreciate the intelligent and manly character of his own countrymen, nor did he comprehend the nature of that government of specified powers and divided sovereignty which was the embodiment of their spirit and principles. Placed at the head of the Financial Department of a new government, he was surrounded with many difficulties. The war had left the Confederation and the States burdened with debt; and, exhausted of resources, it became his duty to devise means to resuscitate the one, and to pay off the other. With no experience in his own country, it was natural he should look to the successful example of others. He is considered a wise statesman, who is guided by established precedents, does not strike into unknown paths, but prudently follows the course that has been pursued before him. Judging him by this rule, it would be hard to say how far he ought to have acted otherwise than he did, without hazarding the censure of rashness. "The chief outlines of these plans," says he, in his report on public credit, "are not original, but it is no ill recommendation that they have been tried with success." He recommended that the debts which had been contracted by the several States in the War of Independence, and for which they were bound, as independent sovereignties, should be assumed by the new government,—that these assumed debts, and those contracted by the Confederation, amounting in all to some eighty millions of dollars, though greatly depreciated, and passed from the hands of the original owner, should be funded at their par value; the interest to be paid regularly by an excise and an impost duty, but the capital to be viewed in the light of an annuity, at the rate of six per centum per annum, redeemable at the pleasure of the government. He also advised the incorporation of a National Bank, as "an institution of primary importance to the prosperous administration of the finances, and of the greatest utility in the operations connected with the support of the public credit." In his Reports, he labors, at great length, to prove the utility of a well-funded National Debt. "It is a well known fact," says he, "that in countries where the national debt is properly funded, it answers most of the purposes of money. Transfers of stock, or public debt, are there equivalent to payments in specie; or, in other words, stock in the principal transactions of business passes current as specie. Trade is extended by it, because there is a larger capital to carry it on. Agriculture and manufactures are promoted by it for a like reason. The interest of money will be lowered by it, for this is always in ratio to the quantity of money, and to the quickness of circulation. From the combination of these effects, additional aids will be furnished to labor, to industry, and to arts of every kind. But these good effects of a public debt are only to be looked for when, by being well funded, it has acquired an adequate and stable value." These arguments, viewed in connection with the obvious tendency of his policy, led the enemies of Hamilton to declare that he regarded a national debt as a national blessing. Though this inference might be drawn from his doctrine and policy, he yet, in express terms, declared himself against it. "Persuaded as the Secretary is," says he, "that the proper funding of the present debt will render it a national blessing, yet he is so far from acceding to the proposition, in the latitude in which it is sometimes laid down, that 'public debts are public benefits'—a position inviting to prodigality, and liable to dangerous abuse—that he ardently wishes to see it incorporated, as a fundamental maxim, in the system of public credit of the United States, that the creation of debt should always be accompanied with the means of extinguishment." Had those schemes of Hamilton been laid before a British Parliament, they would have been viewed as clearly and ably expressed, and adopted as practicable and expedient; but with us, far other and higher considerations than those of expediency or practicability had to be weighed before the adoption of any measure. The British Parliament was omnipotent; the American Congress limited to a few, well defined, and specified powers. Parliament was only guided by precedent and usage; Congress were controlled by the words of a written Constitution. There was with us, therefore, a primary and fundamental inquiry to be made on all subjects of legislation, unknown to the British statesman. Whenever a measure is proposed, the first question should be, Is it constitutional? Is it authorized by the specified powers laid down in the Charter? or does it encroach on the reserved rights of the States? How does it affect the balance of power between the Executive, Legislative, and Judiciary Departments, or how does it operate on the morals and integrity of the people, upon whose purity depends the existence of a free government? Unless these preliminary questions are always honestly and fairly settled, it is obvious that a republican and a written Constitution cannot long be of any avail. But these considerations did not occur to the mind of Hamilton, in projecting his schemes of finance; they are never started, nor is the slightest allusion made to them in his Reports. He views every subject in its financial aspect, without regard to its political bearing on the new, peculiar, and delicately balanced institutions of his country. This was his great and fatal error. Thomas Jefferson perceived it, and battled against all his schemes as unconstitutional, destructive to the independence of the States, and corrupting to the rulers and to the people.

Posterity, therefore, in pronouncing judgment on these great rivals, would be constrained to say that Hamilton was the able financier, but Jefferson the profound statesman. While the one, with *averted countenance*, looked back upon the lights the world had already *passed;* the other, with prophetic vision, caught the rays of a new constellation, just dawning upon it. Gathering up in his capacious mind the tendency and influences of those feelings and opinions, recently developed in American history and institutions, Jefferson conceived a theory of government that embodied the growing sentiments of the people, and fulfilled their idea of what free Republic should be. He stands in relation to the Constitution as Aristotle to the Iliad; Homer wrote the poem, the philosopher deduced thence the rules of poetry. Mason and other sages made the Constitution, the statesman abstracted from it the doctrines of a federative, representative, republican government; and demonstrated that they alone are adapted to a wide-spread and diversified country, and suited to the genius of a free and enlightened people. Were the question asked, What has America done for the amelioration of mankind? the answer would not be found in her discoveries in science or improvements in art, but in her political philosophy, as conceived by Jefferson, and developed by his disciples. Though he was the acknowledged leader of what may be called the great American movement, he never spoke in public, and never wrote an essay for the newspapers. His great skill lay in infusing his sentiments into the minds of others by conversation, or correspondence, and making them the instruments of their propagation. Gathering about him the influential men of the new party, he imparted to them more comprehensive views of their own doctrines, and made them the enthusiastic defenders of those principles, the importance of which they had but dimly perceived. Over no one did he exert a greater influence than the young and ardent subject of this memoir. His connection with the family of Edmund Randolph, and his near relationship to Mr. Jefferson himself, brought him frequently within the sphere of that fascinating conversation, which was never spared in the propagation of his opinions. But John Randolph, although a youth, was not the character to yield a blind allegiance to any leader. The disciple differed widely in many doctrines from the master. The grounds of that difference may be found in the writings of another great statesman that begun about that time to take hold on his mind, and deeply impress his character. So great was their influence in after life, that the writings of Edmund Burke became the key to the political opinions of John Randolph. With him Edmund Burke was the great master of political philosophy.

CHAPTER XI.

SMALL BEGINNINGS—EDMUND BURKE—THOMAS PAINE.

Soon after the adjournment of Congress, the 4th of March, 1791, General Washington left the seat of government, and commenced his tour through the Southern States. The secretaries at the head of the different departments, were left as a kind of committee to conduct affairs in his absence.

About this time the public mind began to be greatly agitated not only by the wonderful events of the French Revolution, but the various speculations on those extraordinary occurrences that daily teemed from our own political press. The two leading productions, that were held up on both sides as setting forth most clearly and fully the views they respectively entertained, proceeded from men who were well and favorably known in America as the friends of liberty.

Edmund Burke had not only defended the colonies, in the British Parliament, against the unjust and oppressive taxation of the ministry, but had nobly vindicated their character and their motives. Throughout America his name was venerated and beloved. Well might he exclaim, " I love a manly, moral, regulated liberty as well as any man, be he who he will; and perhaps I have given as good proofs of my attachment to that cause in the whole course of my public conduct."

Thomas Paine was in America during the struggle of the Colonies for independence, and greatly aided the cause by his spirited and patriotic essays. It was generally conceded that in the darkest hour of the Revolution, when our armies were disbanded, and the hearts of the people despondent, he helped to rally the one, and to animate the other by his bold and patriotic appeals. The first men of the nation forgot his many vices, and cherished his person and his reputation in grateful remembrance of his valuable services.

General Washington was his constant correspondent while abroad, and while in America the house of Jefferson was his home.

In the great struggle for liberty which had now commenced on the other side of the Atlantic, these two champions of the cause took opposite sides. Burke expressed a hearty wish that France might be animated by a spirit of rational liberty, and provide a permanent body in which that spirit might reside, and an effectual organ by which it might act; but, he said, it was his misfortune to entertain great doubts concerning several material points in their late transactions. Paine, on the other hand, had no doubts; inflamed by the spirit of liberty, suddenly burst forth in the hearts of the French people, and dazzled by its brilliant achievements, he threw himself warmly into the popular cause without knowing or caring for the consequences.

The habits, education, social position, and natural temperament of the two men led to this wide difference. Burke had been long trained in the school of experience, Paine was the mere speculative theorist. The one judged of the future by the past, the other projected the future not from the solid ground of experience, but the hopeful theories of his own sanguine imagination. Burke was the cautious statesman, Paine the enthusiastic patriot.

The statesman cannot stand forward and give praise or blame to any thing which relates to human actions, and human concerns, on a simple view of the object, as it stands stripped of every relation, in all the nakedness and solitude of metaphysical abstraction. Circumstances which with some pass for nothing, give in reality to every political principle its distinguishing color, and discriminating effect. The circumstances are what render every civil and political scheme beneficial or noxious to mankind. Burke was guided by this great political maxim, the truth of which he had been taught by long experience. "I must be tolerably sure," said he, "before I venture publicly to congratulate men upon a blessing, that they have really received one. Flattery corrupts both the receiver and the giver; and adulation is not of more service to the people than to kings. I should therefore suspend my congratulations on the new liberty of France, until I was informed how it had been combined with government, with public force, with the discipline and obedience of armies, with the collection of an effective and well distributed revenue, with morality and religion, with solidity and property, with peace and order, with civil and social manners. The effect of liberty to individuals is, that they may do what they please; we ought to see what it will please them to do, before we risk congratulations, which may soon be turned into complaints. Prudence would dictate this in the case of separate insulated private men; but liberty, when men act in bodies, *is power*. Considerate people, before they declare themselves, will observe the use which is made of power; and particularly of so trying a thing as *new* power in *new* persons, of whose principles, tempers, and dispositions, they have little or no experience. Better to be despised for too anxious apprehensions, than ruined by too confident a security."

Paine, on the other hand, with all the inexperienced statesmen of France, followed a transcendental idea. He saw a great and powerful nation burst the oppressive and galling fetters of feudal ages, and proclaim themselves a free people. With all the lovers of mankind through the world, he lifted up his hands and clapped for joy. He beheld the event and rejoiced. But how this new power might be used by the new men, of whose principles, tempers, and dispositions he had no experience, he did not stop to inquire; he did not consult the maxims of prudence, or the principles of reason, but obeyed the impulses of a warm, enthusiastic and patriotic heart. Dictated by such a spirit, his writings might serve to animate, but not to instruct, to inspire a kindred enthusiasm, but to afford no nourishment to the hungering mind. They have perished with the occasion that gave them birth, while the immortal truths scattered as gems through the writings of Edmund Burke, are set like stars in the firmament for lights and guides to mankind.

Burke wrote his reflections on the Revolution in France in the month of May, 1790; and some short time thereafter gave them to the public. Paine's answer, entitled the Rights of Man, soon followed. The first and only copy of this latter production made its appearance in Philadelphia about the first of May, 1791; it was in the hands of Beckley. He lent the pamphlet to Mr. Jefferson, with a request, that when he should have read it, he would send it to Smith the printer, who wished it for re-publication. As he was a stranger to Smith, Mr. Jefferson, in sending the pamphlet, wrote him a note, stating why he, a stranger, had sent it, namely, that Mr.

Beckley had desired it; and, to take off a little of the dryness of a note, he added, that he was glad to find it was to be reprinted, that something would at length be publicly said against the political heresies which had lately sprung up amongst us, and that he did not doubt our citizens would rally again around the standard of Common Sense. In these allusions, Mr. Jefferson had reference to the *Discourses on Davila*, which had filled Fenno's paper for a twelvemonth without contradiction. Mr. Adams, the Vice-President, was the reputed author of those Discourses. When the reprint of Paine's pamphlet appeared, it had prefixed to it the note of Mr. Jefferson, which the printer had appended without giving him the slightest intimation of such an intention. In this unexpected way was the leader of the new and rising Democratic Party identified with the political doctrines of Paine, the principles of the French Revolution, and made publicly to avow his hostility to the political heresies which had lately sprung up in our own country. In addition to this, Paine's pamphlet, though without authority, had been dedicated to General Washington. The pamphlet, accompanied with these circumstances, produced a considerable excitement in the political circles of Philadelphia. Major Beckwith, an unofficial British agent, made it a subject of formal complaint to the private secretary of the President. He expressed surprise that the pamphlet should be dedicated to the President of the United States, and averred that it had received the unequivocal official sanction of the Secretary of State, not as Mr. Jefferson, but as the Secretary of State.

On the other hand, Mr. Adams was not slow in declaring his opposition to the sentiments expressed in Paine's pamphlet. In the most pointed manner, he expressed his detestation of the book and its tendency. "I was at the Vice-President's house," says the private secretary, writing to General Washington, "and while there, the Doctor and Mrs. Rush came in. The conversation turned on this book, and Dr. Rush asked the Vice-President what he thought of it. After a little hesitation, he laid his hand upon his breast, and said in a very solemn manner, 'I detest that book and its tendency, from the bottom of my heart.'"

Mr. Jefferson, in writing to the President about the same time, says: "Paine's answer to Burke's pamphlet begins to produce some squibs in our public papers. In Fenno's paper they are Burkites;

in the others, they are Painites. One of Fenno's was evidently from the author of the *Discourses on Davila.* I am afraid the indiscretion of a printer has committed me with my friend Mr. Adams, for whom, as one of the most honest and disinterested men alive, I have a cordial esteem, increased by long habits of concurrence in opinion in the days of his republicanism; and ever since his apostasy to hereditary monarchy and nobility, though we differ, we differ as friends should do.

"Mr. Adams will unquestionably take to himself the charge of political heresy, as conscious of his own views of drawing the present government to the form of the English constitution, and, I fear, will consider me as meaning to injure him in the public eye. I certainly never made a secret of my being anti-monarchical, and anti-aristocratical; but I am sincerely mortified to be thus brought foward on the public stage, where to remain, to advance, or to retire, will be equally against my love of silence and quiet, and my abhorrence of dispute."

We have given the minute history of this transaction, not only because of its important bearing on the subject of this memoir, but because it traces up to the fountain head one of the many streams which, flowing together in after times, have conspired to swell the mighty tide of party spirit that now sweeps through the land.

John Randolph was in Philadelphia during this time; participated in the interest and excitement of the occasion; heard the discussions in the various circles into which he was freely admitted; saw people become inflamed with the Anglomania or the Gallomania, and arrange themselves under the banners of their respective champions as Burkites or Painites, according as they were inclined to admire the British Constitution, or the more free and levelling doctrines of the French Revolution, and plainly perceived that that great event was destined to swallow up every minor consideration, and to give character and complexion to the politics of his own country. But while he was a democratic republican, a follower of Jefferson in all that pertained to his political doctrines and interpretation of the Constitution, pre-eminently a disciple of the Mason and Henry school of States' rights, yet he did not become a Painite in the sense that term was used by Mr. Jefferson. In the expressive language of Governor Tazewell, he could not bear Tom Paine; he ad mired Burke, though himself a jacobin! While he rejoiced in the overthrow of despotism by the French people, he could not fail to perceive that they were better fitted to destroy tyrants than obey the laws; and hastened to learn those lessons of wisdom that fell from the lips of the great master of political philosophy, who, from the few events already transpired, foretold with the clearness of a Hebrew prophet, the wretched end to which they were hastening. We regard this as a most remarkable fact in the history of that young man. The design of Burke was eminently conservative. He saw the consequences of a dissemination of French revolutionary doctrines among the English people; his purpose was to shut out from England what the kings of Europe called the *French evil.*

With this design, he gives a most beautiful and masterly exposition of the British Constitution, from Magna Charta to the declaration of rights. He calls it an entailed inheritance, derived to us (the people of England) from our forefathers, and to be transmitted to our posterity; as an estate specially belonging to the people of this kingdom—an inheritable crown—an inheritable peerage; and a House of Commons, and a people inheriting privileges, franchises, and liberties from a long line of ancestors.

With the same masterly hand he makes bare the composition of the French National Assembly—the characters that compose it—the few acts they had already performed during a single year; and then predicts, from these elements of calculation, that France will be wholly governed by the agitators in corporations, by societies in the towns formed of directors in assignats, and trustees for the sale of church lands, attorneys, agents, money-jobbers, speculators, and adventurers, composing an ignoble oligarchy, founded on the destruction of the crown, the church, the nobility, and the people. Here end all the deceitful dreams and visions of this equality, and the rights of man. In the *Serbonian bog* of this base oligarchy, they are all absorbed, sunk, and lost for ever. The present form of the French commonwealth, he says, cannot remain; but before its final settlement it may be obliged to pass, as one of our poets says, "through great varieties of untried being;" and in all its transmigrations to be purified by fire and blood!

It is not surprising that such a book as this should be seized upon by the partisans of England, and held up as a justification of their doctrine that the British Constitution, with all its corruptions, was the best model of a government the world ever saw; and as a vindication of the abhorrence they had expressed for the doctrines of the French Revolution, and their tendency.

But it is a matter of no little surprise that a mere stripling, a youth of some eighteen or twenty years of age, himself a republican and a jacobin, with an ardent temperament and a lively imagination, should have the independence to ponder over the pages of a book condemned by his associates; the judgment to perceive its value, and the discrimination to leave out that which peculiarly belonged to England or to France, without being inflamed by its arguments, and to appropriate to himself those rich treasures of wisdom to be found in its pages: the massive ingots of gold that constitute the greater part of that magnificent monument of human intellect. As we have said, the writings of Edmund Burke are the key to the political opinions of John Randolph.

In after life, as he grew in experience, those opinions became more and more assimilated to the doctrines of his great master.

His position in society, his large hereditary possessions, his pride of ancestry, his veneration for the commonwealth of Virginia, her ancient laws and institutions; his high estimation of the rights of property in the business of legislation,—all conspired to shape his thoughts, and mould them in matters pertaining to domestic polity after the fashion of those who have faith in the old, the long-established, and the venerable. No one can trace his course in the Virginia Convention, or read his speeches, which had a remarkable influence on the deliberations of that body, without perceiving that his deep and practical wisdom is of the same stamp, and but little inferior to the great Gamaliel at whose feet he was taught.

CHAPTER XII.

YOUTHFUL COMPANIONS.

We are not to suppose that a youth, in the joyous hours of his dawning faculties, devoted his time, or any great portion of it, to the society of sober statesmen, or to the grave study of political science. Far other were the associates and companions of John Randolph during his residence in the Quaker city, even at that day renowned for its intelligent, polished, gay, and fashionable society.

With occasional visits to Virginia, and a short residence of a few weeks in Williamsburg during the autumn of 1793, Philadelphia, till the spring of 1794, continued to be his place of abode. His companions were Batte, Carter, Epps, Marshall, and Rose of Virginia; Bryan of Georgia, and Rutledge of South Carolina. Most of these were young men of wealth, education, refined manners, high sense of honor, and of noble bearing. John W. Epps afterwards became a leading member of Congress, married the daughter of Mr. Jefferson, and in 1813 was the successful rival of Randolph on the hustings before the people. Joseph Bryan likewise in a short time became a leading character in Georgia, was a member of Congress from that State, and to the day of his untimely death continued to be the bosom friend of the associate of his youth. Most of the others, though unknown to fame, adorned the social sphere in which they moved, and were noble specimens of the unambitious scholar and the gentleman. Thomas Marshall, the brother of the Chief Justice, and father of Thomas Marshall, the late member of Congress, is still living. He is a man of extraordinary powers, and great learning: his wit and genial humor are not to be surpassed. Those who knew them well agree that his natural talents surpass those of his late illustrious brother, the Chief Justice. Robert Rose was a man of genius; he married the sister of Mr. Madison, and might have risen to any station in his profession (which he merely studied as an ornament), in letters, or in politics, that he aspired to; but, like too many in his sphere and station in society, he lived a life of inglorious ease, and wasted his gifts, like the rose its sweets, on the desert air. With such companions, we may readily suppose there was fun and frolic enough; but nothing low or mean, or vulgar or sordid, in all their intercourse. The correspondence of some of those young men at that period is now before the writer. It is very clear that Randolph was the centre of attraction in that joyous circle of boon companions. And while there can be no doubt that they indulged in all the license allowed at that time to young men of their rank and fortune, yet he passed through that critical period of life without the contamination of a single vice. Though many years afterwards, he said, "I know by fatal experience the fascinations of a town life, how they estrange the mind from its old habits and attachments." Bryan, in February, 1794, wishes him all the happiness that is attendant on *virtue and regularity*. Again, in speaking of one of their companions, to whom Randolph had become strongly attached, he expresses a hope that he may prove worthy of the friendship,—"possessing as you do," says he, "a considerable knowledge of mankind, your soul would not have knit so firmly to an unworthy object."

Most of those young men were students of medicine. Randolph also attended with them several courses of lectures in anatomy and physiology—sciences that are indispensable not only to a professional, but to a liberal and gentlemanly education. We do not learn, as many have supposed, that he studied law at that time in the office of his relation, Edmund Randolph, the Attorney General. Two years after leaving Philadelphia, Bryan writes that he is rejoiced to hear his friend has serious thoughts of *attacking the law*. He tells us himself that he never, after Theodorick broke up his regular habits at New-York, devoted himself to any systematic study, except for the few weeks he was in Williamsburg, in the autumn of 1793. So we conclude that he never made the law a matter of serious study, certainly never with the view of making it a profession.

In April, 1794, he returned to Virginia. In June he was twenty-one years of age, and then took upon himself the management of his patrimonial estates, which were heavily encumbered with a British debt. Matoax was still in the family, but was sold about this time for *three thousand pounds sterling*, to pay off a part of the above debt. The mansion house has since been burnt, but the same estate now would not bring three hundred dollars, although it is within three miles of Petersburg.

Richard Randolph, the elder brother, lived at Bizarre, an estate on the Appomatox, about ninety miles above Petersburg. It is near Farmville, but on the opposite side of the river, in Cumberland county. John made his brother's house his home, while his own estate, called Roanoke, lay about thirty miles south on the Roanoke river, in the county of Charlotte.

CHAPTER XIII

RICHARD RANDOLPH.

With Richard the reader has already formed some slight acquaintance. In 1789 he married Judith Randolph, the daughter of Thomas Mann Randolph, of Tuckahoe. Judith was a relation in both the direct and collateral lines. Her father, Thomas Mann, was the son of William, who was the son of Thomas of Tuckahoe, the son of William, the first founder of the family in Virginia. Her mother was Anne Cary, the daughter of Mary Cary, who was the daughter of the first Richard of Curles, and the sister of the second Richard of Curles, the grandfather of Richard her husband. This lady was remarkable for her great strength of mind, for her many virtues, and high accomplishments. Richard was regarded as the most promising young man in Virginia. His talents were only surpassed by his extraordinary goodness of character.

Let his own grateful acknowledgments to his father-in-law, Judge Tucker, speak for him. "Accept," says he, "once more, my beloved father, the warmest effusions of a heart that knows but one tie superior to that which binds him to the best of parental friends. When I look back to those times wherein I was occupied in forming my mind for the reception of professional knowledge, and indeed to whatever period of my life I cast my eyes, something presents itself to remind me of the source whence sprung all my present advantages and happiness. Something continually shows my father to me in the double light of parent and friend. While I recognize all the attention I have received from him, all the precepts inculcated by him; while I feel that if I have any virtuous emotions or pleasures, they are all derived from him, that to him I owe whatever capacity I possess of being useful in the world I am in—while all these reflections are crowding into my mind, I feel a sensation that all are strangers to, who have not known such a friend. The feelings which arise from a sense of gratitude for the kindness and friendship of my father—the tender affection inspired by his virtues and his love, are as delightful to my soul, as the knowledge of being obliged by those we despise is painful and oppressive." A grateful heart obliged by a worthy and beloved object, as Milton finely says, "*by owing owes not*, but finds itself at once indebted and discharged." And again:—"The time is now at hand, when I hope you will be relieved from all further anxiety, and the embarrassments you have too long endured in the management of our patrimony; when my brother and myself will take on ourselves our own troubles, and when the end of your administration of our little affairs will furnish the world with one complete and perhaps solitary example, shall I only say, of an unerring guardian of infant education and property? An example, I glory in boasting it, of an adopted father surpassing in parental affection, and unremitted attention to his adopted children, all the real fathers who are known to any one. I can most sincerely and truly declare, that in no one moment of my whole life, have I ever felt the loss in the least trifle."

One of the debts owing by the father to creditors in England, was a simple open account, that might have been easily avoided, as it was not binding on the estate devised to the sons. But Richard wrote to Judge Tucker, "I urge the propriety, indeed necessity, of paying the open account which my mother always said was recognized by my father as a true one, and ought therefore honestly to be discharged. For myself I can never bear the idea of a just debt due from my father to *any* one, remaining unsatisfied while I have property of his, firmly convinced as I am that he had no equitable right, whatever power the law may have given him, of devising me land or any thing else, to the loss of any of his just creditors, and that under this conviction, it will be equally iniquitous in me to retain such property, suffering these just claims to pass unnoticed."

Nor did this noble-minded man stop here in his high sense of right and justice. He again writes to his late guardian:—"With regard to the division of the estate, I have only to say, that I want not a single negro for any other purpose than his immediate liberation. I consider every individual thus unshackled as the source of future generations, not to say nations of freemen; and I shudder when I think that so insignificant an animal as I am, is invested with this monstrous, this horrid power. For the land I care not a jot. I am ready to yield all my claim to it. I am ready to yield Matoax or its profits, and all of my Prince Edward and Cumberland land, except a bare support, rather than see those wretches sacrificed at the shrine of unjust and lawless power."

Richard was bred to the profession of law, but never could be induced to engage in the practice. Nothing but necessity, he declared, could overcome his disinclination. It was not the fatigue and disgust that repelled him so much as the chicane and low cunning, which his observation led him to conclude were the essential qualifications of a county court lawyer. "What inducement," exclaimed he, "have I to leave a happy and comfortable home to search for bustle, fatigue and disappointment? I have a comfortable subsistence, which is enough to make me happy."

The family circle was composed of Richard, his wife, Nancy the sister of Mrs. Randolph, John (Theodorick had died in February, 1791), and Mrs. Anna Bland Dudley and her children. Mrs. Dudley was the daughter of Mrs. Eaton, the sister of John Randolph's mother. They lived in North Carolina. Her husband was unfortunate, had died and left his family poor and dependent on their friends. Richard went himself to North Carolina, brought Mrs. Dudley and her children to Virginia, and gave them an asylum under the hospitable roof of Bizarre.

John did not confine himself much to home or business. He kept up a regular correspondence with many of his old companions; amused himself with his dog and gun, and visited from place to place among his friends. As a specimen of his wanderings, we give the following memorandum made by himself:

November, 1795.

Monday, 30.—Bizarre to D. Meade's.

December.

Tuesday, 1.—Capt. Murray's.
3.—Richmond.
Wednesday, 9.—Petersburg.
Thursday, 17.—Left Petersburg to Jenito.
Friday, 18.—To F. Archer's and D. Meade's.
Saturday, 19.—D. Meade's to Bizarre; received letter from Rutledge.
Sunday, 20.—Roanoke.
Sunday, 27.—From Roanoke to Bizarre.
Tuesday, 29.—To Roanoke.
Thursday, 31.—To Bizarre.
January, '96, New-Year's day at Bizarre.
Saturday, 2.—To Major Eggleston's.
Sunday, 3.—Colonel Botts.
Monday, 4.—Petersburg.
Friday, 15.—At Jenito Bridge.
Saturday, 16.—At D. Meade's. } rain.
Sunday, 17.—At D. Meade's. }

CHAPTER XIV.

VISIT TO CHARLESTON AND GEORGIA.

His old friends, Bryan and Rutledge, had for some time been urging him to pay them a visit. Bryan directed his letters to "Citizen John Randolph, of Charlotte county, Virginia," and says, "I am happy to hear you are settled in a healthy part of Virginia, but I am almost inclined to think my friend premature in settling so early, as you will in a great measure be deprived of that freedom you know so well how to enjoy." He then urges him to visit Georgia. "You will find me on the sea-coast," says he, "and as you bribe me with a pipe, I can promise in return best Spanish segars and the best of liquors—good horses, deer-hunting in perfection—good companions, that is to say, not merely bottle crackers, Jack, but good, sound, well-informed Democrats."

This long-expected visit was made in the spring of 1796. On the back of a letter received from Rutledge, he lays out the programme of his journey, with the various distances and stages, from Bizarre to Charleston; then concludes the memorandum with these words: "Where I hope to embrace the friend of my youth; the sight of whom will ten thousand times repay this tedious journey."

E. S. Thomas, in his Reminiscences of the last Sixty-five Years, printed at Hartford, in 1840, thus speaks of him: "On a bright sunny morning, early in February, 1796, might have been seen entering my bookstore in Charleston, S. C., a fine-looking, florid complexioned old gentleman, with hair white as snow, which, contrasted with his own complexion, showed him to have been a free liver, or *bon-vivant* of the first order. Along with him was a tall, gawky-looking flaxen-haired stripling, apparently of the age from sixteen to eighteen, with a complexion of a good parchment color, beardless chin, and as much assumed self-consequence as any two-footed animal I ever saw. This was John Randolph. I handed him from the shelves volume after volume, which he tumbled carelessly over, and handed back again. At length he hit upon something that struck his fancy. My eye happened to be fixed upon his face at the moment, and never did I witness so sudden, so perfect a change of the human countenance. That which before was dull and heavy, in a moment became animated and flushed with the brightest beams of intellect. He stepped up to the old gray-headed gentleman, and, giving him a thundering slap on the shoulder, said, "Jack, look at this!!" I was young, then, but I never can forget the thought that rushed upon my mind at the moment, which was that he was the most impudent youth I ever saw. He had come to Charleston to attend the races. There was then living in Charleston a Scotch Baronet, by the name of Sir John Nesbit, with his younger brother Alexander, of the ancient house of Nesbits, of Dean Hall, some fifteen miles from Edinburgh. Sir John was a very handsome man, and as 'gallant gay Lothario' as could be found in the city. He and Randolph became intimate, which led to a banter between them for a race, in which each was to ride his own horse. The race came off during the same week, and Randolph won; some of the ladies exclaiming at the time, 'though Mr. Randolph had won the race, Sir John had won their hearts.' This was not so much to be wondered at, when you contrasted the elegant form and graceful style of riding of the Baronet, with the uncouth and awkward manner of his competitor."

From Charleston, Randolph pursued his journey into Georgia, and spent several months with his friend Bryan.

We cannot doubt that these young men enjoyed themselves in the manner that young men usually enjoy themselves on such occasions. Bryan, in his subsequent letters, frequently alludes to some amusing incident that occurred during the sojourn of his friend in Georgia. "My eldest brother," says he, "still bears a friendly remembrance of the *rum ducking* you gave him."

But the all-absorbing subject in Georgia, at the time of Randolph's visit, was the Yazoo question.

On the 7th day of February, 1795, the Legislature of Georgia passed an act authorizing the sale of four tracts of land, therein described, and comprehending the greater part of the country west of the Alabama river, to four companies, called the Georgia, the Georgia Mississippi, the Upper Mississippi, and the Tennessean Companies, for which they were to pay five hundred thousand dollars. The land contained within the boundaries of the several companies was estimated by the claimants at *forty millions* of acres. The sale of a country so extensive, for a sum so far below its value, excited immediate and universal indignation in the State of Georgia. The motives of the Legislature were questioned and examined. Their corruption was established on the most indisputable evidence. Upwards of sixty-four depositions were taken, that developed a scene of villany and swindling unparalleled in the history of any country. On comparing a list of the names of the companies with the names of the persons who voted for the land, it appeared that all the members in the Senate and House of Representatives of Georgia, who voted in favor of the law, were, with one single exception, interested in and parties to the purchase. Every member who voted for the law received either money or land for his vote. The guardians of the rights of the people united with swindlers, defrauded their constituents, sold their votes, betrayed the delegated trust reposed in them, and basely divided among themselves the lands of the people of Georgia. This flagrant abuse of power, this enormous act of corruption, was viewed with abhorrence by every honest man. The press through the country burst out in a blaze of indignation. All the grand juries of the State (except in two counties, where there were corrupt majorities of Yazoo men,) presented this law as a public robbery, and a deliberate fraud. The Convention which met in the month of May, 1795, at Louisville, was crowded with petitions from every part of the State, which, by an order of the Convention, was referred to the succeeding Legislature. This Legislature was elected solely with reference to that question. Repeal or no repeal, Yazoo and anti-Yazoo, was the only subject canvassed before the people. On the 30th of January, 1796, an act was passed, with only three dissenting voices, declaring the usurped act of February, 1795, void, and expunging the same from the public records. At a subsequent period, this expunging act was engrafted on the Constitution, and made a fundamental law of the land.

Randolph arrived in Georgia in the midst of this excitement, and shared with his friends their indignation at that flagrant act of corruption on the part of the agents of the people. The famous Yazoo claim, which afterwards made such a noise in Congress, was preferred by the New England Mississippi Land Company, to recover from Congress the value of the lands thus fraudulently obtained. It was in opposition to this application, that Randolph immortalized himself in speeches that will stand the test of time, and of criticism the severest scrutiny. It was among those who had been betrayed, in the midst of the people who were burning with shame at the insult and indignity offered them, that he caught the fire of inspiration that winged his words with such a withering power as to drive from the halls of Congress for more than ten years, so long as he had a seat there, all those who were interested in the nefarious scheme.

John Randolph returned from this visit of friendship, and arrived in Virginia about the first of July. He was destined to experience a shock such as he had never felt before. His brother Richard died the 14th of June, on Tuesday, about 4 o'clock in the morning; such was the minute record made of it himself. This sudden and unexpected calamity crushed him down.

Next to the death of his mother this was the severest blow he had ever received. His mother died when he was a child. Though mournful, yet sweet was the memory of her image, associated with those days of innocence and brightness. But the strong bonds of fraternal affection in grown up men, were now torn asunder; the much prized treasure of a brother's love is suddenly taken from him, leaving no pleasant memories to soothe the pain of so deep a wound. His best friend and counsellor, the first born of his father's house, its pride, and cherished representative, hurried away in his absence to an untimely grave—he not present to receive his last breath, and to close his lifeless eyes. He never recovered from this stroke. The anguish of his heart was as fresh on the fiftieth anniversary of the birthday of that brother, as when first he experienced the desolation made in the domestic circle at Bizarre by the hand of death. How touching is the following simple note addressed to his brother, Henry St. George Tucker, many, many years after this sad event! "Dear Henry:—Our poor brother Richard was born 1770. He would have been fifty-six years old on the 9th of this month. I can no more. J. R. of R." In the deep solitude of his heart, the only green spot was the memory of the days of his youth.

Few events exerted a greater influence over the mind and character of John Randolph than the death, the untimely and sudden death, of his brother. Richard, as we have said, was the most promising man in Virginia. John Thompson, himself a man of brilliant genius, nipped also in the blooming, thus writes: "Grief like yours, my dear friend, is not to be alleviated by letters of condolence. The anguish of hearts like yours cannot be mitigated by the maxims of an unfeeling and unnatural philosophy. Let such consolation be administered to the insensible being, who mourns without sorrow, whose tears fall from a sense of decorum, and whose melancholy ceases the instant fashion permits. Let some obdurate moralist instruct this selfish being, that the death of a friend is not a misfortune, and that sensibility is weakness. Nothing but sympathy ought to be offered to you. Accept that offering from one of your sincerest friends. My heart was long divided between you and your brother. His death has left a void which you will occupy. I will fondly cherish his memory. Painful as the retrospect is, I will often contemplate his virtues and his talents. Never shall I perform that holy exercise without feeling new virtue infused into my soul. To you I will give that friendship, of which he can no longer be sensible. Take it, and return it if you can. I cannot write your brother's eulogium. Although his fame was only in the dawn, although like a meteor he perished as soon as he began to dazzle, I cannot sound his praise. His life would be a pathetic tale of persecuted genius and oppressed innocence. The fictions of romance cannot present so affecting a story. When his country was preparing to do him ample justice, and to recompense his sufferings by her warmest admiration,

Death marked him for his victim. Modern degeneracy had not reached him.

"Nervous eloquence and dauntless courage fitted him to save his sinking country. He has left no memorial of his talents behind. He was born to enlighten posterity, but posterity will not hear of him.

"O Providence, thy dispensations are dark! We cannot comprehend them! His amiable wife, his children—but here my heart begins to bleed—I cannot go on."

CHAPTER XV.

AT HOME.

John Randolph, now became the head of a large household, was suddenly thrown into a position of great responsibility. His own estate was very large; so was his brother's—and both were heavily encumbered with a British debt, contracted by the father many years before.

Richard liberated his slaves. This was a mark of his great benevolence of feeling and nobleness of character. But it proved in the end to be a mistaken philanthropy. Left in the country where they had been slaves, those negroes soon became idle and profligate vagabonds and thieves; a burthen to themselves, and a pest to the neighborhood. The family at Bizarre consisted of Mrs. Randolph, her two infant children, St. George and Tudor, Mrs. Dudley and her children, Nancy and John Randolph. For nearly fifteen years, till Bizarre was destroyed by fire, he continued at the head of the household. Though twenty-three years of age at the death of his brother, he had the appearance of a youth of sixteen, and was not grown. He grew a full head taller after this period.

His extreme sensibility had been deeply touched—the quick irritability of his temper exasperated by the tragic events of his family. A father's face he had never seen, save what his lively imagination would picture to itself from the lines of a miniature likeness which he always wore in his bosom. The fond caresses of a tender mother, *who alone knew him*, were torn from him in his childhood. The second brother had died in his youth; and now the oldest, the best, the pride and hope of the family, after years of suffering and persecution, just as he had triumphed over calumny and oppression, was suddenly called away. We may well imagine how deep, how poignant was his grief, when thirty years thereafter, in the solitude of his hermitage at Roanoke, his lively fancy brought back those early scenes with all the freshness of recent events, and caused him to exclaim with the Indian Chief, who had been deprived of all his children by the white man's hand—"Not a drop of Logan's blood—father's blood except St. George, the most bereaved and pitiable of the step-sons of nature!"

His room at Bizarre was immediately under the chamber of Mrs. Dudley. She never waked in the night that she did not hear him moving about, sometimes striding across the floor, and exclaiming, "*Macbeth hath murdered sleep!* Macbeth hath murdered sleep!" She has known him to have his horse saddled in the dead of night, and ride over the plantation with loaded pistols.

His natural temper became more repulsive; he had no confidential friend, nor would any tie, however sacred, excuse inquiry. Why should it? for who can minister to a mind diseased, or pluck from the heart its rooted sorrow? Why then expose, even to friendship's eye, the lacerated wounds that no balm can cure?

He grew more restless than ever, though his home had every external arrangement to make it agreeable. Hear him describe it: "Mrs. Randolph, of Bizarre, my brother's widow, was, beyond all comparison, the nicest and best housewife that I ever saw. Not one drop of water was ever suffered to stand on her sideboard, except what was in the pitcher; the house, from cellar to garret, and in every part, as clean as hands could make it; and every thing as it should be to suit even my fastidious taste. Never did I see or smell any thing to offend my senses, or my imagination." Those who lived there had been taught in the school of affliction. Chastened and subdued by their own sorrows, they had learned to feel for the misfortunes of others. That home, which could not fill the aching void of its youthful master's heart, or soothe the earnest longings of his wounded soul, was made the delightful retreat and asylum of the distressed and the unfortunate. There could they find sympathy and encouragement.

To escape from the burden and pain of his own thoughts, John Randolph often fled to his friends in distant parts of the country. For the next three years he was frequently found at the residence of his father-in-law, in Williamsburg. He often visited Mr. Wickham, who lived in the same city. That gentleman had taken a great liking to him. He was the agent of the British creditors, who held a mortgage on the Randolph estates. His forbearance and indulgence were highly appreciated by him on whom the whole burthen of payment had now fallen. He returned this act of kindness by an ardent affection for the man, and a high admiration of his character. He has said, "John Wickham was my best of friends without making any professions of friendship for me; and the best and wisest man I ever knew except Mr. Macon."

When interrogated by Mr. Wickham as to what he had been doing, Governor Tazewell, who was his youthful companion on those visits, says his answer was—*Nothing, sir, nothing!* Yet he showed that he had been reading, and that he had digested well what he had read. The conversation was generally on the politics of the day—the French Revolution, and Burke, which was his political Bible.

That he pursued no systematic course of reading at this time is certain. Mrs. Dudley says his habits of study one could not ascertain, as he was never long enough in one place to study much. She has frequently heard him lament that he was fond of light reading—has known him to seat himself by the candle, where she and Mrs. Randolph were knitting, turn over the leaves of a book carelessly, like a child, without seeming to read, and then lay it down and tell more about it than those who had studied it. He had a fine taste for music, but it was uncultivated. "I inherited from your grandmother," says he, writing to his niece, Mrs. Bryan, "an exquisite ear, which has never received the slightest cultivation. This is owing in a great measure to the low estimate that I saw the fiddling, piping gentry held in when I was young; but partly to the torture that my poor brother used to inflict upon me, when essaying to learn to play upon the violin, now about forty years ago. I have a taste for painting, but never attempted drawing. I had read a great deal upon it and had seen a few good pictures before I went to England: there I astonished some of their connoisseurs as much by the facility with which I pointed out the hand of a particular master, without reference to the catalogue (I never mistook the hand of Van Dyke—I had seen specimens of his and Reuben's pencil, and some other great masters, at Mr. Geo. Calvert's, near Bladensburg—they were since sold in Europe), as by my exact knowledge of the geography, topography and statistics of the country.

"For poetry I have had a decided taste from my childhood, yet never attempted to write one line of it. This taste I have sedulously cultivated. I believe that I was deterred from attempting poetry by the verses of Billy Mumford, and some other taggers of rhyme, which I heard praised (I allude to epistles in verse, written at 12 or 13 years old), but secretly in my heart despised. I also remember to have heard some poetry of Lord Chatham and of Mr. Fox, which I thought then, and still think, to be unworthy of their illustrious names—and before Horace had taught me that 'neither gods, nor men, nor booksellers' stalls could endure middling poetry,' I thought none but an inspired pen should attempt the task."

Among the youthful companions that he most valued and cherished about this time, were John Thompson, the author of the letter in a preceding chapter, and his brother William Thompson. The following is a memorandum in his own handwriting, and found among his papers: "John Thompson, Jr., son of John and Anne Thompson, of Sussex, born 3d Nov. 1776, died 25th January, 1799. He was the author of Graccus, Cassius, Curtius, written on the subject of American politics—*speak they for him.*" And surely for one of his age they were remarkable productions, especially the latter addressed to General Marshall, afterwards Chief Justice, then a candidate for Congress on the Federal side of politics. William Thompson was born the 20th of August, 1778. In the year 1798 he and his friend John Randolph undertook a pedestrian tour to the Mountains, to visit Richard Kidder Meade, a relation of the latter. They started from Bizarre, each with a small bundle on a cane. Mrs. Dudley was an eye-witness of their departure and of their return. She was informed that they performed the whole journey on foot. They both returned in fine health and spirits. Soon after this Thompson went to Europe, wandered over Germany, studied medicine, then abandoned it for the law, returned to Virginia, went on foot to Canada in the fall of 1801. Having squandered his patrimony, falling into dissipated habits, with a genius equally as brilliant, though far more eccentric than his deceased brother, he was rapidly throwing away the great gifts of nature, and sinking into a hopeless vagabond and outcast, when his friend Randolph took him by the hand, brought him to Bizarre, made it his home, encouraged him, and cherished him with the affection of a brother so long as he could be persuaded to remain in Virginia. With him hereafter the reader will become more intimately acquainted. Writing from Bizarre to Randolph, in his absence, he says: "My dear brother—Since you left us I have been deeply engaged in what you advised. I have reviewed the Roman and the Grecian History. I have done more; I have reviewed my own. Believe me, Jack, that I am less calculated for society than almost any man in existence. I am not, perhaps, a vain fool, but I have too much vanity, and I am too susceptible of flattery. I have that fluency which will attract attention and receive applause from an unthinking multitude. Content with my superiority, I should be too indolent to acquire real, useful knowledge. I am stimulated by gratitude, by friendship, and by love, to make exertions now. I feel confident that you will view my foibles with a lenient eye—that you will see me prosper, and in my progress be delighted."

CHAPTER XVI.

CANDIDATE FOR CONGRESS—HISTORY OF THE TIMES.

We have now approached an important period in the life of John Randolph. In the winter of 1799, in the twenty-sixth year of his age, he was announced as a candidate for Congress in the district which afterwards became so celebrated as the Charlotte district.

John Thompson, writing to his brother, then in Europe, says, "Our friend John Randolph *offers* for Congress, and will probably be elected. He is a brilliant and noble young man. He will be an object of admiration and terror to the enemies of liberty." In 1831, in the last political speech he ever made, he is reported to have said that when he commenced his political career he had waged a warfare, remarkable for its fierceness—he had almost said for its ferocity—against certain principles, and those who advocated them. When he drew his sword to carry on that warfare, he had thrown away the scabbard, and as he never asked for quarter, so he did not always give it. It becomes necessary, therefore, in order to understand his position, to give a brief and general outline of the most important events which had occurred up to the time that he made his appearance on the political stage. We have already seen that the source of party division is to be traced to the Federal Convention; that those elements of discord which have continued to agitate the country up to this day, had their birth in the cradle of the Constitution. Patrick Henry and George Mason were the fathers of the doctrine of States-rights. At a subsequent period, under the auspices of Thomas Jefferson, those doctrines were digested into the canon of a regularly organized party that exerted a powerful influence on the administration of government. The difference between the two parties, Federalist and Republican, as they respectively called themselves at that time, was not confined to the interpretation of the Constitution.

While the one desired and the other deprecated a strong government, the spirit that inclined them to bend that instrument to their wishes, is to be found in the mental and moral organization of the men themselves. Those who doubted the capacity of the people for self-government (and there were many at that time when our experiment was untried), and believed that the only efficient control was to be found in a strong government in the hands of the *rich and well born*, naturally inclined to an interpretation that would authorize such measures as might bring about such a state of things. Those, on the other hand, who had full faith in the capacity of the people, combatted every doctrine which in their judgment tended to steal power from the many and place it in the hands of the few. This radical difference of sentiment, which originated in natural temperament, and was modified by education and position in society, influenced the judgment in its interpretation of every measure of government, and men inclined to the one or the other side, according as they believed the measure originated in the one or the other doctrine above mentioned. The Republicans accused the other party of being monarchists in principle, and of a design so to shape the administration of affairs, that in time the government might assume that form.

The Republicans again were charged by their opponents with being disorganizing levellers, and the enemies of all government. The first great questions on which they divided were the financial schemes of Alexander Hamilton, then Secretary of the Treasury. With these the reader has already been made acquainted. The legislative measures enacted from time to time to carry them into effect, finally brought on a crisis in the whisky insurrection, as it was called, when the people in the western counties of Pennsylvania, by armed force, resisted the execution of the excise law. The Federalists were accused of goading on this rebellion, that they might have a pretext to raise a standing army, to be used as an instrument for forcing their schemes on the country. The Republicans were charged with promoting discontent and insurrection, that they might destroy all government. Unhappily, neither party gave the other credit for honesty or patriotism; and the people, in the heat of the contest, were well nigh driven, in blindness and in rage, on the bayonets of each other. The occasion, however, passed away without serious difficulty; but the bitter and hostile feelings engendered by so violent a contest still remained, and were ready to expand themselves with increased fury on any other occasion that might arise.

In the mean time the French Revolution had made rapid progress. When the news of that event was first wafted across the Atlantic, it was hailed with acclamation as the effort of a great nation to shake off the yoke of despotism, and to assume their position among people with a free and enlightened government. The events of a single year led many to doubt the success of the experiment, and to predict that the whole would end in anarchy. Among the prophets of evil omen was Edmund Burke, the great master of political philosophy. We have already seen how his great work was seized upon by the Federalists as the ablest expounder of their general doctrines, and of their views in particular in regard to the tendency of the principles of the French Revolution. This was to throw the other party to the other extreme: for true it is that the great masses are more influenced by impulses of the heart, than the judgments of the understanding. Paine's "Rights of Man" was set forth as the exponent of the doctrines of the Republicans. Burke, in his spirit of conservatism, pronounced a glowing eulogy on the British Constitution. Paine denounced it as the instrument of oppression and tyranny. It is easy to perceive the bias in the minds of those who took Burke and those who took Paine as their standard of orthodoxy. When these great masters wrote, the monarchy in France was still in existence. It was soon overturned, and a republic, one and indivisible, proclaimed in its stead. This event, more than any thing that had transpired before, stirred up the elements of party-strife in the United States. Free and republican themselves, the American people did not pause on the horrors that were perpetrated, did not consider the consequences of the doctrines that were brought into practice by the rash theorists of France; they only saw a great people, taking themselves as a model, struggling for their independence. Their sympathies were awakened, and all their feelings enlisted in behalf of the republican cause in France. Those who paused—those who suggested a doubt—were denounced as enemies of the people. The deep enthusiasm of a free people in favor of those who, however erroneous, were, like themselves, seeking freedom, did more than any other cause to build up the Republican party in America. The cautions of a cold judgment, however true, cannot weigh against the generous impulses of a warm heart. What is true of individuals in this particular, is ten thousand times more true of the multitude.

But the elastic spirit of freedom could not be restrained within the limits of France. It began to spread to other kingdoms, and to alarm, by its rapid diffusion, the monarchs of Europe. They combined to suppress what they called the *French evil.* England was at the head of the coalition. A furious war commenced—a desperate death-struggle for existence. One or the other must be crushed and destroyed. Republicanism and monarchy could not exist together on the same continent. All the deep passions of the human heart were aroused—all the elements of destruction brought into active operation. It was a war of Titans, and nature groaned under the mighty toils of her warring sons. There could be no neutrality in such a contest. Their wide-sweeping arms drew in, as instruments or agents of strife, the remotest nations. America, though remote, could not hope to escape.

Her position was too conspicuous—her example in producing the present state of things in France too well known for her to escape. England sought to drag her into the contest on the side of the allies. France stretched forth her arms to embrace her ancient ally, and to stand by her side on the hills of Ardenne in the same cause that had seen them side by side on the plains of Yorktown.

The true policy of the United States was to pursue a line of strict neutrality. In accordance with the unanimous vote of his cabinet, Thomas Jefferson at the head as Secretary of State, General Washington issued his proclamation, April 22d, 1793, declaring that a state of war exists between Austria, Prussia, Sardinia, Great Britain, and the United Netherlands, on the one part, and France on the other; and that the duty and interest of the United States require that they should with sincerity and good faith adopt and pursue a conduct friendly and impartial toward the belligerent powers. The citizens of the United States at the same time were warned carefully to avoid all acts and proceedings whatsoever, which might in any manner tend to contravene such disposition. It was impossible, however, to repress the enthusiasm of the people in favor of the French cause. When their minister landed at Charleston, about the time of the above proclamation, he was marched in triumph through the Southern States and principal towns to the capitol at Philadelphia. Presuming on certain privileges which he assumed to have been granted to France in her treaty of alliance with the United States, 1778,—emboldened by the ardent devotion of the people to the cause of liberty, so eagerly manifested towards himself as the representative of a sister republic, he soon threw off all restraint, treated the government with contempt, and assumed acts of sovereignty not only inconsistent with our rights of neutrality, but our existence as an independent and respectable nation. This conduct led to correspondence, remonstrance, and irritation on both sides.

Great Britain at all times doubted the sincerity of our declaration of impartiality, and treated with the utmost contempt our rights of neutrality. Her naval officers insulted and menaced us in our own ports—violated our national rights, by searching vessels and impressing seamen within our acknowledged jurisdiction, and in an outrageous manner seizing *entire crews* in the West Indies, and other parts of the world. Her licensed privateers committed the most atrocious depredations and violences on our commerce, both in the capture and in the after-adjudication, such as were never tolerated in any well-organized and efficient government. The Governor of Upper Canada, in an official and formal manner, ordered settlers within our own territory, and far removed from the posts they had unjustly withheld from us, to withdraw, and forbade others to settle on the same. The persons to whom their Indian affairs were intrusted took unusual pains and practised every deception to keep those people in a temper of hostility towards us.

The agents sent amongst us, as with a design to insult the country, were ungracious and obnoxious characters, rancorous refugees, who retaining all their former enmity, could see nothing through a proper medium, and were the source of constant misrepresentation and falsehood. The government were encouraged to permit all these outrages, because they were told there was a British party in America that would not suffer the country to be involved in a war with England.

France, seeing with what boldness and impunity England committed her depredations, was not slow in doing the same. She avowed her purpose, and fulfilled it to the letter, of treating us in the same manner we permitted her enemies to treat us. Such was the deplorable condition of things within one year from the proclamation of neutrality. As the last resort, willing to exhaust all the means of conciliation before a declaration of war, the administration, on the 19th of April, 1794, commissioned John Jay as minister extraordinary to the court of London, with instructions to demand redress for our grievances, and if occasion suited, to negotiate a treaty of amity and commerce. A few weeks thereafter, the 28th of May, James Monroe was sent as minister plenipotentiary to the French government, with similar instructions. The occasion was most favorable for a negotiation with England. The campaign of 1793–4 proved disastrous to the allied powers. The coalition was dissolved. The hot lava fires France poured forth from her volcanic bosom consumed her enemies. The star of the republic was in the ascendant. At such a moment it seemed plain to the ministry that it would not do to break with the United States. If they should drive the two republics into a close alliance, events had already proved that the two united would be invincible. A different line of policy, therefore, must be pursued. Hence, when Mr. Jay arrived at the Court of St. James, he was most graciously received. Lord Granville was all conciliation and compromise. He had not been engaged in the business of negotiation many days, when the King—tough old George, who was the last to surrender in the Revolution—said to him, " Well, sir, I imagine you begin to see that your mission will probably be successful." " I am happy, may it please your majesty, to find that you entertain that idea." " Well, but don't you perceive that it is likely to be so ?" " There are some recent circumstances (the answer to Jay's representations) which induce me to flatter myself that it will be so." The king nodded with a smile, signifying that it was to those circumstances that he alluded. It was a foregone conclusion. Peace with the United States had now become essential to England : and that wise nation never stands on trifles when an important object is to be attained.

Never did negotiator, beginning with such anxious forebodings, find himself proceeding so smoothly, so satisfactorily. The treaty was concluded and signed in London, on the 19th of November, 1794; was received by the President the 7th of March following, and on the 8th of June was submitted to the Senate for their consideration. On the 24th, by precisely a constitutional majority, they advised and consented to its ratification. Although in the mind of the President several objections had occurred, they were overbalanced by what he conceived to be its advantages ; and before transmitting it to the Senate he had resolved to ratify it, if approved by that body. But before he had given his signature to the treaty, it was well ascertained that the British order in council of the 8th of June, 1793, for the seizure of provisions going to French ports, had been renewed. Apprehensive that this might be regarded as a practical interpretation of an article in the treaty in regard to provisions not being contraband of war unless in particular cases, the President wisely determined to reconsider his decision. Marshall, in his Life of Washington, says : " Of the result of this reconsideration there is no conclusive testimony." It has become a matter of importance in history to determine this fact.

It was charged that a war with France, and a consequent alliance with England, had been the object of the executive council, from the commencement of hostilities between those two great European powers. The treaty, it was alleged, originated in that spirit. And the circumstances and manner of its consummation were confidently alluded to as evidence of that fact. It was well known that the President made up his judgment with great deliberation; and that when once fixed he was unalterable; he had an invincible repugnance to retract an opinion, or retrace a step once taken.

While he was deliberating on the treaty—when in fact, as it was alleged, he had determined not to sign for the present, an intercepted letter addressed by the French minister to his government, was placed in the President's hands. This letter contained many facts bearing on the character of the President, the influences that were working on him, and deeply implicating the reputation of the Secretary of State. It was alleged that the other Secretaries, into whose hands the letter had fallen, made an unwarrantable use of it to prejudice the mind of the President against their obnoxious colleague and the French cause, and thereby to induce him hastily to ratify the treaty contrary to his better judgment—to drive from his cabinet the only republican remaining in office, and to lend his aid, though unconsciously and indirectly, to the destruction of the republican cause in the United States.

Mr. Jefferson retired from the State Department in 1794, early in January. He says that he suffered martyrdom all the time he was in office—alluding to his single-handed and unaided efforts to combat the heresies of Hamilton, and to resist the tendencies of the government to yield to British influence. He was succeeded by the Attorney General, Edmund Randolph, whose relationship to the subject of this memoir has already been made known to the reader. That gentleman professed to be of no party, but was understood to be a Republican in principle, and favorably inclined to the French cause. "The fact is," says Jefferson, "he has generally given his principles to the one party, and his practice to the other—the oyster to one, the shell to the other. Unfortunately, the shell was generally the lot of his friends, the French and Republicans, and the oyster, of their antagonists. Had he been firm to the principles he professed, in the year 1793, the President would have been kept from an habitual concert with the British and anti-republican party."

Randolph declared that long before the Fauchet letter made its appearance, the British partizans had been industrious in disseminating the most poisonous falsehoods concerning him, and in his absence seized the advantage of uttering uncontradicted slanders; boasting and insisting that in a controversy between them, he (Randolph) must be sacrificed. Hamilton had retired, but was in constant communication with the President on all subjects of importance. The British partisans alluded to, were Pickering and Wolcott, the Secretary of War and of the Treasury.

With these facts before us we can now proceed with the subject in hand. We have said that the President had determined to ratify the treaty, if so advised by the Senate. But soon after their adjournment he became satisfied that the *provision order*, as it was called, had been renewed by the British government. He then began to balance whether to ratify or not. In this state of mind, he required the Secretary of State to hold a conversation with the British Minister on the 29th June, 1795, and to tell him that by the constitution the treaty now rested with the President, and that he had entered into the consideration of the subject. A letter was written to the American Minister at Paris, on the 2d of July, under the President's eye and special correction, in which it was stated that the "President has not yet decided upon the final measure to be adopted by himself." He consulted with all the officers of government on several collateral points in the treaty—consulted, as it was believed, with Hamilton on the treaty at large—and required the Secretary of State to give his written opinion. This opinion of the Secretary was handed in the 12th of July, 1795. Among other things, he says: "I take the liberty of suggesting that a personal interview be immediately had between the Secretary of State and Mr. Hammond, and that the substance of the address to him be this"—(after some preliminary remarks): "But we are informed by the public gazettes, and by letters tolerably authentic, that vessels, even American vessels, laden with provisions for France, may be captured and dealt with as carrying a kind of contraband. Upon the supposition of its truth, the President cannot persuade himself that he ought to ratify during the existence of the order. His reasons will be detailed in a proper representation through you (Mr. Hammond) to his Britannic Majesty. At the same time, that order being removed, he will ratify without delay or further scruple." In the morning of the 13th of July, the President instructed the Secretary to have the proposed interview immediately with Mr. Hammond, and to address him as had been suggested.

Mr. Hammond asked, in the course of the interview, if it would not be sufficient to remove the order out of the way; and after the ratification to rescind it?

The Secretary replied with some warmth, that this would be a mere shift, as the principle was the important thing. He then asked, if the President was irrevocably determined, not to ratify, if the provision order was not removed? The Secretary answered, that he was not instructed upon that point. This conversation was immediately related to the President. He told the Secretary *that he might have informed Mr. Hammond that he never would ratify, if the provision order was not removed out of the way.*

The President left Philadelphia for Mount Vernon, the 15th day of July, 1795; and soon afterwards, the Secretary commenced drafting the memorial that was to be addressed to his Britannic Majesty. After discussing the article of the treaty in reference to provisions, and showing the inconsistency of the order of the 8th of June, 1793, with that article, the memorial concludes: "The chief obstacle, which is dependent for its removal on his Britannic Majesty, is the order above stated. The President is too much deprived of its particulars, to declare what shall be his irrevocable determination: but the sensibility which it has excited in his mind, cannot be allayed without the most unequivocal stipulation, to reduce to the only construction in which he can acquiesce, the article of the treaty."

Before the President had received the memorial which he had ordered to be drafted, he wrote to the Secretary on the 22d July, from Mount Vernon, thus: "In my hurry I did not signify the propriety of letting those gentlemen (the Secretaries of War and the Treasury, and the Attorney General) know fully my determination with respect to the ratification of the treaty, and the train it was in; but as this was necessary, in order to enable them to form their opinions on the subject submitted, I take it for granted, that both were communicated to them by you, as a matter of course. The first, that is the conditional ratification, (if the late order, which we have heard of respecting provision-vessels, is not in operation,) may on all fit occasions be spoken of as my determination, unless from any thing you have heard, or met with since I left the city, it should be thought more advisable to communicate with me on the subject. My opinion respecting the treaty is the same now that it was; that is, not favorable to it; but that it is better to ratify it in the manner the Senate have advised, (*and with the reservation already mentioned,*) than to suffer matters to remain as they are—unsettled."

In answer to this the Secretary writes: "I had communicated fully your determination with respect to the ratification. I have no doubt that the order for seizing provision-vessels exists. Nothing has occurred to prevent the speaking of that determination."

On the 29th July the President writes: "I also return, under cover of this letter, the draft of the *memorial*, and the rough draft of a *ratification*. These are very important papers, and, with the instructions which follow, will require great attention and consideration, and are the primary cause of my returning to Philadelphia."

On the 31st he writes: "The *memorial* seems well designed to answer the end proposed."

While the memorial was in the hands of the President at Mount Vernon, it became the subject of conversation with the Heads of Departments. Wolcott and Pickering were both opposed to any delay in concluding the business. Wolcott observed that it would give the French Government an opportunity of professing to make very extensive overtures to the United States, and thus embarrass the treaty with Great Britain.

Pickering, on hearing the memorial, exclaimed, "This, as the sailors say, is throwing the whole up in the wind."

The President returned to Philadelphia on the 11th of August. The same evening, in presence of Pickering and Bradford, the Secretary of State observed, "that the sooner the memorial was revised by the gentlemen jointly, who were prepared with their opinions, the better." The President replied, "that he supposed every thing of this sort had been settled. The Secretary said that it was not so, as Colonel Pickering was for an immediate ratification. To this Pickering responded: "I told Mr. Randolph that I thought the postponement of ratification was a ruinous step."

On the morning of the 13th of August, the letters which had been written to foreign ministers in his absence, were laid before the President. The one addressed to Mr. Monroe was in these words: —"The treaty is not yet ratified by the President; nor will it be ratified, I believe, until it returns from England—if then. The late British order for seizing provisions, is a weighty obstacle to a ratification. I do not suppose that such an attempt to starve France will be countenanced." Other letters were written of the same tenor, and laid before the President. He made no objection to the strong expressions contained in them.

There can be no question from the evidence, that up to the 13th of August, 1795, and for a month previous, the President had deliberately made up his mind not to sign the treaty so long as the provision order was in existence. What caused the great change between that time and the 18th; for on that day he gave to the treaty an unconditional ratification? Marshall, in his Life of Washington, intimates, that the great clamor raised against the treaty in the commercial towns, was the cause of this change in the mind of the President. He thought that by signing the treaty at once he would put an end to all hope of influencing the executive will by agitation. This solution is not consistent with the character of the man. No one despised mere popular clamor more than he did; no one valued more the opinion of his fellow-citizens. With a mind not suggestive, but eminently judicious, he sought for counsel in all quarters, and profited more by advice than any other man that ever held a public station.

He considered that the occasion called for wise and temperate measures. In his letter of the 31st of July, to the Secretary of State, he says: "In time, when passion shall have yielded to sober reason, the current may possibly turn; but in the mean while, this Government, in relation to France and England, may be compared to a ship between the rocks Scylla and Charybdis. If the treaty is ratified, the partisans of the French (or rather of war and confusion) will excite them to hostile measures, or at least to unfriendly sentiments: if it is not, there is no foreseeing all the consequences which may follow, as it respects Great Britain. It is not to be inferred from hence, that I am, or shall be disposed to quit the ground I have taken, unless circumstances more imperious than have yet come to my knowledge, should compel it; for there is but one *straight* course in these things, and that is, to seek truth and pursue it steadily." He then instructs the Secretary to be attentive to all the resolutions that might come in, and to all the newspaper publications, that he might have all the objections against the treaty which had any weight in them, embodied in the *memorial* addressed to the British king, or in the instructions to the American Minister at London. It cannot be presumed, therefore, that the excitement in the country against the treaty, was the cause, or at least the principal cause of the sudden change in the determination of the President. We must look to some other source for a solution of this difficulty.

CHAPTER XVII.

THE FAUCHET LETTER.

On the 31st day of October, 1794, about the time of the wh.sky insurrection, and Jay's negotiation in London, the French Minister forwarded a dispatch to his government, entitled "Private Correspondence of the Minister on Politics, No. 10."

This letter on its way was captured by a British cruiser, placed in the hands of Lord Grenville, and by him forwarded to the Minister here (Mr. Hammond), with instructions to use it for the benefit of his Majesty's service. When the letter came to Hammond, he made known the contents to Mr. Wolcott, Secretary of the Treasury, but did not intimate a desire that it might be communicated to the President. Wolcott himself suggested it, and asked that it might be placed in his hands for that purpose. Hammond at first declined, but finally consented, on condition that a certified copy should be left in his hands. Wolcott received the letter the 28th day of July, 1795, while the President was at Mount Vernon. He immediately showed it to Mr. Pickering. It was their opinion that its contents were of so delicate and important a nature that they ought to be imparted to the President without delay, *and with the utmost secrecy.* Any open attempt to effect this end, they thought *might excite the suspicion of Mr. Randolph.* The first hint of the matter was communicated to the President in a letter from Mr. Pickering in the following words: "July 31st—On the subject of the treaty, I confess I feel extreme solicitude, and, *for a special reason*, which can be communicated to you only in person. I entreat, therefore, that you will return with all convenient speed to the seat of government. In the mean time, for the reason above referred to, I pray you to decide on no important political measure in whatever form it may be presented to you. Mr. Wolcott and I (Mr. Bradford concurring) waited on Mr. Randolph, and *urged his writing to request your return. He wrote in our presence.*" Just the day before, Randolph had written to the President—"As soon as I had the honor of receiving your letter of the 24th instant, I conferred with the Secretaries of the Treasury and of War upon the necessity or expediency of your return hither at this time. *We all concurred* that neither the one nor the other existed, and that the circumstance would confer upon the things which had been and are still carried on, an importance which it would not be convenient to give them." After receiving the above mysterious letter from Pickering, which perhaps arrived the same day with Randolph's, the President hastened to the seat of government. He arrived on the 11th of August, and the contents of Fauchet's intercepted letter were made known to him the same day.

In this *private correspondence*, after stating that the dispatches of himself and colleagues had been confined to a naked recital of facts, the Minister thus proceeds:—"I have reserved myself to give you, as far as I am able, a key to the facts detailed in our reports. * * * The previous confessions of Mr. Randolph alone throw a satisfactory light upon every thing that comes to pass. * * * I shall, then, endeavor to give you a clue to all the measures, of which the common dispatches give you an account; and to discover the true causes of the explosion, which it is *obstinately* resolved to repress with great means (the whisky insurrection), although the state of things has no longer any thing alarming." * * * He then undertakes to give a history of the primitive division of parties—Federalists and Anti-Federalists. Speaks of the whimsical contrast between the name and the real opinion of the parties—the former aiming with all their power to *annihilate Federalism*, while the latter were striving to preserve it. These divisions, he proceeds to say, originated in the system of finances, which had its birth in the cradle of the constitution. It created a financiering class, who threaten to become the aristocratical order of the State. He then continues, in the fifth paragraph, in these words: "It is useless to stop longer to prove that the monarchical system was interwoven with those novelties of finance, and that the friends of the latter favored the attempts which were made, in order to bring the constitution to the former by insensible gradations. The writings of influential men of this party prove it (alluding to Mr. Adams's Discourses on Davila); their real opinions, too, avow it, and the journals of the Senate are the depository of the first attempts."

He speaks of the sympathy of this party with the regenerating movements of France, *while running in monarchical paths;* and after an account of the rapid increase and consolidation of the Anti-Federal party, under the name of patriots and republicans, he thus proceeds:—"In every quarter are arraigned the imbecility of the Government towards Great Britain, the defenceless state of the country against possible invasions, the coldness towards the French Republic—the system of finance is attacked, which threatens eternizing the debt, under pretext of making it the guarantee of public happiness; the complication of that system which withholds from general inspection all its operations—the alarming power of the influence it procures to a man whose principles are regarded as dangerous—the preponderance which that man acquires from day to day in public measures, and, in a word, the *immoral* and impolitic modes of taxation which he at first presents as expedients, and afterwards raises to permanency."

He then speaks of the *excise law*—the navigation of the Mississippi, and the system for the sale of public lands, as being the principal sources of discontent to the Western people, and the cause of their rebellion. "At last," says he, "the local explosion is effected. * * * The Government which had foreseen it, reproduced, under various forms, the demand of a disposable force which might put it in a state of respectable defence. Defeated in this measure, who can aver that it may not have hastened the local eruption, in order to make an advantageous diversion, and to lay the more general storm which it saw gathering? Am I not authorized in forming this conjecture from the conversation which the Secretary of State had with me and Le Blanc, above, an account of which you have in my dispatch, No. 3? But how may we expect that this new plan will be executed?—By exasperating and severe measures, authorized by a law which was not solicited till the close of the session. This law gave to the one already existing for collecting the *excise*, a coercive force which hitherto it had not possessed, and a demand of which was not before ventured to be made. * * * * This was undoubtedly what Mr. Randolph meant in telling me *that under pretext of giving energy to the Government, it was intended to introduce absolute power, and to mislead the President in paths which would conduct him to unpopularity.*"

He then proceeds to describe the successful efforts to raise an army, and to gain over certain influential characters, and continues thus: "The Secretary of this State possessed great influence in the popular societies of Philadelphia, which in its turn influenced those of other States: of course he merited attention. It appears, therefore, that those men, with others unknown to me, all having, without doubt, Randolph at their head, were balancing to decide on this party. Two or three days before the proclamation was published (in reference to the whisky insurrection 25th September, 1794), and of course before the cabinet had resolved on its measures, Mr. Randolph came to see me with an air of great eagerness, and made to me the overtures of which I have given you an account in my No. 6. Thus, with some thousands of dollars, the republic would have decided on civil war, or on peace. Thus the consciences of the pretended patriots of America have already their prices. * * * What will be the old age of this Government if it is thus early decrepit. Such, citizen, is the evident consequence of the system of finances conceived by Mr. Hamilton. He has made of a whole nation, a stock-jobbing, speculating, selfish people. * * * * Still, there are patriots of whom I delight to entertain an idea worthy of that imposing title. Consult Monroe—he is of this number; he had apprised me of the men whom the current of events had dragged along as bodies devoid of weight. His friend Madison is also an honest man. Jefferson, on whom the patriots cast their eyes to succeed the President, had foreseen these crises. He prudently retired, in order to avoid making a figure against his inclination in scenes, the secret of which will soon or late be brought to light."

These are the leading and essential facts in the intercepted letter. And they certainly contain very grave charges. The men in power are accused of a design of changing the government into a monarchy; clothing the President with absolute power, and fomenting a rebellion, that they might have a pretext to raise a standing army to enforce their designs. The pretended patriots of the country are accused of venality and corruption—the highest officer under Government charged with making overtures to the minister of a foreign power for money; and it is alleged that none but those who are opposed to the Administration are trustworthy and honest.

It is not surprising that a communication of this sort, addressed by a foreign minister to his Government, whose feeling of friendship to our own was extremely questionable, falling into the hands of one of the parties implicated, should excite his indignation and create in him a desire to have the truth of the charges investigated. But the use made of that letter by the triumvirate, Wolcott, Pickering, and Bradford, to destroy an obnoxious rival and to crush the rising energies of a hateful party, cannot be justified. The wicked and jesuitical doctrine, that *all is fair in politics*, may sanction the means in the end; but the pen of the historian must condemn, under all circumstances, both the principle and its application. Randolph was a colleague of those men—held the highest station in the executive department of Government—was in the most intimate relations with them, holding daily and hourly communications on the gravest subjects of state. He was reputed to be among the first gentlemen of his age—possessed a high reputation, and an unblemished character for integrity and honor. A paper falls into the hands of his intimate and daily associates, written by an ignorant and prejudiced foreigner, in which this man is charged with being accessible to a bribe. What line of conduct do they pursue? It seems that in a formal dispatch of the foreign minister, No. 6, the facts are stated from which he draws his injurious inference. Did the triumvirate call for that document so obviously necessary as a means of explaining the injurious charges? It was in the hands of the same individual from whom they had obtained the first communication. But they made no inquiry for it; did not seem to wish to know that the means of explanation were in their reach, or in existence. Did they communicate the contents of the letter to their implicated colleague, that he might exculpate himself from its charges? They kept it a profound secret from him—held frequent conclaves over it—considered it extremely important, and concluded that the President must be informed of it, but in the most secret manner, lest the implicated person might take the alarm. They even go to him, and induce him in their presence to write to the President, requesting his immediate return to the seat of government. Not content with this, one of the party writes himself, stating that he is very solicitous about the treaty, and *for a special reason*, thus connecting the fate of the treaty with the contents of the intercepted letter. Was this acting fairly towards their colleague? It was not treating him even as a gentleman. Their conduct can only be compared to that of a bailiff or town beadle, who has gotten some clue on a suspected character, towards whom he must act with the utmost caution and secrecy, lest he might snuff suspicion in the wind and take to flight.

Nor was their conduct at all mitigated by the return of the President. They beset him the moment of his arrival; the intercepted letter was placed in his hands the same evening; a cabinet council was called the next morning to deliberate on the treaty. Not a breath was uttered to Randolph by the President, that he was suspected of treachery to himself, and of having made overtures for a bribe to betray his country. On the contrary, an unusually cordial manner is observed towards him. He is called on to give his opinion on the subject of ratification. He repeats the same arguments he had used before; he contended that the treaty did not warrant the provision order, and that the President could not sign the treaty so long as the order existed; because we had already acknowledged, on the 7th of September, 1793, that a permission to Great Britain to exercise such a power, would be a just cause of war to France; that we should be inconsistent in our discussions with the French minister; because when he remonstrated upon the extension of contraband by the treaty, it was answered that we did not alter the law of nations; but now we should desert what was contended to be the law of nations, in two letters to Mr. Hammond; that we should run the hazard of a war with France, by combining to starve her; and that her discontents were the only possible chance remaining to the British partisans for throwing us into the arms of Great Britain, by creating a seeming necessity of an alliance with the latter power. These cogent arguments had already been urged on the President; he felt their force, and had determined, as the reader cannot doubt, not to sign so long as the provision order existed, and had taken his measures accordingly. How are these arguments met now? Let it be remembered that on the morning of this very day, it was circulated in the coffee-houses by Hammond, the British minister, and his partisans, that Randolph was at the bottom of the town meetings which had been gotten up to denounce the treaty (and which actually burnt a copy of the treaty in front of Hammond's house, by the hands of the common hangman), and that there was a conspiracy, of which Randolph was a member, to destroy the popularity of the President, and to thrust Mr. Jefferson into his chair. No one can doubt that these rumors designedly put afloat, were carefully related to the President by his faithful and disinterested ministers, so that when Randolph concluded his speech, the very arguments that had weighed with the President before, were now evidences of his guilt—*confirmations strong as proofs of Holy Writ.* Pickering and Wolcott answered in the most excited and intemperate manner; urged the immediate ratification of the treaty, and charged that the struggle to defeat it was the act of a *detestable and nefarious conspiracy.* There was a unanimous vote for immediate unconditional ratification, so far as the provision order was concerned; but to be accompanied with a remonstrance on that subject. The President receded from his determination, and consented to ratify. The necessary papers were prepared, and on the 18th of August, 1795, the President affixed his signature to the treaty. All this struck the Secretary of State with astonishment. He did not know how to account for it. All the while he was treated with unusual courtesy. Two days after the President had determined to sign the treaty, on the 14th of the month, he paid a private and friendly visit to Mr. Randolph's house; invited him next day in the most cordial manner to dine with a party of chosen friends, and placed him at the foot of the table as a mark of respect and confidence. On the 18th, the day of the ratification, the same air of cordiality was assumed. But good, easy man, while his honors were thus ripening, next day there came a nipping frost.

On Wednesday, the 19th of August, 1795, while going to the President's at the usual hour, *nine o'clock* in the morning, he was met by the steward, who informed him that the President desired him to postpone his visit till half past ten. On reaching the door at the appointed hour, he was surprised to learn that the President had been closeted with his colleagues for more than an hour. On entering the room, the President rose from his chair, and received him with marked formality. After a few words, the President drew a letter from his pocket, and said: "Mr. Randolph, here is a letter which I desire you to read, and make such explanations as you choose."

After he had read the letter, and some little conversation had ensued, the President requested Messrs. Wolcott and Pickering to interrogate him! In a short time he was requested to leave the room, that they might consult on what had been said! Can the reader come to any other conclusion, than that the mind of the President had been worked up to prejudge the case? Can any one believe that the great and good Washington would have acted in a manner so precipitate in itself, so injurious and humiliating to a long tried friend, and a faithful, confidential officer, unless his passions had been excited by some undue influence, exerted over his peculiar temper and character?

Who can doubt, after a review of all the facts connected with this transaction, that Randolph, as he declared himself, *was the meditated victim of party spirit?* Who can doubt that Wolcott and Pickering, by their artful insinuations, and earnest commentaries on the intercepted letter, had induced the President to believe that there was in truth a *detestable* and *nefarious* conspiracy to defeat the treaty?—that there was a dark design of replacing him by another President; and that his Secretary of State, in whom he had placed the most unbounded confidence, had been convicted of a corrupt attachment to France, and of perfidy to himself. The more we read and learn of Washington and his acts, the more exalted our judgment becomes of his virtue and purity. The more the days of his mortality recede from us, the more sublime and godlike his character appears. But when we go back to the times when he wrought on earth with other men, and performed his part on the public stage, we perceive that he had like passions with ourselves, and like us, was liable to err.

The ratification of such a treaty would at any time have created a strong hostility to the administration that advised it. It was certainly very defective. We say nothing about the objections raised against it, under the influence of the party excitement of the times. Much allowance must be made for them; but the negotiator himself admitted that the subjects of difficulty were merged in the treaty, but not settled. Time has proved the truth of his admission. The late war with Great Britain—the more recent difficulties on the boundary question, all grew out of the unsettled questions of dispute merged in the treaty. It was evidently made for a temporary purpose—*to serve the nonce*—and perhaps that was all that could have been expected. The President did not approve it. The more he thought of it, the less he liked it. But that there might be some settlement of the perplexing and threatening difficulties between the two nations, he consented to ratify, if the Senate advised. The ratification of such a treaty, under any circumstances, would have encountered formidable opposition. But when it was made known that the President, under the influence of a party intrigue, had been hurried into a premature ratification, contrary to his better judgment, with the British order in council staring him in the face, which seemed to have been issued in contempt of the treaty, as a license to plunder our defenceless commerce, the storm that was raised cannot well be imagined. The great Washington rose into the pure empyrean of a clear conscience; but the guilty beings below were swept away by the tempest. All who had any thing to do with this business were *treaty-foundered*, and ingulfed in the torrent that soon swept over the land.

It was predicted, as a sequel to these transactions, that Monroe would be recalled from Paris. In December, 1795, only three months after the ratification, Mr. Jefferson writes: "I should not wonder if Monroe were to be recalled, under the idea of his being of the partisans of France, whom the President considers as the partisans of *war and confusion*, in his letter of July 31st, and as disposed to excite them to hostile measures, or at least to unfriendly sentiments; a most infatuated blindness to the true character of the sentiments entertained in favor of France." Sure enough, the subject was soon made the theme of cabinet consultation; and on the 2d day of July, 1796, it was resolved to recall him. "We think," said the Heads of Department, in their communication to the President, "the great interests of the United States require that they have near the French government some faithful organ to explain their real views, and to ascertain those of the French. Our duty obliges us to be explicit. Although the present Minister Plenipotentiary of the United States at Paris has been amply furnished with documents to explain the views and conduct of the United States, yet his own letters authorize us to say, that he has omitted to use them, and thereby exposed the United States to all the mischiefs which would flow from jealousies and erroneous conceptions of their views and conduct. Whether this dangerous omission arose from such an attachment to the cause of France as rendered him too little mindful of the interests of his own country, or from mistaken views of the latter, or from any other cause, the evil is the same." After speaking of his confidential correspondence with the *notorious enemies of the whole system of government*, and of certain anonymous letters, which they entertained no doubt were written with the privity of Mr. Monroe, they proceed: "The anonymous communications from officers of the United States in a foreign country, on matters of a public nature, and which deeply concern the interests of the United States in relation to that foreign country, *are proofs of sinister designs*, and show that the public interests are no longer safe in the hands of such men." On the 8th of July, from Mount Vernon, the President invited Charles Cotesworth Pinkney, of Charleston, to succeed Mr. Monroe. In his private and confidential letter to that gentleman, he says: "The situation of affairs, and the interests of this country, as they relate to France, render it indispensably necessary, that a *faithful organ* near that Government, able and willing to explain its views and to ascertain those of France, should immediately fill the place of our present Minister Plenipotentiary at Paris."

From this period not a friend of the French cause remained in the administration of affairs. Jefferson, foreseeing the tendency of events, had prudently retired, after having suffered a three years' martyrdom. Randolph had been ignominiously driven from the cabinet; and Monroe recalled, not only with the charge of infidelity to his Government, but under the accusation of *sinister designs* against his country.

It was proclaimed in the newspapers, in political meetings, on the hustings, every where, *that the friends of liberty are for an intimate union with France. The partisans of slavery prefer an alliance with England.* On the other hand, the President had declared and acted on the belief, that the friends of France were the partisans of *war and confusion.* "*A most infatuated blindness*," said Jefferson, "*to the true character of the sentiments entertained in favor of France!*"

The reader cannot mistake, at this rate, how things were tending.

The person and character of the President were no longer respected. The Republicans were resolved that their opponents should not shelter themselves behind the *ægis* of his fame. They considered that he had descended into the arena of strife, and were determined that he should share the fate of other combatants.

Happily for him, he soon sought repose in voluntary retirement. The reins of government fell into other hands. On the 4th of March, 1797, this pure patriot entered the shades of Mount Vernon with infinitely more pleasure than he had ever passed the threshold into the cabinet of power. However much some of the measures of his administration may be condemned, his own motives are above suspicion. If ever a man had in view the exaltation of the character of his own country, impressing on it a pure American stamp, free from all foreign alloy, he had. Whether all the measures advocated by him tended to that end is another question. The historian must not be deterred from a critical examination into them from the fear of tarnishing his great name. That is impossible! From the clouds of party it has come out all the brighter for the mists by which it was temporarily enveloped.

CHAPTER XIX.

MR. MONROE—FRANCE—MR. ADAMS ELECTED PRESIDENT.

THE charges against Mr. Monroe were unjust, and his recall an impolitic measure, unless the Government had determined not to send a successor, for which there was sufficient reason. Nothing but the intemperate zeal of such partisans as Pickering and Wolcott could have advised the course pursued. The strangest part of the business is that General Washington should have yielded so completely to their views. He speaks more harshly, if possible, than they do, not only of Mr. Monroe's conduct, but of his motives. He charges him with misrepresenting his own Government, an undue condescension to that of France, and alleges that he was promoting the views of a party in his own country, that were obstructing every measure of the

Administration, and, by their attachment to France, were hurrying it (*if not with design*, at least in its consequences), into a war with Great Britain, in order to favor France. He further charges that this *French party* had brought the country to a most degraded and humiliating condition; and that our Minister at Paris had been the principal actor in its accomplishment. That he was timid in his demands of justice, and over zealous in his efforts to conciliate the French people, cannot be doubted. But he had a most difficult part to perform. His open reception by the National Convention—the fraternal embrace in the midst of shouts and acclamation, and his unreserved declarations of attachment to the French cause, were not at all diplomatic. The people of Paris, who were the Government in fact, would have consented to no other kind of reception. Fond of exhibition and excitement at all times, they could not let an occasion of that sort pass quietly by without considering that they had cast a slight on the representative of a sister Republic. At the same time, the whole nation were thoroughly impressed with the belief that we owed our existence to them; that their timely alliance had sustained our cause against the arms of England, and their powerful influence in negotiation had secured our Independence. They were taught this lesson not only by their own Government, and the thousands of Frenchmen who fought in our armies, but they were taught it by the statesmen of America, her orators, her poets, her historians, and all her diplomatic agents abroad. All France was penetrated with a belief that we owed them a debt of gratitude that no service could repay. Whether right or wrong, such was the national faith. They were now engaged in a war with the very nation from whose tyrannous oppression they had plucked us—their own hereditary enemy of a thousand years—a war destructive, vindictive, exterminating. So soon, therefore, as it was known that the United States had sent an envoy to negotiate a treaty with England, their suspicions were awakened. They doubted the sincerity of our declarations of friendship, and insisted that Mr. Monroe was merely sent to blind and lull them into repose, while the real design was a close alliance with their mortal foe. In vain did the Minister declare that no treaty would be made with England that would affect the rights of France. There is no reasoning in detail with the multitude; special facts make but a slight impression, they are governed by broad and universal truths.

It was impossible to persuade the French mind that the United States meant well in seeking to form a treaty with their enemies, while they were impressed with the belief that they owed their existence, independence, and an immense debt of gratitude to France. Whenever Mr. Monroe made a demand for the redress of our many grievances, he was at once met with the charge of ingratitude, and was threatened with the displeasure and hostility of France, if the treaty then in progress at London should be consummated. So soon as it was known that a treaty had been made, and that it had been advised by the Senate and ratified by the President, the hostility of the French Government and the indignation of the people knew no bounds. The harassing decrees of Government, the depredations on American commerce, the atrocious cruelties committed on her seamen and citizens were worse than if there had been an open declaration of war; for then all merchant vessels would have been kept at home. It was declared by the Government that these things were done in consequence of the British treaty. They now began to draw a distinction between the Administration and the people of the United States. They imagined that a large majority were friendly to an alliance with France. The first appeal was made by the minister Adet, in the autumn of 1796, with a view of influencing the presidential election. Mr. Adams was considered as the representative of the Administration, or English party, and Mr. Jefferson the representative of the French party. The next occasion on which this spirit was manifested in the most remarkable degree, was in the month of December, 1796, by the Directory. When Mr. Monroe presented his letters of recall, and the letters of credence of General Pinckney, who the reader knows had been appointed to succeed him, he was told that the Directory would not acknowledge nor receive another Minister Plenipotentiary from the United States, until after the redress of grievances demanded of the American Government, and which the French Government had a right to expect from it. He was, at the same time, told that this determination allowed to subsist between the French Republic and the *American people*, the affection founded upon former benefits and reciprocal interests, and that he himself had cultivated this affection by every means in his power. And to his valedictory address, the President of the Executive Directory thus replied :—" Mr. Minister Plenipotentiary of the

United States of America, by presenting to-day your letters of recall to the Executive Directory, you give to Europe a very strange spectacle. France, rich in her liberty, surrounded by a train of victories, strong in the esteem of her allies, will not abase herself by calculating the consequences of the condescension of the *American Government to the suggestions of her former tyrants.* Moreover, the French Republic hopes that the successors of Columbus, Raleigh, and Penn—always proud of their liberty—*will never forget that they owe it to France.* They will weigh in their wisdom the magnanimous benevolence of the French people, with the crafty caresses of certain perfidious persons who meditate bringing them back to their former slavery. Assure the good American people, sir, that, like them, we adore liberty; that they will always have our esteem, and that they will find in the French people republican generosity, which knows how to grant peace, as it does to cause its sovereignty to be respected."

While Mr. Monroe was assured that he had combated for principles, had known the true interests of his country, and that they parted from him with regret, General Pinckney was treated in the most disrespectful manner. In no manner was he recognized in his official capacity,—was refused the usual cards of hospitality on which his personal safety depended, and like an ordinary stranger, was left wholly to the regulations of the Paris police. And about the first of February, 1797, the very day that Bonaparte's brilliant termination of the Italian campaigns was announced, he was ordered to quit Paris, and to pass beyond the confines of France.

The news of the election of Mr. Adams to the presidency, arrived in Paris about the first of March. This filled the measure of hostile feelings on the part of the Directory: they were now ready for any extremity. The unfriendly sentiments of Mr. Adams were well known in France; and they were cordially reciprocated. Those feelings began to develope themselves at an early period. And it is important at this point of our history, that the reader should know their origin.

In the summer of 1780 Mr. Adams was in Paris, charged with three distinct commissions from the Congress of the Confederation: first, to take a share in any future negotiations for peace; second, to conclude a treaty of commerce with Great Britain; third, to represent the United States at the Court of London. At that time there was not the slightest prospect of peace. Cornwallis was marching triumphantly through the southern provinces, and England was in high hopes of subjugating her revolted colonies. At this conjuncture, Mr. Adams proposed to make known to the Court of London that he held a commission to conclude a treaty of commerce with Great Britain, and to represent the United States at the Court of London. As he was required to do, he consulted the Count de Vergennes on the subject. That nobleman, the Secretary for Foreign Affairs, ridiculed it as an ill-timed and visionary proposition. To be solicitous about a treaty of commerce, before independence was established, he thought was like being busy about furnishing a house before the foundation was laid. He told Mr. Adams that the British ministry would consider the communication as ridiculous, and would either return no answer, or an insolent one.

Mr. Adams still insisted on the propriety of his course, entered into an elaborate argument to prove it, and was very intemperate in his language and insinuations as to the motives of France, and showed an overweening desire either to figure himself in the Court of London, or to form a close commercial alliance with England as the best means of securing independence to his country. He evidently showed no disposition to rely on the good intentions of France in the business.

The Count de Vergennes at length inclosed a copy of his correspondence with Mr. Adams, to Dr. Franklin, accompanied with these remarks:—"You will find, I think, in the letters of that plenipotentiary, *opinions and a tone* which do not correspond either with the manner I explained myself to him, or with the intimate connection which subsists between the king and the United States. You will make that use of these pieces which your prudence shall suggest. As to myself, I desire that you will transmit them to Congress, that they may know the line of conduct which Mr. Adams pursues with regard to us, and that they may judge whether he is endowed, as Congress no doubt desires, *with that conciliating spirit* which is necessary for the important and delicate business with which he is intrusted."

The communication was made to Congress; and that body responded to Mr. Adams, that they did not doubt his correspondence with the Count de Vergennes flowed from his zeal and assiduity in the service of his country, but that the opinions of that minister were well-founded, and that he must be more cautious in future. Mr. Adams never forgot or forgave this insult to his vanity and self-esteem, which were ruling traits in his character. He soon left for Holland, where he remained till negotiations for peace had commenced in Paris, in November, 1782. When he arrived on the scene of action, Mr. Jay and Dr. Franklin, two of the associate commissioners, had made considerable progress in the negotiation. The whole matter was talked over to him, and he very soon displayed his suspicions of the sincerity and motives of France. In his correspondence he thus writes :—" Paris, Nov. 1782. When I speak of this (French) Court, I know not that any other minister (Count de Vergennes) is included than that of Foreign Affairs. A whole system of policy is now as glaring as the day, which perhaps Congress and the people of America have little suspicion of. The evidence now results from a large view of all our European negotiations. The same principle and the same system have been uniformly pursued from the beginning of my knowledge in Europe, in April, 1778, to this hour. In substance it has been this :—In assistance afforded us in naval force and in money, to keep us from succumbing, and nothing more : To prevent us from ridding ourselves wholly of our enemies, and from growing rich and powerful : To prevent us from obtaining acknowledgments of our independence by other foreign powers, and from acquiring consideration in Europe, or any advantage in the peace, but what is expressly stipulated in the treaties : To deprive us of the Grand Fishery, the Mississippi river, the Western lands, and to saddle us with the tories." The friends of Mr. Adams even went so far as to say, that Dr. Franklin favored, or did not oppose the designs of France against the United States ; and that it was entirely owing to the firmness, sagacity, and disinterestedness of Mr. Adams, with whom Mr. Jay united, that we had obtained those important advantages. Dr. Franklin, in allusion to this subject, says : " He (Mr. Adams) thinks the French minister one of the greatest enemies of our country ; that he would have straitened our boundaries, to prevent the growth of our people ; contracted our fishery to obstruct the increase of our seamen ; and retained the royalists amongst us, to keep us divided ; that he privately opposed all our negotiations with foreign courts, and afforded us, during the war, the assistance we received, only to keep it alive, that we might be so much the more weakened by it; that to think of gratitude to France is the greatest of follies, and that to be influenced by it would ruin us. He makes no secret of his having these opinions—expresses them publicly, sometimes in presence of the English ministers, and speaks of hundreds of instances, which he could produce in proof of them. If I were not convinced of the real inability of this Court to furnish the further supplies we asked, I should suspect these discourses of a person in his station might have influenced the refusal—(at that very moment, the king of France had postponed his own creditors, that he might furnish means to sustain the credit of the United States;)—but I think they have gone no further than to occasion a suspicion, *that we have a considerable party of anti-Gallicans* in America, who are not tories, and consequently, to produce some doubts of the continuance of our friendship. As such doubts may hereafter have a bad effect, I think we cannot take too much care to remove them; and it is, therefore, I write this to put you on your guard (believing it my duty, though I know I hazard by it a mortal enmity), and to caution you respecting the insinuations of this gentleman against this Court, and the instances he supposes of their ill will to us, which I take to be as imaginary as I know his fancies to be, that Count de Vergennes and myself are continually plotting against him, and employing the news-writers of Europe to depreciate his character. But as Shakspeare says, "Trifles light as air," &c. I am persuaded, however, that he means well for his country, is always an honest man, often a wise one, but sometimes, and in some things, absolutely out of his senses."

This was the man elected President of the United States. Such were the opinions and sentiments entertained by him in regard to France, which time and the revolution in that country had only developed and strengthened.

So soon as this election was known, and avowedly in consequence of it, the Executive Directory, on the 2d of March, 1797, decreed that the treaty concluded on the sixth of February, 1778, between France and the United States, was modified of full right by that which had been concluded at London on the nineteenth of November, 1794, between the United States of America and England; and in consequence thereof, decreed further, that all merchandise of the enemy's, all merchandise not sufficiently ascertained to be neutral, conveyed under American flags, shall be confiscated; that every thing which serves directly or indirectly to the arming and equipping of vessels, shall be contraband—that every American who shall hold a commission from the enemies of France, as well as every seaman of that nation, composing the crew of the ships and vessels, shall, by this fact alone, be declared piratical, and treated as such, without suffering the party to establish that the act was the consequence of threats or violence; that every American ship shall be deemed a lawful prize, which shall not have on board a bill of lading (*role d'equipage*) in due form, according to the plan annexed to the treaty of the sixth of February, 1778. This was in fact a declaration of war in disguise. It was so intended. The Government avowed their determination to *fleece* the American citizens of their property, to a sufficient degree to bring them to their feeling in the only nerve in which it was presumed their sensibility lay, which was their pecuniary interest.

When Mr. Adams was inaugurated on the fourth of March, 1797, he was ignorant of this decree; he only knew that General Pinckney had been refused credence as Minister Plenipotentiary, and had been ordered to leave France.

Notwithstanding this, he expressed a desire for reconciliation. Meeting with Mr. Jefferson, who had come to Philadelphia to take upon himself the duties of Vice-President, to which office he had just been elected, Mr. Adams entered immediately on an explanation of the situation of our affairs with France, and the danger of rupture with that nation, a rupture which would convulse the attachments of this country; that he was impressed with the necessity of an immediate mission to the Directory, and had concluded to send one, which, by its dignity, should satisfy France, and by its selection from the three great divisions of the continent, should satisfy all parts of the United States; in short, that he had determined to join Gerry and Madison to Pinckney, and he requested Mr. Jefferson to consult Mr. Madison for him. On the *sixth of March*, when Mr. Jefferson reported the result of his negotiation with Mr. Madison, the President replied, that, on consultation, some objections to that nomination had been raised, which he had not contemplated; the subject was then dropped, and never afterwards resumed. The consultation alluded to was with Pickering, Wolcott, McHenry and Lee, the late Cabinet of General Washington, which he had transmitted entire to his successor. The feelings and opinions of those gentlemen are well known to the reader. So that the kind intentions of Mr. Adams, in the first enthusiasm of office, towards the Republican party, and his spirit of conciliation towards France, were soon dissipated by the advice of his counsellors. In less than three weeks from this date, the President's proclamation was issued, requiring an extraordinary session of Congress to be convened on the fifteenth day of May.

It is obvious that the President was *advised* to this measure, and that the design of his advisers was to procure, if not a declaration of war, at least the enactment of such strong retaliatory measures as would lead to that result. There could have been no other motive in convening the legislative department at that unusual season; and when the decree of the 2d of March was made known, there was no other alternative left to the Administration. The President might have dismissed his ministers, and taken into his Cabinet such men as Madison, Gallatin and Gerry. With their advice he could have sent to France, as he proposed at first, such envoys as would at once have satisfied that nation, smothered every asperity, caused the repeal of every obnoxious decree, and the institution of a tribunal to try all questions of dispute between the two nations. But not choosing to follow this course, there was no alternative in the line of policy to be pursued but war or disgrace.

The President's opening speech on the 17th of May, was considered by his friends sufficiently spirited. After giving a history of the rejection of the American Minister by the Executive Directory, and the indignities offered to the nation through him, he thus proceeds: "With this conduct of the French Government, it will be proper to take into view the public audience given to the late Minister of the United States on his taking leave of the Executive Directory—the speech of the President discloses sentiments more alarming than the refusal of a Minister, because more dangerous to our independence and union; and at the same time studiously marked with indignities towards the Government of the United States: it evinces a disposition to separate the people of the United States from the Government, to persuade them that they have different affections, principles, and interests, from those of their fellow-citizens whom they themselves have chosen to manage their common concerns; and thus to produce divisions fatal to our peace. Such attempts ought to be repelled with a decision which shall convince France and the world, that we are not a degraded people, humiliated under a colonial spirit of fear and sense of inferiority, fitted to be the miserable instruments of foreign influence, and regardless of national honor, character, and interest."

While he intended to make another effort to adjust all our differences with France by amicable negotiation, the threatening aspect of affairs rendered it his indispensable duty to recommend to the consideration of Congress *effectual measures of defence.* "The present situation of our country," says he, in conclusion, "imposes an obligation on all the departments of Government to adopt an explicit and decided conduct. . . . . It is impossible to conceal from ourselves, or the world, what has been before observed, that endeavors have been employed to foster and establish a division between the Government and the people of the United States. To investigate the causes which have encouraged this attempt is not necessary; but to repel, by decided and united councils, insinuations so derogatory to the honor, and aggressions so dangerous to the constitution, union, and even independence of the nation, is an indispensable duty. . . . . Convinced that the conduct of this Government has been just and impartial to foreign nations; that those internal regulations which have been established by land for the preservation of peace, are in their nature proper, and that they have been fairly executed; nothing will ever be done by me to impair the national engagements, to innovate upon principles which have been so deliberately and uprightly established, *or to surrender in any manner the rights of the Government.*"

This energetic speech of the President was not responded to by the Representatives in the same spirit. The original draft of the address intending to be fully responsive to the speech, contained the following clause: "Knowing as we do the confidence reposed by the people of the United States in their Government, we cannot hesitate in expressing our indignation at the sentiments disclosed by the President of the Executive Directory of France in his speech to the Minister of the United States. Such sentiments serve to discover the imperfect knowledge which France possesses of the real opinions of our constituents." This very pointed and spirited paragraph was stricken out by a vote of *forty-eight* to *forty-six*, and the following substituted in its place: "Any sentiments tending to derogate from the confidence; such sentiments, wherever entertained, serve to evince an imperfect knowledge of the real opinion of our constituents."

The address contained the following paragraph: "We therefore receive, with the utmost satisfaction, your information that a fresh attempt at negotiation will be instituted; and we cherish the hope that a mutual spirit of conciliation, and a disposition on the part of the United States to place France on grounds similar to those of other countries, in their relation and connection with us, if any irregularities shall be found to exist, will produce an accommodation compatible with the engagements, rights, duties, and honor of the United States." A motion was made to strike out the latter part of this clause, in regard to France. It was negatived by a vote of *forty-nine* to *fifty*. Thus it seems that there were forty-nine members opposed to placing France on similar grounds to those of other countries, in their relation and connection with us.

A motion was then made to strike out the whole paragraph. Only *forty-one* voted for this proposition; so that there were at least that many opposed to any farther negotiation, or conciliation with France.

A motion was made to strike from the address the following paragraph: "Believing, with you, that the conduct of the Government has been just and impartial to foreign nations; that the laws for the preservation of peace have been proper, and that they have been fairly executed, the representatives of the people do not hesitate to declare, that they will give their most cordial support to the execution of principles so deliberately and uprightly established." This motion was made by Mr. Gallatin, who was a native of Geneva, and spoke English with a very broken accent. It was opposed by Mr. Allen, who said he was sure such a motion could never pass while there was a drop of *American* blood in the House, and an American *accent* to say *no*. *Forty-five* voted to strike out, thereby expressing their belief that the Government had not been just and impartial to foreign nations—that laws proper for the preservation of peace had not been enacted, nor fairly executed.

The House of Representatives was composed of one hundred members, leaving out the Speaker; ninety-nine remained to vote on all questions. Fifty made the majority. Thus the reader will perceive that a very large and powerful minority were opposed to all the measures of the administration. Much the larger portion of its friends were desirous of no further attempts at negotiation with France, and were prepared to push matters to the extremity of war; but the two or three timid, vacillating, and as it was asserted, venal men, necessary to make the majority, could not be relied on. All the labors of Congress, after a two months' session, resulted in a perfect abortion. A few insignificant acts of a defensive character were passed, but nothing energetic or decisive was done.

The republican party, or French partisans as they were called, were reproached for this failure. General Washington had long before said they were the friends of war and confusion; it was now asserted that they were prepared to sacrifice the independence of their own country to the ambition of France. Had it been merely a subject of foreign policy that divided them from the administration, it might be a question how far they were justified in giving the least countenance to the indignities and the atrocities of the French Government. But it must be remembered that great principles, deep and radical, not only in regard to the interpretation of the Constitution, but the basis and design of all government, divided them from the party of the administration. They were firmly impressed with the belief that the latter desired to absorb all the powers distributed among the States, and left to the people, into the federal head; to concentrate them in the Executive, and then to consolidate and confirm these usurpations by a close alliance with Great Britain, whose government and policy were to be taken as a model for our own; and that all their measures, the British treaty, disgrace of Randolph, recall of Monroe, and unconciliating temper towards France, were taken with a view to the consummation of these great designs. Thus impressed, it could not be expected that those men would yield to the policy of the administration. The lasting welfare of the country was of more importance than the removal of a mere temporary shadow that overhung the shield of its fame. They saw the administration in a dilemma; they did not consider it their duty to extricate them from it, that they might pursue measures detrimental to the interests of the country.

Mr. Adams never pursued any well-digested plan of any sort.

He was the creature of impulse. His first impulse, as we have seen, was to send Madison and Gerry to France. This feeling he yielded to the wishes of his counsellors, who were evidently for war. The representatives of the people were called together to second these designs. But falling far short of the expectations of those who had advised the call, the President was compelled to fall back on his original plan, and resort once more to negotiation. But it was now too late. He found himself in this awkward position. He had said to France, I was indignant at your insults and malicious attempts to divide the people from their government, and intended to repel them with becoming spirit; but when I called on the popular branch of government, those who more immediately represented the feelings and wishes of the people, to furnish me the means, I found that a very formidable minority were of your way of thinking; very few prepared to retaliate your insults with war, and a large majority disposed to conciliate you by further negotiations. I am compelled to yield to their wishes, as they are the war-making power; and as a token of my sincerity, I send you three envoys—Messrs. Pinckney, Marshall, and Dana—gentlemen, one of whom you know, of high-toned character, great devotion to my administration and the policy of my predecessor—indignant at the insults you have offered their government, hostile to your principles, shocked at your merciless barbarities at home and abroad, and prepared with unyielding energy and spirit to demand redress for the depredations you have committed on our commerce, and the injuries you have done to our seamen.

What could have been expected from such a mission but disappointment and additional insult? It is true Mr. Dana resigned, and Gerry was put in his place; but the majority of the commission were precisely such men as were the least agreeable to the Directory. It was just as well known to Barras, Merlin, and Talleyrand, as it was to Gallatin, Madison, and Jefferson, that the administration were in a difficulty from which they could not easily escape. They saw plainly from the proceedings and the debates of Congress, that Mr. Adams would be compelled to yield to the republican party, or make war on France. and ally himself with England, or retire in disgrace. A war with France, and a consequent alliance with England, they knew would not be attempted with so formidable an opposition as the late Congress had displayed. They had every reason to expect, that by a steady resistance to the overtures of the administration, they would finally secure a triumph to their friends in America. Governments are conducted by men; men are influenced by human motives, too often by the basest passions and prejudices—(Quam parva sapientia regitur mundus.) Judging from these premises, it was preposterous in Mr. Adams to suppose that his embassy would be received by the Directory in any other than the haughtiest spirit. The defeat of such a mission must have been foreseen from the beginning. Pickering, Wolcott and Company had too much political sagacity not to have anticipated it. And perhaps it is not uncharitable to suppose, that it was projected with the view of creating additional causes of irritation on the part of France.

CHAPTER XIX.

THE X. Y. Z. BUSINESS.

The envoys arrived in Paris about the first of October, 1797. On the *eighth* they were introduced to the minister, M. Talleyrand, and produced their letters of credence. The minister informed them that he was engaged in preparing for the Executive Directory, a report relative to the situation of the United States with regard to France; and that when it was finished he would let them know what steps were to follow. They then retired with the promise that cards of hospitality, in a style suitable to their official character, should be furnished them. No further notice was taken of them for ten days. They complained to unofficial persons that they had been treated with great slight and disrespect since their arrival. Talleyrand, on the other hand, complained that they had not been to see him. He sent his private secretary, Mr. Z., to wait on them. They had not yet been received by the Directory; and, of course, their Minister of Foreign Affairs could not recognize them publicly as ambassadors. But he did all in his power to do: he sent his secretary, who informed them that M. Talleyrand, Minister of Foreign Relations, professed to be well disposed towards the United States; had expected to have seen the American Ministers frequently in their private capacities; and to have conferred with them individually on the objects of their mission; and had authorized him to make the communication. This, from the circumstances in which the parties were placed, seems not to have been an unreasonable expectation on the part of M. Talleyrand. But two of the envoys excused themselves on the ground of etiquette. General Pinckney and General Marshall expressed their opinion, that, not being acquainted with M. Talleyrand, they could not, with propriety, call on him; but that, according to the custom of France, he might expect this of Mr. Gerry, from a previous acquaintance in America. This Mr. Gerry reluctantly complied with, and appointed a day for an interview. While thus standing off in this ceremonious manner, and unrecognized by the Government, our envoys had some strange adventures. In the morning of October the eighteenth, Mr. W * * * *, of the house of * * * * * * * *, called on General Pinckney, and informed him that a Mr. X. who was in Paris, and whom the General had seen, * * * * * * * *, was a gentleman of considerable credit and reputation, * * * * * * * *, and that we might place great reliance on him. In the evening of the same day, Mr. X., the gentleman so mysteriously announced, called on General Pinckney, and after having sat some time, whispered him, that he had a message from M. Talleyrand to communicate when he was at leisure. General Pinckney immediately withdrew with him into another room; and when they were alone Mr. X. said, that he was charged with a business in which he was a novice; that he had been acquainted with M. Talleyrand, * * * * * * * * * *, and that he was sure he had a great regard for America and its citizens; and was very desirous that a reconciliation should be brought about with France; that to effectuate that end, he was ready, if it was thought proper, to suggest a plan, confidentially, that M. Talleyrand expected would answer the purpose. General Pinckney said he would be glad to hear it. Mr. X. replied, that the Directory, and particularly two of the members of it, were exceedingly irritated at some passages of the President's speech at the opening of Congress in May, and desired that they should be softened; and that this step would be necessary previous to our reception; that, besides this, a sum of money was required for the pocket of the Directory and ministers (about fifty thousand pounds sterling), which would be at the disposal of M. Talleyrand; and that a loan would also be insisted on. Mr. X. said, if we acceded to these measures, M. Talleyrand had no doubt that all our difficulties with France might be accommodated. At the same time, he said his communication was not immediately with M. Talleyrand, but through another gentleman, in whom M. Talleyrand had great confidence.

Next day Mr. X., and Mr. Y., the confidential friend alluded to, called on the envoys. Mr. Y., having been introduced as the confidential friend of M. Talleyrand, commenced the conversation, and proceeded pretty much in the same strain as Mr. X. on the day preceding. He said the minister could not see them himself, as they had not been received by the Directory, but had authorized his friend Mr. Y. to communicate certain propositions, and to promise on his part, that if they could be considered as the basis of the proposed negotiation, he would intercede with the Directory to acknowledge them, and to give them a public audience. Mr. Y. stated explicitly and repeatedly that he was clothed with no authority; that he was not a diplomatic character; that he was not * * * * * * * *; he was only the friend of M. Talleyrand, and trusted by him. He then read the parts of the President's speech that were objectionable, and dilated very much upon the keenness of the resentment it had produced, and expatiated largely on the satisfaction he said was indispensably necessary as a preliminary to negotiation. "But," said he, "gentlemen, I will not disguise from you that this satisfaction being made, the essential part of the treaty remains to be adjusted: Il faut de l'argent—il faut beaucoup d'argent;" *you must pay money—you must pay a great deal of money.* He said that the reception of the money might be so disguised as to prevent its being considered a breach of neutrality by England; and thus save us from being embroiled with that power. Concerning the twelve hundred thousand livres (£50,000), little was said.

Next day (October 21st) Mr. X. and Mr. Y. again called on the envoys, and commenced their private and unofficial negotiation. It was explained more fully, how the loan might be accomplished by the purchase of certain Dutch inscriptions held by the French government; and it was delicately intimated, that if the envoys would search a little, they might find means to soothe the angry feelings of Merlin and Company, and avert the demand concerning the President's speech.

The envoys replied, that the proposition of a loan in the form of Dutch inscriptions, or in any other form, was not within the limits of their instructions, and that upon this point the Government must be consulted; and one of the American ministers would, for the purpose, forthwith embark for America.

Mr. Y. seemed disappointed at this conclusion. He said the envoys treated the money part of the proposition as if it had proceeded from the Directory; whereas, in fact, it did not even proceed from the minister, but was only a suggestion from himself, as a substitute to be proposed by them, in order to avoid the painful acknowledgment that the Directory had determined to demand.

These unofficial gentlemen, X. and Y., who, the envoys admitted, had brought no testimonials of their speaking any thing from authority, continued their visits from day to day, and urged their propositions with all the earnestness and eloquence they possessed. They told the envoys that France had just concluded a treaty with the Emperor of Austria; and that the Directory, since this peace, had taken a higher and more decided tone with respect to the United States, and all other neutral nations, than had been before taken; that it had been determined that all nations should aid them, or be considered and treated as their enemies. They expatiated on the power and violence of France, urged the danger of our situation, and pressed the policy of softening them, and of thereby obtaining time.

While these strange conferences were held with men unconnected with the Government, and one a foreigner, Mr. Gerry, on the 28th of October, according to appointment, paid his first visit to the minister since the day of their presentation. The others, standing on etiquette, refused to go. After the first introduction, M. Talleyrand began the conference. He said the Directory had passed an arrête, which he offered for perusal, in which they had demanded of the envoys an explanation of some parts, and a reparation for others, of the President's speech to Congress, of the 16th of May last. He was sensible, he said, that difficulties would exist on the part of the envoys relative to this demand; but that by their offering money, he thought he could prevent the effect of the arrête. It having been stated that the envoys had no such power, M. Talleyrand replied, they can in such case take a power on themselves, *and proposed that they should make a loan.* Mr. Gerry then stated that the uneasiness of the Directory resulting from the President's speech, was a subject unconnected with the objects of their mission; that the powers of the envoys, as they conceived, were adequate to the discussion and adjustment of all points of real difference between the two nations; that they could alter and amend the treaty, or, if necessary, form a new one; that as to a loan, they had no powers whatever to make one; but that they could send one of their number for instructions on this proposition, if deemed expedient. M. Talleyrand, in answer, said he should be glad to confer with the other envoys individually; but that this matter about the money must be settled directly, without sending to America; that he would not communicate the arrête for a week; and that if they could adjust the matter about the speech, an application would, nevertheless, go to the United States for a loan. In this private interview between M. Talleyrand and one of the envoys, that minister intimates that a loan will be asked, and will be expected to be granted on the part of the United States; but not the slightest allusion is made to a douceur for the use of the members of the Directory.

On the 11th of November the envoys transmitted an official letter for the first time to the Minister of Foreign Affairs, in which they state that his declaration at the time of their arrival, that a report on American affairs was then preparing, and would, in a few days be laid before the Directory, whose decision thereon should, without delay, be made known, had hitherto imposed silence on them. For this communication they had waited with that anxious solicitude which so interesting an event could not fail to excite, and with that respect which was due to the government of France. They disclosed their full powers to treat on all differences between the two nations; and expressed their anxiety to commence the task of restoring that friendship, that mutual interchange of good offices, which it was alike their wish and their duty to effect between the citizens of the two republics. Having received no answer, on the 21st they sent their secretary to wait on the minister, and inquire of him whether he had communicated the letter to the Directory, and whether an answer might be expected. He replied that he had submitted the letter, and that when he was directed what steps to pursue, they should be informed.

On the 24th of December the envoys wrote to the Secretary of State, that they had received no answer to their official letter to the Minister of Foreign Affairs, dated the 11th of November; but that reiterated attempts had been made to engage them in negotiation with persons not officially authorized. They further stated it as their opinion, that if they were to remain six months longer, unless they were to stipulate the payment of money, and a great deal of it, in some shape or other, they would not be able to effectuate the object of their mission, nor would they even be officially received.

The President of the United States, in a message to Congress, March 19th, 1798, stated that the dispatches from the envoys extraordinary to the French Republic had been received, examined, maturely considered, and that he perceived no ground of expectation that the objects of their mission could be accomplished, on terms compatible with the safety, honor, or the essential interests of the nation.

On the 27th of January, 1798, the envoys addressed a letter to the Minister of Foreign Affairs, on the subject of a late law, authorizing the capture of neutral vessels, on board of which any productions of Great Britain or its possessions should be laden showing how incompatible such law was with the rights of neutral nations and the treaty between France and America, its direct tendency to destroy the remaining commerce of this country, and the particular hardships to which it would subject the agricultural as well as commercial interests of their countrymen, from the peculiar situation of the United States. They added, that under existing circumstances, they could no longer resist the conviction, that the demands of France rendered it entirely impracticable to effect the objects of their mission. On the 19th of February, having received no answer to this communication, they sent their secretary to know of the minister whether he had any response to make. He replied that he had none, as the Directory had taken no order on the subject. At length, on the 27th of February, for the first time since their arrival in Paris, the envoys solicited a personal interview on the subject of their mission. The minister promptly acceded to the request, and fixed on the 2d day of March for the interview. On that occasion, the minister said, that, without doubt, the Directory wished very sincerely, on the arrival of the envoys, to see a solid friendship established between France and the United States, and had manifested this disposition, by the readiness with which orders for their passports were given. That the Directory had been extremely wounded by the last speech of General Washington, made to Congress when about to quit the office of President of the United States; and by the first and last speech of Mr. Adams. That explanations of these speeches were expected and required of us. He said, that the original favorable disposition of the Directory had been a good deal altered by the coldness and distance which the envoys had observed. That instead of seeing him often, and endeavoring to remove the obstacles to a mutual approach, *they had not once waited on him.* In this state of things some proof, he said, would be required on the part of the United States, of a friendly disposition, previous to a treaty with them. The envoys ought to search for, and propose some means which might furnish this proof. In this he alluded very intelligibly to a loan. He said he must exact from them, on the part of his Government, some proposition of this sort; that to prove their friendship, there must be some immediate aid, or something which might avail them; that the principles of reciprocity would require it. This once done, he said, the adjustment of complaints would be easy; that would be matter of inquiry; and if France had done wrong, it would be repaired; but that if this was refused, it would increase the distance and coldness between the two republics. It was replied that the envoys had no power to make a loan. One of them, Mr. Gerry, then observed, that the Government of France must judge for itself; but that it appeared to him, that a treaty on liberal principles, such as those on which the treaty of commerce between the two nations was first established, would be infinitely more advantageous to France than the trifling advantages she could derive from a loan. Such a treaty would produce a friendship and attachment on the part of the United States to France, which would be solid and permanent, and produce benefits far superior to those of a loan, even if they had powers to make it. To this observation, M. Talleyrand made no reply. Nor did he express any sentiment as to the propriety of one of the envoys going home to consult the Government on the expediency of giving powers to negotiate a loan. He had already expressed his opinion that they had the power, or might assume it, without violating their instructions.

On the 18th of March, M. Talleyrand addressed a letter to the envoys in answer to theirs of the 17th January. In this he elaborately reviews the whole course of the two Governments, and justifies France in every particular. It might appear incredible, he said, that the Republic, and her alliance, were sacrificed at the moment when she had redoubled her regards for her ally; and that the corresponding demonstrations of the Federal Government had no other object but to keep her, as well as her Government in a false security. And yet it is now known, that, at this very period, Mr. Jay, who had been sent to London solely, as it was then said, to negotiate arrangements relative to the depredations committed upon the American commerce by the cruisers of Great Britain, signed a treaty of amity, navigation and commerce, the negotiation and signing of which had been kept a profound secret at Paris and at Philadelphia. Observing that, in this treaty every thing having been calculated to turn the neutrality of the United States to the disadvantage of the French Republic, and to the advantage of England; that the Federal Government having in this act made to Great Britain concessions the most unheard of, the most incompatible with the interests of the United States, the most derogatory to the alliance which subsisted between the said States and the French Republic; the latter was perfectly free, in order to avoid the inconveniences of the treaty of London, to avail itself of the preservative means with which the laws of nature, the law of nations, and prior treaties furnished it. Such were the reasons which had produced the decrees of the Directory, of which the United States complained.

He then proceeded to declare that newspapers, known to be under the immediate control of the Cabinet, had, since the treaty, redoubled their invectives and calumnies against the Republic and against her principles, her magistrates and her envoys. Pamphlets, openly paid for by the minister of Great Britain, had reproduced in every form those insults and calumnies. The Government itself was intent on encouraging this scandal in its public acts. The Executive Directory had been denounced in a speech delivered by the President as endeavoring to propagate anarchy and division within the United States In fine, he said, one could not help discovering in the tone of the speech and of the publications which had just been pointed to, a latent enmity that only wanted an opportunity to break out. Facts being thus established, it was disagreeable, he said, to be obliged to think that the instructions under which the commissioners acted, had not been drawn up with the sincere intention of attaining pacific ends. The intentions which he had attributed to the Government of the United States, were so little disguised, that nothing seemed to have been neglected at Philadelphia to manifest them to every eye. And it was probably with this view that it was thought proper to send to the French Republic, persons whose opinions and connections were too well known to hope from them dispositions sincerely conciliatory. Penetrated with the justice of these reflections, and their consequences, the Executive Directory had authorized him to express himself with all the frankness which became the French nation. It was only to smooth the way of discussions that he had entered into the preceding explanations. It was with the same view that he declared to the commissioners and envoys extraordinary, that, notwithstanding the kind of prejudice which had been entertained with respect to them, the Executive Directory was disposed to treat with that one of the three whose opinions, presumed to be more impartial, promised, in the course of the explanations, more of that reciprocal confidence which was indispensable.

To the communication of Talleyrand, the envoys returned a very elaborate reply, in which they reviewed all the points of difficulty raised by him, endeavored to disabuse his mind as to the motives of the Government of the United States, and the prejudices which he imagined to exist in the minds of the envoys themselves, and concluded by declaring that no one of them was authorized to take upon himself a negotiation indirectly intrusted by the tenor of their powers and instructions to the whole; nor were there any two of them who could propose to withdraw themselves from the task committed to them by their Government, while there remained a possibility of performing it.

The very day the answer of the envoys was sent to the minister (3d April) Mr. Gerry received a note from him in which he said:—"I suppose that Messrs. Pinckney and Marshall have thought it useful and proper, in consequence of the intimations given in the end of my note of the 28th Ventose last (18th March), and the obstacle which their known opinions have interposed to the desired reconciliation, to quit the territory of the Republic. On this supposition, I have the honor to point out to you the 5th or 7th of this decade, to resume our reciprocal communications upon the interests of the French Republic and the United States of America."

Mr. Gerry replied (April 4th), that as his colleagues were expected to quit the territory of France, he had no authority to act in their absence. He could only confer informally, he said, and unaccredited, on any subject respecting their mission, and communicate to the Government of the United States the result of such conferences, being in his individual capacity unauthorized to give them an official stamp. Nevertheless, every measure in his power, he said, and in conformity with the duty he owed his country, should be zealously pursued, to restore harmony and a cordial friendship between the two republics.

In consequence of the above intimation from the minister, Messrs. Marshall and Pinckney soon left Paris. In a letter to the President, dated the 16th of April, Mr. Gerry said he had expected his passports with his colleagues, but was informed that the Directory would not consent to his leaving France; and, to bring on an immediate rupture by adopting this measure, contrary to their wishes, would be in his mind unwarrantable, and therefore he concluded to remain.

Thus ended this extraordinary mission; a conclusion which must have been foreseen—must have been anticipated by those who projected it. So soon as the dispatches containing those transactions, of which the above is intended to be a faithful though succinct narrative, were made known to the public, the political barometer at once rose to the storm point. At the time of their reception, Congress was debating the proposition, *that it is inexpedient to resort to war against the French Republic.* It was expected to be carried by a majority of two or three; but it was now laid aside, and the most vigorous war measures introduced. "The most artful misrepresentations of the contents of those papers," says Mr. Jefferson, April 6th, "were published yesterday, and produced such a shock in the republican mind as had never been since our independence. We are to dread the effects of this dismay till their fuller information The spirit kindled up in the towns is wonderful. These and New Jersey are pouring in their addresses, offering life and fortune. The answers of the President are more thrasonic than the addresses. Nor is it France alone, but his own fellow-citizens, against whom his threats are extended. *The delusions*, says he, *and misrepresen-*

tations which have misled so many citizens must be discountenanced by authority, as well as by the citizens at large. . . . . At present the warhawks talk of Septembrizing, deportation, and the examples of quelling sedition set by the French Executive. Early in April the war party, with passionate exclamation, declared that they would soon pass a citizens' bill, an alien bill, and a sedition bill, with the view of disfranchising such men as Gallatin, banishing Volney, Collot, and other unfortunate Frenchmen who had taken refuge in the country, and of silencing Bache, Carey, and other republican presses."

The excitement spread far and wide among the people. The cry was, *millions for defence, not a cent for tribute.* This broad, comprehensive, self-evident proposition to a brave and independent people, soon became the watchword of the multitude: *millions for defence, not a cent for tribute.* This happy and pithy appeal to the pride of a nation was level to the capacity of all; every body could understand it; and, what was more important, every body could feel it. 'Twas vain to attempt to reason down this excited feeling of national pride. 'Twas vain to tell the people that France had demanded no tribute—that our envoys had never held but one interview with the minister of foreign affairs, and that the only proposition on that occasion was the bare suggestion that the United States, as proof of her friendship, might make a loan to France in her present necessities, by way of reciprocity for a similar loan made to us in the war of revolution, when our credit and very existence were dependent on the timely aid then extended to us; that the demand of tribute was made by a couple of swindlers, unconnected with the Government, who had imposed on the credulity of our envoys, and who, in fact, encouraged the intrigue, that they might make political capital, in order to create the very excitement it had occasioned; that the only obstacle in the way of an amicable settlement of all our differences with France was the intemperate speeches of the President, the haughty, reserved and unconciliatory temper of the envoys themselves; that France had only done what she had a right to do according to the laws of nations, to show her displeasure to ministers plenipotentiary who were disagreeable to her, who were hostile to her principles, unfriendly to her Government, and of such a temper as not to be able to secure her confidence; that she had only signified her desire that those envoys should depart, and the one in whom she had confidence might remain, with whom she was ready to negotiate on terms of the utmost fairness and equality. 'Twas vain to state the plain facts to an excited multitude. *Millions for defence, not a cent for tribute*, was the ready and comprehensive answer. The fever was up, and must run its course. The multitude are not only fond of broad and comprehensive phrases that will serve them on all occasions, and save the necessity of thought, but they must always have some sign, or outward symbol of their feelings. On this occasion the *black cockade* of England was mounted as a badge of hostility to the *tri-color* of France. The handwriting, it was said, at the bottom of an address is seen but by few persons; whereas a cockade will be seen by the whole city, by the friends and the foes of the wearer; it will be the visible sign of the sentiments of his heart, and will prove that he is not ashamed to avow those sentiments. Persons who marched to the President's house to present their warlike addresses were encouraged to wear the *American cockade*. Those who dare not designate themselves, they were told, by this lasting mark of resolution, may, indeed, walk up Market-street, but their part of the procession will only serve to recall to our minds the old battered French gasconade—

> "The King of France, with forty thousand men,
> Marched up the hill, and thén—*marched down again.*"

Congress, under the war-excitement, passed in rapid succession, a stamp-act, an excise law, an act, entering into minute and vexatious details, laying a direct tax on lands, slaves, houses, and other property; two acts authorizing the President to borrow large sums of money at usurious interest; several acts authorizing the purchasing of vessels, creating a naval armament, and a navy department in the Government; acts prohibiting the exportation of arms, and authorizing the purchase of cannon, and the fortification of ports and harbors; acts creating additional regiments in the army, augmenting those in existence, and authorizing the President to call out and organize a *provisional* army of *ten thousand men*, if in his opinion there existed an imminent danger of invasion; acts prohibiting all intercourse with France or her dependencies, and authorizing the capture of all French armed vessels; an act making it lawful for the President of the United States to cause all such aliens as he shall judge dangerous to the peace and safety of the United States, or shall have reasonable grounds to suspect are concerned in any treasonable or secret machinations against the Government thereof, to depart out of the territory of the United States; and an act declaring, that if any person shall write, print, utter, or publish, or aid in the same, any false, scandalous, and malicious writings against the Government of the United States, Congress, or the President, with intent to defame, or bring them into contempt or disrepute, being thereof convicted before any court of the United States, shall be punished by fine and imprisonment. To crown all these vast military preparations, General Washington was appointed Commander-in-chief of the Army. "We must have your name," said the President, in a letter to him, "if you will in any way permit us to use it. There will be more efficiency in it than in many an army." Without waiting for an answer, on the 2d of July he nominated to the Senate, "George Washington, of Mount Vernon, to be Lieutenant-General and Commander-in-chief of all the armies, raised and to be raised in the United States."

Washington accepted the appointment; and in his reply to the President, said: "It was not possible for me to remain ignorant of, or indifferent to, recent transactions. The conduct of the Directory of France towards our country, their insidious hostilities to its Government, their various practices to withdraw the affections of the people from it, the evident tendency of their arts, and those of their agents, to countenance and invigorate opposition, their disregard of solemn treaties and the laws of nations, their war upon our defenceless commerce, their treatment of our minister of peace, and their demands, amounting to tribute, could not fail to excite in me corresponding sentiments with those which my countrymen had so generally expressed in their affectionate addresses to you. Believe me, sir, no one can more cordially approve of the wise and prudent measures of your administration. They ought to inspire universal confifidence, and will no doubt, combined with the state of things, call from Congress such laws and means as will enable you to meet the full force and extent of the crisis. Satisfied, therefore, that you have sincerely wished and endeavored to avert war, and exhausted to the last drop the cup of reconciliation, we can with pure hearts appeal to Heaven for the justice of our cause, and may confidently trust the final result to that kind Providence, which has heretofore, and so often, signally favored the people of these United States."

The war excitement was kept up through the summer and autumn. The republican party found it difficult to separate in the public mind the principles for which they contended, from the acts of the French Directory. Having been regarded through the country as the French party, they had now to bear much of the odium that was attached to the French cause. The war fever began to abate as winter approached. Mr. Gerry, our envoy, who remained in France after the departure of his colleagues, and other eminent citizens of the United States, had now returned from Europe, and reported that the French Directory were in a most friendly temper towards the United States, and were prepared to treat with any minister they might send, on terms of perfect reciprocity. The Virginia legislature, early in the session of 1798–9, passed a series of resolutions denouncing the Alien and Sedition Laws as unconstitutional. The heavy taxes also began to work their usual effect on the public mind. It was soon perceived that some effort must be made to prevent the popular current from turning against the administration. The great object was to keep up the majority in Congress, so as to continue their war measures. The spring elections of 1799 were coming on, and every effort was made by both sides to influence them. It was perceived that the future destiny of the country depended on the result. Virginia was the great battle-ground: all eyes were turned in that direction.

There was the stronghold of republicanism—there were its renowned chiefs to be found—Jefferson, Madison, Monroe, Giles, Taylor, besides a host of others of less fame, but equal zeal in the cause. There, also, was Washington, who had thrown himself into the opposite scale, and, with energy, exerted all his influence to give preponderance to the side he espoused. No man did more to bring out influential characters to represent the State, both in Congress and the legislature. "At such a crisis as this," said he, "when every thing dear and valuable to us is assailed; when this party hangs upon the wheels of government as a dead weight, opposing every measure that is calculated for defence and self-preservation; abetting the nefarious views of another nation upon our rights; preferring, as long as they dare contend openly against the spirit and resentment of the people, the interest of France to the welfare of their own country; justifying the former, at the expense of the latter; when every act of their own government is tortured, by constructions they will not bear, into attempts to infringe and trample upon the constitution, with a view to introduce monarchy; when the most unceasing and the purest exertions, which were making to maintain a neutrality, proclaimed by the executive, approved unequivocally by Congress, by the State legislatures, nay, by the people themselves, in various meetings, and to preserve the country in peace, are charged with being measures calculated to favor Great Britain at the expense of France; and all those who had any agency in it, are accused of being under the influence of the former, and her pensioners; when measures are systematically and pertinaciously pursued, which must, eventually, dissolve the Union, or produce coercion; I say, when these things have become so obvious, ought characters who are best able to rescue their country from the pending evil, to remain at home? Rather ought they not to come forward, and, by their talents and influence, stand in the breach, which such conduct has made on the peace and happiness of this country?"

By such persuasions as this, General Lee was induced to offer himself as a candidate for Congress in the Westmoreland district—Westmoreland, the birth-place of Washington! On the other hand, by the persuasions of Mr. Jefferson, Dr. Walter Jones came out in opposition to him. The canvass between these two champions of adverse wishes and sentiments, was very animated. In colloquial eloquence and irony, no man could surpass Dr. Jones; but he was overmatched by his antagonist, in popular address and public eloquence. In the Richmond district, John Clopton, the sitting member, and a republican, was opposed by General Marshall, the late envoy to France, and, by all odds, the ablest champion of the federal cause in Virginia. But the great field of contest—the citadel that must be carried—was the State legislature. That body had recently pronounced the Alien and Sedition Laws unconstitutional. The great object was now to obtain a majority to reverse that decision. It was well known that Mr. Madison would be in the next legislature, with his matchless logic, to develope, explain and enforce the doctrines of the resolutions recently passed. Some one must be found to oppose him. General Washington found the man—that man was Patrick Henry. And by him the trembling old warrior was induced to buckle on the harness for his last battle. In a confidential letter, dated 15th January, 1799, Washington says: "It would be a waste of time to attempt to bring to the view of a person of your observation and discernment, the endeavors of a certain party among us to disquiet the public mind with unfounded alarms; to arraign every act of the administration; to set the people at variance with their government; and to embarrass all its measures. Equally useless would it be to predict what must be the inevitable consequences of such a policy, if it cannot be arrested. Unfortunately, and extremely do I regret it, the State of Virginia has taken the lead in this opposition. I have said the *State*, because the conduct of its legislature in the eyes of the world will authorize the expression. I come now, my good sir, to the object of my letter, which is to express the hope, and an earnest wish, that you will come forward at the ensuing elections (if not for Congress, which you may think would take you too long from home) as a candidate for representative in the General Assembly of this Commonwealth. Your weight of character and influence in the House of Representatives would be a bulwark against such dangerous sentiments as are delivered there at present. It would be a rallying-point for the timid, and an attraction for the wavering. In a word, I conceive it to be of immense importance, at this crisis, that you should be there; and I would fain hope that all minor considerations will be made to yield to the measure." All minor considerations were made to yield; and the old veteran, bowed with age and disease, was announced as a candidate to represent the county of Charlotte in the General Assembly of Virginia. Powhatan Bolling was the candidate for Congress, on the federal side; he was opposed by John Randolph. On March court day, Patrick Henry and John Randolph met, for the first time, on the hustings at Charlotte Court House—the one the champion of the Federal—the other the champion of the Republican cause.

CHAPTER XX.

PATRICK HENRY.

Patrick Henry, the advocate of the Alien and Sedition Laws, the defender of federal measures leading to consolidation! Let the reader look back and contemplate his course in the Virginia Convention, called to ratify the Constitution—let him hear the eloquent defence of the Articles of Confederation, which had borne us safely through so many perils, and which needed only amendment, not annihilation—let him witness the ardent devotion to the State government as the bulwark of liberty—the uncompromising opposition to the new Government, its consolidation, its destruction of State independence, its awful squinting towards monarchy—let him behold the vivid picture drawn by the orator of the patriot of *seventy-six*, and the citizen of *eighty-eight;* then it was liberty, give me liberty! now the cry was energy, energy, give me a strong and energetic government—then let him turn and see the same man, in little more than ten years, stand forth, his prophecies all tending to rapid fulfilment, the advocate of the principles, the defender of the measures that had so agitated his mind and awakened his fears—let the reader meditate on these things, and have charity for the mutations of political opinion in his own day, which he so often unfeelingly denounces.

It is true that Patrick Henry had been in retirement since the adoption of the new Constitution, and had no part in the organization of those parties which had arisen under it, but it is certain that they took their origin in those principles which on the one side he so eloquently defended, and on the other so warmly deprecated. Federalist and Republican were names unknown in his day; but from his past history no one could mistake the inclination of his feelings, or the conclusions of his judgment on the great events transpiring around him. Up to 1795 he was known to be on the republican side. In a letter, dated the 27th of June in that year, he says: "Since the adoption of the present Constitution I have generally moved in a narrow circle. But in that I have never omitted to inculcate a strict adherence to the principles of it. . . . . . Although a democrat myself, I like not the late democratic societies. As little do I like their suppression by law." On another occasion he writes: "The treaty (Jay's treaty) is, in my opinion, a very bad one indeed . . . . Sure I am, my first principle is, that from the British we have every thing to dread, when opportunities of oppressing us shall offer." He then proceeds to express his concern at the abusive manner in which his old commander-in-chief was treated; and that his long and great services were not remembered as an apology for his mistakes in an office to which he was totally unaccustomed.

A man of his talents, his eloquence, his weight of character and influence in the State, was well worth gaining over to the side of the administration. Some of the first characters in Virginia undertook to accomplish that end. Early in the summer of 1794, General Lee, then governor of Virginia, and commander-in-chief of the forces ordered out against the whisky insurrection, had frequent and earnest conferences with him on public affairs. He was at first very impracticable. It seems that the old man had been informed that General Washington, in passing through the State on his return from the South in the summer of 1791, while speaking of Mr. Henry on several occasions, considered him a *factious and seditious character*. General Lee undertook to remove these impressions, and combated his opinions as groundless; but his endeavors were unavailing. He seemed to be deeply and sorely affected. General Washington denied the charge. All he had said on the occasion alluded to was, that he had heard Mr. Henry was acquiescent in his conduct, and that, though he could not give up his opinion respecting the Constitution, yet, unless he should be called upon by official duty, he would express no sentiment unfriendly to the exercise of the powers of a government, which had been chosen by a majority of the people.

It was a long time before General Lee had an opportunity of communicating to Mr. Henry the kind feelings of Washington towards him. In June, 1795, about a year after the subject had been broached to him, Mr. Henry writes: "Every insinuation that taught me to believe I had forfeited the good will of that personage, to whom the world had agreed to ascribe the appellation of *good* and *great*, must needs give me pain; particularly as he had opportunities of knowing my character both in public and in private life. The intimation now given me, that there was no ground to believe I had incurred his censure, gives very great pleasure." In inclosing Mr. Henry's letter to General Washington for perusal, Lee thus writes (17th July, 1795): "I am very confident that Mr. Henry possesses the highest and truest regard for you, and that he continues friendly to the General Government, notwithstanding the unwearied efforts applied for the end of uniting him to the opposition; and I must think he would be an important official acquisition to the Government."

One month and two days from this date (19th August) as the reader remembers, Edmund Randolph resigned the office of Secretary of State. On the 9th of October it was tendered to Patrick Henry. In his letter of invitation General Washington stated that the office had been offered to others; but it was from a conviction that he would not accept it. But in a conversation with General Lee, that gentleman dropped sentiments that made it less doubtful. "I persuade myself, sir," said the President, "it has not escaped your observation that a crisis is approaching that must, if it cannot be arrested, soon decide whether order and good government shall be preserved, or anarchy and confusion ensue."

This letter of invitation was inclosed to Mr. Carrington, a confidential friend of Washington, with instructions to hold it back till he could hear from Colonel Innis, to whom the attorney-generalship had been offered. But on consultation with General Marshall, another confidential friend, they were so anxious to make an impression on Patrick Henry, and gain him over, if possible, by those marks of confidence, that they disobeyed orders, reversed the order in which the letters were to be sent, and dispatched Mr. Henry's first, by express.

"In this determination we were governed," say they, "by the following reasons." (We give the reasons entire, that the reader may see that great men and statesmen in those days were influenced by the same motives they are now, and that men are the same in every age.) "First, his non-acceptance, from domestic considerations may be calculated on. In this event, be his sentiments on either point what they may, he will properly estimate your letter, and if he has any asperities, it must tend to soften them, and render him, instead of a silent observer of the present tendency of things, in some degree active on the side of government and order. Secondly, should he feel an inclination to go into the office proposed, we are confident—very confident—he has too high a sense of honor to do so with sentiments hostile to either of the points in view. This we should rely on, upon general grounds; but under your letter a different conduct is, we conceive from our knowledge of Mr. Henry, impossible. Thirdly, we are fully persuaded that a more deadly blow could not be given to the faction in Virginia, and perhaps elsewhere, than that gentleman's acceptance of the office in question, convinced as we are of the sentiments he must carry with him. So much have the opposers of government held him up as their oracle, even since he has ceased to respond to them, that any event demonstrating his active support to government could not but give the party a severe shock."

A very good reason for disobeying instructions, and making the first demonstration on so important a personage. Mr. Henry did not accept the appointment, but the impression intended to be made was nearly as complete as the parties intended.

"It gives us pleasure to find," says Mr. Carrington, "that although Mr. Henry is rather to be understood as probably not an approver of the treaty, his conduct and sentiments generally, both as to the government and yourself, are such as we calculated on, and that he received your letter with impresssions which assure us of his discountenancing calumny and disorder of every description."

These great movements somehow got wind, and came to the ears of the leader of the faction they were designed to crush. In a letter addressed to Monroe, dated July 10th, 1796, Jefferson says: "Most assiduous court is paid to Patrick Henry. He has been offered every thing, which they knew he would not accept. Some impression is thought to be made: but we do not believe it is radical. If they thought they could count upon him, they would run him for their Vice-President, their first object being to produce a schism in this State." A move was now made to prevent the old man from going over altogether. In November following, the democratic legislature of Virginia elected him, for the third time, governor of the State. In his letter declining an acceptance of the office, he merely expresses his acknowledgments and gratitude for the signal honor conferred on him, excuses himself on the ground that he could not persuade himself that his abilities were commensurate to the duties of the office, but let fall no expression that could indicate his present political inclinations.

Early in January, 1799, soon after the passage of the resolutions declaring the alien and sedition laws unconstitutional, and before he had received the letter from Washington urging him to become a candidate for the Virginia legislature, Patrick Henry, in writing to a friend, thus expresses himself: "There is much cause for lamentation over the present state of things in Virginia. It is possible that most of the individuals who compose the contending factions are sincere, and act from honest motives. But it is more than probable that certain leaders meditate a change in government. To effect this, I see no way so practicable as dissolving the confederacy; and I am free to own that, in my judgment, most of the measures lately pursued by the opposition party directly and certainly lead to that end. If this is not the system of the party, they have none, and act *extempore*."

In February following, the President nominated Mr. Henry as one of the Envoys Extraordinary and Ministers Plenipotentiary to the French Republic. Perhaps the very day he appeared before the people at Charlotte Court, he held the commission in his pocket. In his letter declining the appointment, he says: "That nothing short of absolute necessity could induce me to withhold my little aid from an administration whose abilities, patriotism, and virtue, deserve the gratitude and reverence of all their fellow-citizens."

In March, *eighty-nine*, Decius said, *I want to crush that anti-federal champion*—the cunning and deceitful Cromwell, who, under the guise of amendment, seeks to destroy the Constitution, break up the confederacy, and reign *the tyrant of popularity* over his own devoted Virginia. In *ninety-nine*, we find this anti-federal champion veered round to the support of doctrines he once condemned, and given in his allegiance to an administration, which a majority of his countrymen had declared, and all those who had followed him as their oracle declared, was rapidly hastening the Government into consolidation and monarchy.

Let no man boast of his consistency. Such is the subtlety of human motives, that, like a deep, unseen under-current, they unconsciously glide us into a position to-day different from that we occupied yesterday, while we perceive it not, and stoutly deny it.

Patrick Henry for years was sorely afflicted with the belief that the *greatest* and *best* of mankind considered him a *factious* and *seditious* character: to disabuse the mind of Washington, whose good opinion all men desired—to justify the flattering attentions of those distinguished men who had assiduously cultivated his society and correspondence, and showered bright honors on his head, he unconsciously receded from his old opinions, and embraced doctrines which he had, with the clearness and power of a Hebrew prophet, portrayed and made bare in all their naked deformity.

CHAPTER XXI.

MARCH COURT—THE RISING AND THE SETTING SUN.

It was soon noised abroad that Patrick Henry was to address the people at March Court. Great was the political excitement—still greater the anxiety to hear the first orator of the age for the last time. They came from far and near, with eager hope depicted on every countenance. It was a treat that many had not enjoyed for years. Much the largest portion of those who flocked together that day, had only heard from the glowing lips of their fathers the wonderful powers of the man they were about to see and hear for the first time. The college in Prince Edward was emptied not only of its students, but of its professors. Dr. Moses Hogue, John H. Rice, Drury Lacy, eloquent men and learned divines, came up to enjoy the expected feast. The young man who was to answer Mr. Henry, if indeed the multitude suspected that any one would dare venture on a reply, was unknown to fame. A tall, slender, effeminate looking youth was he; light hair, combed back into a well-adjusted cue—pale countenance, a beardless chin, bright quick hazel eye, blue frock, buff small clothes, and fair-top boots. He was doubtless known to many on the court green as the little Jack Randolph they had frequently seen dashing by on wild horses, riding *a la mode Anglais*, from Roanoke to Bizarre, and back from Bizarre to Roanoke. A few knew him more intimately, but none had ever heard him speak in public, or even suspected that he could make a speech. "My first attempt at public speaking," says he, in a letter to Mrs. Bryan, his niece, "was in opposition to Patrick Henry at Charlotte March Court, 1799; for neither of us was present at the election in April, as Mr. Wirt avers of Mr. Henry." The very thought of his attempting to answer Mr. Henry, seemed to strike the grave and reflecting men of the place as preposterous. "Mr. Taylor," said Col. Reid, the clerk of the county, to Mr. Creed Taylor, a friend and neighbor of Randolph, and a good lawyer, "Mr. Taylor, don't you or Peter Johnson mean to appear for that young man to-day?" "Never mind," replied Taylor, "he can take care of himself." His friends knew his powers, his fluency in conversation, his ready wit, his polished satire, his extraordinary knowledge of men and affairs; but still he was about to enter on an untried field, and all those brilliant faculties might fail him, as they had so often failed men of genius before. They might well have felt some anxiety on his first appearance upon the hustings in presence of a popular assembly, and in reply to a man of Mr. Henry's reputation. But it seems they had no fear for the result—*he can take care of himself.* The reader can well imagine the remarks that might have been made by the crowd as he passed carelessly among them, shaking hands with this one and that one of his acquaintance. "And is that the man who is a candidate for Congress?" "Is he going to speak against Old Pat?" "Why, he is nothing but a boy—he's got no beard!" "He looks wormy!" "Old Pat will eat him up bodily!" There, also, was Powhatan Bolling, the other candidate for Congress, dressed in his scarlet coat—tall, proud in his bearing, and a fair representative of the old aristocracy fast melting away under the subdivisions of the law that had abolished the system of primogeniture.

Creed Taylor and others undertook to banter him about his scarlet coat. "Very well, gentlemen," replied he coolly, bristling up with a quick temper, "if my coat does not suit you, I can meet you in any other color that may suit your fancy." Seeing the gentleman not in a bantering mood, he was soon left to his own reflections. But the candidates for Congress were overlooked and forgotten by the crowd in their eagerness to behold and admire the great orator, whose fame had filled their imagination for so many years. "As soon as he appeared on the ground," says Wirt, "he was surrounded by the admiring and adoring crowd, and whithersoever he moved, the concourse followed him. A preacher of the Baptist church, whose piety was wounded by this homage paid to a mortal, asked the people aloud, why they thus followed Mr. Henry about? "Mr. Henry," said he, "is not a god!" "No," said Mr. Henry, deeply affected by the scene and the remark, "no, indeed, my friend; I am but a poor worm of the dust—as fleeting and unsubstantial as the shadow of the cloud that flies over your fields, and is remembered no more." The tone with which this was uttered, and the look which accompanied it, affected every heart, and silenced every voice.

Presently James Adams rose upon a platform that had been erected by the side of the tavern porch where Mr. Henry was seated, and proclaimed—"O yes! O yes! Colonel Henry will address the people from this stand, for the last time and at the risk of his life!" The grand-jury were in session at the moment, they burst through the doors, some leaped the windows, and came running up with the crowd, that they might not lose a word that fell from the old man's lips.

While Adams was lifting him on the stand, "Why Jimmy," says he, "you have made a better speech for me than I can make for myself." "Speak out, father," said Jimmy, "and let us hear how it is."

Old and feeble, more with disease than age, Mr. Henry rose and addressed the people to the following effect:—(Wirt's Life of Patrick Henry, page 393.) He told them that the late proceedings of the Virginia Assembly had filled him with apprehensions and alarm; that they had planted thorns upon his pillow; that they had drawn him from that happy retirement which it had pleased a bountiful Providence to bestow, and in which he had hoped to pass, in quiet, the remainder of his days; that the State had quitted the sphere in which she had been placed by the Constitution; and in daring to pronounce upon the validity of federal laws, had gone out of her jurisdiction in a manner not warranted by any authority, and in the highest degree alarming to every considerate mind; that such opposition, on the part of Virginia, to the acts of the General Government, must beget their enforcement by military power; that this would probably produce civil war; civil war, foreign alliances; and that foreign alliances must necessarily end in subjugation to the powers called in. He conjured the people to pause and consider well, before they rushed into such a desperate condition, from which there could be no retreat. He painted to their imaginations, Washington, at the head of a numerous and well appointed army, inflicting upon them military execution. "And where (he asked) are our resources to meet such a conflict? Where is the citizen of America who will dare to lift his hand against the father of his country?" A drunken man in the crowd threw up his arm and exclaimed that he dared to do it. "No," answered Mr. Henry, rising aloft in all his majesty, "*you dare not do it; in such a parricidal attempt, the steel would drop from your nerveless arm.*"

Proceeding, he asked "Whether the county of Charlotte would have any authority to dispute an obedience to the laws of Virginia;" and he pronounced Virginia to be to the Union what the county of Charlotte was to *her*. Having denied the right of a State to decide upon the constitutionality of federal laws, he added, that perhaps it might be necessary to say something of the laws in question. His private opinion was, that they were *good* and *proper*. But whatever might be their merits, it belonged to the people, who held the reins over the head of Congress, and to them alone, to say whether they were acceptable or otherwise to Virginians; and that this must be done by way of petition. That Congress were as much our representatives as the Assembly, and had as good a right to our confidence. He had seen, with regret, the unlimited power over the purse and sword consigned to the General Government; but that he had been overruled, and it was now necessary to submit to the constitutional exercise of that power. "If," said he, "I am asked what is to be done when a people feel themselves intolerably oppressed, my answer is ready—*overturn the Government.* But do not, I beseech you, carry matters to this length without provocation. Wait, at least, until *some* infringement is made upon your rights, and which cannot otherwise be redressed; for if ever you recur to another changé, you may bid adieu forever to representative government. You can never exchange the present government but for a monarchy. If the administration have done wrong, let us all go wrong together rather than split into factions, which must destroy that *Union* upon which our existence hangs. Let us preserve our strength for the French, the English, the Germans, or whoever else shall dare to invade our territory, and not exhaust it in civil commotions and intestine wars."

When he concluded, his audience were deeply affected; it is said that they wept like children, so powerfully were they moved by the emphasis of his language, the tone of his voice, the commanding expression of his eye, the earnestness with which he declared his design to exert himself to allay the heart-burnings and jealousies which had been fomented in the State legislature, and the fervent manner in which he prayed that if he were deemed unworthy to effect it, that it might be reserved to some other and abler hand to extend this blessing over the community. As he concluded, he literally sunk into the arms of the tumultuous throng: at that moment John H. Rice exclaimed, "the sun has set in all his glory!"

Randolph rose to reply. For some moments he stood in silence, his lips quivering, his eye swimming in tears; at length he began a modest though beautiful apology for rising to address the people in opposition to the venerable father who had just taken his seat; it was an honest difference of opinion, and he hoped to be pardoned while he boldly and freely, as it became the occasion, expressed his sentiments on the great questions that so much divided and agitated the minds of the people.

"The gentleman tells you," said he, "that the late proceedings of the Virginia Assembly have filled him with apprehension and alarm. He seems to be impressed with the conviction, that the State has quitted the sphere in which she was placed by the Constitution; and in daring to pronounce on the validity of federal laws, has gone out of her jurisdiction in a manner not warranted by any authority. I am sorry the gentleman has been disturbed in his repose; still more grieved am I, that the particular occasion to which he alludes should have been the cause of his anxiety. I once cherished the hope that his alarms would have been awakened, had Virginia failed to exert herself in warding off the evils he so prophetically warned us of on another memorable occasion. Her supineness and inactivity, now that those awful squintings towards monarchy, so eloquently described by the gentleman, are fast growing into realities, I had hoped would have planted thorns in his pillow, and awakened him to a sense of the danger now threatening us, and the necessity of exerting once more his powerful faculties in warning the people, and rousing them from their fatal lethargy.

"Has the gentleman forgotten that we owe to him those obnoxious principles, as he now would have them, that guided the Legislature in its recent course? He is alarmed at the rapid growth of the seed he himself hath sowed—he seems to be disappointed that they fell, not by the wayside, but into vigorous and fruitful soil. He has conjured up spirits from the vasty deep, and growing alarmed at the potency of his own magic wand, he would say to them, 'Down, wantons! down!' but, like Banquo's ghost, I trust they will not down. But to drop metaphor—In the Virginia Convention, that was called to ratify the Constitution, this gentleman declared that the government delineated in that instrument was peculiar in its nature—partly national, partly federal. In this description he hit upon the true definition—there are certain powers of a national character that extend to the people and operate on them without regard to their division into States—these powers, acting alone, tend to consolidate the government into one head, and to obliterate State divisions and to destroy State authority; but there are other powers, many and important ones, that are purely federal in their nature—that look to the States, and recognize their existence as bodies politic, endowed with many of the most important attributes of sovereignty. These two opposing forces act as checks on each other, and keep the complicated system *in equilibrium*. They are like the centrifugal and centripetal forces in the law of gravitation, that serve to keep the spheres in their harmonious courses through the universe.

"Should the Federal Government, therefore, attempt to exercise powers that do not belong to it—and those that do belong to it are few, specified, well-defined—all others being reserved to the people and to the States—should it step beyond its province, and encroach on rights that have not been delegated, it is the duty of the States to interpose. There is no other power that can interpose. The counterweight, the opposing force of the State, is the only check to overaction known to the system.

"In questions of *meum et tuum*, where rights of property are concerned, and some other cases specified in the Constitution, I grant you that the Federal Judiciary may pronounce on the validity of the law. But in questions involving the right to power, whether this or that power has been delegated or reserved, they cannot and ought not to be the arbiter; that question has been left, as it always was, and always must be left, to be determined among sovereignties in the best way they can. Political wisdom has not yet discovered any infallible mathematical rule, by which to determine the assumptions of power between those who know no other law or limitation save that imposed on them by their own consent, and which they can abrogate at pleasure. Pray let me ask the gentleman—and no one knows better than himself—who ordained this Constitution? Who defined its powers, and said, thus far shalt thou go, but no farther? Was it not the people of the States in their sovereign capacity? Did they commit an act of suicide by so doing?—an act of self-annihilation? No, thank God, they did not; but are still alive, and, I trust, are becoming sensible of the importance of those rights reserved to them, and prohibited to that government which they ordained for their common defence. Shall the creature of the States be the sole judge of the legality or constitutionality of its own acts, in a question of power between them and the States? Shall they who assert a right, be the sole judges of their authority to claim and to exercise it? Does not all power seek to enlarge itself?—grow on that it feeds upon? Has not that been the history of all encroachment, all usurpation? If this Federal Government, in all its departments, then, is to be the sole judge of its own usurpations, neither the people nor the States, in a short time, will have any thing to contend for; this creature of their making will become their sovereign, and the only result of the labors of our revolutionary heroes, in which patriotic band this venerable gentleman was most conspicuous, will have been a change of our masters—New England for Old England—for which change I cannot find it in my heart to thank them.

"But the gentleman has taught me a very different lesson from that he is now disposed to enjoin on us. I fear that time has wrought its influence on him, as on all other men; and that age makes him willing to endure what in former years he would have spurned with indignation. I have learned my first lessons in his school. He is the high-priest from whom I received the little wisdom my poor abilities were able to carry away from the droppings of the political sanctuary. He was the inspired statesman that taught me to be jealous of power, to watch its encroachments, and to sound the alarm on the first movement of usurpation.

"Inspired by his eloquent appeals—encouraged by his example—alarmed by the rapid strides of Federal usurpation, of which he had warned them—the legislature of Virginia has nobly stepped forth in defence of the rights of the States, and interposed to arrest that encroachment and usurpation of power that threaten the destruction of the Republic.

"And what is the subject of alarm? What are the laws they have dared to pronounce upon as unconstitutional and tyrannical? The first, is a law authorizing the President of the United States to order any alien he may judge dangerous, any unfortunate refugee that may happen to fall under his royal suspicion, forthwith to quit the country. It is true that the law says he must have *reasonable* grounds to suspect. Who is to judge of that reason but himself? Who can look into his breast and say what motives have dominion there? 'Tis a mockery to give one man absolute power over the liberty of another, and *then* ask him, when the power is gone, and cannot be recalled, to exercise it reasonably! Power knows no other check but power. Let the poor patriot who may have fallen under the frowns of government, because he dared assert the rights of his countrymen, seek refuge on our shores of boasted liberty; the moment he touches the soil of freedom, hoping here to find a period to all his persecutions, he is greeted, not with the smiles of welcome, or the cheerful voice of freemen, but the stern demands of an officer of the law—the executor of a tyrant's will—who summons him to depart. What crime has he perpetrated? Vain inquiry! He is a *suspected* person. He is judged dangerous to the peace of the country—rebellious at home, he may be alike factious and seditious here. What remedy? What hope? He who condemns is judge—the sole judge in the first and the last resort. There is no appeal from his arbitrary will. Who can escape the suspicion of a jealous and vindictive mind?

"The very men who fought your battles, who spent their fortunes, and shed their blood to win for you that independence that was once your boast, may be the first victims of this tyrannical law. Kosciusko is now on your shores; though poor in purse and emaciated in body, from the many sacrifices he has made in your cause, he has yet a proud spirit that loves freedom, and will speak boldly of oppression. Is not this enough to bring him under the frowns of power, and to cause the mandate to be issued, ordering him to depart from the country? What may be true of one to whom we owe so much, has already been fulfilled in the person of many a patriot, scholar, and philosopher, whose only crime was, that of seeking refuge from oppression and wrong, on these shores of boasted freedom.

"And what is that other law that so fully meets the approbation of my venerable friend? It is a law that makes it an act of sedition, punishable by fine and imprisonment, to utter or write a sentiment that any prejudiced judge or juror may think proper to construe into disrespect to the President of the United States. Do you understand me? I dare proclaim to the people of Charlotte my opinion to be, that John Adams, so-called President, is a weak-minded man, vain, jealous, and vindictive; that influenced by evil passions and prejudices, and goaded on by wicked counsel, he has been striving to force the country into a war with our best friend and ally. I say that I dare repeat this before the people of Charlotte, and avow it as my opinion. But let me write it down, and print it as a warning to my countrymen. What then? *I subject myself to an indictment for sedition!* I make myself liable to be dragged away from my home and friends, and to be put on my trial in some distant Federal Court, before a judge who receives his appointment from the man that seeks my condemnation; and to be tried by a prejudiced jury, who have been gathered from remote parts of the country, strangers to me, and any thing but my peers; and have been packed by the minions of power for my destruction. Is the man dreaming! do you exclaim? Is this a fancy picture, he has drawn for our amusement? I am no fancy man, people of Charlotte! I speak the truth—I deal only in stern realities! There is such a law on your Statute Book in spite of your Constitution—in open contempt of those solemn guarantees that insure the freedom of speech and of the press to every American citizen. Not only is there such a statute, but, with shame be it spoken, even England blushes at your sedition law. Would that I could stop here, and say that, though it may be found enrolled among the the public archives, it is a dead letter. Alas! alas! not only does it exist, but at this hour is most rigidly enforced, not against the ordinary citizen only, but against men in official stations, even those who are clothed by the people with the sacred duties of their representatives—men, the sanctity of whose persons cannot be reached by any law known to a representative government, are hunted down, condemned, and incarcerated by this odious, tyrannical, and unconstitutional enactment. At this moment, while I am addressing you, men of Charlotte! with the free air of heaven fanning my locks—and God knows how long I shall be permitted to enjoy that blessing—a representative of the people of Vermont—Matthew Lyon his name—lies immured in a dungeon, not six feet square, where he has dragged out the miserable hours of a protracted winter, for daring to violate the royal maxim that the king can do no wrong. This was his only crime—he told his people, and caused it to be printed for their information, that the President, 'rejecting men of age, experience, wisdom, and independency of sentiment,' appointed those who had no other merit but devotion to their master; and he intimated that the 'President was fond of ridiculous pomp, idle parade, and selfish avarice.' I speak the language of the indictment. I give in technical and official words the high crime with which he was charged. He pleaded justification—I think the lawyers call it—and offered to prove the truth of his allegations. But the court would allow no time to procure witnesses or counsel; he was hurried into trial all unprepared; and this representative of the people, for speaking the truth of those in authority, was arraigned like a felon, condemned, fined, and imprisoned. These are the laws, the venerable gentlemen would have you believe, are not only sanctioned by the Constitution, but demanded by the necessity of the times—laws at which even monarchs blush—banishing from your shores the hapless victim that only sought refuge from oppression, and making craven, fawning spaniels, aye! dumb dogs, of your own people! He tells you, moreover, that if you do not agree with him in opinion—cannot consent that these vile enactments are either constitutional or necessary—your only remedy, your only hope of redress, is in petition.

"*Petition!* Whom are we to petition? But one solitary member from Virginia, whose name is doomed to everlasting infamy, dared to record his vote—dared to record, did I say? I beg pardon—but one who did not spurn from them this hideous offspring of a tyrant's lust. Whom, then, I repeat, are we to petition? those who are the projectors of these measures, who voted for them, and forced them upon you in spite of your will? Would not these men laugh at your petition, and, in the pride and insolence of new-born power, trample it under their feet with disdain? Shall we petition his majesty, who, by virtue of these very laws, holds your liberties in his sacred hands? I tell you he would spurn your petition from the foot of the throne, as those of your fathers, on a like occasion, were spurned from the throne of George the Third of England. From whose lips do we hear that word petition—an abject term, fit only for the use of subjects and of slaves? Can it be that *he* is now willing to petition and to supplicate his co-equals in a common confederacy, who proudly disdained entreaty and supplication to the greatest monarch on earth—whose fleets covered our seas, whose armies darkened our shores—sent over to bind and to rivet those chains that had been so long forging for our unfettered limbs! Has age so tamed his proud spirit that he will gently yield to a domestic usurper what he scorned to grant to a foreign master? I fear he has deceived himself, and would deceive you; let not his siren song of peace lull you into a fatal repose. For what is this large standing army quartered on the country? why those recruiting officers insulting every hamlet and village with their pride and insolence, and decoying the honest farmer from his labor, to become the idle, corrupt, and profligate drone of a military camp? Why this large naval establishment? Why such burthensome and odious taxes imposed on the industry of the country? Why those enormous loans at usurious interest in times of peace; and, above all, why those unconstitutional laws to banish innocence—to silence inquiry—stifle investigation, and to make dumb the complaining mouths of the people? Are these vast preparations in consequence of some imminent peril overhanging the country? Are we threatened with war? With whom? with France? France has showed that this wicked administration cannot *drive* her into a war with her ancient friend and ally. She has almost compelled them to keep a minister of peace within her borders, and offered them almost any terms of conciliation consistent with justice and dignity. Yet do you see any abatement in the warlike energies of the Government?

"For what, I ask, are these vast and hostile preparations? Let the late pretended whisky insurrection in the western counties of Pennsylvania answer the question. I am no alarmist; but I cannot close my eyes to the truth when I see it glaring before me. These "provisional" armies, as they have chosen to call them, are meant for you; they are intended, not to meet the troops of France, which they know will never insult the soil of this republic, but to awe you, the people, into submission, and to force upon you, by a display of military power, the destructive measures of this vaulting and ambitious administration. And yet the gentleman tells you we must wait until *some* infringement is made on our rights! Your Constitution broken, your citizens dragged to prison for daring to exercise the freedom of speech, armies levied, and you threatened with immediate invasion for your audacious interference with the business of the Federal Government; and still you are told to wait for *some infringement* of your rights! How long are we to wait? Till the chains are fastened upon us, and we can no longer help ourselves? But the gentleman says your course may lead to civil war, and where are your resources? I answer him in his own words, handed down by the tradition of the past generation, and engraven on the hearts of his grateful countrymen. I answer, in his own words: 'Shall we gather strength by irresolution and inaction? Shall we acquire the means of effectual resistance by lying supinely on our backs, and hugging the delusive phantom of hope, until our enemies shall have bound us hand and foot? Sir, we are not weak, if we make a proper use of those means which the God of nature hath placed in our power. The battle, sir, is not to the strong alone; it is to the vigilant, the active, the brave.'

"But we are not only to have an invading army marching into our borders, but the gentleman's vivid imagination has pictured Washington at the head of it, coming to inflict military chastisement on his native State; and who, exclaims he, would dare lift his hand against the father of his country? Sternly has he rebuked one of you for venturing, in the outburst of patriotic feeling, to declare that he would do it. I bow with as much respect as any man at the name of Washington. I have been taught to look upon it with a veneration little short of that of my Creator. But while I love Cæsar, I love Rome more. Should he, forgetful of the past, grown ambitious of power, and, seduced by the artful machinations of those who seek to use his great name in the subjugation of his country, lift a parricidal hand against the bosom of the State that gave him birth and crowned him with his glory, because she has dared to assert those rights that belong to her, not by the laws of nature, but those rights that have been reserved to her by this very Constitution that she partly ordained, and without which she must drag out an existence of helpless and hopeless imbecility, I trust there will be found many a Brutus to avenge her wrongs. I promise, for one, so help me God!—and it is in no boastful spirit I speak—that I will not be an idle spectator of the tyrannical and murderous tragedy, so long as I have an arm to wield a weapon, or a voice to cry shame! Shame on you for inflicting this deadly blow in the bosom of the mother that gave you existence, and cherished your fame as her own brightest jewel."

We do not pretend, reader, to give you the language of John Randolph on this occasion; nor are we certain even that the thoughts are his. We have nothing but the faint tradition of near fifty years to go upon; and happy are we if all our researches have enabled us to make even a tolerable approximation to what was said. He spoke for three hours; all that time the people, standing on their feet, hung with breathless silence on his lips. His youthful appearance, boyish tones, clear, distinct, thrilling utterance; his graceful action, bold expressions, fiery energy, and manly thoughts, struck them with astonishment. A bold genius and an orator of the first order suddenly burst upon them, and dazzled them with his power and brilliancy. A prophet was among them, and they knew it not. When he concluded, an old planter, turning to his neighbor, exclaimed; "He's no bug-eater now, I tell you." Dr. Hogue turned from the stand, and went away, repeating to himself these lines from the "Deserted Village:"

"Amazed, the gazing rustics ranged around,
And still they gazed, and still the wonder grew,
That one small head could carry all he knew."

Mr. Henry, turning to some by-stander, said: "I haven't seen the little dog before, since he was at school; he was a great atheist then." He made no reply to the speech; but, approaching Mr. Randolph, he took him by the hand, and said: "Young man, you call me father; then, my son, I have somewhat to say unto thee (holding both his hands)—*keep justice, keep truth,* and you will live to think differently."

They dined together, and Randolph, ever after venerated the memory of his friend, who died in a few weeks from that day.

They were both elected in April; the one to Congress, the other to the State Legislature; and, doubtless, many of the good freeholders of Charlotte voted for both. Who can blame them? Happy people of Charlotte! it was your lot to behold the bright golden sunset of the great luminary whose meridian power melted away the chains of British despotism and withered up the cankered heart of disaffected Toryism; then, turning with tearful eyes from the last rays of the sinking orb, to hail, dawning on the same horizon, another sun, just springing, as it were, from the night of chaos, mounting majestically into his destined sphere, and driving clouds and darkness before his youthful beams.

CHAPTER XXII.

FRANCE AND THE ADMINISTRATION.

Mr. Adams saved the country from a war with France, and a consequent alliance with Great Britain, and all the unimaginable events that must have followed that connection; but in so doing he destroyed his party, and defeated his own re-election. No one, to our knowledge, has ever attributed these results to a foreseen and predetermined self-sacrifice on his part for the good of the country. Those who were associated with him and knew him best attribute his course to far other causes. Before we proceed with our narrative, we will give the reader a further insight into the character of this man, so necessary to understand the complicated history of those times. A mere detail of facts, without a knowledge of the causes that produced them, or the character and motives of the men that acted them, can afford no instruction to the student of history. Without some such insight, the battle of the frogs or the wars of the giants would be equally as instructive as the Punic Wars or the conflicts in the forum.

What we say of Mr. Adams is drawn from cotemporary history, and in the language of those who were most intimately associated him. The reader is already aware of his course before and during the negotiations for the treaty of Paris, in 1782, and Dr. Franklin's opinion of his character.

General Hamilton, a very good judge, said of him while President, and during the great events we are now discoursing of, and in explanation of their causes, that he possessed patriotism and integrity, and even talents, of a certain kind; but that he did not possess the talents adapted to the administration of government, and that there were great and intrinsic defects in his character, which unfitted him for the office of Chief Magistrate. With all his virtues, he was tainted with a disgusting egotism, a distempered jealousy, and an ungovernable indiscretion of temper. When he and General Washington were run together as candidates for the presidential and vice-presidential office, it was thought all-important to secure the first office to General Washington (a majority at that time determining the question), by dropping a few votes from Mr. Adams. He complained of this as unfair treatment—said he ought to have been permitted to take an equal chance with General Washington. When, at a subsequent period, he and Mr. Pinckney were on the same ticket, it was thought, by the federal party, that the success of their cause ought not to be hazarded by dropping any of the votes; it was not a matter of such importance that Mr. Adams or Mr. Pinckney should be elected President, as that Mr. Jefferson should be defeated. He was enraged with all those who thought that Mr. Pinckney ought to have an equal chance with himself. To this circumstance, in a great measure, may be attributed the serious schism which, at a subsequent period, grew up in the federal party. Mr. Adams never could forgive the men who were engaged in the plan, though it embraced some of his most partial admirers. He discovered bitter animosity against several of them. His rage against General Hamilton was so vehement, that he could not restrain himself within the forms of civility or decorum, in the presence of that gentleman. His jealousy of the Pinckneys was notorious, and it dated as far back as the appointment of Mr. Thomas Pinckney, by Washington, as envoy to the Court of London. Mr. Adams desired the appointment for himself, notwithstanding the impropriety—he being the Vice-President—and next he desired it for his son-in-law. In the bitterness of disappointment, he played into the hands of the opposition party, and charged upon General Washington that the appointment had been made under British influence.

Soon after his own appointment of General Washington, in July, 1798, as Commander-in-Chief of all the armies of the United States, he became jealous of the overshadowing influence of that great character, and did all he could, consistently with his station, to thwart the plans, to delay and derange the measures, that Washington thought most essential to the service.

His conduct in the appointment of general officers, proved that he was fickle, inconsistent, and under the baneful influence of a distempered jealousy.

With the country in imminent danger of a war; with Washington and Hamilton and C. C. Pinckney at the head of her armies, it was natural that those who felt themselves responsible for the measures that had brought the nation into that predicament, should look to those great men as their guides, instead of the impulsive, aimless, and unsteady character, nominally at the head of affairs. Even his own cabinet had more frequent, intimate, and confidential communications, on all public affairs, with the head of the army than with himself. He did not fail to perceive this; and soon became enraged with his own counsellors. Not long afterwards, some of them were dismissed. A prominent charge against McHenry was, that the Secretary, in a report to the House of Representatives, had eulogized General Washington, and had attempted to eulogize General Hamilton, which was adduced as one proof of a combination, in which the Secretary was engaged, to depreciate and injure him, the President. Here, then, was the secret. His jealous and distempered fancy, stimulated by evil counsel, had conjured up a formidable conspiracy, in which his cabinet were implicated, the object of which was to depreciate and injure him, and to exalt Hamilton or Pinckney above him. To this cause may be attributed his extraordinary course in regard to French affairs; and those fatal aberrations, as they were called by his friends, that resulted in peace with the French nation, but in the destruction of himself and of his party.

We now proceed with the current of events, down to the meeting of Congress, in 1798.

As our object is not a history of the country, but only of those leading causes of history, a knowledge of which is essential to understand the position of political characters who figured at the time, we shall confine ourselves to a development of French affairs, because they absorbed all others, gave weight to the political atmosphere, and indicated, by the elevation or depression of the barometer, the advance or retrograde position of the two great parties that divided men and controlled the politics of the country.

The reader is already aware, that on the departure of Messrs. Pinckney and Marshall from Paris, in the spring of 1798, Mr. Gerry was induced to remain; but he obstinately persisted in refusing to enter into any negotiation. About the last of May, 1798, the X. Y. Z. dispatches, which had been published in America, found their way to the hands of the French Minister of Foreign Affairs, M. Talleyrand. He immediately inclosed the *very strange publication*, as he called it, to Mr. Gerry, and added: "I cannot observe without surprise that intriguers have profited of the insulated condition in which the envoys of the United States have kept themselves to make proposals and hold conversations, the object of which was, evidently, to deceive you." He demanded the names of the parties implicated, and to be informed whether any of the citizens attached to his service, and authorized by him to see the envoys, told them a word which had the least relation to the disgusting proposition which was made by X. and Y., to give any sum whatever for corrupt distribution.

Mr. Gerry disclosed the names of the parties. Two of them, the most conspicuous characters, X. and Y., were foreigners, and unknown to the French Government; the third, Mr. Z., made himself known, and proved that the part he had acted was wholly honorable. Mr. Gerry added; further, that in regard to the citizens attached to the employments of M. Talleyrand, and authorized by him to see the envoys on official communications, not a word had fallen from any of them which had the least relation to the proposition made by X. and Y. in their informal negotiations, to pay money for corrupt purposes.

It is not at all improbable that members of the Directory, whose term of office was exceedingly precarious, and even Talleyrand himself, were not too virtuous to receive a douceur, or a bribe, to secure their influence in the negotiation of a treaty; but that they were, in a roundabout way, actually fishing for one on this occasion, depends solely on the statement of the two principal actors in the business, who, in a most remarkable degree, gained the confidence of the envoys, but who were, in fact, foreigners, unknown to the Government, and corrupt persons, who fled the country on the discovery of the plot. There is not one corroborating circumstance to strengthen their story.

Mr. Gerry admits that every member of the Government with whom they communicated acted with the utmost propriety; and that no corrupt proposition came either from them or M. Talleyrand.

Napoleon, in his Revelations from St. Helena, in giving a history of these transactions, says: "Certain intriguing agents, with which sort of instruments the office of foreign relations was at that period abundantly supplied, insinuated that the demand of a loan would be desisted from, upon the advance of twelve hundred thousand francs, to be divided between the Director Barras and the Minister Talleyrand." This whole narrative of Bonaparte, when carefully examined, is obviously drawn from public documents; just such materials as we have before us at this time. There is not the slightest evidence that he had any personal knowledge of the transactions, and that he knew from any other source than common report growing out of the publications of the day, that Barras, or Talleyrand, had, through intriguing agents, made an overture for a bribe.

Notwithstanding the publication of those X. Y. Z. dispatches, so questionable in their character and design, so well calculated to irritate, yet the French Government would not be excited into a feeling of hostility. "As to the French Government," says Talleyrand, on the 10th of June, "superior to all personalities, to all the manœuvres of its enemies, it perseveres in the intention of conciliating with sincerity all the differences which have happened between the two countries. I confirm it to you anew." He then proposes to proceed with Mr. Gerry on the business of negotiation, discards any further demand for a loan, and rests the whole negotiation on three simple propositions, which might have been speedily and satisfactorily adjusted; and he urged on Mr. Gerry to send home for authority to conclude the treaty, if he did not feel that he was already clothed with sufficient power for the purpose. But he strangely persisted in doing neither one thing nor another: he would not send home and ask *for instruments* necessary to the negotiation, nor for a successor to be put in his stead for that purpose, nor would he enter into a full description of all the points necessarily involved in a treaty, that he might lay before his Government the terms of one he had informally entered into, for their ratification or rejection. He had it in his power, by a firm and manly course of statesmanship, to throw upon the administration the responsibility of closing at once all subjects of difference with the French Republic, or by rejecting a favorable treaty, to involve the country in war with that formidable power. His only thought seems to have been to avoid doing any thing that might hurt the feelings of his late colleagues, and to devise means to get home. He never ceased begging Talleyrand to let him go home. Talleyrand never ceased begging him to stay, and to attend to the important and pressing affairs of his country. At length, finding Mr. Gerry wholly impracticable, he sent him his passports about the last of July, and added, "As long as I could flatter myself, sir, with fulfilling the wish of the Executive Directory, by endeavoring with you to establish the good understanding between the French Republic and the United States, I used my efforts, both in our conferences and in my correspondence with you, to smooth the paths, to establish the basis, to enter on the business, and to convince you of the utility of your presence in Paris. It is in your character of Envoy of the American Government I received you and wrote to you; it depended on yourself to be publicly received by the Executive Directory. . . . You cannot dissemble, that if nothing prevented you from pursuing with me the examining and reconciling of the grievances which divide the two countries, we should not long stand in need of any thing but the respective ratifications. . . . When scarcely informed of the departure of Messrs. Pinckney and Marshall, I endeavored in every conference I afterwards had with you to demonstrate to you the urgency, the propriety, and the possibility of an active negotiation. I collected your ideas; they differed from my own—I endeavored to reconcile them. On the 18th June I transmitted to you a complete plan of the negotiations. On the 27th I sent you my first note for discussion upon one of the points of the treaty; you declined answering it. On the 6th of July I sent you two others. In vain I accompanied these documents with the most cordial invitation rapidly to run over with me this series of indispensable discussions upon all our grievances. You have not even given me an opportunity of proving what liberality the Executive Directory would use on the occasion. *You never wrote, in fact, but for your departure.*" In a postscript, dated three days later, and after receiving advices from America giving an account of the warlike acts of Congress, passed in May and June, M. Talleyrand adds: "It seems that, hurried beyond every limit, your Government no longer preserves appearances." . . . . . .

(He then cites the various acts that have been passed.) "The long-suffering of the Executive Directory," continues he, "is about to manifest itself in the most unquestionable manner. Perfidy will no longer be able to throw a veil over the pacific dispositions, which it has never ceased to manifest. It is at the very moment of this fresh provocation, which would appear to leave no honorable choice but war, that it confirms the assurances I have given you on its behalf. It is yet ready, it is as much disposed as ever, to terminate by a candid negotiation the differences which subsist between the two countries. Such is its repugnance to consider the United States as enemies, that notwithstanding their hostile demonstrations, it means to wait until it be irresistibly forced to it by real hostilities. Since you will depart, sir, hasten, at least, to transmit to your Government this solemn declaration."

Mr. Gerry did hasten to lay these declarations before his Government on the *first day of October*, and added, that *from the best information he could obtain relative to the disposition of the Executive Directory, they were very desirous for a reconciliation between the Republics.*

No sooner had Mr. Gerry left the shores of France, than M. Talleyrand opened a correspondence on American affairs with M. Pichon, Secretary of Legation of the French Republic, near the Batavian Republic, and requested that gentleman to give copies of the same to the American minister, Mr. Murray, doubtless with an expectation that they would be forwarded to the President of the United States. In his letter of August the 28th, just twenty days from the departure of Mr. Gerry, he says: "I see between France and the United States no clashing of interests, no motives of jealousy. Where is, therefore, the cause of the misunderstanding, which, if France did not show herself the wisest, would bring from this moment a great rupture between the two Republics? There are neither incompatible interests, nor projects of aggrandizement, which divide them. *Lately*, *distrust* has done all the mischief. The Government of the United States has believed that France wished to have revolutionized America; France has believed that the Government of the United States wished to throw itself into the arms of England. It is because acrimony, having mingled itself with distrust, neither side has taken true conciliatory means. It has been supposed, in the

United States, that the French Government temporized, in order to strike with greater safety. Hence followed a crowd of measures, each one more aggravating than the other. In France, it has been supposed that the Government of the United States wished only to support the appearances of negotiation. *Thence there was a certain insisting on pledges of good faith.* Let us substitute calmness to passions, confidence to suspicions, and we shall soon agree. I have made my efforts to wind up a negotiation, in this manner, with Mr. Gerry. My correspondence with him, until the day of his departure, is a curious monument of advances from me, and of evasions from him. I wished to encourage Mr. Gerry, by the marks of regard which his good intention deserved, though I cannot dissemble to myself that he had been wanting decision, at the moment when he might easily have settled every thing properly." In a word, he winds up with giving Mr. Murray, through M. Pichon, the most solemn assurances that a new plenipotentiary would be received without hesitation, and that an act of confidence towards them would encourage confidence on their part. This letter, so unequivocal in its nature, and another, of a like tenor, making more direct overtures, if possible, towards re-opening negotiations, must have reached the President before the meeting of Congress in December. The President had other unequivocal, though less direct, evidences of the pacific disposition of the French Directory. Dr. George Logan, a native of Pennsylvania, while in France, was introduced to the Director Merlin, and afterwards visited him on the footing of a private friend. On one of these occasions, Merlin informed him that France had not the least intention to interfere in the public affairs of the United States; that his country had acquired great reputation in having assisted America to become a free republic, and that they never would disgrace their own revolution by attempting the destruction of the United States. Dr. Logan returned home early in November, and hastened to communicate what he thought good news, to the Secretary of State. He was coldly received by Mr. Pickering, and informed that his news was of no importance. General Washington was at the seat of government about the time (Nov., 1798), arranging his military operations with Generals Hamilton, Pinckney, and the Secretary of War. Dr. Logan called on him. His reception was even more cold and repulsive than that of the Secretary.

When Logan repeated to him the conversation with Merlin, he replied, that it was very singular; that he, who could only be viewed as a private character, unarmed with proper powers, and presumptively unknown in France, could effect what three gentlemen of the first respectability in our country, specially charged under the authority of the Government, were unable to do. "*You*, sir," with some emphasis on the word, "were more fortunate than our envoys, for they would neither be received nor heard by M. Merlin, nor the Directory."

It is very evident that General Washington, at that time, was highly exasperated with France; that all his feelings were enlisted against her; and that, had he been at the head of affairs, it would have taken much more than Talleyrand's overtures to have induced him to recommence negotiations. Had Washington been President in 1798, or Hamilton, or Pinckney, or had Mr. Adams yielded more readily to the counsel of his cabinet, who were wholly under the influence of the Triumvirate, the United States would unquestionably have been involved in a war with the French Republic. But Mr. Adams, whether from the motives assigned, or from higher patriotic considerations, refused the dictation, and saved the country from so calamitous a war as that would have been with the French Republic. Just before the meeting of Congress, he arrived in Philadelphia, from his seat at Quincy. The tone of his mind seemed to have been raised, rather than depressed. It was suggested to him (by the *military conclave*—says Mr. Jefferson) that it might be expedient to insert in the speech to Congress, a sentiment of this import—that after the repeatedly rejected advances of this country, its dignity required that it should be left with France, in future, to make the first overture; that if, desirous of reconciliation, she should evince the disposition by sending a minister to this Government, he would be received with the respect due to his character, and treated with in the frankness of a sincere desire of accommodation.

The suggestion was received in a manner both indignant and intemperate. Mr. Adams declared as a sentiment, which he had adopted on mature reflection, *That if France should send a minister to-morrow, he would order him back the next day.*

So imprudent an idea was easily refuted. But yet, in less than forty-eight hours from this extraordinary sally, the mind of Mr.

Adams underwent a total revolution. He resolved not only to insert in his speech the sentiment which had been proposed to him, but to go farther, and to declare, that if France would give explicit assurances of receiving a minister from this country, with due respect, he would send one.

In vain was this extension of the sentiment opposed by all his ministers, as being equally incompatible with good policy and with the dignity of the nation. He obstinately persisted, and the declaration was introduced. The reader may account for this change in the mind of the President in two ways. In the first place, we may presume that he knew nothing of the dispatches containing the correspondence of Mr. Gerry with M. Talleyrand, which might have been received in his absence; but that on perusing the correspondence, he was forcibly struck with the fact that a reconciliation with France depended solely on him. That correspondence presented the business in this light: France says—Two of the ministers you sent to treat with me are personally offensive, on account of their hostile opinions and haughty demeanor, a sentiment, according to the laws of nations, we have a right to express, without giving offence to you. I early expressed a desire that those gentlemen would depart, and a readiness to open negotiation with the third, who evinced better dispositions towards conciliation. I told him to send home for additional powers, if he doubted his authority to act alone, or to inform his Government that another minister would be received to treat in his stead, or to agree informally on the terms of a treaty, which he might submit for consideration on his return to the United States. But declining to act on the one or the other of these propositions, and still insisting on his return home, I then told him distinctly to say to his Government, France has no cause of quarrel with America, does not desire war, and is ready to receive in good faith a minister of peace, whenever one may be sent. Such was the attitude of the subject exhibited by the dispatches of Mr. Gerry.

It was impossible for a President of the United States to understand them, and then to take upon himself the responsibility of rejecting those overtures of peace. In this way we may account for the sudden change in the mind of Mr. Adams, and do credit to his firmness and patriotism. But is it reasonable to suppose that he was ignorant of those dispatches, or their contents, till so late a period?

Mr. Gerry had arrived, and communicated them to the State Department on the first day of October. He himself was an intimate personal friend of the President, and lived in the same State and neighborhood. The most reasonable conclusion, therefore, is, that Mr. Adams was well informed on the whole subject when he arrived in Philadelpha, and that the change in his course was produced by the motives assigned at the time—that is, a jealousy of Hamilton and Pinckney, and a belief that a plot was on foot in which his cabinet were implicated, to degrade and injure him, and to exalt the one or the other of those military characters in his place.

But, notwithstanding this apparent change in his mind towards the most pacific measures, he kept back from Congress those important dispatches of Mr. Gerry, and other information of a pacific kind, till the 18th of January, 1799. They were then accompanied by an elaborate report of the Secretary of State, in which he says the points chiefly meriting attention are the attempts of the French Government; 1. To exculpate itself from the charge of corruption; 2. To detach Mr. Gerry from his colleagues, and to inveigle him into a separate negotiation; and 3. Its design, if the negotiation failed, and a war should take place between the United States and France, to throw the blame of the rupture on the United States. The Secretary labors to keep up the spirit of distrust towards France, and to prove that all the overtures of her minister are insincere, merely intended to deceive the United States, and to gain time. "Warmly professing its desire of reconciliation," says he in conclusion, "it gives no evidence of its sincerity; but proofs, in abundance, demonstrate that it is not sincere. From standing erect, and in that commanding attitude requiring implicit obedience, cowering, it renounces some of its unfounded demands. But I hope we shall remember that *the tiger crouches before he leaps upon his prey.*" A very different temper this from that of the President in his opening speech to Congress in December; nor does it show a very harmonious co-operation between the Chief Magistrate and his ministers.

Just one month from the communication of the Secretary's report to Congress—that is, on the 18th of February, the President nominated William Vans Murray as envoy to the French Republic. This measure was taken without any previous consultation with his ministers. The nomination was, to each of them, even to the Secretary of State, his constitutional counsellor in such affairs, the first notice of the project. The nomination was accompanied with a letter of Talleyrand to M. Pichon, dated 28th September, 1798; and the second, of like tenor, giving assurances that a minister from the United States would be received and accredited.

The precipitate nomination of Mr. Murray brought Mr. Adams into an awkward predicament. He found it necessary to change his plan in its progress, and, instead of one, to nominate three envoys, and to superadd a promise, that, though appointed, they should not leave the United States till further and more perfect assurances were given by the French Government. This remodification of the measure was a virtual acknowledgment that it had been premature. It argued either instability of views, or want of sufficient consideration beforehand.

General Washington disapproved very highly of the measure. He was immediately informed of it by the Secretary of State: and in reply, said—"The unexpectedness of the event communicated in your letter of the 21st ultimo did, as you may suppose, surprise me not a little. But far, very far indeed was this surprise short of what I experienced the next day, when, by a very intelligent gentleman, immediately from Philadelphia, I was informed that there had been no *direct* overture from the Government of France to that of the United States for a negotiation; on the contrary, that M. Talleyrand was playing the same loose and round-about game he had attempted the year before with our wrongs; and which, as in that case, might mean any thing or nothing, as would subserve his purpose best."

The speculations of the Republicans on the other hand were to the following effect. "I inform you," says Mr. Jefferson in a letter to Madison, "of the nomination of Murray. There is evidence that the letter of Talleyrand was known to one of the Secretaries, and therefore probably to all; the nomination, however, is declared by one of them to have been kept secret from them all. He added that he was glad of it, as, had they been consulted, the advice would have been against making the nomination. To the rest of the party, however, the whole was a secret till the nomination was announced. Never did a party show a stronger mortification, and consequently, that war had been their object. Dana declared in debate (as I have from those who were present), that we had done every thing which might provoke France to a war; that we had given her insults which no nation ought to have borne; and yet she would not declare war. The conjecture as to the Executive is, that they received Talleyrand's letter before or about the meeting of Congress: that not meaning to meet the overture effectually, they kept it secret, and let all the war measures go on; but that just before the separation of the Senate, the President, not thinking he could justify the concealing such an overture, nor indeed that it could be concealed, made a nomination, hoping that his friends in the Senate would take on their own shoulders the odium of rejecting it; but they did not choose it. The Hamiltonians would not, and the others could not, alone. The whole artillery of the phalanx, therefore, was played secretly on the President, and he was obliged himself to take a step which should parry the overture while it wears the face of acceding to it. (Mark that I state this as conjecture; but founded on workings and indications which have been under our eyes.) Yesterday, therefore (25th Feb.), he sent in a nomination of Oliver Ellsworth, Patrick Henry, and William Vans Murray, Envoys Extraordinary and Ministers Plenipotentiary to the French Republic, but declaring the two former should not leave this country, till they should receive from France assurances that they should be received with the respect due by the laws of nations to their character. This, if not impossible, must keep off at least the day so hateful and so *fatal* to them, of reconciliation, and leave more time for new projects of provocation."

The truth is, the friends of the Government were not agreed as to ulterior measures. Some were for immediate and unqualified war—of this class were Hamilton and most of the military gentry—others were for a more mitigated course: the dissolution of treaties, preparation of force by land and sea, partial hostilities of a defensive tendency; leaving to France the option of seeking accommodation, or proceeding to open war. As most of the responsibility rested on members of Congress, this latter course was preferred by them, and prevailed. Either course was consistent with itself and admitted of a steady line of policy. But the President, having no fixed object, and governed by the impulse of the moment, came athwart all their plans and destroyed them. Notwithstanding the modifications of his embassy, it was very evident that most of the federal members of both branches of Congress carried home with them a settled dislike to the measure. They regarded it as ill-timed, built upon too slight grounds, and, therefore, humiliating to the United States; as calculated to revive French principles, strengthen the party against Government, and produce changes in the sentiments and conduct of some of the European powers, that might materially affect the interests and growing commercial prospects of the United States.

Before the envoys departed, intelligence was received of a new revolution in the French Government, and the expulsion of two of the Directory. This was thought to be a valid motive for delay—at least till it could be known whether the new Directory would ratify the assurances of the old one. When the news of the revolution in the Directory arrived, Mr. Adams was at his seat in Massachusetts. His ministers addressed to him a joint letter, communicating the intelligence, and submitting to his consideration, whether that event ought to suspend the projected mission. In a letter which he afterwards wrote from the same place, he directed the preparation of a draft of instructions for the envoys, and intimated that their departure would be suspended for some time.

Shortly after, about the middle of October 1799, he came to the seat of government, when he adjusted with his ministers the tenor of the instructions to be given; but observed a profound silence on the question whether it was expedient that the mission should proceed. The ministers expected a consultation on the great question, whether the mission to France would be suspended until the fate of its Government could be known. But they were disappointed. The President alone considered and decided. The morning after the instructions were settled, he signified to the Secretary of State that the envoys *were immediately to depart.*

Though uncommunicative to his constitutional advisers, he was very free in his conversations with the envoys as to his expectations in regard to their embassy. He told them that the French Government would not accept the terms, which they were instructed to propose; that they would speedily return: and that he should have to recommend to Congress a declaration of war. "But as to the French negotiation producing a war with England," said he, "if it did, England could not hurt us." "When," Mr. Ellsworth says, "Pickering recited this last idea to me and Mr. Wolcott, I had not patience to hear more. And yet the President has several times, in his letters to me, from Quincy, mentioned the vast importance of keeping on good terms with England."

The reader cannot be surprised that such a man should work the destruction of any party that regarded him as its head; indeed that, with him, there was no such thing as party; either he was elevated above ordinary mortals, and studied the good of the country alone, without regard to his own interests, or sunk below the level of common-trading politicians who care for neither measures nor men, only so far as they may conspire to their own personal elevation.

When the new Congress, of which John Randolph was a member, assembled at the Capitol in December, 1799, the federal party apparently compact, and with a majority of at least twenty in the House of Representatives, carried within it all the elements of dissolution. The death blow had been given by its own friends, and it required time only to discover the causes of its rapid decay. When the extraordinary events of which we have spoken were made known to Washington, on the 17th of November, 1799, but a few weeks before his death, he would answer nothing to them, but exclaimed, "*I have been stricken dumb!* I have, some time past," says he, "viewed the political concerns of the United States with an anxious and painful eye. They appear to me to be moving by hasty strides to a crisis; but in what it will result, that Being who sees, foresees, and directs all things, alone can tell. The vessel is afloat, or very nearly so, and considering myself as a passenger only, I shall trust to the mariners, whose duty it is to watch, to steer it into a safe port." Thou great and good man! *the ship is afloat!* When first launched upon the deep, thine own seamanship guided the untried vessel o'er many a stormy billow, with Scylla and Charybdis on either hand; thy wakeful eye didst steer right onward; but never was it permitted thee, thou good Palinurus, to see the ship *steered into a safe port!* From amidst thy fellow-passengers, all weeping and gazing in the heavens, thou wert borne aloft in a chariot of fire, and, by bands of celestial spirits heralded into realms of immortal glory. And now, the old Iron-sides having buffeted many a stormy sea, and riding gallantly with all her banners streaming, hails thee her first, her best, her greatest Captain!

CHAPTER XXIII.

SCENE IN THE PLAYHOUSE—STANDING ARMY.

On the first day of January, *eighteen hundred*, Washington was dead; Bonaparte First Consul of France. Our envoys had been favorably received. Every prospect of a satisfactory adjustment of the differences between the two republics, and no further need for the large army which had been established, and the other vast and expensive military preparations that had been projected with so much vigor under the X. Y. Z. excitement. Accordingly, on the 7th of January, Mr. Nicholas, a leading member of the republican party, moved in the House a resolution to repeal the act passed the 16th of July, 1798, entitled "An act to augment the army of the United States." The debate lasted for several days, and was warm and animated. On the 10th the motion was lost by a vote of *sixty* to *thirty-nine*. It was a strict party vote, and showed a majority of *twenty-one* for the federalists. John Randolph, for the first time, participated in the debate this day. The part he performed will be given in his own words. "In the course of the debates upon the resolution of Mr. Nicholas, I took occasion to say that the people of the United States ought not to depend for their safety on the soldiers enlisted under the laws, the repeal of which was the object of the resolution, and casually, but justly, applied to them the epithet of *ragamuffins*. I also declared that standing, or mercenary armies, were inconsistent with the spirit of our Constitution, or the genius of a free people. General Lee, and others, dilated upon these terms. He affirmed the last to be misapplied, and defined the word *mercenary* so as to give it an application only to troops hired for the defence of a country *other than their own*. In reply, I contended that there was no etymology which would warrant his construction; that the term was derived from a Latin word which signified *wages*, and did not embrace, as he had declared my meaning would justify, the militia, which likewise receives pay when in actual service, but was exclusively appropriated to such men (whether foreigners, or otherwise) as made the art military a profession, or trade, and was properly expressive of a *stand-*

ing army who served for *wages* and by contract, in contradistinction to a militia, or patriotic army, which was composed of all ranks of citizens, equally bound to fight the battles of their country, and in which each contributed his share to the public safety, and who received pay only when in actual service, to enable the poorer citizen to perform his military duty.

"In consequence of my application of these terms to the existing establishment—the first of which I confined to such recruits as had been picked up in my own country—a party of officers, the principal agents among whom were a Captain M'Knight and a Lieutenant Michael Reynolds, both belonging to the marine corps, being apprised that I was in the playhouse on Friday evening last (on which day the resolution was lost, about six o'clock), came into the box where I was, and commenced their operations by frequent allusions, *aimed at me*, to what was going on in the house. The play was The Stranger, and the after-piece Bluebeard. They asked one another if the soldiers on the stage did not act very well for mercenaries; said they supposed from their color (Turks) they were Virginians; squeezed into the seat with evident intention to incommode us, particularly myself; and when we were leaving the box, gave me a twitch by the coat; but upon the author being demanded, they had disappeared. On going down stairs, some of the gentlemen said they tried to push us all down in mass, and in the street they passed with a rude quickness, jostling one of the gentlemen, and striking another's foot. In their aim upon me they were disappointed. I regarded all they said with the most perfect nonchalance; was unmoved by their attempts to insult me, except when they offered personal violence; and in conformity to what I thought my duty, laid a written complaint before the President. To-day (Tuesday, the 14th) he sent it to the House with a letter, in which he lays it before us 'without any comment upon its style.' I must not omit telling you that my feelings were strongly excited. A motion was made to provide a committee of privileges, to whom it was to be referred. This I opposed, expressing my surprise that the letter had been laid before us, a measure which I had not contemplated when I wrote it; that I had addressed it to the authority whose particular duty it was to suppress such conduct in the military, and disclaimed all wish to throw myself upon the protection of himself or of that House; that the privileges of

Congress being expressly defined by the Constitution, I was unwilling to give my assent to any measure which might lead to enlarge them, and which, even if we had a right to adopt it, would hereafter be prostituted to nefarious designs. My objection was overruled, and a committee appointed of seven, on which the speaker had the uncommon goodness to nominate *three* republicans.

"Perhaps some misguided persons may be induced to depreciate the motives by which I have been actuated. I cannot help it. My business is to do what I conceive right, careless of the opinion of all. I was delighted to find my sentiments upon this subject coincided with those of Dr. Tucker; it is no bad criterion of the truth of any opinion that it meets his assent. I sometimes look back upon the principles which once governed my moral conduct with astonishment—how much to be regretted it is, that the painted phantom of honor should be dressed in such captivating colors as to suffer few of the nobler minds to escape her contagious embrace."

The letter addressed to the President, after stating the affair in the theatre, proceeds thus—"Having stated the fact, it would be derogatory to your character for me to point out the remedy. So far as they relate to this application addressed to you in a public capacity, they can only be supposed by you to be of a public nature. It is enough for me to state, that the independence of the legislature has been attacked, and the majesty of the people, of which you are the principal representative, insulted, and your authority contemned. In their name, I demand that a provision commensurate with the evil be made, and which will be calculated to deter others from any future attempt to introduce the reign of terror into our country. In addressing you in this plain language of man, I give you, sir, the best proof I can afford of the estimation in which I hold your office and your understanding; and I assure you with truth, that I am with respect, your fellow-citizen,

"JOHN RANDOLPH.

"Chamber H. Representatives Jan. 11,—24th Independence.

"To the President of the U. States."

The reader perceives here none of those courtly and unmeaning (if not worse) phrases that usually begin and end the epistles addressed to high functionaries by those who seek to gain their favor by obsequiousness and flattery—*To his Excellency, thê President of the United States—Your most obedient and humble servant*—none of that, but an unvarnished, straight-forward statement of facts; he tells the President that the independence of the legislature has been attacked, the majesty of the people insulted, and demands that he, their chief representative, shall make some provision adequate to prevent the reign of terror from being introduced into the country. The whole letter was conceived in a stern, independent, republican spirit, and ought not, we would suppose, to have given offence to any one who understood and duly appreciated the term *fellow-citizen.*

This letter the President thought proper on the 14th of the month to communicate to the House—"As the inclosed letter," says he, "from a member of your body, received by me on the night of Saturday the 11th inst., relates to the privileges of the House, which in my opinion ought to be inquired into by the House itself, *if any where.* I have thought proper to submit the whole letter and *its tendencies* to your consideration, without any other *comments on its matter and style.*" It is very plain what he and Pickering thought about both.

The committee appointed to take this matter of privilege into consideration, consisted of Messrs. Chauncey, Goodrich, Macon, Kittera, Jones, Sewell, Robert Williams, and Bayard—Mr. Macon was excused and Mr. Hanna appointed in his stead.

Messrs. Goodrich, Kittera, Sewell, and Bayard, constituting the majority of the committee, were the most distinguished and influential members of the federal party in the House.

On the 18th, Mr. Randolph addressed the following communication to the Chairman of the Committee:—"A mature consideration of the subject induces me to suspect, that a refusal on my part to communicate the information requested by you a few days ago, could only have originated in a false delicacy, under whose impulse I am determined never to act; I shall therefore proceed to state some instances of the misconduct of Capt. M'Knight and Lieut. Reynolds, on the night of Friday, the 10th instant.

"Exclusive of repeated assertions to what passed in the House of Representatives during the debate of the preceding day, and a frequent repetition of some words which fell from me during that discussion, in a manner so marked as to leave no doubt on *my* mind, or that of Messrs. Van Rensselaer, Christie, or Macon, of their intention to insult me personally; finding me determined to take no notice of their *words*, they adopted a conduct which placed their designs beyond every possibility of doubt, and which they probably conceived to be calculated to *force* me into their measures. Mr. Christie had left his seat between me and the partition of the box; after which, Mr. Van Rensselaer, who sat on the other side of me, laid down, so as to occupy a more than ordinary portion of room, and occasioned my removal to a part of Mr. Christie's former seat, leaving a very small vacancy between myself and the partition. Into this Lieut. Reynolds *suddenly*, and without requesting or giving time for room to be made for him, dropped with such violence as to bring our hips into contact. The shock was sufficient to occasion a slight degree of pain on my part, and for which it is probable he would in some degree have apologized, had not the act been intentional. Just before I left the box, one of them, I believe M'Knight, gave me a sudden and violent pull by the cape of my coat. Upon my demanding who it was, (this was the first instance in which I noticed their proceedings,) no answer was given. I then added, that I had long perceived an intention to insult me, and that the person offering it was a puppy. No reply that I heard was made.

"It will be impossible for me, sir, to specify the various minute actions of these persons and their associates, which tended to the same point. Suffice it to say, that their whole deportment exhibited an insolence, and their every act betokened a bold defiance, which can nether be *defined* nor *mistaken*, and which, according to the generally received opinions of the world, not only would have justified, but demanded chastisement.

"Referring the committee to the numerous and authentic accounts of this transaction, which the gentlemen present are so well calculated to give, I remain with respect, sir,

"Your fellow-citizen,

"JOHN RANDOLPH."

Those gentlemen, Mr. Christie, Mr. Macon, Mr. Nicholson, and others, men of great respectability, and members of Congress, did confirm in every particular the above statement. There rested not the shadow of a doubt on their mind, that Reynolds and M'Knight intended to insult Mr. Randolph, and to inflict personal injury on him, for words spoken in debate.

The only testimony in opposition to those gentlemen of such high respectability, and Mr. Randolph's own statement, so detailed and explicit, was the declaration of those persons themselves. Their testimony is evidently an equivocation: they say they did not go to the theatre with the intention of insulting Mr. Randolph. "I did not know," says M'Knight, "Mr. Randolph was to be at the theatre, nor do I ever recollect seeing him previous to Friday evening; and, from his *youthful appearance and dress, I had no idea of his being a member of the House of Representatives.*" All this may be very true, and yet after reaching there, it is very evident they conceived the idea of insulting and injuring him.

The committee, after collecting all the evidence they could find material in the case, report the following resolutions:

Resolved, That this House entertains a respectful sense of the regard which the President of the United States has shown to its rights and privileges, in his message of the 14th instant, accompanied by a letter addressed to him by John Randolph, Jun., a member of this House.

Resolved, That in respect to the charge alleged by John Randolph, Jun., a member of this House, in his letter addressed to the President of the United States, on the eleventh instant, and by him submitted to the consideration of this House, that sufficient cause does not appear for the interposition of this House, on the ground of a breach of its privileges.

The first resolution was passed without a division. To the second, several amendments were offered, going to censure M'Knight and Reynolds, but were rejected. Then the resolution itself was rejected, by a majority of *twelve*, showing that even that House were not prepared to sacrifice their privileges, which had been so evidently and wantonly insulted and trampled on. The Speaker then ruled all further action on the subject out of order, and so shoved it aside.

We leave Mr. Randolph's friend and contemporary, William Thompson, to make his commentaries on these transactions, the more valuable as the spontaneous effusions of an ingenuous and noble mind:—"The committee," says he, "who sat to examine the charge against several minions of executive power, which, of all that can be brought against men, was most serious, as being most destructive to the liberties of America—the committee who were called on to say whether the privileges of the House should be prostrated, as the privileges of the people have been—the committee who were called on to decide whether a set of armed ruffians should surround the capitol, and dictate our laws—this committee have determined, that although there were *some circumstances* (language of the report) which deserved censure, yet they were not of such a nature as to be considered a breach of the privileges of the House. Admit the meaning which they wish to give to *some circumstances*, I say, if there were any circumstance, no matter how trivial in its nature it may be, if on the most rigid inquiry it can be found that a legislator is insulted for his *official conduct*, that the man who insults offers an insult to the people; and that the men who do not, when called on, inflict all the punishment their power licenses, is an enemy, are enemies to the liberty of America. What, sir, will result from the decision of that committee? The republicans are liable to daily and hourly insults—the soldiers of Philadelphia are to be raised to a Pretorian band—our measures are to be dictated by the willing foes of our liberty—and virtuous opposition is to be silenced by the bayonet. Let me not be told that these apprehensions are ridiculous; I say they are grounded in the full conviction, that the military mob is supported by the administration, and that administration will make great sacrifices to their love of power. I say it is grounded on a conviction that this army is not now kept up to secure us from invasion; but that it contemplates something, and I fear that something is injurious to my country. That the insults you received were not offered to you as an individual, is certain; for as an individual, separate from your principles, I perceive they knew you not; it is certain, because your words were quoted. Not content with debasing us in fact, they wish to debase us even in appearance—*they cavil at your words.* Had you addressed the President in courtly style, *they* would forgive the contents of your letter; addressing him as you have done, we applaud the conduct, and we rejoice there is one man left us whose principles and whose manners stand uncorrupted in these corrupted times. I say we, for I speak the language of many; I say we, for I speak the language of your State. The persecutions of a faction have made you more dear to us. Not that your merits are increased by circumstances, but because this is a glaring instance amongst many, that men are persecuted as the organs of principles. This committee have done more, anxious that no opportunity should be lost to liquidate part of the great debt of adulation, they have interwoven a motion of thanks to the President for the respectful sense he has shown of their privileges. Whither does this lead? Is it not to be apprehended, that by this conduct your rights are to be changed into courtesy, that your rights are to hang on the nod of your President? Does this man deserve thanks for the compliance with his official duties? Does he deserve thanks for doing that for which he is paid by his country? The friends of America look at this affair with wonder and with horror. The timid part of the community say we will not send a man whose principles are obnoxious, for fear of consequences; the patriots of your State say we will send men who dare to speak the truth, no matter in whose ears it is grating. But it was disrespectful to call him fellow-citizen! Yes, he is not a fellow-citizen, because he is chief officer, he is alienated by promotion. There is more truth in his having been aliened than they would admit. I will forget for a moment that I am personally acquainted with you, and state, that you evinced in this affair an intrepid coolness, a firmness, and calmness, which must convince every man, not sworn to partiality, that every word of your evidence is most rigid truth. But your remark of mercenary and ragamuffin was galling to certain men in that House; your arguments throughout the whole were unanswerable; and your *naked* truths (for I will adopt your very appropriate expression) were dangerous to men who, unveiled, are damned."

This affair created, at the time, great excitement through the country. It was considered as but one of a series of events that had for their end the subjugation of the people to the will of the federal oligarchy. The enormous public debt, which was daily increasing by heavy loans at usurious interest, the funding system, the National Bank, the recently-created navy establishment, and large standing army without an enemy or the prospect of an enemy, the alien and the sedition laws in active operation, sparing neither station nor age, had given an alarming and a powerful centralizing action to the Government. And it was thought that the evil tendencies of all those measures were now consummated in the humiliation of the legislature to executive authority, and its tame submission to the arrogance of military pride. The trivial occurrence in the theatre, giving an opportunity to the President to display his petulant temper and his high sense of official consequence, and to the House of Representatives to manifest their subservient spirit, proved to be a very serious business. The people, more sagacious than they have credit for among some politicians, saw at once the tendency of these proceedings; and Randolph was hailed throughout the Union as the champion of the rights of the people. The very morning (15th January) his correspondence with the President appeared in the Philadelphia papers, and before any action thereon by the House, he received a communication professing to convey *the sentiments of a number of respectable citizens.* "It is our decided opinion," say they, "that the person of a delegate in Congress ought to be as sacred from public or private insult as the person of an ambassador to a foreign power. Should this flagrant violation of the privilege of a member of your House which has been offered to your person be *winked at*, may not enterprising men introduce parties into the House, which, by putting its members in bodily fear, will completely shackle the freedom of debate, and thereby injure the public good?" They then proceed to thank him for having the boldness *candidly to avow the real sentiments* of his heart, with a huge capital *R* and a tremendous underscoring of the word *real* in the original document, which is now before us. We might infer from this that such boldness was very unusual at that time. And indeed it was true. Madison had retired before the storm; so had Giles and the plain blunt-spoken Finlay, of Pennsylvania. Gallatin was still there; but he was not the man for the crisis; he was a foreigner, modest, plain in his elocution, and dealt more in facts and figures of arithmetic than those bold metaphors and figures of speech so essential to arouse and interest the people. The whole House might slumber under Gallatin's demonstrations, while one schrill echo of Randolph's voice would wake the seven sleepers. Matthew Lyon is seen among the silent voters; but three months' imprisonment last winter in a dungeon, not six feet square, under the sedition law, for daring to *publish* words in disparagement of the President, has cooled his Irish temper, and awed him into silence. This Harry Hotspur, therefore, or young cornet of horse, burst suddenly among them like a sky-rocket. His boldness, his eloquence, his youthful appearance, struck them with astonishment. But who can tell the effect of those *naked truths*, which fell like hot shot among the enemy, all intrenched and secure, as they supposed themselves, behind their formidable walls! John Thompson's prediction was fulfilled in the very outset of his career: *He will become an object of admiration and terror to the enemies of liberty!*

CHAPTER XXIV.

MAKE TO YOURSELF AN IDOL, AND, IN SPITE OF THE DECALOGUE, WORSHIP IT.

During the winter and spring of 1800 he kept up a regular correspondence with his friend, William Thompson, who, the reader knows, had found a home and an asylum in his misfortunes under the hospitable roof of Bizarre. The soothing temper he manifests towards that unfortunate youth, the sound advice he gave him, so fraught with wisdom and a knowledge of human nature, and his judicious and well-timed encouragement, to arouse from his lethargy and become the man he was capable of being, present the character of John Randolph in a pleasing point of view, and explain in a measure those traits of mind and disposition, known only to a few, that made him such an object of devoted friendship on the part of those who were honored by his intimate regard.

John Randolph, jun to his friend and brother, William Thompson.

Philadelphia, Dec. 31, 24th year.

"Your letter was peculiarly acceptable to me. It relieved me from considerable anxiety on account of your health, to the ill state of which I attributed that suspension of our correspondence, which has originated in the derangement of the post office department; it contained assurances of that regard of which I never entertained a doubt, but which, nevertheless, were extremely gratifying to me; but above all it put my mind at ease upon a subject which has been productive of considerable concern. I mean your change of residence, which, as you will find by my last, I understood you had removed to Chinquepin Church—not knowing your reasons for leaving Bizarre, I could not combat. Great, however, was my surprise and pleasure to receive a letter from Judy (Mrs. Richard Randolph) and yourself; both of which relieved my anxiety upon this head. I am, moreover, charmed, my friend, that you are resolutely bent upon study, and have made some progress therein. Let me conjure you to adhere inflexibly to this rational pursuit. Your destiny is in your own hands. Regular employment is of all medicines the most effectual for a wounded mind. If the sympathy of a friend who loves you because you are amiable and unfortunate; because you are the representative of that person (John Thompson died January, 1799) who held the first place in his heart, and the first rank in the intellectual order; if my uniform friendship, my dear Thompson, could heal the wounds of your heart, never should it know a pang. Your situation is of all others the one most eminently calculated to repair, so far as it is possible, the ills which you have sustained. An amiable woman, who regards you as a brother, who shares your griefs, and will administer as far as she can to your consolation, who unites to talents of the first order a degree of cultivation uncommon in any country, but especially in ours—such a woman is under the same roof with you. Cultivate a familiarity with her; each day will give you new and unexpected proof of the strength of her mind, and the extent of her information. Books you have at command; your retirement is unbroken. Such a situation is, in my opinion, the best calculated for a young man (under any circumstances) who will study; or even for one who is determined to be indolent. Female society, in my eye, is an indispensable requisite in forming the manly character. That which is offered to you is not to be paralleled, perhaps, in the world. You call on me, my friend, for advice. You bid me regard your foibles with a lenient eye; you anticipate the joy which I shall derive from your success. I will not permit myself to doubt of it. You shall succeed—you must. You have it in your power. Exertion only is necessary. You owe it to the memory of our departed brother, to yourself, to me, to your country, to humanity! Apprised that you have foibles to eradicate, the work is more than half accomplished. I will point them out with a friendly yet lenient hand. You will not shrink from the probe, knowing that in communicating present pain your ultimate cure and safety is the object of the friendly operator. If I supposed myself capable of inflicting intentional and wanton pain upon your feelings, I should shrink with abhorrence from myself. In the course of my strictures I may, perhaps, appear abrupt. I am now pressed for time.

"Self-examination, when cool and impartial, is the best of all correctives. It is a general and trite observation that man knows his fellows better than himself. This is too true; but it depends upon every individual to exhibit, in himself, a refutation of this received maxim. Retirement and virtuous society fit the mind for this task.

"Among your foibles I have principally observed unsteadiness; a precipitate decision, and the want of mature reflection, *generally*. It would be uncandid to determine your character by these traits, which originate, perhaps, or are at least heightened, by the uneasiness which preys upon your mind, which renders you more than usually restless. Endeavor, my friend, to act less upon momentary impulse; pause, reflect; think much and speak little; form a steadiness of demeanor, and having once resolved, persevere. Read, but do not devour, books. Compare your information; digest it. In short, according to the old proverb, "Make haste slowly." There is one point upon which I must enjoin you to beware. You appeared restless, when I saw you, to change your property. Let things stand as they are a little. Facilis discensus, sed revocare gradum, hoc opus. (Excuse, I beseech you, this pitiful display of learning.)

"The Duc de la Rochefoucault—who, by the by, is a bad moral preceptor—has, among others, this very excellent maxim: 'We are never made so ridiculous by the qualities we possess, as by those which we affect to have.' I never knew a man who would not profit of this observation. To preserve your own esteem, merit it. I have no fear that you will ever render yourself unworthy of its greatest good. Yet, a man who is so unfortunate as to lose his own good opinion, is wrong to despair. It may be retrieved. He ought to set about it immediately, as the only reparation which he can make to himself or society. The ill opinion of mankind is often misplaced; *but our own of ourselves never.*

"Pardon, my dear brother, this pedantic and didactic letter. Its sententiousness is intolerable, yet it was almost unavoidable. I had written till my fingers were cramped. The hour of closing the mail approached, and I was obliged to throw my sentiments into the offensive form of dogmas. That I, who abound in foibles, and, to speak truth, *vices*—that I should pretend to dogmatize, may appear to many arrogant indeed. Yet, let them recollect that we are all frail, and should sustain each other; and that the truth of a precept is not determined by the practice of him who promulges it. Go on, my dear Thompson, and prosper. I regret that I am debarred the pleasure of sharing your literary labors, and of that interchange of sentiment which constitutes one of the chief sources of my enjoyment. To our amiable sister—for such she considers herself with respect to you—I commit you, confident that your own exertion, aided by her society, will form you such as your friend will rejoice to behold you. Write to him frequently I beseech you; cheer his solitary and miserable existence with the well known characters of friendship. Adieu, my dear brother."

William Thompson to John Randolph.

"Dear Jack,—I am not ceremonious. I feel a conviction that your silence does not proceed from a want of regard, but from a cause more important to the world, to yourself, and, if possible, more distressing to me than the loss of that place in your heart, on which depends my future prosperity. I had fondly hoped that the change of scene, and the novelty of business, would have dissipated that melancholy which overhung you. To see my friend return happy and well, was the only wish of my heart.

"To the man who is not devoted to unnatural dissipations, a great city has no charms: it awakens the most painful sensations in the breast of the philanthropist and patriot. It is disgusting to behold such a mass of vice, and all its attendant deformities, cherished in the bosom of an enlightened country. Prostitutions of body, and still greater prostitution of mind, excite our pity and hatred. The political life has not those attractions to the virtuous which it once had, and which it ought still to have in this country. The spirit of party has extinguished the spirit of liberty. The enlightened orator must be shocked at the willing stupidity of his auditors. Our exertions are vain and impotent. Every man is the avowed friend of a party. Converts to reason are not to be found; whilst converts to interest are innumerable.

"You know I promised not to visit Richmond. I have rigidly adhered to that. I felt a necessity of *cooling down.* I foreboded the acquirement of dissipated habits, which would haunt me unceasingly. I saw that the patronage of the virtuous would awaken an emulation in me to attain their perfection. I feel confident that if my friends bear a little longer with my foibles, they will be corrected. I look forward with honest pride to the day when I shall merit the regard—when, by my conduct and by my principles, I shall make some retribution for the exalted generosity which I have met with from your family. I am not made of such stern stuff as to resist singly; but the idea of friendship will steel my heart against temptation. Since you left me, I have been generally at *home*, conscious how little I merit regard. That which I feel for your amiable family may perhaps appear presumption, yet the thought of losing it is stinging. * * * To your sister, your most amiable sister, I try to render myself agreeable. There is a gentleness of manners, an uniformity of conduct, and a majesty of virtue, which seem to render admiration presumptuous."

John Randolph to his brother, William Thompson.

"Your letter, my dear Thompson, has communicated to my heart a satisfaction to which it has not been at all familiar. It has proved beyond dispute that the energies of your mind, however neglected by yourself, or relaxed by misfortune, have been suspended, but not impaired; and that the strength of your understanding has not been unequal to the ordeal of misfortune, of which few are calculated to bear the test. Proceed, my friend, in the path in which you now move; justify those lively hopes which I have never ceased to entertain, or to express, of your future attainments: in the words, although not in the sense of the poet, let me exhort you, 'carpe diem.' The past is not in our power to recall. The future we can neither foresee nor control. The present alone is at our disposal: on the use to which it is applied, depends the whole of what is estimable or amiable in human character."

Poor Thompson went to Petersburg about this time (February, or March, 1800), and got entangled in a way that most young men of his temper are apt to be. He shall tell the story in his own way. After getting back to Bizarre, in April, he thus writes:

"You will be surprised, dear brother, when you are informed, that my stay in Petersburg was protracted by a circumstance against which you warned me in a letter some time past. I allude to Mrs. B——. Nature has compensated for mental imperfection, by bodily perfection in that woman. And my attachment to her corroborates a heresy in love, that desire is a powerful ingredient. Her mind is not cultivated, her disposition is not calculated to make a man of my enthusiasm in regard *happy*. Fully aware of these circumstances, I cherished her name as dear. Thus situated, let me ask you a question. Had you been told—nay, had you known that this woman was the victim of infamous oppression—that these charms had been wrested from your possession by unfeeling relations (they were engaged when he went to Europe in 1798), that your name was dear, her husband's name odious—that on you she looked with tenderness, and on him with hatred, what line of conduct would you adopt? * * * I had resolved to shun her, and in truth did; but that fate, which shows refinement in its policy, forced me to an interview. * * * * * * After several resolutions, some ridiculous (as is usual in such cases), and one which had near proved fatal, I fled to the asylum of the distressed (wisely thought of), to the spot where tender friendship forms a character exalted to a height, which makes the feebler of her sex look low indeed, would make me blush at my folly, and banish the idea of a baneful passion. I will not recapitulate the wrongs of fortune, but I fondly hope that they will plead in apology for the failings of your friend."

Now for the answer; and let every young man, and young woman too, ponder well upon it.

"April 19, 24 year.—To-day I received your letter of the 12th. It has unravelled a mystery, for whose solution I have before searched in vain. That you should have been in Petersburg, sighing at the feet of the fair Mrs. B., is what I did not expect to learn, since I supposed you all the while in Sussex. I am now not at all surprised at your silence, during this period of amorous intoxication; since nothing so completely unfits a man for intercourse with any other than the object of his infatuation.

"The answer to your questions is altogether easy. In the first place, it is not true, because it cannot be true, that this lady was compelled to the step which she has taken. What *force* could be brought to act upon her, which materials as hard as wax would not resist? The truth is, if ever she felt an attachment to you, she sacrificed it to avarice; not because money was the end, but the means, of gratification; her vanity, the ruling passion of every mind as imbecile as her own, delighted in the splendor which wealth alone could procure. At this time the same passion, which is one of the vilest modifications of self-love, would gratify itself with a little coquetry; and if your prudence has not exceeded that of the lady, it has gone, I fear, greater lengths than she at first apprehended. Nor have you, my friend, done this woman a good office, in rendering her discontented with her lot, by suffering her to persuade herself that she is in love with you, and that oppression alone has driven her to a detested union with a detestable brute, for such (on all hands, I believe, it is agreed) is Mr. B. Never did I see a woman apparently better pleased with her situation. She did not lose one pennyweight of her very comfortable quantity of flesh; and, however she *might have hesitated between* my friend and the cash, minus the possessor, had you been on the spot to contest your right to her very fair hand, yet W. T., on the other side of the Atlantic, or perhaps at the bottom of it, was no rival to the *solid* worth of her now cara sposa. Perhaps, in the first instance, she might have disliked the man, for good reasons; and in the second, for no reason at all, but because her relations were very anxious for the match; but be assured her imagination was not sufficiently lively to induce her to *shed one tear* on your account.

"You ask me, my friend, what conduct you ought to pursue; and you talk of revenge. B. has never injured you; he has acted like a fool, I grant, in marrying a woman whose only inducement to the match, he must be conscious, was his wealth; but he has committed no crime; at least he was unconscious of any. That the fellow should wear antlers, is no great matter of regret, because the os frontis is certainly substantial enough to bear their weight. Yet I do not wish them to be planted by you, *for your sake.* I will allow that this lady is as fair as she is *fat*—that she is a very inviting object; yet why should you prevent her leading a life of as much happiness as she is susceptible of—fruges consumere, &c. Has not her conduct in relation to *you* and to her husband been such as renders her unworthy of any man of worth? Has he not conferred on you a

benefit, by preventing the possibility of an alliance with a woman capable of carrying on a correspondence with any other than her husband; and can you, who enjoy the society of that pattern of female virtue, feel for this woman any sentiment but contempt? . . .
So far from injuring you, B. is the injured person, if at all. His impenetrable stupidity has alone shielded him from sensations not the most enviable, I imagine. Do not suppose from my style that I am unfeeling, or have too low an estimate of the sex; on the contrary, I am the warmest of their admirers. But silly and depraved women, and stupid, unprincipled men, are both objects of my pity and contempt. I wish you to form a just estimate of what is valuable in female character—then seek out a proper object and marry. Intrigue will blast your reputation, and, what is more to the purpose, your peace of mind; it will be a stumbling-block to you through life. An acquaintance with loose women has incapacitated you from forming a proper estimate of female worth. . . . .
I must congratulate you on your escape, and on your resolution to behold no more the fascinating object which has caused you so much uneasiness. I shall shortly have the pleasure of embracing you.

"P. S. My servant (Johnny?) has been packing up some effects, which I am about sending to Petersburg by water, and at every three words I have had a query to solve. This will account for my incoherence.

"P. S. (Characteristic, two postscripts.) I have been so hurried, as perhaps to betray myself into an inaccuracy of expression. But let me suggest two ideas to you. Has not your conduct been such as to injure a woman for whom you have felt and professed a regard? is it a liberal or disinterested passion (passion is never liberal or disinterested), which risks the reputation of the beloved object? Has not her conduct in admitting your attentions rendered her unworthy of any man but her present possessor? View this matter in its proper light and you will never think more of her. . . . . Success attend your study of law."

About the middle of May, Essex was dispatched with Jacobin and other horses, to meet his young master at the Bolling-green. He took along with him the following letter from William Thompson:

"What are my emotions, dearest brother, at seeing your horse thus far on his way to return you among us! How eagerly do I await the appointed day! Ryland (Randolph) has returned (some unsuccessful adventure), and another of the children of misfortune will seek refuge and consolation under this hospitable roof. He has promised me by letter to be with us in a day or two,—what pleasure do I anticipate in the society of our incomparable sister, in yours, in Ryland's! I wish I had the vanity to suppose I was worthy of it.

"We have been visited by the young ladies of Liberty Neck, and by its mentor, Major Scott. I had rather have his wisdom than Newton's or Locke's; for depend on it, he has dipped deep in the science of mind. According to the laws of gallantry, I should have escorted them to Amelia; but I am not fitted for society, and the continued round of company in the Neck is painful instead of pleasing.

"Our sister is now asleep; she would have written but for her being busy in finishing the children's clothes, and being obliged to write to Mrs. Harrison. When I came in last evening, I found her in the passage, a candle on the chair, sewing. I could hardly help exclaiming, what a pattern for her sex. The boys are well; they have both grown—the Saint particularly, whose activity will astonish you. Every body is cheerful—your arrival in anticipation is the cause. Farewell, dearest brother—hasten to join us.

"W. Thompson.

"Take care how you ride Jacobin, and if not for your own, at least for our sakes, run no risks by putting him in a carriage—we all dread the attempt."

He returned safely, to the joy of more people (ladies too?) than those at Bizarre. This delightful society was now complete; books, high discourse on philosophy, morals, government, the destiny of man—intermingled with the charming conversation and the music of elegant and accomplished women—exercise on the high-mettled steed, and frequent visits and dining parties at neighbors' houses, whose warm reception, bountiful hospitality, and unostentatious refinement of manner (universal with the gentlemen of the olden time), made the guest perfectly at home, and at ease in heart and in behavior. Such was the Old Dominion, half-a-century ago, such is she now in some degree; but, alas! the difference!

But poor Thompson, the hapless child of misfortune, was not long permitted to enjoy the sweets of this paradise. Some wicked and envious Mephistophiles looked in with his jealous eyes on the happy beings that composed it; and sought to blast it with his malicious tongue. It was rumored that Thompson staid at Bizarre for a selfish purpose; that, besides the convenience of the thing in his condition, his object was to win the affection of its fair mistress What if it were true? But this base world will allow nothing but a base motive for the most generous action. The insinuation was enough for the high-minded Thompson. He immediately left Bizarre, and wrote the following letter:—"The letter which I have transmitted by the same opportunity to that most amiable of women our sister, communicates intelligence of a report, the effects of which on my mind you will be fully aware of, from a former conversation on the subject. Would you suppose, my dearest brother, that the world would have dared to insinuate, that my object in remaining at Bizarre is to solicit the affections of our friend! Time, and the apprehension that I shall be intruded on, compel me to conciseness. My abode will be Ryland's until I receive letters from you both. View the subject with impartiality—enter into my feelings, for you know my heart—tell me with candor whether I am not bound to leave the abode of innocence and friendship? Tell me whether refined friendship does not demand on my part a sacrifice of every prospect of happiness, to the amiable, to the benevolent and virtuous woman who is wronged from her generous sympathy to the hapless."

A most delicate task this imposed on a friend—particularly one holding the relation of Mr. Randolph to the lady in question. But see how nobly, how manfully he discharged the duty: "For the first time I perceive myself embarrassed how to comply with the requisition of friendship. But yesterday, and I should have been unable to comprehend the speculative possibility of that which to-day is reduced to practice. If I decline the task which you have allotted me, it is not because I am disposed to shrink from the sacred obligations which I owe to you. My silence is not the effect of unfeeling indifference, of timid indecision, or cautious reserve. It is the result of the firmest conviction that it is not for *me* to advise you in the present crisis. It is a task to which I am indeed unequal. Consult your own heart, it is *alone* capable of advising you. The truly fraternal regard which you feel for our most amiable sister, does not require to be admonished of the respect which is due to her feelings. You alone are a competent judge of that conduct which is best calculated not to wound her delicacy; and it is that alone which you are capable of pursuing. Whatever may be your determination, you will not be the less dear to me. That spirit of impertinent malice, which mankind seem determined to cherish at the expense of all that should constitute their enjoyment, may, indeed, intrude upon our arrangements and deprive me of your society; but it can never rob me of the pure attachment which I have conceived for you, and which can never cease to animate me. I hold this portion of good, at least, in contempt of an unfeeling and calumnious world—invulnerable to every shaft, it derides their impotent malice.

"Let me suggest to you to pursue that line of conduct which you shall be disposed to adopt, as if it were the result of your previous determination. Prosecute, therefore, your intended journey, and do not permit malicious curiosity to enjoy the wretched satisfaction of supposing that IT has the power of influencing your actions.

"I have perceived, with extreme pleasure, that your mind has for some time been rapidly regaining its pristine energy. Keep it, therefore, I beseech you, my friend, in constant exercise. Get up some object of pursuit. Make to yourself an image, and, in defiance of the decalogue, worship it. Whether it be excellence in medicine or law, or political eminence, determine not to relax your endeavors until you have attained it. You must not suffer your mind, whose activity must be employed, to prey upon *itself*. The greatest blessing which falls to the lot of man is thus converted into the deadliest curse. I need not admonish you to keep up the intercourse which subsists between us, and which nothing shall compel me to relinquish.

"I trust that I shall hear from you in the space of a week at farthest. Meanwhile rest assured of the undiminished affection of the firmest of your friends."

Poor Thompson! why could he not follow the advice so delicately given—pursue the line of conduct he had previously determined on—which was, doubtless, to stay at Bizarre—prosecute his journey, and then come back, without regard to the malicious surmises of a wicked world? He did not sacrifice his happiness to that amiable, benevolent and virtuous woman, as he supposed; she did not need it or require it—but to malicious curiosity. He had not strength of mind to resist the vague impression of the world's censure; and suffered the spirit of impertinent malice to enjoy the wretched satisfaction of supposing that *it* had the power of influencing his actions. He never came back to Bizarre as a home again—soon fell into his old habits—wandered over Canada a-foot, seeking rest but finding none—a wandering spirit that rapidly glided into irregular courses; the world, erewhile so bright and smooth, had suddenly become dark and slippery to him; ne'er again could he find rest for the sole of his foot;—turned out from that paradise, a world of turbid waters was all his wearied eye could light upon. What further befell him shall be made known to the reader in the sequel.

CHAPTER XXV.

THE COURSE OF TRUE LOVE NEVER DID RUN SMOOTH.

THE reader is already aware that John Randolph was the centre of a very extensive correspondence with some of the first young men of the country—among others, Joseph Bryan, of Georgia. In the month of January, last winter (1800), Bryan informed him that he was about to embark soon for England, and wished his friend to procure certificates of citizenship for himself and companion from Mr. Jefferson; and promised in his next to give the reason for quitting his native country—which accordingly he did in the following words: "I have in that time, my friend (since this time twelve months), been on the verge of becoming a member of the fraternity of Benedicts, as you humorously style married men. In short, I paid my addresses to an accomplished young woman, of both family and fortune, in Carolina—quarrelled with my father and mother because I would not relinquish the pursuit—followed her with every prospect of the desired success for eighteen months—went to her abode last Christmas, with the comfortable idea of marrying her on the commencement of the new year—and was discarded by her parents because mine would not consent to the match. There were one or two other trifling objections, such as—I was a ———, a man of no religion—a Georgian; and would take their child where they might never see her face again, &c. All this you may think apocryphal—'tis true, upon my word. Yet 'my heart does not bleed at every pore from the bitterest of recollections;' to be sure I was in a hell of a taking for two or three days. But I found that keeping myself employed, made it wear off to a miracle. So much for my love affairs. You may perhaps be a little surprised at my going to England; 'twas a sudden resolution, I must confess; I'll tell you how it happened. While I was laboring under the horrors of my dismission, I swore to my little grisette, in order to melt her, that if she would not quit father and mother and run away with me, I would go off immediately and fight the Russians! She would not do that, so I am obliged by a point of honor to make the attempt, at least.

"If, after my arrival in England, I can conveniently get to France, I shall go there; if not, I shall spend the money I carry with me, and come home again.

"I don't know whether 'twill be proper to apply to Mr. Jefferson for the certificate I wrote to you for—my reasons were these: I knew that he was better known and better liked in France than any distinguished person in our country, therefore, a certificate from him would do me more service than from any other; besides, I don't like any of the Adamites well enough to receive a favor of that kind from their hands.

"I expect to sail from Savannah about the 20th instant (February, 1800); as soon as I arrive you will hear from me. One of my *principal reasons* for going to Europe, is to improve my health, which is very indifferent at this time."

So then it was your own pleasure and convenience at last, and not the sting of disappointed love, that drove you away to France! The girls are very much deceived when they flatter themselves that men generally will do rash things for their sweet sakes; they may be in *a hell of a taking* for a time, but the fever soon wears off. Men are no better treated. This girl, in his absence, while he was fighting for liberty under the banners of France, did the very thing she refused to do with him—ran away and got married against the will of her parents.

But the answer to the first letter, and in anticipation of the one above: "Your letter of the 7th of last month was this moment put into my hands. Need I say that it distresses me beyond measure? Ah, my friend, it is then too true! My suspicions were but too well grounded! The eagle-eye of friendship finds no difficulty in piercing the veil which shrouds you; which, until now, I did not dare to lift. You have related nothing, yet I know every thing. This omission, for which you promise to atone in another letter, is but too well supplied by conjectures which cannot, I fear, deceive me.

"Bryan, my friend, you are about to render yourself, me, all who are interested in your happiness, wretched, perhaps, for ever. These are more numerous than you are at present willing to allow. At one stroke you are about to sever all those ties which bind you to the soil which gave you birth, to the tender connections of your childhood, to the most constant of friends—relations which give to existence its only value. Your sickly taste loathes that domestic happiness which is yet in store for you—perhaps you deny that it can have, for yourself, any existence; you prefer to it, *trash* of foreign growth. You seek in vain, my friend, to fly from misery. It will accompany you—it will rankle in that heart in whose cruel wounds it rejoices to dwell. It is of no country, but *yourself*, and time alone can soothe its rage.

"Among the dangers you are about to encounter, I will not enumerate those of a personal nature; not because they are in themselves contemptible, however they may be despised by yourself, but because in comparison to the gigantic mischiefs which you are about to court, they are indeed insignificant. I mean in respect to yourself—to your friends they are but too formidable. Recall then, I beseech you, your rash determination—pause, at least, upon the rash step which you meditate! It is, however, the privilege of friendship *only* to *advise*. The certificates which you require, I will endeavor to procure time enough to accompany this letter. This is Saturday, and after the hour of doing business at the offices; and to be valid they must issue from that of the Secretary of State. Be not impatient, they shall be forwarded by Tuesday's mail, *in any event;* letters from Jefferson to some of his European friends shall follow them."

Thus we find this young man, not yet twenty-seven years of age, the grave Mentor to his young friends. They confide to his friendship, constant and pure, all their cares and troubles, and confidently expect in return his sympathy, his advice, and the practical lessons of a sage wisdom. But was he without care? Had he no troubles of his own to perplex his bosom? Had this young Mentor so soon fought the battle of life, and gained the victory? Was his heart serene and lifted above the storm of passion that raged around him? *I, too, am wretched!* "To the procuring and transmitting," continues he, "of these certificates of birth and citizenship, I annex a condition of which I will not brook the refusal—a compliance is due to that attachment which has so long subsisted between us; it is an exertion certainly not too great to be yielded to a friendship, whose constancy has been rarely equalled, but never surpassed. Listen, therefore:

"I, too, am wretched; misery is not your exclusive charter. I have for some months meditated a temporary relinquishment of my country. The execution of this scheme has no connection with yours. The motives which produced it originated in events which happened before I took my seat in Congress, although I was then ignorant of their existence; they were, indeed, prior to my election to an office, of which nothing but a high sense of the obligations of public duty has prevented the resignation. A second election could not, in that event, have been practicable, until the present session was somewhat advanced. I determined, therefore, not to relinquish my seat until its expiration; then to resign it, and bid adieu to my native shores for a few years, at least. In this determination I still remain. If, therefore, you refuse to rescind your hasty resolution, I desire permission to be the companion of your voyage—to partake your sorrows and to share with you my own—to be the friend of him who is to accompany you, because he is *yours*. Yet, believe me, Joe, and it is unnecessary to declare by what motives I am influenced to the assertion, that I shall be glad to hear that I am to prosecute my voyage alone—to be informed that you have receded from a project which has not, like my own, been the fruit of deliberate resolve. I had, indeed, hoped that the relation of your own domestic enjoyment would have beguiled many a sad hour of my life. But, pardon me, my dear fellow, I see my indiscretion. It shall not be repeated.

If, then, you persist in carrying into execution your plan, take a passage with your friend for New-York, or the Delaware, it is open; meet me here about the middle of March—we rise in April—there is a resolution laid upon our table to adjourn on the first of the month; it will certainly be carried; they even talk of substituting 'March.' We will then embark together for any part of the other continent that you may prefer; I am indifferent about places. But if I go alone, I shall take shipping for some English port, London or Liverpool. I wish I could join you in Savannah; but it would be extremely inconvenient. I fear the climate; a passage would be more uncertain too from thence, and the accommodations perhaps not so good. Yet I will even meet you there, or in Charleston, in case you are resolved to leave America, if I can have your company on no other terms. Write immediately and solve this business. I repeat, that it will be very inconvenient to take my passage from a southern port; it will likewise occasion delay. I shall have a voyage to make thither, and then to wait the sailing of a vessel; whereas, if you meet me here, I can fix myself for any ship bound to Europe about the time of the rising of Congress; and in the great ports of New-York, Philadelphia, or Baltimore, we cannot fail to procure a speedy embarkation, and agreeable berths. Again I entreat you to write to me immediately upon the receipt of this: in expectation of the answer, I shall remain under no common anxiety until its arrival. Meantime, remember, my friend, that there is one person, at least, and he an unshaken friend, who is not insensible to your worth. Farewell, dear Joseph.

"P. S. I had like to have omitted enjoining you to preserve inviolable secrecy with respect to my designs. The reason I will detail to you at meeting. It is unnecessary to say that they are not such as I should be ashamed to avow; yet I do not wish it to be known that I am about to leave the country until a week or ten days before my departure. Adieu!"

Bryan did not receive this letter before his embarkation. Had it come to hand in time, there can be no question that he would have gladly accepted the offer of his friend, and gone to Philadelphia and awaited the adjournment of Congress, that they might have the pleasure of a voyage together.

But it is certain Randolph did not go abroad at that time. Had his friend arrived in Philadelphia, in obedience to his wishes, he would unquestionably have strained a point, and, at all hazards, fulfilled an engagement he had so solemnly made. In that case, the events of history would have been changed. But he did not go; the reason why is unknown to us. It may have been pecuniary embarrassment. He was paying large instalments of the British debt about that time to Mr. Wickham. In 1824, writing to a friend from Paris, he says: "Here, then, am I, where I ought to have been thirty years ago, and where I would have been, had I not been plundered and oppressed."

But he did not escape from his sorrows at that time by flying across the sea. He staid at home to brood over them. *I, too, am wretched.*

"My character" (says he in a letter to a friend about this time August, 1800), "like many other sublunary things, hath lately undergone an almost total revolution." It seems that he had some special sorrow that weighed upon his heart, the cause of which originated before his election in April, 1799, but was unknown to him for some months afterwards. That it was of the same nature with that which drove one friend across the Atlantic and the other to Canada—that it was the malady of love which brought him into trouble, and that oppressed his soul, cannot be questioned.

Soon after he took his seat in Congress Thompson wrote to him, detailing the circumstances of a report which had been fabricated and secretly circulated to his injury, tracing it to its source, and proving it to be an idle tale without foundation, and confined to the knowledge of a few only. He then continues: "Repose on thy pillow and heed not the shafts that are thrown against you. The world has not injured me, and it has not despised you. Mrs. M. assured me that in your honor she placed the most implicit confidence. When you communicate with M——a, as probably you have already done, she will declare herself unaffected by this tale, which has disturbed your peace. I have spoken with candor, but I have spoken with truth. Demand the author, and if he be given up, you will find it a child. The time of telling it, the month of August.

"Alas, my brother, what are not you destined to suffer! What tremendous trials of fortitude have you not undergone! In the enthusiasm of friendship I look forward to your happiness, and each day brings to life some new pang which is unfeelingly inflicted. Let not this affair make too deep an impression on your mind—command my services if they be required; for be assured that the mind which personifies irregularity and want of system in the affairs of the world, is nerved to act with dauntless energy in the cause of my brother. Prudence, caution, all the requisites of successful friendship, are at the command of him, who in the walk of life is eccentric and unsteady."

About the time of the correspondence with Bryan, and his determination to go abroad, Thompson again writes:—"I have mingled with society; I have purposely spoken of you and Miss W——d to ascertain precisely the public opinion; and I can repeat with joy, that my brother has not been wronged by the world. As to the idle suggestions of babbling men and women, shall they be heaped together and transformed into most serious charges, that even your confidence of yourself may be shaken if possible, and thus your peace of mind be for ever blasted? Enough on this subject. I have violated my common rule of conduct by being aggressor on the topic."

On another occasion he says:—"In our lives, my brother, we have seen two fine women (Mrs. Judith Randolph and Miss M——a W—d); never extend your list; never trust your eyes, or your ears, for they stand alone." And in his voluntary banishment from the asylum of the wretched and unfortunate, when he deeply felt his bereavement and forlorn condition, he thus writes: "M——a, the amiable, the good M——a, has honored me with a short letter; such tokens of esteem, such evidences of generous pity, for a man cast on the wide world unfriended and unprotected, create a gratitude not to be expressed. It is not until we are humiliated by misfortune that we feel these things, for in the height of worldly prosperity the wish and the pursuit go hand in hand, and successive gratifications blunt the sensibilities of our nature. Whilst we rejoice in a mortality as the termination of lives mutually painful, in which we have been called on to exercise a fortitude sufficient to overwhelm minds less noble and less firm, in which every fair prospect has been blighted, every brilliant expectation thwarted, and every tender emotion hatefully disappointed, let us linger out a remnant which cannot be long, mutually cherishing and supporting each other on the tedious road. My dear friend, let us not leave each other behind; for, alas! how sterile and how barren would creation then be! United, we are strong, but unsupported we could not stand against the increasing pressure of misfortune. Often do I exclaim, Would that you and I were cast on some desert island, there to live out the remainder of our days unpolluted by the communication with man. Separated from each other, our lips are sealed, for the expression of sentiments which exult and ennoble humanity. Even in the support of virtue, the cautious language of vice must be adopted; even in the defence of truth we must descend to the artifice of error."

Here, reader, we let drop the curtain. Its thick folds of half a century are impervious to the light of mortal eyes; ask not a look beyond the mysterious veil. There are secrets we trust not to a friend, that we betray not to ourselves, and which none but the impious curiosity of a heartless world would ever dare to penetrate. Let the gross impulses, the base considerations of worldly gain, that constitute the ground and the motive of most human associations, suffice as fit subjects for your cold observation, your ridicule and contempt; but hold sacred, or look with awe, on that deep self-sacrificing passion, which, springing from the soul of man, is all-embracing in its love, fathomless, infinite, and divine. Enough to know, that in the bosom of this man there glowed the fires of such a love, that continued to burn through life, and were only extinguished amid the crumbling ruins of the altar by the damp dews that gathered over them in the dark valley and the shadow of death. He hath said: "*One* I loved better than my own soul, or him that created it." "My apathy is not natural, but superinduced. There *was* a volcano under my ice, but it is burnt out, and a face of desolation has come on, not to be rectified in ages, could my life be prolonged to a patriarchal longevity. The necessity *of loving and being beloved* was never felt by the imaginary beings of Rousseau and Byron's creation more imperiously than by myself. My heart was offered up with a devotion that knew no reserve. Long an object of proscription and treachery, I have at last (more mortifying to the pride of man) become one of utter indifference."

To you, reader, he is far from being an object of indifference, and we trust that before the end of these volumes he will be drawn to your heart by the cords of affection, and that his memory will ever hereafter awaken in your bosom those noblest emotions of sympathy and veneration.

CHAPTER XXVI.

PRESIDENTIAL ELECTION, 1800–1—MIDNIGHT JUDGES.

The reader is already aware of the intense political excitement raging through the country at this time. The civil wars, and violent upturning of the whole social system in Europe, spread the contagion of their influence across the Atlantic. The efforts of the belligerent powers to draw the United States into the war, and the anxiety of leading politicians here at home to cast on their political adversaries the odium of their foreign associations—Anglo-mania and Gallo-mania—threw into the contest a bitterness and violence little short of actual civil commotion. The excited political campaign in the spring of 1799, was but a prelude to the more violent presidential election that was to take place in the autumn of 1800. The fate of the Republic depended on that election. Had the federalists succeeded, there can be no doubt that a degradation of the States and a concentration of all power in a splendid central empire, would have been the final result. Happily for the cause of human freedom, the election terminated in the triumph of the republican cause.

Thomas Jefferson and Aaron Burr being the candidates of the republicans, got seventy-three votes, John Adams sixty-five votes, Charles Cotesworth Pinckney sixty-four votes, and John Jay one vote. But a difficulty grew out of this result that could not have been anticipated. The Constitution, by an amendment made in consequence of this difficulty, now requires the electors to designate the person they vote for as president, and the person they vote for as vice-president; but at that time there was no means of discrimination; they voted for two persons, and the one getting the highest number of votes was declared to be elected president, and the person getting the next highest number of votes was declared to be elected vice-president. Mr. Jefferson and Mr. Burr had an equal number of votes; neither of them could be declared as being elected president; and the question had to be decided by the House of Representatives voting by States. So soon as this state of things was known, a high degree of uneasiness and alarm was excited in the minds of the republicans, lest the will of the people might be frustrated by intrigue and corruption. Mr. Jefferson charged the federalists with a design of preventing an election altogether. In a letter to Mr. Madison he says: "The federalists appear determined to prevent an election, and to pass a bill giving the government to Mr. Jay, reappointed chief justice, or to Marshall, as secretary of state." This would have been an act of revolution; and some of the more violent and unprincipled may have carried their designs thus far; but there can be no question that the aim of the party was to defeat Mr. Jefferson and to elect Burr. This was carrying their opposition to the will of the people very far. Aaron Burr never was thought of for president; not a single vote was cast for him with that view, and the mere accident of his having the same number of votes with the favorite of the people, brought his name into the House of Representatives; and yet the federalists determined to take advantage of this circumstance, and to elevate him to the presidency, in spite of the popular will. They justified themselves on the ground that the public will could only be expressed to them through the constitutional organs. There were two candidates, they said, for the office of president, who were presented to the House of Representatives with equal suffrages. The Constitution gave them the right, and made it their duty, to elect that one of the two whom they thought preferable. Neither of them was the man of their choice, but the Constitution confined their election to one of the two, and they gave their vote to the one they thought the greater and the better man. That vote they repeated, and in that vote they declared their determination to persist, had they not been driven from it by imperious necessity. The prospect ceased of the vote being effectual, and the alternative only remained of taking one man for president, or having no president at all. They chose, as they thought, the lesser evil. The republicans, on the other hand, condemned their course as factious and revolutionary; and, had they succeeded in electing Burr to the presidency, in all probability he would have been driven from his seat at the point of the bayonet. From all quarters the sound came up, "We will obey no other president but Mr. Jefferson." There are many interesting facts and important lessons connected with this election that come within the province of the general historian, but which we must pass over as inappropriate to this Biography. The part that John Randolph took in these affairs was that of a silent voter and watchful observer. He dispatched daily bulletins to his father-in-law, giving the result of each balloting as it took place. After the nineteenth ballot he writes: "No election will, in my opinion, take place." But on the 17th of February he writes: "On the thirty-sixth ballot there appeared, this day, ten States for Thomas Jefferson; four (New England) for A. Burr, and two blank ballots (Delaware and South Carolina). This was the second time that we balloted to-day. The four Burrites of Maryland put blanks into the box of that State; the vote was, therefore, unanimous. Mr. Morris, of Vermont, left his seat, and the result was, therefore, Jeffersonian. I need not add that Mr. J. was declared duly elected."

Mr. Randolph attributed this result to the patriotism of Alexander Hamilton. That gentleman was the influential and popular leader of the federal party, and when he saw the extremity to which things were likely to be driven by a longer persistence in their course, he advised his friends, rather than to produce a revolution in the government, or excite popular commotion, to give way and suffer Mr. Jefferson to be elected. Mr. Randolph often expressed the opinion, in after life, that we owed the safety of the Republic to Hamilton, and that his course on that trying occasion had elevated him very much in his estimation.

The federalists perpetrated another act during the session that excited a great deal of indignation. They so altered and enlarged the judiciary system as to require the appointment of a great many new judges. It was urged as an objection to the bill, that it was made by a party at the moment when they were sensible that their power was expiring and passing into other hands. They replied it was enough for them that the full and legitimate power existed. The remnant left them (the bill passed 15th February, 1801) was plenary and efficient—and it was their duty to employ it according to their judgments and consciences for the good of the country. They thought the bill a salutary measure, and there was no obligation upon them to leave it as a work for their successors. They had no hesitation in avowing that they had no confidence in the persons who were to follow them, and were, therefore, the more anxious to accomplish a work which they believed would contribute to the safety and stability of the government. It was further urged as an objection to the bill, that it was merely designed to create sinecures and retreats for broken-down political hacks—and to erect battlements and fortresses in which the discomfited leaders of federalism might rally their scattered forces for another contest. Mr. Jefferson said of this measure, "I dread this above all the measures meditated, because appointments in the nature of freehold render it difficult to undo what is done." Yet the next Congress did not hesitate to undo what was done. The first regular speech made by Mr. Randolph was on the proposition to repeal this law. It was in answer to Mr. Bayard, the leader and the ablest champion on the opposite side. This speech was published, many years ago, in a collection intended to be specimens of American eloquence; and notwithstanding he was so young a man, it will bear a comparison, in point of style and argument, with the very best that were delivered at that day. In justifying a repeal of the law, and thereby displacing judges, who by the Constitution hold their appointments during good behavior, Mr. Randolph argued—"I agree that the Constitution is a limited grant of power, and that none of its general phrases are to be construed into an extension of that grant. I am free to declare, that if the extent of this bill is to get rid of the judges, it is a perversion of your power to a base purpose; it is an unconstitutional act. If, on the contrary, it aims not at the displacing one set of men from whom you differ in political opinion, with a view to introduce others, but for the general good, by abolishing useless offices, it is a constitutional act. The *quo animo* determines the nature of this act, as it determines the innocence or guilt of other acts. But we are told that this is to declare the judiciary, which the Constitution has attempted to fortify against the other branches of government, dependent on the will of the legislature, whose discretion alone is to limit their encroachments. Whilst I contend that the legislature possesses this discretion, I am sensible of the delicacy with which it is to be used. It is like the power of impeachment, or the declaring of war, to be exercised under a high responsibility. But the power is denied—for, say they, its exercise will enable flagitious men to overturn the judiciary, in order to put their creatures into office, and to wreak their vengeance on those who have become obnoxious by their merit; and yet the gentleman expressly says, that arguments drawn from a supposition of extreme political depravity prove nothing; that every government presupposes a certain degree of honesty in its rulers, and that to argue from extreme cases is totally inadmissible. Nevertheless, the whole of his argument is founded on the supposition of a total want of principle in the legislature and executive."

While speaking on the subject of the judiciary in the Virginia Convention, nearly thirty years after this transaction, Mr. Randolph thus alludes to it: "At the very commencement of my public life, or nearly so, I was called to give a decision on the construction of that clause in the Federal Constitution which relates to the tenure of the judicial office; and I am happy to find that, after the lapse of thirty years, I remain precisely of the same opinion that I then held."

If a law should be passed *bona fide*, for the abolition of a court which was a nuisance, and ought to be abolished, he considered such a law as no infringement of judicial independence; but, if the law was enacted *mala fide*, and abolished a useful court, for the purpose of getting rid of the judge who presided in it, such a law was undoubtedly a violation of that independence; just as the killing of a man might be murder or not, according to the intention, the *quo animo* with which it was done. He said that it could not be necessary to recount to the gentleman who occupied the chair (Mr. Barbour) the history of the decision which was given in Congress, as to the true intent and meaning of this part of the Federal Constitution. Parties had never run higher than at the close of the administration of the elder Adams, and the commencement of that of Mr. Jefferson. After efforts the most unparalleled, Mr. Adams was ejected from power, and the downfall of the party attached to him was near at hand. After this decision by the American people, when they were compelled to perceive that the kingdom was passing from them, in the last agonies and throes of dissolution, they cast about them to make some provision for the broken-down hacks of the party; and at midnight, and after midnight, on the last day of Mr. Adams's administration, a batch of judges was created, and bequeathed as a legacy to those who followed.

The succeeding party on coming into power, found that they must consult the construction of the Constitution, to prevent the recurrence of such a practice; because, if the construction should be allowed under which this had been done, it would enable every political party, having three months notice of their departure from the helm of affairs, to provide for themselves and their adherents, by getting up a judiciary system, which would be irrevocable; a city of refuge where they would be safe from all approach of danger. To avoid such a result it became necessary to abolish the system, which was then believed to be injurious, and which experience has proved to be unnecessary. Mr. Randolph said, that he was one of those who voted for the decision which declared that the court might be abolished *bona fide*, and that the office of the judge should cease with it.

Shortly after these midnight appointments, Mr. Adams left the city, under the cover of darkness, that he might not witness, the next day, the inauguration of his successful rival. Many of his friends were deeply mortified at this undignified and unmanly retreat.

On reaching an inn beyond Baltimore, 'tis said (we speak on the authority of Mr. Randolph) that Mr. Adams, walking up to a portrait of Washington, and placing his finger on his lips, exclaimed, "If I had kept my lips as close as that man, I should now be the President of the United States."

It is very true, Mr. Adams had no judgment, no discretion. He possessed a brilliant imagination, a bold and an ardent temper, that made him the impassioned and powerful orator of the Revolution; but he could lay claim to few of those faculties that fit a man to conduct wisely and prudently the affairs of a great republic.

CHAPTER XXVII.

THE SEVENTH AND EIGHTH CONGRESSES.—CHAIRMAN OF THE COMMITTEE OF WAYS AND MEANS.—THE WORKING PERIOD.—THE YAZOO BUSINESS.

At the opening of the first Congress under the new administration, in December, 1801, Mr. Randolph had the satisfaction of seeing his friend, Nathaniel Macon, elected Speaker of the House of Representatives. Mr. Randolph was placed at the head of the Committee of

Ways and Means. Some notion may be formed of the duties of this committee from the resolution calling for its appointment.

"*Resolved*, That a Standing Committee of Ways and Means be appointed, whose duty it shall be to take into consideration all such reports of the Treasury Department, and all such propositions relative to the revenue, as may be referred to them by the House; to inquire into the state of the public debt, of the revenue, and of the expenditures; and to report, from time to time, their opinion thereon."

The duties of this committee, as we may perceive, embraced a wide field of inquiry. The new administration had pledged itself to the people to place the "ship of state on its republican tack," and to furnish a model of a simple and economical government. All unnecessary offices and useless expenditures were to be abolished, the army and navy reduced, and the national debt was to be redeemed. All the necessary inquiries, investigations, reports, and bills, touching these important subjects, had to emanate from the Committee of Ways and Means. The chairman of that committee had to be brought in daily official communication with the executive departments; his relation towards them was of a most confidential character; and he was regarded as the leader of the friends of the administration in the representative department.

Mr. Randolph and the President were intimate friends; they were on terms of unreserved intercourse—personally and politically they cordially agreed, and heartily co-operated in accomplishing the great ends of the administration. In accordance with the recommendation of the President, Mr. Randolph introduced a proposition, "that a committee be appointed to inquire whether any, and what alterations can be made in the judiciary department of the United States, and to provide for securing the impartial selection of juries in the courts of the United States;" and also another resolution, to inquire what reductions could be made in the civil government of the United States. They were referred to a select committee, of which he was chairman. On the 4th of February, he reported a bill to repeal the laws of the last session with respect to the judiciary, and after undergoing considerable discussion in committee of the whole, it was finally passed by the House on the 3d March, 1802, by a large majority. Mr. Randolph's speech on this subject we have already alluded to in the preceding chapter. On the 20th January he introduced a resolution, directing the Secretary of the Treasury to lay before the House a list of the exports to the Mediterranean, distinguishing those of the growth of the United States. He also took part in the debate on the apportionment under the census of 1800. Mr. Randolph took a lively interest in this subject, and long foresaw the effect each succeeding census would have on the political power of his native State. He introduced on the 9th of June, a resolution to reduce the military establishment. Having been appointed chairman of the select committee to see what could be done to expedite the public printing, he reported a resolution to appoint a public printer; and to his exertions may be justly attributed an economical improvement in the printing of the House.

But one of the most important subjects to which Mr. Randolph turned his attention was the public debt. On the 9th of April, 1802, he reported a bill making provision for the redemption of the public debt of the United States. It provided that so much of the duties on merchandise and tonnage, &c., as will amount to an annual sum of seven millions three hundred thousand dollars, be yearly appropriated as a sinking fund; and said sums were declared to be vested in Commissioners of the Sinking Fund, to be applied by them to the payment of interest and charges, and to the redemption of the principal of the public debt. After this appropriation he kept a watchful eye on its faithful disbursement. The subject was frequently before the Committee of Ways and Means, and the conduct and management of the commissioners minutely criticised.

The chief subject that attracted the attention of Congress during the next session, which began in December, 1802, was the navigation of the Mississippi and the cession of Louisiana to France. In the preceding October, the Governor of New Orleans, Don Morales, had issued a proclamation, excluding that port as a dépôt for our commerce, a privilege we had a right to enjoy under our treaty with Spain. This conduct on the part of the Spanish authorities had created great excitement in the western country. In addition to this, it was rumored abroad that Louisiana had been transferred to the dominion of the all-powerful and all-grasping French Republic, now under the sway of the ambitious Bonaparte. These important facts, together with the private information he had obtained on the subject, were deemed by the President as being worthy of a secret and confidential communication to Congress, which was made the 22d of December. Additional information was communicated on the 31st, and on the 5th of January Mr. Griswold moved that the President be requested to lay before the House copies of such official documents as have been received by the Government, announcing the cession of Louisiana to France, together with a report explaining the stipulations, circumstances, and conditions, under which that province is to be delivered up. Those private messages, which called forth this resolution, had, on motion of Mr. Randolph, been referred to a committee, and had been under consideration in the House with closed doors. He now moved to refer Mr. Griswold's resolution to a Committee of the Whole on the state of the Union. The motion, after some discussion, was carried, and the House went into committee. Mr. Randolph observed that he had in his hand certain resolutions connected with the message, relative to the late proceedings at New Orleans, the discussion of which had been ordered to be conducted with closed doors. He asked the decision of the question, whether, previously to offering his resolutions, the doors ought not to be closed. Much opposition was made to this motion. Mr. Griswold's resolution, it was said, was one for information, and ought to be discussed with open doors. Mr. Randolph observed, that he had already more than once stated his objections to discuss this subject in public. He had observations, which, he had said, must be made in secret. "The gentleman from Connecticut says he is willing the resolution should be fully discussed, and therefore concludes that it must not be referred to a select committee, as he is pleased to term it, where alone, as we contend, and have informed him, the discussion can take place. Sir, this may be logic, but it is new to me. A message from the President relative to New Orleans has been referred to a certain committee, and we propose to refer the resolution to the same committee. Gentlemen exclaim that this is denying them information. Does it follow of necessity that we deny the information because we choose to consider the subject with closed doors? Cannot the resolution be as fully discussed in private as in public? Do all the reasoning faculties of the House cease to exist the moment the doors are closed? Cannot the eloquence of the gentleman be exerted unless when addressed to the ladies who do us the honor of attending in this hall?" Mr. Randolph's motion prevailed. The House was cleared, and he offered, with closed doors, the following resolution, to which he had alluded in debate; "Resolved—That this House receive, with great sensibility, the information of a disposition in certain officers of the Spanish Government at New Orleans to obstruct the navigation of the river Mississippi, as secured to the United States by the most solemn stipulations. That, adhering to the humane and wise policy which ought ever to characterize a free people, and by which the United States have always professed to be governed, willing, at the same time, to ascribe this breach of compact to the unauthorized misconduct of certain individuals, rather than to a want of good faith on the part of his Catholic Majesty, and relying with perfect confidence on the vigilance and wisdom of the Executive, they will wait the issue of such measures as that department of the Government shall have pursued for asserting the rights and vindicating the injuries of the United States; holding it to be their duty, at the same time, to express their unalterable determination to maintain the boundaries and the rights of navigation and commerce through the river Mississippi, as established by existing treaties."

One of the measures of the Executive to which Mr. Randolph alludes, was a pending negotiation for the purchase of Louisiana. Mr. Livingston, our minister at Paris, had received ample instructions on this subject, and, about this time, Mr. Monroe had been dispatched as envoy extraordinary, to aid him in the negotiation. The proposition happened to have been made at a most fortunate juncture of affairs, when Bonaparte was preparing for a war with England. He wished to keep on good terms with the United States—feared that the British navy might wrest his newly acquired province from him during the coming war, and was much in need of money. These considerations induced him to listen favorably to the proposition of the United States to purchase Louisiana for a large sum of money.

Mr. Livingston conducted the business with great ability, and when Mr. Monroe arrived, he had but little more to do than sign the articles of the treaty. Bonaparte, in a very short time, repented of this measure. He saw the great blunder he had committed in parting with a country so large, so rich, and so important, in a political and commercial point of view; and would have availed himself of any pretext to break the treaty, and take back the province. The

President was apprised of all these facts, and warned by our ministers, that if there should be the slightest delay in the ratification, and in the provisions to be made by Congress to pay the instalments of the purchase, we should lose it altogether. The treaty was signed at Paris, the 30th of April, 1803. So soon as it reached the United States, the President, by proclamation, called Congress on the first Monday in October, to take measures to carry it into effect.

In all his efforts to bring this business to a successful issue, the President received the hearty co-operation of the leader of the House of Representatives. Mr. Randolph's quick and comprehensive mind saw, at a glance, the importance of the crisis, and, as chairman of the Committee of Ways and Means, his aid was most prompt and efficient in getting over the difficulty. By the 10th of November, a bill had been passed, and approved by the President, creating certificates of stock in favor of the French Republic, for the sum of eleven millions two hundred and fifty thousand dollars, bearing an interest of six per centum per annum, from the time when possession of Louisiana shall have been obtained, in conformity with the treaty of the thirtieth day of April, one thousand eight hundred and three, between the United States of America and the French Republic. Possession was given the 20th of December following; and all the measures adopted by Congress in regard to the newly acquired territory, were either matured by the Committee of Ways and Means, of which Mr. Randolph was chairman, or by some select committee, appointed at his instance. Few men did more than he to secure the purchase of Louisiana, when once made, and then to provide for it a good and efficient government. Next to the Declaration of Independence, and the adoption of the present Constitution, the acquisition of Louisiana has had more influence than any other thing on the destiny of the United States.

Mr. Jefferson was a strict constructionist, and held that no powers should be exercised but those specifically granted. The Constitution contemplates no territory beyond that in possession of the Confederacy or of the States at the time of its adoption. The purchase of foreign territory was a thing not dreamed of by its framers, nor is there any clause authorizing such a measure. Mr. Jefferson was fully aware of this; but he considered that there was such an imperious necessity in this case, requiring such immediate action—now or never—that he would be justified in making the acquisition, and procuring a sanction of it afterwards, by an amendment of the Constitution. "The Constitution has made no provision for our holding foreign territory," says he, "still less for incorporating foreign nations into our Union. The Executive, in seizing the fugitive occurrence, which so much advances the good of their country, have done an act beyond the Constitution. The legislature, in casting behind them metaphysical subtleties, and risking themselves like faithful servants, must ratify and pay for it, and throw themselves on their country, for doing for them, unauthorized, what we know they would have done for themselves, had they been in a situation to do it. But we shall not be disavowed by the nation, and their act of indemnity will confirm and not weaken the Constitution, by more strongly marking out its lines."

But unfortunately this act of indemnity was never performed—the amendment of the Constitution was never made. What was an exception, justified only by necessity, has now become a precedent; and nearly all the difficulties that threaten a dissolution of the Union, growing out of the slavery question, and the acquisition of new territory, have been occasioned by that fatal omission. Had the Constitution been amended, as contemplated, by first sanctioning that which had been admitted as a violation of it, and then by defining minutely the powers to be exercised in future by Congress, the present embarrassments of the country could never have happened. We see also in this transaction the insufficiency of a paper constitution to resist the current of the popular will—unless there be power to restrain power, nothing else can withstand it—the plea of necessity has been urged by Congress for nearly every unconstitutional act they have perpetrated.

The next subject of importance to which Mr. Randolph's attention was turned, was the impeachment and trial of Judge Chase. On Thursday the 5th of January, 1804, he moved that a committee be appointed to inquire into the official conduct of Samuel Chase, one of the associate justices of the Supreme Court of the United States, and report their opinion whether the said Samuel Chase had so acted in his judicial capacity as to require the interposition of the constitutional power of the House. The committee reported seven articles of impeachment drafted by their chairman, and detailing charges of misconduct on the part of the judge in the trial of John Fries, for high treason, in levying war against the United States during the Whisky Insurrection in Pennsylvania; and also in the trial of Thomas Cooper and James Callender, for sedition or libel against the President.

This trial was a very important one, as Judge Chase had been one of those high-handed federalists, who not only approved the Alien and Sedition Laws, but had transcended all bounds in his eagerness to enforce them.

For want of time the subject was postponed to the next session. On the 30th November, 1804, the articles of impeachment were again reported, and Mr. Randolph was appointed chief manager to conduct the trial before the Senate. The proceedings were very tedious—many witnesses were examined—and many arguments during the progress of the examination were delivered on both sides. Mr. Randolph conducted the cause on the part of the prosecution with the skill of a practised attorney. He opened the case on the part of the House, the 14th February, 1805, in a speech of one hour and a half. Though it is out of the line of his usual forensic efforts, it will well repay a perusal. As two-thirds of the senators present were required to concur in sustaining an impeachment, and as only a majority concurred in sustaining some of the articles, Judge Chase was acquitted.

There was scarcely any subject of importance before Congress at this period that did not attract the personal attention of Mr. Randolph. Not content with the laborious duties of the Finance Committee, furnishing work enough for any ordinary mind, we find him on innumerable select committees, embracing the widest range of investigation on all subjects of legislation. Nothing escaped his vigilant eye—nothing too laborious for him to undertake. These four years, from the opening of Mr. Jefferson's administration to the 4th of March, 1805, the close of the eighth Congress, were indeed his working days. He was abstemious in his habits, unceasing in his labors, unremitting in his attention to public duties.

No man had ever risen so rapidly, or attained a higher degree of eminence and influence; his career was brilliant and successful. The President in the executive department, and he as the leader of the legislative, had done all that was expected of them in the great work of reforming the government, and bringing it back to its original simplicity. Many years afterwards he recurred to this period with just pride. "Sir, (said he in a speech on retrenchment, in 1828,) I have never seen but one administration, which seriously, and in good faith, was disposed to give up its patronage, and was willing to go farther than Congress, or even the people themselves, so far as Congress represents their feelings, desired—and that was the first administration of Thomas Jefferson. He, sir, was the only man I ever knew or heard of, who really, truly, and honestly, not only said "*nolo episcopari*," but actually refused the mitre. It was a part of my duty, and one of the most pleasant parts of public duty that I ever performed, under his recommendation—not because he recommended it, thank God!—to move, in this House, to relieve the public at once from the whole burden of that system of internal taxation, the practical effect of which was, whatever might have been its object, to produce patronage rather than revenue. He, too, had really at heart, and showed it by his conduct, the reduction of the national debt; and that in the only mode by which it can ever be reduced, by lessening the expenses of the Government till they are below its receipts."——"Never was there an administration," says he, "more brilliant than that of Mr. Jefferson, up to this period. We were indeed in the full tide of successful experiment! Taxes repealed; the public debt amply provided for, both principal and interest; sinecures abolished; Louisiana acquired; public confidence unbounded."

None deserved more than himself a large portion of that unbounded public confidence, which attached to the administration—and he was, indeed, looked to from all quarters as the fearless champion of truth and justice. But no man ever drank of the cup of life unmingled with bitter waters. The mean and the envious had grown jealous of his greatness, and were seeking by low and cunning arts to destroy his influence, and to withdraw from him the confidence of the people. It was a trait of his character never to abandon principle for policy; never to relinquish a favorite measure however hopeless of success; never to quit his books and his study for idle conversation; never to permit a vulgar familiarity for the sake of gaining popularity with those who were to vote on his measures.

Hence, they began to speak of him as a person possessing proud and haughty manners; and as a leader, having failed to harmonize the republican members of Congress. "Great God!" exclaims Thompson, "to think that measures of the highest import to our country are opposed, because their advocate does not make a bow in the right way! This is the fact: I have taken the liberty of asking, what your manner has to do with your public character—whether there are laws penal against study, reading, and devotion to the welfare of your country." But the cause of offence lay not in his reserved and retiring deportment—his proud and haughty manners—it was found in that keen sense of injustice and wrong that made him detect baseness and corruption in their most secret hiding-places, and in that manly independent spirit that made him fearless in dragging out the perpetrators into the light of day, and drawing on them the scorn and indignation of the world. Mr. Randolph was one that never could tolerate corruption in public men. There were many of that class—or many that he suspected to be of that class—connected with the administration. He was unsparing in his denunciations of them. This was the cause of the growing discontent, and the desire to throw him off as a leader.

His patriotic endeavors to overturn that colossus of turpitude, the Yazoo speculation, was the cause of the hostility which soon manifested itself against him in the ranks of the administration. Unfortunately, too many were interested in upholding this gigantic robbery. The reader has already been made acquainted with its character; by a reference to chapter thirteen of this volume, he will see something of its history. Randolph was in Georgia at the time of the perpetration of this villany, and participated in the shame and mortification of his friends at seeing persons, reputed religious and respectable, effecting a public robbery, by bribing the legislators of the State, and reducing them to the horrors of treachery and perjury. A more detestable, impudent, and dangerous villany is not to be found on record. Notwithstanding the notoriety of these transactions in the State of Georgia—the law was not only pronounced unconstitutional, fraudulent and void, was not only repealed, but it was burnt by the common hangman, and the record of it expunged from the statute book—notwithstanding these facts, known to all men, a company of individuals in other States purchased up this fraudulent title and presented their petition to Congress, asking remuneration for the land, which in the mean time had been transferred by Georgia to the United States.

In the "Articles of Agreement and Cession" between Georgia and the United States, is a proviso that the United States may dis pose of, or appropriate a portion of the said lands, not exceeding five millions of acres, or the proceeds of the five millions of acres, or any part thereof, for the purpose of satisfying, quieting, or compensating for any claims, other than those recognized in the articles of agreement, which may be made to the said lands. It was under this provision, that the New England and Mississippi Land Company, who in the mean time had purchased the spurious title of the original grantees of a corrupt legislature, petitioned Congress to satisfy their claim by a fair purchase or commutation. In the session of 1802–3, this subject was first brought to the attention of the legislature. Mr. Madison and Mr. Gallatin, members of the President's cabinet, and Mr. Levi Lincoln, were appointed commissioners to investigate this subject. They made an elaborate report, and concluded with a proposition, that so much of the five millions of acres as shall remain after having satisfied the claims of settlers and others, not recognized by the agreement with Georgia, which shall be confirmed by the United States, be appropriated for the purpose of satisfying and quieting the claims of the persons who derive their titles from an Act of the State of Georgia, passed on the 7th day of January, 1795. Thus we see that the leading members of the administration were pledged to the justice of this claim, and the propriety of some compensation on the part of the United States.

Gideon Granger, the Postmaster General, was at the head of the New England and Mississippi Land Company, and was its agent to prosecute the claim before Congress. He wrote an extended and elaborate argument to prove that the Company were innocent purchasers without notice; and indeed he undertook to cast censure on the people of Georgia for repudiating and repealing the act of a bribed legislature, and to charge that State and the United States with injustice in appropriating to themselves lands which had been legally sold by the State and purchased by his Company. Not only, therefore, was the cabinet of the President committed as to the justice of this claim; but one of its most active and influential members was deeply interested personally in its success.

Mr. Randolph opposed it, however, from the beginning: he knew its origin, its history; and no consideration of prudence or policy could induce him for a moment to tolerate the monstrous iniquity.

On the 25th of January, 1805, a resolution was introduced into the House, that three commisssioners be appointed to receive propositions of compromise and settlement from the several companies or persons holding claims to lands within the present limits of the Mississippi Territory, in such manner as in their opinion shall conduce to the interests of the United States, provided such settlement shall not exceed the limit prescribed by the convention with the State of Georgia. This resolution was introduced by a few remarks from Mr. Dana, chairman of the Committee of Claims.

Mr. Randolph then rose:—"Perhaps," said he, "it may be supposed from the course which this business has taken, that the adversaries of the present measure indulge the expectation of being able to come forward at a future day—not to this House, for that hope was desperate, but to the public—with a more matured opposition than it is in their power now to make. But past experience has shown to them that this is one of those subjects which pollution has sanctified, that the hallowed mysteries of corruption are not to be profaned by the eye of public curiosity. No, sir, the orgies of Yazoo speculation are not to be laid open to the public gaze. None but the initiated are permitted to behold the monstrous sacrifice of the best interest of the nation on the altar of corruption. When this abomination is to be practised, we go into conclave. Do we apply to the press, that potent engine, the dread of tyrants and of villains, but the shield of freedom and of worth? No, sir, the press is gagged. On this subject we have a virtual sedition law; not with a specious title, but irresistible in its operations, which goes directly to its object. This demon of speculation has wrested from the nation at one sweep, their best, their only defence, and has closed the avenue of information. But a day of retribution may yet come. If their rights are to be bartered away, and their property squandered, the people must not, they shall not be kept in ignorance by whom it is done. We have often heard of party spirit, of caucuses, as they are termed, to settle legislative questions, but never have I seen that spirit so visible as at present. The out-door intrigue is too palpable to be disguised. When it was proposed to abolish the judiciary system, reared in the last moments of an expiring administration, the detested offspring of a midnight hour; when the question of repeal was before the House; it could not be taken until midnight in the third or fourth week of the discussion. When the great and good man who now fills, and who (whatever may be the wishes of our opponents) I hope and trust will long fill the executive chair, not less to his own honor than to the happiness of his fellow-citizens—when he recommended the repeal of the internal taxes, delay succeeded delay, till patience itself was worn threadbare. But now, when public plunder is the order of the day, how are we treated? Driven into a committee of the whole, and out again in a breath by an inflexible majority, exulting in their strength, a decision must be had immediately. The advocates for the proposed measure feel that it will not bear scrutiny. Hence this precipitancy. They wince from the touch of examination, and are willing to hurry through a painful and disgraceful discussion. As if animated by one spirit, they perform all their evolutions with the most exact discipline, and march in firm phalanx directly up to their object. Is it that men combined together to effect some evil purpose, acting on previous pledge to each other, are even more in unison than those who, seeking only to discover truth, obey the impulse of that conscience which God has placed in their bosom? Such men will not stand compromited. They will not stifle the suggestions of their own minds, and sacrifice their private opinions to the attainment of some nefarious object.

"The memorialists plead ignorance of that fraud by which the act from which their present title was derived, was passed. As it has been a pretext for exciting the compassion of the legislature, I wish to examine the ground upon which this allegation rests. When the act of stupendous villany was passed, in 1795, attempting under the form and semblance of law to rob unborn millions of their birthright and inheritance, and to convey to a band of unprincipled and flagitious men, a territory more extensive, more fertile than any State in the Union, it caused a sensation scarcely less violent than that caused by the passage of the Stamp Act, or the shutting up of the port of Boston: with this difference, that when the Port Bill of Boston passed, her Southern brethren did not take advantage of the forms of law, by which a corrupt legislature attempted to defraud her of the bounties of nature; they did not speculate on the wrongs of their insulted countrymen. * * * * * Sanction this claim, derived from the act of 1795, and what, in effect, do you declare? You record a solemn acknowledgment that Congress has unfairly and dishonestly obtained from Georgia a grant of land to which that State had no title, having previously sold it to others for a valuable consideration, of which transaction Congress was at the time fully apprised. The agents of this Mississippi Land Company set out with an attempt to prove that they are entitled to the whole fifty millions of acres of land, under the act of 1795; and thus they make their plea to be admitted to a proportional share of five. If they really believed what they say, would they be willing to commute a good legal or equitable claim for one-tenth of its value! * * * * We are told that we stand pledged, and that an appropriation for British grants, not granted by Spain especially, was made for the especial benefit of a particular class of claimants, branded too by the deepest odium, who dare talk to us of the public faith, and appeal to the national honor! * * * * The right of the State of Georgia to sell is denied by your own statute book. So far from being able to transfer to others the right to extinguish the Indian title to land, she has not been able to exercise it for her own benefit. It is only through the agency of the United States that she can obtain the extinguishment of the Indian title to the sale of land within her limits; much less could she delegate it to a few Yazoo men. * * * * * The present case presents a monstrous anomaly, to which the ordinary and narrow maxims of municipal jurisprudence cannot be applied. It is from great first principles, to which the patriots of Georgia so gloriously appealed, that we must look for aid in such extremity. Extreme cases, like this, call for extreme remedies. They bid defiance to palliatives, and it is only by the knife, or the actual cautery, that you can expect relief. There is no cure short of extirpation. Attorneys and judges do not decide the fate of empires. * * * * * The Government of the United States, on a former occasion, did not, indeed, act in this firm and decided manner. But those were hard, unconstitutional times, that never ought to be drawn into precedent. The first year I had the honor of a seat in this House, an act was passed somewhat of a similar nature to the one now proposed. I allude to the case of the Connecticut Reserve, by which the nation was swindled out of three or four millions of acres, which, like other bad titles, had fallen into the hands of innocent purchasers. When I advert to the applicants by whom we were then beset, I find among them one of the persons who styled themselves the Agents of the New England Mississippi Land Company, who seems to have an unfortunate knack of buying bad titles. His gigantic grasp embraces with one hand the shores of Lake Erie, and with the other stretches to the Bay of Mobile. Millions of acres are easily digested by such stomachs. Goaded by avarice, they buy only to sell, and sell only to buy. The retail trade of fraud and imposture yields too small and slow a profit to gratify their cupidity. They buy and sell corruption in the gross, and a few millions of acres, more or less, is hardly felt in the account. The deeper the play, the greater their zest in the game; and the stake which is set upon the throw is nothing less than the patrimony of the people. Mr. Speaker, when I see the agency which is employed on this occasion, I must own that it fills me with apprehension and alarm. The same agent is at the head of an executive department of our Government, and inferior to none in the influence attached to it. * * * * This officer presents himself at your bar, at once a party and an advocate. Sir, when I see such a tremendous influence brought to bear upon us, I do confess it strikes me with consternation and despair. Are the heads of executive departments, with the influence and patronage attached to them, to extort from us now, what we refused at the last session of Congress? * * * * * I will pin myself upon this text, and preach upon it as long as I have life. If no other reason could be adduced, but for a regard for our own fame—if it were only to rescue ourselves from this foul imputation—this weak and dishonorable compromise ought to receive a prompt and decisive rejection. Is the voice of patriotism lulled to rest, that we no longer hear the cry against an overbearing majority, determined to put down the Constitution, and deaf to every proposition of compromise? Such were the dire forebodings to which we have been compelled heretofore to listen. But if the enmity of such men be formidable, their friendship is deadly destruction, their touch deadly pollution! What is the spirit against which we now struggle—which we have vainly endeavored to stifle? A monster generated by fraud, nursed in corruption, that in grim silence awaits its prey. It is the spirit of Federalism."

* * * * * * *

It may readily be conceived what effect this and similar speeches which had been delivered, whenever the subject was presented, would have on the members of the republican party who were interested, for themselves or their friends, in the Yazoo speculation. An intrigue was set on foot to supplant Mr. Randolph. It was determined that he should be put down. The Postmaster General openly declared that he or Randolph—one must fall. This expression was understood as intimating an intention to call him out. Some one observed that Randolph would not be backward in answering to a call of that kind. He replied, not in that way—"*I mean, as a public man—as a political character*." After the adjournment of Congress, March, 1805, he made a tour of the New England States, for the purpose of organizing a party to *pull down* Randolph. Some of the republican members from that quarter gave countenance to the plan, and Mr. Barnabas Bidwell was put forward as their file-leader. These men insinuated themselves into favor, and assumed to be the exclusive friends of the President; but they were charged, many of them, with being in league with Burr, and having no other design but to embarrass the Executive, and to force the President into a sanction of their views. "If some members of Congress," says a leading journal of that day, "are to be *bribed with post-office contracts* to obtain their votes for a nefarious speculation, on one hand; and if a member of Congress, superior to all corruption, and all pollution or dishonor, is to be *pulled down;* and the offices of Government are to be employed to such ends; it is vain to pretend that republican government can stand, if such corruption and such corrupt men are suffered to retain all the power, which they prostitute; and if men of virtue, honor, talents and integrity, are to be made victims of intrigue, bottomed on such corruption."

CHAPTER XXVIII.

FRIENDSHIP.

We have seen what an immense task, and what a weight of responsibility, devolved on Mr. Randolph for the last four years. He found time, nevertheless, to keep up an extensive correspondence with his friends. He had now added to the list his two half-brothers and their sister, who were just growing up. His sentiments in regard to the conduct of a family towards those "worthy lads," who just begin to feel the pride and self-importance of budding manhood, are so true and so worthy of imitation, that we give them to the reader.—"Give to dear Beverly," says he, "my warmest love. Let me, my dear sister, caution you (and be not offended at it) respecting that worthy lad. Treat him with a marked attention. I know you love him tenderly—he is deserving of it. Display that affection by a manner the most *considerate* and *kind*. Cherish him; for he is a jewel above price. Beverly is now of an age to receive from every body the treatment due to a *man*—a young one, I grant—and to a *gentleman*. No consideration should dispense with this conduct on any part. It does not imply *formality*, but *respect*—not coldness, but kind attention. These, I pronounce, are *essentially requisite*, and in a *greater degree* than usual, to the development of his amiable character."

But poor Thompson continued, by his erratic ways, to keep alive the anxious solicitude of his friend. That brilliant, though wayward genius, had fallen into desperate courses. Calumny, acting on a morbid sensibility, had banished him from that home where alone he could find sympathy and encouragement. Misfortune had so perverted his feelings, as to make him, in the spirit of misanthropy, shun the observation of those that once knew and respected him, and to seek oblivion and forgetfulness in the haunts of low dissipation. Now was the time to test true friendship. The cold world would pass him by with averted look, and protest they never knew him; the friend would take him by the hand, and gently and affectionately draw him back to the paths of virtue. Randolph professed to be his friend—how nobly did he redeem that pledge! In the following letter, he speaks to him in plainness and in truth. But whilst he does not spare his erring friend, his censure is accompanied with such a tone of delicacy and affection, as to melt the most obdurate heart, and kindle emotions of reformation in the most desperate outcast.

"Whatever may be the motives," says he, "which have determined you to renounce all intercourse with me, it becomes me, perhaps, to respect them; yet to be deterred from my present purpose by punctilio would evince a coldness of temper which I trust does not belong to me, and would, at the same time, convict me to myself of the most pitiful insincerity, in professing for you a regard which has never been inferior to my professions, and which is not in any circumstance entirely to destroy. To tell you that during the last three months I have observed your progress through life with uninterrupted and increasing anxiety, would be to give you a faint idea of what has passed in my mind. The mortification which I have experienced on hearing you spoken of in terms of frigid and scanty approbation, can only be exceeded by that which I have felt on the silent embarrassment which my inquiries have occasioned those who were unwilling to wound your character or my feelings. You know me too well, William, to suppose that my inquiries have been directed by the miserable spirit which seeks to exalt itself on the depression of others. They have, on the contrary, been very few, and made with the most guarded circumspection. To say the truth, I have never felt myself equal to the task of hearing the recital of details which were too often within my reach, and which not unfrequently courted my attention. They have always received from me the most decisive repulse. My own pride would never bear the humiliation of permitting any one to witness the mortification which I felt. After all this preamble, let me endeavor to effect the purpose of this address. Let me beg of you to ask yourself what are your present pursuits, and how far congenial to your feelings or character. I have not, I cannot, so far have mistaken you; you cannot so successfully have deceived yourself. Yours is not the mind which can derive any real or lasting gratification from the pursuits or the attainments of a grovelling ambition. These may afford a temporary and imperfect relief from that voice which tells you who you are, and what is expected from you. The world is well disposed to forgive the aberrations of youthful indiscretion from the straight road of prudence; but there is a point beyond which its temper can no longer be played upon. After a certain degree of resistance, it becomes more prone to asperity than it had ever been to indulgence. But grant that its good nature were unlimited, you are not the character who can be content to hold by so humiliating a tenure that which you can and ought to demand of right. Can you be content to repose on the courtesy of mankind for that respect which you may challenge as your due, and which may be enforced when withheld? Can you quit the high ground and imposing attitude of self-esteem to solicit the precarious bounty of a contemptuous and contemptible world? I can scarcely forgive myself for dwelling so long on so invidious a theme. I have long meditated to address you on this subject. One of the dissuasives from the plan is now removed. Let me again conjure you to ask yourself seriously, What are your present objects of pursuit? How far any laudable acquirement can be attained by a town residence, particularly in a tavern? Whether such a life be compatible with the maintenance of that respectability of character which is necessary to give us value in the eyes of others or of ourselves? And let me conjure you to dissolve by a single exertion the spell which now enchains you. The only tie which could have bound you is no more. Town fetters are but those of habit, and that of but short standing. Were it confirmed, there would indeed be but little hope, and this letter would never have been penned. As it would be improper to urge the dissolution of your present plan of life without pointing out some alternative, I recommend a residence of twelve or eighteen months with Taylor, and a serious application, before it be too late, to that profession which will be a friend to you when the sunshine insects who have laughed with you in your prosperity shall have passed away with the genial season which gave them birth. The hour is fast approaching, be assured, when it will be in vain to attempt the acquirement of professional knowledge. Too well I know that readiness of apprehension and sprightliness of imagination will not make amends for application. The latter serves but to light up our ignorance.

"There is one topic on which I cannot trust even my pen. Did I not believe that this letter would occasion you pain, it certainly never had been written. Yet to write it with that view would be a purpose truly diabolical. You are a physician; you probe not the wounds of the dead. Yet 'tis to heal, and not to agonize, that you insert your instrument into the living body. Whatever may be the effect of this attempt—whatever may be the disposition which it creates in you, I shall never, while you live, cease to feel an interest in your fate. Every one here remembers you with undiminished affection. If I judge from myself, you are more than ever interesting to them, and whenever, if ever, you revisit Bizarre, you will recognize in every member of the family your unchanged friends.

"Adieu,

"J. R., Jr."

This last and noble effort to redeem a fallen friend was not in vain. The advice was followed. Thompson spent a few months with Creed Taylor, in the neighborhood of Bizarre; he then went to Richmond and read law, in the office of George Hay, Esq., a distinguished lawyer and politician of that day. From this time, with few exceptions, his letters are more cheerful, and replete with sallies of his fine genius; he communicates much instructive and amusing information about the proceedings of the legislature, and the leading characters of Richmond; and never failed to give vent to those deep feelings of gratitude that swelled in his bosom, towards one who had been to him a brother indeed, in his hour of degradation and misfortune.

Having obtained a competent knowledge of his profession, Mr. Randolph procured for him an office in the newly acquired territory of Louisiana—encouraged him to break off from his old associations, and to seek his fortune anew, in a land of strangers. In the spring of 1804, he married a virtuous and accomplished wife, and set out on his journey to the far west, with all those bright prospects that his ardent imagination knew so well how to picture before him. This is the last letter ever addressed to him by his friend:

BIZARRE, 13 May, 1804.

"When I requested you to inquire at the post-office at Abington for a letter from me, it did not occur to me by how circuitous a route my communication must travel before it could reach that place. To guard against accidents, therefore, I have directed it to be forwarded to Nashville, in case you should have left Abington before its arrival there. We have been every day suggesting to ourselves the inconvenience to which you must have been exposed by the bad weather which we have invariably experienced ever since your departure, and regretting that the situation of your affairs would not permit you to continue with us until a change took place. You, however, my good friend, have embarked upon too serious a voyage to take into consideration a little rough weather upon the passage. The wish which I feel to add my mite to the counsels through which alone it can prove prosperous, is repressed by the reflection, that your success depends upon the *discovery* of no *new principle* of human affairs, but upon the *application* of such as are familiar to all, and which none know better how to estimate than yourself. Decision, firmness, independence, which equally scorns to yield our own rights as to detract from those of others, are the only guides to the esteem of the world, or of ourselves. A reliance upon our resources for all things, but especially for relief against that arch fiend the tædium vitæ, can alone guard us against a state of dependence and contempt. But I am growing sententious, and, of course, pedantic. Judy joins me in every good wish to yourself and Mrs. Thompson. Permit me to add that there is one being in the world who will ever be ready to receive you with open arms, whatsoever may be the fate of the laudable endeavors which you are now making.

"Yours, truly,

"JOHN RANDOLPH.

"WM. THOMPSON."

Poor Thompson did not live to test the strength of his redeemed virtue, and to make a new application of those principles that he had learned in the school of adversity so well how to estimate. He died by the way-side, and all the renewed hopes of himself and of his friend, were swallowed up in the oblivious night of death. On the back of the copy of the foregoing letter, which is written in Mr. Randolph's own handwriting, is found the following endorsement: "W. T., May 13, 1804. Alas!" What more could he write as an epitaph on the lonely tomb of this wandering, ill-starred young man? Alas! alas! was all that could be said of the misfortunes and the untimely end of poor William Thompson.

Joseph Bryan, in the meantime, had returned from his travels; the joyous, free-hearted Bryan had ceased "fighting the Russians," recrossed the broad Atlantic main, and from his sea-girt isle was inditing letters to his friend, describing the cities he had seen, the men and their manners—if not with the depth of observation of the wise Ulysses, at least with as much pleasure and freedom of narration. He urged his old companion to visit once more his friends in Georgia: "You are the popular man here," says he, "the federalists to the contrary notwithstanding." But Randolph, ever seeking to make his friends useful to themselves and to their country, turned the thoughts of this volatile young man to a higher aim.

On his solicitation, Bryan became a candidate for Congress; was defeated; renewed the attempt, and was successful. He stood by the side of his gallant friend and fought manfully that Medusa head of fraud, the Yazoo speculation, whenever it reared its horrid front upon the floor of Congress. He had been to Bizarre, and formed an acquaintance with the charming society there, of which he ever afterwards spoke in terms of the highest admiration; he had hunted, fished, flown kites, and played marbles with "the boys;" but above all, his wild fancy had been caught at last, and, like the fly in the spider's web, he was entangled in the inextricable meshes of all-conquering love. Miss Delia Foreman, daughter of General Foreman, of the Eastern Shore of Maryland, intimate friends of Mr. Randolph, was the charming object of attraction. The summer recess of 1804 was spent in Georgia, but the island in the sea, with all its means of pleasure, had lost its charm, and he was about to desert it, and to go in search of the fair nymph whose dwelling looked out on the broad waters of the Chesapeake.

On the 8th of September, 1804, from Bizarre his friend writes to him: "Should this find you at Wilmington, which I heartily wish it may not, I trust, my dear Bryan, that you will derive the most satisfactory information from the inclosed respecting your fair tyrant. To *me* the Major says not a word on the subject of his daughter, but I infer from a variety of circumstances that she is about this time on a visit to her aunt, Mrs. Van Bibber, in Gloucester, about eighty miles from Richmond; I hope, therefore, very soon to see you in Virginia.

"I have nothing worth relating, except that Mrs. Randolph was almost as much disappointed as myself when our messenger arrived last night from the post-office without a letter from you. How easy would it be, once a week, to say 'I am at such a place, in such health, and to-morrow shall go to ———.' These little bulletins of your well-being and motions would be a thousand times more interesting to me than those of his Britannic Majesty's health, or his Corsican Highness's expeditions. Let me beg of you to make dispatch.

"Yours as ever,

"JOHN RANDOLPH."

After the adjournment of Congress, March, 1805, Bryan hastened on to Chestertown to be married. On the 8th of March he writes from that place: "You will hardly believe me when I tell you, that my tyrants have had the unparalleled barbarity to postpone my marriage until the 25th of this month. Sumptuousness, pomp, parade, &c., must be observed in giving away a jewel worth more than the kingdoms of this world.—I rather suspect I shall be myself the most awkward and ungraceful movable used on the occasion: curse it, I hate to be exhibited; and nothing but the possession of the jewel itself would induce me to run the gauntlet of felicitation I shall receive from the whole file of collaterals.————Lovely as her person is, I prize her heart more. Jack! what have I done to induce the good God to favor me so highly? Sinner that I am, I deserve not the smallest of his gifts, and behold I am treated more kindly than even Abraham, who saw God face to face, and was called his friend; he, poor fellow, had to put up with his sister Sarah, who, beside other exceptionable qualities, was cursed with a bad temper; while I, having sought among the beauties of the earth, have found and obtained the loveliest and best, which I am willing to prove against all comers on foot or on horseback, in the tented field with sword and spear, or on the roaring ocean at the cannon's mouth. If you will come and see us (on their island in the sea), my Delia will make one of her best puddings for your entertainment. In the course of a year or two you may expect to see your friend *Brain* metamorphosed into a gentleman of high polish, able to make as spruce a bow, and to hand a lady to her carriage with all the graces of an Adonis. Adieu! may heaven prosper and bless you."

In the course of a year or two, alas! he *was* metamorphosed; the beautiful Delia also faded away; and their two little boys were left orphans! John Randolph showed his attachment to the father by his devotion to the sons; they were raised partly in his own house, and educated at his expense. The oldest and the namesake, John Randolph Bryan, many years after this period, when he grew up to manhood, married Miss Elizabeth Coulter, the niece of Mr. Randolph; "my charming niece," as he used to call her, and the daughter of his beloved and only sister. Mr. Bryan and his accomplished wife now live in Gloucester county, Virginia, on the Bay Shore. A bountiful soil blesses them with its abundant fruits; and the tide, that daily flows at their feet, wafts to their door the rich treasures of the sea. May they long live to enjoy in their "happy nook" the blessings of a peaceful home; and to dispense that elegant hospitality, so rare now, but, at the time their father first visited Bizarre, so common in the Old Dominion.

The causes of this great change, or at least some of them, we are now about to investigate. John Randolph has said that "The embargo, like Achilles' wrath, was the source of our Iliad of woes!"

CHAPTER XXIX.

NINTH CONGRESS.—FOREIGN RELATIONS.—DIFFICULTIES WITH FRANCE AND SPAIN.

Never had an administration a more difficult task to perform than that of Mr. Jefferson at this time. Ever since the French revolution there had been a constant warfare, with short breathing intervals, between France and England. The hostility of their political principles, added to old national antipathies, now made it a war of extermination. These great belligerent powers strove to involve the United States in the controversy. But our policy was neutrality: General Washington early announced this course, and his firm hand steadily pursued it so long as he grasped the helm of affairs. Mr. Adams was not so successful—his English predilections swerved him from the straight path of neutrality, and involved his administration in a "quasi war" with France. Mr. Jefferson had hitherto been eminently successful in all his domestic and foreign policy. But now, in 1805, he seemed to be involved in almost inextricable difficulties. Our embarrassments with Spain, France, and England, had grown so complicated and critical, that it seemed impossible to escape without war, or national disgrace. The purchase of Louisiana removed a present peril, but brought with it a train of difficulties. Bonaparte made the sale just before his meditated rupture of the treaty of Amiens, and at a time when he feared the province would be wrested from him by the superior maritime power of England. But he soon repented of his bargain, and sought every opportunity to regain his lost empire beyond the Atlantic. Spain, but three years before, had made an exchange of it with France, and had not surrendered possession. She was much displeased at the transfer made by the First Consul, and between them they embarrassed the United States as much as they could, and threw every obstacle in the way of a full and peaceable possession of the new territory. England still retained much of her old grudge towards the United States as revolted provinces—looked with a jealous eye on their growing commerce, their rising greatness—and sought every opportunity to clip the wing of the aspiring eagle. Entertaining these feelings towards the peaceful and neutral government beyond the Atlantic, these two great powers were involved in a war of life and death between themselves; all Europe was in battalion; every engine of destruction was brought to play; like the Titans of old, they tore up mountains, islands, whole continents, and hurled them at each other; the globe itself seemed as though it might tumble into ruins beneath their giant warfare. What chance had the commerce or the neutral rights of the United States to be respected in such a strife? The President, in his opening message, the 3d of December, 1805, describes in glowing terms the destructive course of the great belligerents towards his own country. Again, on the 6th of December, three days after the opening of Congress, he sent a special message on the subject of Spanish aggressions; they seemed to be first and most urgent. The depredations, he said, which had been committed on the commerce of the United States during a preceding war, by persons under the authority of Spain, had been adjusted by a convention; so also the spoliations committed by Spanish subjects and carried into ports of Spain; it had been likewise agreed that those committed by French subjects and carried into Spanish ports should remain for further discussion. Before this convention was returned to Spain with our ratification, the transfer of Louisiana by France to the United States took place, an event as unexpected as disagreeable to Spain. From that moment she seemed to change her conduct and dispositions towards us; it was first manifested by her protest against the right of France to alienate Louisiana to us, which, however, was soon retracted, and the right confirmed. Her high offence was manifested at the act of Congress establishing a collection district on the Mobile, although by an authentic declaration, immediately made, it was expressly confirmed to our acknowledged limits; and she now refused to ratify the convention signed by her own minister under the eye of his sovereign, unless we would consent to alterations of its terms, which would have affected our claims against her for spoliations by French subjects carried into Spanish ports.

To obtain justice, as well as to restore friendship, the President thought proper to send Mr. Monroe on a special mission to Spain. "After nearly five months of fruitless endeavors," says the message, "to bring them to some definite and satisfactory result, our ministers ended the conferences without having been able to obtain indemnity for spoliations of any description, or any satisfaction as to the boundaries of Louisiana, other than a declaration that we had no right eastward of the Iberville; and that our line to the west was one, which would have left us but a string of land on that bank of the Mississippi. Our injured citizens were thus left without any prospect of retribution from the wrong-doer, and as to boundary, each party was to take its own course. That which they have chosen to pursue will appear from the documents now communicated. They authorize the inference, that it is their intention to advance on our possessions until they *shall be repressed by an opposing force.*"

The message then speaks of the conduct of France in regard to the misunderstanding between the United States and Spain. "She was prompt and decided in her declarations, that her demands on Spain for French spoliations carried into Spanish ports, were included in the settlement between the United States and France. She took at once the ground, that she had acquired no right from Spain, and had meant to deliver us none, eastward of the Iberville."

In conclusion, the President says: "The present crisis in Europe is favorable for pressing a settlement, and not a moment should be lost in availing ourselves of it. Should it pass unimproved, our situation would become much more difficult. Formal war is not necessary; it is not probable it will follow; but the protection of our citizens, *the spirit and honor of our country require, that force should be interposed to a certain degree;* it will probably contribute to advance the object of peace. But the course to be pursued will require the *command of means,* which it belongs to Congress exclusively, to deny or to yield. To them I communicate every fact material for their information, and the documents necessary to enable them to judge for themselves. To their wisdom, then, I look for the course I am to pursue, and will pursue with sincere zeal that which they shall approve."

The President recommends no definite plan of action—leaves, every thing to the discretion of Congress; but it is obvious that he expected them to appropriate means to raise an army of some sort, to repel the invasions of Spain, and to protect the persons and the property of our citizens in the disputed territory.

This message was secret and confidential: all propositions in regard to it were discussed in conclave. The debate is said to have taken a very wide range, and was very animated. On that occasion, John Randolph is said to have delivered the ablest and most eloquent speech ever heard on the floor of Congress. When this message was read in the House of Representatives, it was referred to a select committee, of which Mr. Randolph was chairman. He immediately waited on the President, and informed him of the direction which had been given to the message. We have his authority for saying, that he then learned, not without surprise, *that an appropriation of two millions was wanted to purchase Florida!* He told the President that he would never agree to such a measure, because the money had not been asked for in the message; that he would not consent to shift to his own shoulders, or those of the House, the proper responsibility of the Executive. If the money had been explicitly demanded, he should have been averse to granting it, because, after a total failure of every attempt at negotiation, such a step would disgrace us for ever; because France would never withhold her ill offices, when, by their interposition, she could extort money from us; that it was equally to the interest of the United States, to accommodate the matter by an exchange of territory;—(to this mode of settlement the President seemed much opposed)—that the nations of Europe, like the Barbary powers, would hereafter refuse to look on the credentials of our ministers, without a previous *douceur*.

The committee met on the 7th of December. One of its members (Bidwell of Massachusetts) *construed* the message into a requisition of money for *foreign intercourse*. To draw such a conclusion, it is plain he must have had some other key of interpretation than that of the words in which the message was expressed. He proposed a grant to that effect, which was overruled. On the 14th of December, the chairman was obliged to go to Baltimore, and did not return till the 21st of the month. During this interval, the dispatches from Mr. Monroe, of the 18th and 25th of October, bearing on the subject of Spanish aggressions, were received by Government, but never submitted to the committee. Previous to the chairman's departure for Baltimore, he had occasion to call on the Secretary of State (Madison) to obtain a passport for his nephew, Saint George Randolph, whom he was about sending to Braidwood's and Sicard's schools, near London and Paris. Mr. Madison took this opportunity to enter into an explanation of the policy about to be pursued in regard to Spanish aggression. He concluded his remarks with the declaration, *that France would not permit Spain to adjust her differences with us; that France wanted money, and that we must give it to her, or have a Spanish and French war!*

It will be remembered that this declaration was made to one who was reputed to be the leader of the House of Representatives, and who was chairman of the Committee of Ways and Means. The appropriation here intimated would have to be recommended by that committee, and explained and defended before the House by its chairman. It is not surprising that a man of Mr. Randolph's high sense of honor and of personal dignity; and, above all, that one who had so nice a perception of the rights of the representative, and of the delicate relation existing between him and the Executive, which admitted not of the slightest approach towards influence or dictation, should have fired with indignation at a proposition which seemed to make him and the House of Representatives a mere tool of the Executive, to do that for them which they dare not avow before the world.

When this declaration was made, so different from the sentiments expressed by the President's public and secret messages, and so humiliating to the pride and honor of the country, Mr. Randolph abruptly left the presence of the Secretary with this remarkable exclamation, "Good morning, sir! I see I am not calculated for a politician!"

Mr. Randolph returned from Baltimore, the 21st of December, and convened the committee. As they were assembling, the Secretary of the Treasury (Gallatin) called him aside, and put into his hands a paper headed, "Provision for the purchase of Florida."

Mr. Randolph declared he would not vote a shilling; and expressed himself disgusted with the whole of this proceeding, which he could not but consider as highly disingenuous—the most scrupulous care, he said, had been taken to cover the reputation of the administration, while Congress were expected to act as though they had no character to lose; whilst the official language of the Executive was consistent and dignified, Congress was *privately* required to take upon itself the odium of shrinking from the national honor and national defence, and of delivering the public purse to the first cut-throat that demanded it. From the official communication, from the face of the record, it would appear that the Executive had discharged his duty in recommending manly and vigorous measures, which he had been obliged to abandon, and had been compelled, *by Congress*, to pursue an opposite course; when, in fact, Congress had been acting all the while at Executive instigation. Mr. Randolph further observed, that he did not understand this *double* set of opinions and principles; the one *ostensible*, to go upon the journals and before the *public;* the other, the *efficient* and real motives to action; that he held true wisdom and cunning to be utterly incompatible in the conduct of great affairs; that he had strong objections to the measure itself; but in the shape in which it was presented, his repugnance to it was insuperable. In a subsequent conversation with the President himself, in which those objections were recapitulated, he declared that he too had a character to support and principles to maintain, and avowed his determined opposition to the whole scheme.

On the 3d of January, 1806, Mr. Randolph made a report, under the instructions of the committee, which seems to be fully responsive to the views of the President, as expressed in both his messages. "The committee have beheld," says the report, "with just indignation, the hostile spirit manifested by the court of Madrid towards the government of the United States, in withholding the ratification of its convention with us, although signed by its own minister, under the eye of his sovereign unless with alteration of its terms, affecting claims of the United States which, by the express conditions of the instrument itself, were reserved for future discussion; in piratical depredations upon our fair commerce; in obstructing the navigation of the Mobile; in refusing to come to any fair and amicable adjustment of the boundaries of Louisiana; and in a daring violation, by persons acting under the authority of Spain, and, no doubt, apprised of her sentiments and views, of our undisputed limits, which she had solemnly recognized by treaty.

"To a government having interests distinct from those of its people, and disregarding its welfare, here is ample cause for a declaration of war, on the part of the United States, and such—did they obey the impulse of their feelings alone—is the course which the committee would not hesitate to recommend. But, to a government identified with its citizens, too far removed from the powerful nations of the earth for its safety to be endangered by their hostility, peace must always be desirable, so long as it is compatible with the honor and interest of the community. Whilst the United States continue burdened with a debt which annually absorbs two-thirds of their revenue, and duties upon imports constitute the only resource from which that revenue can be raised, without resorting to systems of taxation not more ruinous and oppressive than they are uncertain and precarious—the best interests of the United States cry aloud for peace. When that debt shall have been discharged, and the resources of the nation thereby liberated, then may we rationally expect to raise, even in time of war, the supplies which our frugal institutions require, without recurring to the hateful and destructive expedient of loans; then, *and not till then*, may we bid defiance to the world. The present moment is peculiarly auspicious for the great and desirable work. Now, *if ever*, the national debt is to be paid, by such financial arrangements as will accelerate its extinguishment, by reaping the rich harvest of neutrality, and thus providing for that diminution of revenue which experience teaches to expect on the general pacification of Europe. And the committee indulge a hope, that in the changed aspect of affairs in that quarter, Spain will find motives for a just fulfilment of her stipulations with us, and an amicable settlement of limits, upon terms not more beneficial to the United States than advantageous to herself; securing to her an ample barrier on the side of Mexico, and to us the countries watered by the Mississippi, and to the eastward of it. But whilst the committee perceive, in the general uproar of Europe, a state of things peculiarly favorable to the peaceable pursuit of our best interests, they are neither insensible to the indignity which has been offered on the part of Spain, nor unwilling to repel similar outrages. On the subject of self-defence, when the territory of the United States is insulted, there can be but one opinion, whatever differences may exist on the question whether that protection, which a vessel finds in our harbors, shall be extended to her by the nation in the Indian or Chinese seas. Under this impression the committee submit the following resolution: That such number of troops (not exceeding ——) as the President of the United States shall deem sufficient to protect the southern frontier of the United States from Spanish inroad and insult, and to chastise the same, be immediately raised."

Mr. Randolph explained, that the peculiar situation of the frontier at that time insulted, had alone induced the committee to recommend the raising of regular troops. It was too remote from the population of the country for the militia to act, in repelling and chastising Spanish incursion. New Orleans and its dependencies were separated by a vast extent of wilderness from the settlements of the United States; filled with disloyal and turbulent people, alien to our institutions, language, and manners, and disaffected toward our government. Little reliance could be placed upon them; and it was plain that if "it was the intention of Spain to advance on our possessions until she should be repulsed by an opposing force," that force must be a regular army, unless we were disposed to abandon all the country south of Tennessee; that if the "protection of our citizens and the spirit and the honor of our country required that force should be interposed," nothing remained but for the legislature to grant the only practicable means, or to shrink from the most sacred of all its duties, to abandon the soil and its inhabitants to the tender mercy of hostile invaders.

Such were the proposition and the views of the committee, in exact correspondence, as they conceived, with the wishes of the President as expressed in his public and secret message.

Yet the report of the committee, moderate as it might seem, was deemed of too strong a character by the House. It was rejected. A proposition, the avowed object of which was, to enable the President to open a negotiation for Florida, was moved as a substitute, by Mr. Bidwell of Massachusetts. Mr. Randolph moved that the sum to be appropriated should be confined to that object; which was agreed to. But afterwards, when the bill was formally brought in, this specific appropriation was rescinded by the House, and the money left at the entire discretion of the Executive, to be used "toward any extraordinary expense which might be incurred in the intercourse between the United States and foreign nations."

Mr. Randolph also moved to limit the amount which the Government might stipulate to pay for the territory in question; upon the ground that if Congress were disposed to acquire Florida by purchase, they should fix the extent to which they were willing to go, and thereby furnish our ministers with a safeguard against the rapacity of France; that there was no probability of our obtaining the country for less, but every reason to believe that without such a precaution on our part, she would extort more. This motion was overruled.

When the bill came under discussion, various objections were urged against it by the same gentleman; among others, that it was in direct opposition to the views of the Executive, as expressed in the President's official communication (it was on this occasion that General Varnum declared the measure to be consonant to the secret wishes of the Executive); that it was a prostration of the national honor at the feet of our adversary; that a concession so humiliating would paralyze our efforts against Great Britain, in case the negotion then pending between that government and ours, should prove abortive; that a partial appropriation towards the purchase of Florida, without limiting the President to some specific amount, would give a previous sanction to any expense which he might incur for that object, and which Congress would stand pledged to make good; that if the Executive, acting entirely upon its own responsibility, and exercising its acknowledged constitutional powers, should negotiate for the purchase of Florida, the House of Representatives would, in that case, be left free to ratify or annul the contract; but that the course which was proposed to be pursued (and which eventually was pursued) would reduce the discretion of the legislature to a mere shadow; that at the ensuing session Congress would find itself, in relation to this subject, a deliberative body but in *name;* that it could not, without a manifest dereliction of its own principles, and, perhaps, without a violation of public faith, refuse to sanction any treaty entered into by the Executive, under the auspices of the legislature, and with powers so unlimited; that, however great his confidence in the Chief Magistrate, he would never consent to give any President so dangerous a proof of it; and that he never would preclude himself, by any previous sanction, from the unbiassed exercise of his judgment on measures which were thereafter to come before him; that the House had no official recommendation for the step which they proposed to take; on the contrary, it was in direct opposition to the sentiments as expressed in the confidential message; and that the responsibility would be exclusively their own; that if he thought proper to ask for an appropriation for the object (the purchase of Florida), the responsibility of the measure would rest on him; but when the legislature undertook to prescribe the course which he should pursue, and which he had pledged himself to pursue, the case was entirely changed; that the House could have no channel through which it could be made acquainted with the opinions of the Executive, but such as was official, responsible, and known to the Constitution; and that it was a prostitution of its high and solemn functions, to act upon an unconstitutional suggestion of the private wishes of the Executive, irresponsibly announced by an irresponsible individual, and in direct hostility to his avowed opinions.

It will be remembered that these proce dings and discussions took place in conclave, on the President's confidential message. Mr. Randolph's course was so grossly misrepresented, and his motives so basely calumniated, that, at a subsequent period of the session, he moved the House to take off the injunction of secrecy from the President's communication, that the world might see what the Executive had really required at the hands of the legislature, and how far they had complied with his publicly expressed wishes, in the report and resolution of the committee.

The secret journal of the House had been published; but, for some reason unaccountable to us, the message, which was the foundation of the whole proceeding, and without which the journal was wholly unintelligible, had been withheld from the public. Mr. Randolph's motion was, to publish the message and the documents—he was willing to abide the decision of an impartial judgment on the perusal. This motion gave rise to much debate and angry recrimination. Mr. Randolph said:

"It is not my wish, Mr. Speaker, to trespass on the patience of the House. But I think it necessary to explain what I am sure the House has not well understood; for my positions have been grossly perverted, whether intentionally or not I will not undertake to say. Gentlemen opposed to us act a very strange and inconsistent part.

They will not give credit to a private individual as to a conversation had with him. I only stated that conversation as a reason for saying I had withdrawn my confidence. And will gentlemen say I am bound, when evidence has come to my private knowledge which is sufficient to damn any man, to legislate on a principle of confidence? When I find misrepresentations made to the public, and insinuations of the most despicable kind on this floor, I come out, and call on any man to deny what I have stated. They cannot—they dare not. For I take it for granted no man will declare in the face of the nation a wilful falsehood. But while gentlemen will not give credit to what has fallen from one individual, they have no hesitation in giving credit to an individual member for the whole course of the Government.

"In my opinion it is of the first importance that the message should be published, from a material fact which took place in this House. A member in his place told you, that the course recommended by a particular individual was consonant with the secret wishes of the Executive. I did then reprehend that language as the most unconstitutional and reprehensible ever uttered on this floor. I did believe that the people of the United States possessed as free a Constitution as the British people, and I had hoped freer; and I knew that such language had in the British Parliament been considered as reprehensible, and had brought forward a vote of indignation in that body. I allude to the case, where the King's name was used for the purpose of throwing out Mr. Fox's India bill. I then reprobated this back-stair influence, this double dealing, the sending one message for the journals and newspapers, and another in whispers to this House. I shall always reprobate such language, and consider it unworthy of any man holding a seat in this House. I had before always flattered myself, that it would be a thousand years hence before our institutions would have given birth to these Charles Jenkinson's in politics. I did not expect them at this time of day, and I now declare it important, in my opinion, that the message should be published, that the public may be enabled to compare the official with the unofficial message which decided the vote.

"There is another reason for its publication. The gentleman from Pennsylvania has said there is no mention of France on the journals; and that we have no cause of complaint against France

I wish the publication of the message to prove what causes of complaint we have against France. Let men of sense take a view of all the papers, and I am willing to abide the issue. It is said France has done us no injury—that the bubble is burst. We are told that this is a plain answer to all the speeches made on this floor. Permit me to say, the gentleman (Mr. Epps) has given a plain answer to all the speeches delivered on this floor; it was impossible to have given a plainer answer to them. He says, I will vote with you, but I will make a speech against you. Permit me to say, this is the first time I would not rather have had his vote than his speech. After this speech there can be no doubt as to the issue of the question. I will go further, after the adjournment on Saturday there could be no doubt. Saturday, it seems, is an unfortunate day, on which no expedition is to be undertaken, no forlorn hope conducted.

"The same gentleman has said that we pursued precisely the same course in 1803 as in 1806, and for obtaining the same object. He says the same course is now pursued, and yet he says he will not undertake to say the cases are not dissimilar; put this and that together, and what do you make of it? The cases are decidedly dissimilar. In 1803 there was no existing misunderstanding between the American and French governments with regard to our differences with Spain. Those differences have started up like a mushroom in the night. We made an appropriation to purchase the Floridas—to buy them—from whom? From their rightful owner. The circumstances would have been similar, if the United States had given money to France to compel Spain to form a treaty with us; then the national honor would have received a deadly wound. But there was nothing of this sort in the formation of the treaty then made. Spain, under the operation of causes in which we had no agency, transferred Louisiana to France, and France transferred it to us. But this is not now the case. We are told that Spain is no longer an independent power, but is under the control of France. What follows? That France is an aggressor on us, which proves every thing I have alleged.

"There is another thing to be observed. The public have been given to understand, that two millions have been appropriated for the purchase of the Floridas. This is not so. The appropriation is only towards doing something; but what that is, is not defined by law.

Now if in 1803 we appropriated two millions for the purchase of the Floridas, and did not get them, what security is there now that by making an appropriation in the same language, we shall obtain them? Although the persons making the appropriation are not the same identical beings, those applying the sum appropriated are. I do not believe that we shall get the Floridas. In this I may be mistaken: I hope I shall be; for after having descended to prostitute the national character, let us at least receive the wages of iniquity.

"But gentlemen inquire, will you become the guardians of Spain? This is a mistake which has run through every attempt at argument I have heard. We never professed to be the guardians of Spain. We profess to be the guardians of our own honor. We care not for France trampling on Spain. Let her pick her pockets, for what we care; but if we instigate her to it, it is no longer a mere question between France and Spain, but a question in which our own honor is engaged, which is at once mortgaged and gone.

"Until the gentleman from Virginia got up, I confess that, what with my exhausted state, the badness of the air, and the tenuity of the arguments of gentlemen, so excessively light that they at once vanished into thin air, that I had not a word to say; for it is not to be supposed that I intended to reply to any thing offered by the gentleman behind me. If I am to fall, let me fall in the face of day, and not be betrayed by a kiss,—I mean no profane allusion. I shall do my duty as an honest man. I came here prepared to co-operate with the government in all its measures. I told them so. But I soon found there was no choice left, and that to co-operate in them would be to destroy the national character. I found I might co-operate, or be an honest man; I have therefore opposed, and will oppose them. Is there an honest man disposed to be the go-between, to carry down secret messages to this House? No. It is because men of character cannot be found to do this business, that agents must be got to carry things into effect, which men of uncompromited character will not soil their fingers, or sully their characters with.

"One word on the subject of voting on unofficial notice, on the representations of individuals, in the place of communications officially received from the officers of the executive department. I have always considered the Executive, in this country, as atanding in the same relation to the two Houses, that the minister or administration bore to the legislature under governments similar to our own. I have always considered that the responsibility for public measures, rested more particularly on them. For those measures they are answerable to the people—and to me it has been a subject of peculiar regret (I do not speak of the general character of the Constitution) that they have not a seat on this floor. For whatever may be supposed to be my feelings, as to the members of the administration, I am ashamed when I see their fame and character committed to such hands as we are in the daily habit of witnessing. If their measures are susceptible of justification, I should like to have a justification at their own hands, instead of hearing Yazoo men defend them. Much less did I expect, on such an occasion, to hear a Yazoo man, assigning his motives for a vote, on a totally different subject, and this in justification of a man with whom he is connected by ties of consanguinity. This reminds me of the intention imputed to me, to bring forward an impeachment against a great officer of state. This, however, is so far from being the truth, that I appeal to those who heard me, whether I did not declare that I washed my hands of impeachments—that I was done with them. No, I will neither directly, nor indirectly, have any thing to do with them. But I will in all questions that shall come before this House, discuss the public character and conduct of any public agents from a secretary to a constable: and I will continue to do it, until it shall be admitted by the Constitution that the king can do no wrong. I say I wish the heads of departments had seats on this floor. Were this the case, to one of them I would immediately propound this question: Did you, or did you not, in your capacity of a public functionary, tell me, in my capacity of a public functionary, that France would not suffer Spain to settle her differences with us, that she wanted money, that we must give her money, or take a Spanish or French war? And did not I answer, that I was neither for a war with Spain or France, but in favor of defending my country? I would put that question to him. I would put this question to another head of department: Was, or was not, an application made to you for money, to be conveyed to Europe to carry on any species of diplomatic negotiation there? I would listen to his answer, and if he put his hand on his heart, and like a man of honor said no, I would believe him, though it would require a great stretch of credulity. I would call into my aid faith, not reason, and believe when I was not convinced. I would then turn to the first magistrate of the nation and say: Did you not buy Louisiana of France? Has France acted in that transaction in a bona fide manner? Has she delivered into your possession the country you believed you had bought from her? Has she not equivocated, prevaricated, and played off Spain against you, with a view of extorting money? I will answer for the reply. There cannot be the smallest doubt about it. I will put the whole business on this issue. All the difficulty has arisen from that quarter.

"Yes, the bubble has burst! It is immaterial to us, whether you publish the President's message or not. But it is material to others that you should; and let me add, the public will not rest satisfied with the conduct of those, who profess to wish it published, while they vote against the publication. The public will not confide in such professions. Gentlemen may show their bunch of rods, may treat them as children, and offer them sugar-plums; but all will not avail them, so long as they refuse to call for the dispatches of our ministers, and other documents, which if published would fix a stain upon some men in the government, and high in office, which all the waters in the ocean would not wash out. Gentlemen may talk about our changing and chopping about, and all that. What is the fact? We are what we profess to be—not courtiers, but republicans, acting on the broad principles we have heretofore professed—applying the same scale with which we measured John Adams to the present administration. Do gentlemen flinch from this and pretend to be republicans? They cannot be republicans, unless they agree that it shall be measured to them as they measured to others. But we are perhaps to be told, that we all have become federalists—or that the federalists have become good republicans. This, however, is a charge which, I am convinced, the federalists will not be more anxious to repel than we to be exonerated from. No, they will never become good republicans. They never did, they never will act with us. What has happened? they are in opposition from system, and we quo ad hoc, as to this particular measure. Like men who have roughed it together, there is a kind of fellow-feeling between us. There is no doubt of it. But as to political principle, we are as much as ever opposed. There is a most excellent alkali by which to test our principles. The Yazoo business is the beginning and the end, the alpha and omega of our alphabet. With that our differences began, and with that they will end; and I pray to God that the liberties of the people may not also end with them.

"When the veracity of a man is called in question it is a serious business. The gentleman from Massachusetts has appealed to the House for the correctness of his statement. I, too, appeal to the House whether this was not his expression, when he undertook to explain away what he had said, for he did not deny it: "That he would vouch that such were the secret wishes of the President;" and whether I did not observe that his attempt to explain was like Judge Chase attempting to draw back a prejudicated opinion in the case of Fries; that he might take back the words, but not the effect they had made on the Assembly; that the Constitution knows only of two ways by which the Executive could influence the Legislature: the one by a recommendation of such measures as he deemed expedient; the other, by a negative on our bills; and that the moment it was attempted to influence the House by whispers and private messages its independence was gone. I stated the proneness of legislative bodies to be governed by Executive influence, and, in illustration, referred to the Senate, who, from its association with the Executive and the length of time for which its members hold their seats, was necessarily made up of gaping expectants of office, and there can be no doubt of the fact. It must be so from the nature of things. Now, if it be necessary, let the House appoint a Committee of Inquiry to ascertain what the gentleman from Massachusetts did say, and let us see who can adduce the most witnesses and swear the hardest. No, the gentleman from Massachusetts had on that occasion so different a countenance, dress and address, that I could not now recognize him for the same man. He seemed thunderstruck and to be in a state of stupefaction at his indiscretion. He appeared humbled in the presence of those who heard what he had said, and beheld his countenance. His words were these, my life on it: 'I will vouch that such are the secret wishes of the President, or the Executive,' I do not know which."

CHAPTER XXX.

DIFFICULTIES WITH GREAT BRITAIN.

THE aggressions of Great Britain on the persons, the property, and the rights of American citizens began at an early period, and were still continued with increased aggravation. It was high time for some firm stand to be taken in regard to them. The peace, prosperity, and honor of the country demanded an effectual system of measures to arrest them. Officers of the British navy had long been in the habit of boarding American vessels, dragging seamen thence, and forcing them into their own service under the pretext that they were British subjects. The law of England did not recognize the right of expatriation. The sovereign claimed the services of all his subjects in time of war, and impressed them wherever they could be found. The similarity of language, of person, and of habits, made it difficult to distinguish an American from an English sailor. Many of the latter had taken refuge from their own hard naval service in the profitable commercial marine of the United States. In re-capturing their own subjects, they not unfrequently dragged American citizens from their homes. They were charged with not being very scrupulous in this regard. Not less than three thousand American sailors, it was said, had been forced to serve in the British navy. The government of the United States denied the right of Great Britain to impress seamen on board any of their vessels on the high seas, or within their own jurisdiction. They contended that a neutral flag on the high seas was a safeguard to those sailing under it. They were sustained in this doctrine by the law of nations.

Although Great Britain had not adopted in the same latitude with most other nations the immunities of a neutral flag, yet she did not deny the general freedom of the high seas, and of neutral vessels navigating them, with such exceptions only as are annexed to it by the law of nations. The exceptions are objects commonly denominated contraband of war; that is, enemies serving in the war, articles going into a blockaded port, and enemy's property of every kind. But nowhere, it was contended, could an exception to the freedom of the seas and of neutral flags be found that justified the taking away of *any person, not an enemy in military service, found on board a neutral vessel.*

The right of impressment, growing out of their different interpretation of the law of nations, was one, and the gravest, of the subjects of dispute between the two nations. The other was in regard to the carrying trade. The question commonly presented itself in this form: Was that commerce allowable in time of war which was prohibited in time of peace? Great Britain, by her powerful marine, had swept the ocean nearly of the whole of the vessels of her enemies. In consequence of this, the produce of the colonies of France, Spain, and Holland, was imported into the mother countries by neu tral ships; in fact, it was almost wholly transported in American bottoms. The restrictive colonial system of these powers did not suffer this transportation by foreigners in times of peace; but the necessities arising from a calamitous naval war induced them to lay their ports open by a forced liberality to this general commerce. French, Spanish, and Dutch property in American bottoms now became neutralized, and was protected, as some contended, by the American flag. But the property was still enemy's property, and fell within the exception of the law of nations. The French navy had been totally annihilated; in consequence, the products of her colonies had to lie rotting on their wharfs, for want of transportation, while the mother country was suffering both from the want of the products and of the revenue arising from the sale and consumption of them. These were the evils intended to be inflicted by a naval victory, in order to force her to an honorable peace. But the United States came in with their ships, and relieved France of these evils, by becoming carriers between her and her colonies.

Can that be a *neutral* commerce which robs one of the belligerent parties of all the advantages of a victory, and relieves the other from nearly all the evils of a defeat? It can hardly seem possible at this day that any one could have contended for such a doctrine; yet Mr. Madison maintained that the contrary principle, denying the neutral character of such a commerce, *was of modern date*—that it was avowed by no other nation than Great Britain, and that it was assumed by her, under the auspices of a maritime ascendency, which rendered such a principle subservient to her particular interests.

This doctrine, however, contended for by a nation that had the power to maintain it, was gotten over by subterfuge and evasion. We will illustrate the manner by an example. A French subject purchases a cargo of coffee at Guadaloupe, intending it for the market of Nantes: to ship it in a vessel belonging to any one of the nations belligerent with England, was absolutely throwing it away; but the ordinary device of sending it under the cover of an American flag is resorted to; the American refuses to carry it directly for the harbor of Nantes, alleging, that if he is captured by an English cruiser, a condemnation must follow such an attempt at an immediate commerce between the mother country and her colony. False owners are created for the ship's cargo, in the character of Americans. The vessel instead of sailing for Nantes, makes for New York, and in due time arrives there; bonds for the payment of duties are given, and the cargo is landed. The vessel loads again with the same coffee; the debentures of the custom-house are produced; the bonds for duties are cancelled, and she now makes her way boldly for Nantes, as a neutral ship, not to be molested. The entire trade of the French, Spanish and Dutch colonies was conducted in American vessels, in this indirect way. A most profitable business it was surely, but it is shocking to contemplate the influence on the moral character of those engaged in it. All this chicanery and duplicity were often forced through by absolute perjury—*always* by a prostration of honorable delicacy.

The British Courts of Admiralty allowed this indirect trade through a neutral port, where there was proof of an actual change of ownership. Whenever the neutral party could show that he had *purchased* the property, he was suffered to pass unmolested; but such a *bona fide* purchase rarely took place; and enemy's property was covered up and protected by neutral names, under false pretences. *Such was the carrying trade.*

These two—the impressment of seamen and the carrying trade—constituted the main difficulties existing between the United States and Great Britain; all others grew out of them, and would necessarily cease on a satisfactory adjustment of those leading subjects of complaint.

These questions were involved in much obscurity. Much might be said on both sides. Each nation had just cause of complaint against the other. Here was a fair field for negotiation and compromise. But we can now perceive the secret motives that would incessantly throw obstacles in the way of a satisfactory arrangement of these difficulties. There was the old grudge against England, cherished in the prejudices of the people; the jealousy of her superior naval power on that element where we were as much at home as she was; the spirit of rivalry that stimulated our merchants to share with her the commerce of the world; the barren results of any settlement of difficulties with her during the wars in Europe—it might secure peace, but could bring no profit. On the other hand, there were the old partialities for our ancient ally; the fraternizing spirit between the two Republics; the enthusiasm enkindled in a martial people, by the daring exploits and brilliant successes of Napoleon; the secret consciousness that his irresistible power would always be interposed between them and any hostile movements of England; the lucrative commerce, and the absolute monopoly of the carrying trade between France, Spain, Holland, and their dependencies, and which must cease on a compromise with England;—add to these causes, that went home to the prejudices and the interests of the people, the all-controlling influence of party spirit—which had long since attached to the friends of England the epithet of monarchists and tories, and to the friends of France that of republicans and friends of the people—and we cannot fail to perceive that every agency which was calculated to give direction to public opinion would bend it against any adjustment of British difficulties during the continuance of the wars in Europe.

The subjects of difference were ably discussed by the Secretary of State in his instructions to our minister at the Court of St. James; but when the President thought proper to bring the matter before Congress, and to call on them for action, he had no plan to propose. He did not recommend, as the Constitution required, any specific mode of adjustment. He left the Legislature to grope their way in the dark, and to adopt such measures as they might think proper, without any previous participation on his part in the responsibility.

Various crude and illy-digested schemes were offered in the House and in the Senate. They all seemed to contemplate coercing England into measures by operating on her commerce. Gregg's resolution—the one principally discussed in the House—went so far as to prohibit all intercourse between the two nations, until England would consent to settle the subjects of dispute between them on fair terms. This professed to be a peace measure, but it was actual war in disguise. Many of its friends discussed it as a war measure. Mr. Randolph so regarded it. "I am not surprised," said he, "to hear this resolution discussed by its friends as a war measure. They say, it is true, that it is not a war measure; but they defend it on principles that would justify none but war measures, and seemed pleased with the idea that it may prove the forerunner of war. If war is necessary, if we have reached this point, let us have war. But while I have life, I will never consent to these incipient war measures, which in their commencement breathe nothing but peace, though they plunge us at last into war. * * * * * What is the question in dispute? The carrying trade. What part of it? The fair, the honest, and the useful trade, that is engaged in carrying our own productions to foreign markets and bringing back their productions in exchange? No, sir; it is that carrying trade which covers enemy's property, and carries the coffee, the sugar, and other West India products to the mother country. No, sir; if this great agricultural nation is to be governed by Salem and Boston, New York and Philadelphia, and Baltimore, and Norfolk, and Charleston, let gentlemen come out and say so; and let a committee of public safety be appointed from these towns to carry on the government. I, for one, will not mortgage my property and my liberty to carry on this trade. The nation said so seven years ago; I said so then, I say so now; it is not for the honest carrying trade of America, but for this mushroom, this fungus of war, for a trade, which as soon as the nations of Europe are at peace will no longer exist—it is for this that the spirit of avaricious traffic would plunge us into war. I am forcibly struck on this occasion by the recollection of a remark, made by one of the ablest, if not the honestest, ministers England ever produced; I mean Sir Robert Walpole; who said that the country gentlemen (poor, meek souls!) came up every year to be sheared, that they laid mute and patient whilst their fleeces were taking off, but if he touched a single bristle of the commercial interest the whole stye was in an uproar. It was, indeed, shearing the hog—great cry and little wool.

"What is the fact? Whilst we boast of our honor on this floor, our name has become a by-word among the nations. Europe, and

Paris especially, swarms with pseudo-Americans, with Anglo and Gallo Americans, and American French and English, who have amassed immense fortunes by trading in the neutral character—by setting it up to auction, and selling it to the best bidder. Men of this description—striplings, without connections or character—have been known to buy rich vessels and their cargoes, in Amsterdam and Antwerp, and trade with them under the American name to the Indies. Neutral character has constituted one of the best remittances for colonial produce, or the goods which purchase it; and the trade in this commodity of neutrality has produced a most lucrative branch of traffic. This it is that has sunk and degraded the American name abroad, and subjected the fair trader to vexatious seizure and detention.

"But yet, sir, I have a more cogent reason against going to war, for the honor of the flag in the narrow seas, or any other maritime punctilio. It springs from my attachment to the principles of the Government under which I live. I declare, in the face of day, that this Government was not instituted for the purposes of offensive war. No; it was framed (to use its own language) for the common defence and general welfare, which are inconsistent with offensive war. I call that offensive war, which goes out of our jurisdiction and limits, for the attainment or protection of objects not within those limits and that jurisdiction. As in 1798, I was opposed to this species of warfare, because I believed it would raze the Constitution to its very foundation—so in 1806, am I opposed to it, and on the same grounds. No sooner do you put the Constitution to this use—to a test which it is by no means calculated to endure, than its incompetency to such purposes becomes manifest and apparent to all. I fear, if you go into a foreign war, for a circuitous, unfair foreign trade, you will come out without your Constitution. Have you not contractors enough in this House? or do you want to be overrun and devoured by commissaries, and all the vermin of contract? I fear, sir, that what are called the energy men, will rise up again—men who will burn the parchment. We shall be told that our Government is too free, or, as they would say, weak and inefficient—much virtue, sir, in terms; that we must give the President power to call forth the resources of the nation—that is, to filch the last shilling from our pockets, or to drain the last drop of blood from our veins. I am against giving this power to any man, be he who he may. The American people must either withhold this power, or resign their liberties. There is no other alternative. Nothing but the most imperious necessity will justify such a grant; and is there a powerful enemy at our door? You may begin with a First Consul. From that chrysalis state he soon becomes an emperor. You have your choice. It depends upon your election whether you will be a free, happy, and united people at home, or the light of your executive majesty shall beam across the Atlantic, in one general blaze of the public liberty.

"But, sir, it seems that we, who are opposed to this resolution, are men of no nerve—who trembled in the days of the British treaty—cowards, I suppose, in the reign of terror. Is this true? Hunt up the journals—let our actions tell. We pursue our old, unshaken course. We care not for the nations of Europe, but make foreign relations bend to our political principles, and serve our country's interests. We have no wish to see another Actium, or Pharsalia, or the lieutenants of a modern Alexander playing at piquet, or all-fours, for the empire of the world. 'Tis poor comfort to us to be told that France has too decided a taste for luxurious things to meddle with us; that Egypt is her object, or the coast of Barbary, and, at the worst, we shall be the last devoured. We are enamored with neither nation. We would play their own game upon them—use them for our interest and convenience. But, with all my abhorrence of the British Government, I should not hesitate between Westminster Hall and a Middlesex jury, on the one hand, and the wood of Vincennes and a file of grenadiers, on the other. That jury trial which walked with Horne Tooke, and Hardy through the flames of ministerial persecution, is, I confess, more to my taste than the trial of the Duke d'Enghein."

But we must forbear any further quotations from Mr. Randolph's speeches against Gregg's resolutions. There were two of them, delivered on the 5th and 6th of March. They were not merely eloquent and forcible in their expression, but display a comprehensive knowledge of our foreign relations, and a deep insight into the motives of men who foment discord between nations that should be at peace with each other. They are patriotic in their tone, and show a warm devotion to the Constitution and the Union, and a profound comprehension of those principles which alone can preserve them in their integrity. While we forbear further quotation, we feel constrained to give the substance of Mr. Randolph's views on the questions therein discussed.

This was an important crisis, not only in his own history, but in that of the country. This was the beginning of a series of measures that separated Mr. Randolph from his old political associations, and that finally involved the country in a disastrous war. The party heats and animosities that rankled in the bosoms of men at that day have all died away. Let impartial history speak the truth, and do justice to one whose name has long been calumniated. We shall give facts as they are condensed from his own speeches, and leave the world to judge how far he acted as a zealous patriot, an honest man, and an enlightened statesman.

It was notorious, says Mr. Randolph, that in regard to the course to be pursued towards Great Britain, no opinion was expressed by the members of the Cabinet, in their collective or individual capacities. On the contrary, the President frequently declared, without reserve, that he had no opinion on the subject. Similar declarations were made by other influential and leading persons presiding over the executive departments—and it is a fact, that no consultation was held between them, from the meeting of Congress, on the 3d of December, till some time in the month of March. This want of concert and decision in the administration, might easily have been inferred (even if there were no other proof of it) from the various, discordant, and undigested projects which were brought forward in the legislature, and to this want of system must be referred much of the mischief which then resulted from this subject, as well as the embarrassment which afterwards ensued.

Mr. Randolph was of opinion that the impressment of our seamen furnished just cause for indignant resentment on our part; but he saw no reason for pushing that matter to extremity at that time, which had not existed in as full force, for the last five years, or even twelve years. Our government, in consideration of the great number of British seamen in our employment, and of the identity of language and manners between that class of their subjects, and the same description of our citizens, but above all, from motives of sound policy (too obvious to need recapitulation), had hitherto deemed it expedient to temporize on this interesting and delicate topic—he could see no just ground, at present, for departing from this system—more especially pending an actual negotiation between the two governments, on the point in dispute. He was of opinion that nothing should be left undone to accommodate our differences amicably, and that no step should be taken which might interrupt or defeat such a settlement—that even if we should resort to war, it must eventuate in a treaty of peace, by which the points in controversy would be adjusted, or left *in statu quo ante bellum*—and that after incurring the incalculable mischiefs of war, the derangement of our finances and the augmentation of the public debt, to an extent which could not now be foreseen; to say nothing of its baneful effects upon our political institutions, and of the danger which must accrue from throwing our weight, at this juncture, into the preponderating scale of Europe; there was no prospect that we should obtain better terms at any future pacification, than were attainable at present—at any rate, he was disposed to give fair play to a fair experiment at negotiation. But if any active measures were to be taken against Great Britain, they should be of the most efficient and decisive nature. He deprecated half measures, as the most injurious to ourselves which could be adopted.

Whilst the Bill was yet under discussion, the news of the death of Mr. Pitt, and of the consequent change of ministry, reached the United States. No circumstance could have afforded a fairer or more honorable pretext, or a more powerful motive, for suspending our measures against Great Britain, than this. The late Premier was known to be decidedly hostile to the institutions, the interests, and the very people, of America.

No administration, not even that of Lord North himself, had been or could be more inimical to the United States, than that of Mr. Pitt. His power, moreover, was connected with, and depended upon, the continuation and duration of the war. He was succeeded by Mr. Fox, unquestionably the most liberal and enlightened statesman of Europe; the man above all others, beyond the Atlantic, the best affected towards the principles of our government, and the illustrious character by whom it was administered.

Never did a fairer occasion present itself to any nation for changing, without any imputation of versatility, or any loss of honor, the course which they had chosen to prescribe to themselves. The excitement of public sentiment, and the measures consequent upon that excitement, might, fairly and honorably, have been referred to the known character of the late Premier, the pupil of Dundas, and the disciple of Charles Jenkinson; and the United States might have awaited, in a dignified and imposing inactivity, the manifestation of a different sentiment by the new ministry. But the new leaders of the House of Representatives were men who soared above, or skimmed below, all considerations of time, place, and circumstance—they gloried in their ignorance of men and things in Europe, and boasted that their policy should not be modified by any change in the aspect of affairs at home, or abroad—and in the pursuit of an abstract metaphysical *ignis fatuus*, they did not hesitate to embark the best interests of the Union.

Against these measures, Mr. Randolph further objected, that during the "*five months which our ministers had spent in fruitless discussion at Madrid*," it had entered into the head of nobody to suggest any proposition of a coercive nature in relation to Spain, and that, even after the total failure of that negotiation, no such measure had been proposed—that Great Britain had indeed impressed our seamen, and advanced certain injurious principles of national law, which, if carried into their full extent, would materially affect our commerce; but that Spain, after having refused to make good her solemn stipulations to compensate us for former spoliations committed on our commerce, had "*renewed the same practices during the present war*." She had not, it was true, impressed our seamen, but her cruisers had "*plundered and sunk our vessels, and maltreated and abandoned their crews in open boats, or on desert shores, without food or covering*." Her Courts of Admiralty had, indeed, advanced no "new principles of the law of nations," but they had confiscated our ships and cargoes, without the pretext of principles of any sort, new or old. She had, moreover, insulted our territory, violated the property and the persons of our citizens, within our acknowledged limits, and insolently rejected every overture to accommodation. With Spain, all our attempts to negotiate had failed—with Great Britain, we had a negotiation actually pending, and which the despatches of our minister at the Court of London gave us every reason to suppose would have a prosperous issue—and even admitting, for the sake of argument, that our vote of money to purchase Florida was, in itself, no derogation from the national honor, inasmuch as we proposed to receive a fair equivalent for it, yet, having refused to take any coercive measures for the unparalleled indignities of Spain, who had peremptorily rejected all our propositions for pacific accommodation, how could we, with any face of impartiality towards the belligerent powers, assume this elevated tone towards Great Britain? Mr. Randolph further declared, that the proposed measure was, in itself, inefficient to every valuable purpose—that its sole operation would be to pique the pride and rouse the resentment of our adversary, and whilst it indicated a strong spirit of hostility on our part, would afford her a fair opening to strike the first effectual blow—that it was indeed showing our teeth, without, at the same time, daring to bite—that Great Britain would have, until the next session of Congress, ample time to devise means for annoying us in the most effective manner, and that, meanwhile, she might withdraw her property from our grasp, and guard every valuable point from our attack. He conjured the House not to suffer themselves, from the honest prejudices of the revolution, from their ancient partiality to France, and their well-grounded antipathy to England, to be legislated into a war, which would involve the best interests of their country.

Another strong objection to the non-importation bill arose from its bearing the aspect (especially when taken in conjunction with our recent conduct towards Spain and France) of a disposition on our part to aid the views of the French governement in cramping the navigation and destroying the manufactures of Great Britain. This constituted one principal source of animosity between those rival nations, and the American government could perhaps take no step which would so strongly excite the resentment of the British ministry. The prompt and decisive conduct of that government towards Prussia, so soon as she manifested a disposition to come into the views of France on this subject, forms the best commentary upon this opinion, and the sudden change in the tone of Mr. Fox towards the United States is no bad criterion of its truth.

When Mr. Randolph declared, that if any coercive measures were to be pursued towards Great Britain they should be of the most energetic stamp, and mentioned an embargo as that which he deemed the most efficient in the outset, he was asked by some "why he did not move such a proposition?" and they declared at the same time, that if he would bring forward the measure, they would support it. To this he answered: That he wished to try the fair experiment of negotiation in the first instance—that he deemed it impolitic, pending that negotiation, to take any step that might defeat it—and that it was astonishing to him, that gentlemen who had remained entirely passive under the aggressions of Spain, who had refused even to concur in measures of self-defence against her inroads—made too after a peremptory rejection of every overture to accommodation, should advocate an opposite course towards another power, with whom we were at that moment actually treating.

Mr. Randolph's powerful opposition was so far successful as to defeat Gregg's resolution, which contemplated a total suspension of commercial intercourse between the two countries. Another was introduced, prohibiting only certain enumerated articles of British manufacture, and passed by a large majority. *Eighty-seven* republicans voted for these restrictive measures, while only *eleven* republicans and the whole body of federalists, being but *four and twenty* in all voted against them.

The Act passed by Congress, it was said by the friends of it, was the first leading step in a system of measures well calculated to awaken England from her delusive dreams; and that it was expressly adopted as a measure equally fitted for producing a change in her conduct, or for standing as a part of our permanent commercial regulations. Here the reader will observe was the beginning of those measures, which if not designedly, indirectly fostered the manufactures of the country (by prohibiting importation) at the expense of its agriculture and commerce.

How far this non-importation scheme of the Legislature was likely to influence the minds of the British Cabinet, may be seen from the following extract taken from an essay styled "Observations on Randolph's Speech," and written by the most eminent British writer of the day, in immediate connection too with the ministry, and well possessed of their views—no less a personage than the author of "War in Disguise," a book that took all Mr. Madison's learning and ability to give a plausible answer to. The author is expressly recommending to the British minister, to send an envoy to the American Government to treat for an adjustment of differences. He concludes thus: "The only objection I can possibly imagine to arise against this expedient is, from the passing of the limited non-importation bill, the fate of which is yet unknown, and which is represented as containing a clause, making its operation depend either on the fiat of the executive government, or on that of its minister in this country; or, as other accounts intimate, on the bare event of our refusing immediate compliance with the demands of the American government.

"Now such a bill either has, or has not been passed by the Congress. In the latter case, the difficulty will not arise; but in the former, I hesitate not to say, that it makes your compliance, consistently with any regard to the dignity and honor of this great nation, absolutely impossible.

"What! Is a rod to be put into the hands of a foreign minister, to whip us into submission; and are we broadly and coarsely to sell our maritime rights, for the sake of passing off a little haberdashery along with them!

"Are we to make a lumping pennyworth to the buyers of our leather wares, our felt and tin wares, and the other commodities enumerated in this insolent bill, by tossing our honor, our justice, and our courage also into the parcel!! I would not consent to disparage even the quality of our manufactures, much less of our public morals, by so shameful a bargain.

"No, sir! if Mr. Monroe is indeed instructed and empowered to treat with us in this humiliating style of huckstering diplomacy, a new reason arises for delay, and for treating beyond the Atlantic.

"Let the threatened prohibition take place. Our hats, our shoes, and our tea-kettles, must find some other market for a few months; unless the American merchants should be impatient enough to import them by smuggling, into that country, in the mean time; which, I doubt not, they will, in a more than usual abundance. Perhaps when our minister arrives, the advanced price of British goods, and the loss of the duties upon them, may form an argument of some weight in our favor."

CHAPTER XXXI.

CLOSING SCENE.

In looking over the House of Representatives of the ninth Congress, who had devolved on them the important duty of giving the first impulse and direction to the policy of the country in regard to foreign nations, at this critical period, when the powers of Europe, not content with destroying one another, seemed to be aiming at the commercial and political annihilation of this transatlantic republic also, we are struck with the very common and unimportant characters of which it was composed. There were, doubtless, some modest and retiring men, of sound judgment, who were content to give their vote in silence, and to pass their opinions on men and things around them without giving the world the benefit of their wisdom. But all those who were most prominent in the lead of affairs, were without reputation, without political experience or information, the mere hacks of a party, possessing none of the qualities of head or heart that constitute the statesman, filled at the same time with all the narrow conceptions and the intolerance of political bigotry. The reputation of not one has survived the age in which he lived. The world is none the wiser for what they have said or done. Their names, with all their acts, have gone down to oblivion. Such men require a head to think for them; without knowledge, or independence of character, they needed a leader to guide and to instruct them in their duty. Coming into office under the auspices of Mr. Jefferson, his opinion was law to their understanding, his will the harmonizing agent to all their actions. The true character of the representative office, and the delicate relationship existing between that and the Executive, was beyond their conception; and they made a boast and a virtue of their unbounded confidence in the source of all power and patronage. In the hands of a virtuous President, these men were the confiding representatives without question to approve his measures; in the hands of a corrupt and ambitious aspirant, they would have been the subtle tools to enregister his edicts of usurpation or oppression. Fortunately for the country, Mr. Jefferson was a pure patriot and an honest man; he seemed to have no other wish but the good of his country. And, perhaps, it was a consciousness of this fact that made his followers place such implicit reliance on the propriety and the wisdom of whatever he did. What is blind fidelity to the leader of an opposition, will soon be converted into corrupt adulation to the bountiful dispenser of all honors and rewards. An honest coincidence of opinion will be the source of allegiance in the one case; but a base affinity for the loaves and fishes will be the means of cohesion in the other. Corruption follows power; and the rapacious and the profligate, like sharks in the sea, are sure to swim in the wake of the rich freighted argosy of state.

The proceedings of Congress, in regard to our foreign relations, furnish a fruitful commentary on the facility with which men will surrender their opinions and their consciences into the keeping of a popular leader; and the readiness with which bodies of men, in a corporate capacity, will do an act that would disgrace an individual of common respectability. As to these foreign affairs, so complicated and so critical, the President had no plan to propose. On this subject, above all others, he had a right to give a direction to the acts of the legislature; the treaty-making power belonged to him and to the Senate. He did not comply with the Constitution; he informed them of the facts in his possession, but did not recommend what should be done. He had no well-digested plan, on which he was willing to stake his reputation as a statesman; but he stimulated the legislature, by an expression of his secret wishes, to do those things which he was not willing to assume the responsibility of recommending. This was certainly degrading the representative body to a menial purpose. But they were wholly unconscious of the part they were made to act; and when the proud and independent spirit of their leader rose in rebellion, they sought to hunt him down like some wild beast that had broken into the quiet close of a browsing herd. But in justice to these men, it must be conceded, that it was not so much the acts of Mr. Randolph on the Spanish question that offended them, as the bitter and sarcastic words used by him on all occasions towards some of those who professed to belong to the same party, and claimed to be his political friends. It is true, he did not mince his words, and in the heat of debate, he spoke the plain truth in strongest terms. There was no diplomatic ambiguity about him;

and often his blunt directness of expression gave offence where it was not intended. But possessing, as he did, a keen insight into the motives of men; having a high sense of the dignity and purity of the representative character, and a strong disgust for selfishness and grovelling meanness in those who should be patterns of truth and nobleness, he was unsparing in his denunciations of men who, under the guise of republicanism, had crept into official places for no other purpose but to rob the treasury. And it must be confessed that there were not a few of this class to be found in all the departments of government. The Yazoo speculation, Proteus-like, had assumed every shape by which it could glide into the councils of the nation, and find favor in the eyes of the people; it was the dry-rot of the body politic, that secretly consumed the very joints of its massive timbers. A member of the President's cabinet, as we already know, was the Hercules on whose shoulders was upreared this vast fabric of speculation; the boundless patronage of his office was prostituted to his purposes; and he insolently boasted of the means that he used and the triumph he anticipated over the public virtue. There were many post-office contractors in the House of Representatives; the evil had grown to such an extent that Randolph moved an amendment to the Constitution, prohibiting all contractors from holding a seat on the floor of Congress. "I have said, and I repeat it," said Mr. Randolph, "that the aspect in which this thing presents itself would alone determine me to resist it. (The Yazoo petitioners.) In one of the petitioners I behold an executive officer, who receives and distributes a yearly revenue of three hundred thousand dollars, yielding scarcely any net profit to the government—a patronage limited only by the extent of our country. Is this right? Is it even decent? Shall political power be made the engine of private interest? Shall such a suspicion tarnish your proceedings? How would you receive a petition from a President of the United States, if such a case can be supposed possible? Sir, I wish to see the same purity pervading every subordinate branch of administration, which I am persuaded exists in its great departments. Shall persons holding appointments under the great and good man who presides over our counsels, draw on the rich fund of his well-earned reputation, to eke out their flimsy and scanty pretensions? Is the relation in which they stand to him to be made the cloak and cover of their dark designs? To the gentleman from New-York, who takes fire at every insinuation against his friend, I have only to observe on this subject, that what I dare say, I dare to justify. To the House I will relate an incident how far I have lightly conceived or expressed an opinion to the prejudice of any man. I owe an apology to my informant for making public what he certainly did not authorize me to reveal. There is no reparation which can be offered by one gentleman and accepted by another that I shall not be ready to make him, but I feel myself already justified to him, since he sees the circumstances under which I act. A few evenings since a profitable contract for carrying the mail was offered to a friend of mine, who is a member of this House. You must know, sir, the person so often alluded to, maintains a jackal; fed not, as you would suppose, upon the offal of contract, but with the fairest pieces in the shambles; and at night, when honest men are abed, does this obscene animal prowl through the streets of this vast and desolate city, seeking whom he may tamper with. Well, sir, when this worthy plenipotentiary had made his proposal in due form, the independent man to whom it was addressed, saw at once its drift. 'Tell your principal,' said he, 'that I will take his contract, but I shall vote against the Yazoo claim, notwithstanding.' Next day he was told that there had been some misunderstanding of the business, that he could not have the contract, as it was previously bespoken by another.

"Sir, I well recollect, when first I had the honor of a seat in this House, we were then members of a small minority—a poor forlorn hope—that this very petitioner appeared at Philadelphia on behalf of another great land company on Lake Erie. He then told us, as an inducement to vote for the Connecticut reserve (as it was called), that if that measure failed, it would ruin the republicans and the cause in that State. You, sir, cannot have forgotten the reply he received: 'That we did not understand the republicanism that was to be paid for; that we feared it was not of the right sort, but spurious.' And having maintained our principles through the ordeal of that day, shall we now abandon them to act with the men and upon the measures which we then abjured? Shall we now condescend to means which we disdained to use in the most desperate crisis of our political fortunes? This is indeed the age of monstrous coalitions; and this corruption has the qualities of connecting the most inveterate enemies, personal as well as political. It has united in close concert those, of whom it has been said, not in the figurative language of prophecy, but in the sober narrative of history, 'I have bruised thy head and thou hast bruised my heel.' Such is the description of persons who would present to the President of the United States an act, to which, when he puts his hand, he signs a libel on his whole political life. But he will never tarnish the unsullied lustre of his fame; he will never sanction the monstrous position (for such it is, dress it up as you will), that a legislator may sell his vote, and a right which cannot be divested will pass under such sale. Establish this doctrine, and there is an end of representative government; from that moment republicanism receives its death-blow.

"The feeble cry of Virginian influence and ambitious leaders, is attempted to be raised. If such insinuations were worthy of a reply, I might appeal to you, Mr. Speaker, for the fact, that no man in this House (yourself perhaps excepted) is oftener in a minority than I am. If by a leader be meant one who speaks his opinion frankly and boldly—who claims something of that independence, of which the gentleman from New-York so loudly vaunts—who will not connive at public robbery, be the robbers who they may,—then the imputation may be just; such is the nature of my ambition: but in the common acceptation of words, nothing can be more false. In the coarse but strong language of the proverb, ''tis the still sow that sucks the draff.'

"No, sir, we are not the leaders. *There* they sit! and well they know it, forcing down our throats the most obnoxious measures. Gentlemen may be silent, but they shall be dragged into public view. If they direct our public counsels, at least let them answer for the result. We will not be responsible for their measures. If we do not hold the reins, we will not be accountable for the accidents which may befall the carriage.

"But, sir, I am a denunciator! Of whom? Of the gentlemen on my left? Not at all; but of those men and their principles whom the people themselves have denounced; on whom they have burnt their indelible curse, deep and lasting as the lightning from heaven.

"Mr. Speaker, I had hoped that we should not be content to live upon the principal of our popularity, that we should go on to deserve the public confidence, and the disapprobation of the gentleman over the way; but if every thing is to be reversed—if official influence is to become the handmaid of private interest—if the old system is to be revived with the old men, or any that can be picked up,—I may deplore the defection, but never will cease to stigmatize it. Never shall I hesitate between any minority, far less that in which I find myself, and such a majority as is opposed to us. I took my degrees, sir, in this House in a minority, much smaller, indeed, but of the same stamp: a minority, whose very act bore the test of rigorous principle, and with them to the last I will exclaim, *Fiat justitia ruat cœlum.*"

It is too plainly to be perceived, that a man of this bold, fearless, and independent character, was not to be tolerated by those who, in their connection with the government, had far other objects in view than pure principle or patriotism; or even by those honest plodding men, whose blundering mediocrity was awed and overshadowed by his superior genius. He must be put down; the *fiat*, we know, had already gone forth. Whole States had been traversed last summer to organize an opposition to him; he must be silenced, or driven into the ranks of the federalists, and then nobody will believe what he says. The plot was now ripe for execution: like Cæsar, he was to fall on the floor of the Senate by the hands of his treacherous friends. The evening of the 21st of April, on the final adjournment of the House, was selected as the time—that parting hour, usually given up to hilarity, to friendship, and an oblivious forgetfulness of all past animosities, was chosen as the fit occasion to stab to the heart one who should have been their pride and their ornament—one, whose only crime was, not that of having conspired against the liberties of his country, but that of having spoken the truth, and maintained right. Alas! for the virtue and the liberties of mankind. This has most usually been the crime they have ignorantly pursued and punished. Corruption opens a path where truth finds an impassable barrier.

As the shades of night were gathering over the legislative hall, while the dim light of the taper served only to make darkness visible, the conspirators, each with his part well conned and prepared, commenced the assault on their unsuspecting victim, who sat as a confiding friend in their midst.

Mr. William Findley, a member from Pennsylvania, rose and addressed the House, without provocation, in a strain of gross and indecent personal abuse of Mr. Randolph, charging him with having designs to pull down the present administration. It was plainly to be perceived, from the language and manner of Findley, that he was at this time very much intoxicated with strong drink; and many of the members then present declared the same opinion. Mr. Findley was so outrageously indecent in his language, that he was repeatedly called to order; but, without regarding the call, he continued to speak in the same strain, until the House was thrown into a state of confusion, perhaps never before witnessed.

As soon as Findley sat down, John Randolph rose, and without taking particular notice of the conduct of the unfortunate old man, observed, in a manner the most mild, dignified and conciliatory, that "he had hoped, however we might have differed in opinion on the various subjects discussed this session, we should, on the eve of separation, have forgiven and forgotten any asperities and political animosities that had occurred during the session; and that we should have parted like men and friends. He had hoped the harmony of that House would not have been disturbed in the last moments of the session, either by those who had been habitual declaimers, or by those who had *kept the noiseless tenor of their way;* that contumely and personal hatred would have been banished from these walls, and that we should at least have separated in good humor." These remarks produced a gleam of pleasure on the countenance of almost every person present. The language he used and the sentiments he expressed were so mild and conciliatory, that Mr. Randolph's friends were particularly delighted. Although there was nothing in his language or manner that would justify in the smallest degree an idea that he intended to make any particular or personal allusion, yet the attention of every member then present was immediately directed to Mr. Thomas Mann Randolph, the President's *son-in-law*, who, under the impression that John Randolph had made some allusion to him (which no person present but himself could have supposed), rose, and in a manner indicative of rage and defiance, vociferated:

"Mr. Speaker, I rise to reply to the gentleman from Virginia. I will not pretend to vie with him in point of talent or of eloquence; in these he is far, very far, my superior. This is not the first time that gentleman has availed himself of the sanction and the presence of this assembly, to apply his personal allusions to me, and to make use of language and conduct here, which he would not do out of this House.

"But, sir, I will tell that gentleman, that however he may be my superior in talents and eloquence, in patriotism I am his superior; yes, sir, his superior. Last year, sir, that gentleman commenced florist, and dealt in flowers and gardening; I saw him with his spade and pitchfork, and rake and manure, cultivating his flower-garden. This, sir, was on the *Yazoo question;* and then I perceived the gentleman launch forth to sea, without compass or rudder, his masts broken, his sails tattered and torn, and his vessel in a leaky condition; and, when I saw that, sir, I thought it high time to quit him, and look out for the land. The gentleman can talk and boast of the arguments of lead, and powder, and steel; with these arguments, sir, I am as expert as himself, and as willing as he may be to use them."

Mr. Thomas Mann Randolph possessed as quick and as fiery a temper as his kinsman; but it is impossible to conceive any motive for the anger, rage, and threatening denunciation exhibited on this occasion, unless it was premeditated, and the deliberate part of a concerted scheme to immolate John Randolph on the altar of party intolerance, for having dared to differ from them as to what they chose to assume and hold forth as the wishes of the Executive. This gentleman had taken no part in the previous debate, and it is impossible that any allusion could have been made to him. As he progressed, towering in rage, astonishment and regret were exhibited in the looks and expressions of the members. This speech had the most strange and alarming effect. The atmosphere seemed to be surcharged with electric fire, and another spark would blow it into a flame.

Coming from the quarter it did, and under existing circumstances, this denunciation excited in the minds of a great part of those present, sentiments of the most serious nature. Where this thing might end, they could not conjecture, but felt the most anxious apprehension. That Randolph was to be denounced on this occasion by all the self-anointed priests of the true faith, and to be cast out of the synagogue, cannot be questioned. The moment Thomas Mann took his seat, he was followed by James Sloan, of New Jersey, who *read* a speech of about two sheets, closely written, and then delivered it over into the hands of the printer, who was present to receive it, and to publish it. Randolph had not been sparing in his ridicule of the crude conceptions of this man, put forth in a series of resolutions on the great and grave questions about which the administration itself had no settled opinion. He called the nostrums of this man "*Sloan's mint-drops.*" Now was the time for revenge—when the whole pack was in full cry, and the noble stag at bay, he could slyly thrust his fangs into his side with impunity. But Randolph did not wait to hear this well-studied lecture, which for false assertions, low scurrility, and personal abuse, cannot be surpassed. If he heard it at all, it fell senseless on his ears. He was after other game. A few minutes after T. M. Randolph closed his remarks, John Randolph left his seat, and desired Mr. Garnett to make a formal application to know whether the remarks that had fallen from that gentleman were addressed to him, and unless he disavowed any such intention, to demand a meeting. Mr. Garnett seemed deeply concerned at this request, and endeavored to dissuade his friend from the step. Randolph replied, that his resolution was irrevocably taken; that, perhaps, on the whole, he had cause to be obliged to Mr. Thomas Mann Randolph; that he had long been a target for every worthless scoundrel in that House to aim his shafts at; and that Mr. T. M. Randolph, by this unprovoked and studied outrage, had given him an opportunity to answer them all, in the person of an adversary who would not disgrace his contest, and under circumstances in which no possible blame could attach to him. Mr. T. M. Randolph replied to Mr. Garnett, that unless he had supposed some of Mr. John Randolph's expressions pointed particularly at him, he should have thought himself highly culpable in saying what he had; but believing that they were intended for him, he felt himself called upon to say something.

Having acknowledged that his observations were levelled at Mr. John Randolph, he was told that that gentleman expected to meet him. He replied that he was ready to do so; but that if Mr. John Randolph would only say that he meant no allusion to him, there was no apology which a man of honor could or ought to make, which he would not be ready to offer. When Mr. Garnett delivered this message, Mr. John Randolph observed that the course which Mr. T. M. Randolph had chosen to pursue precluded any sort of declaration or acknowledgment on his part; that Mr. T. M. R. must make reparation commensurate with the injury aimed at his feelings, or meet him, and give him satisfaction. Mr. Garnett immediately apprised the gentleman of these conditions, and requested that he would choose some friend with whom he might have farther conversation on the subject. Mr. Coles was called in; after a short consultation aside with his friend, he rejoined Mr. Garnett, and said: All that Mr. T. M. R. desired was an assurance that none of Mr. J. R.'s remarks were intended for him, and that he would be willing (in that case) to make any apology a man of honor could offer. Mr. Garnett replied, that there was no doubt on his mind, or, he believed, of any other spectator, that Mr. T. M. R. had entirely misconceived Mr. J. R.'s expressions; but that, after what had passed, Mr. J. R. would make no statement whatever; and if Mr. T. M. R. could not reconcile it to himself to make a suitable apology, Mr. J. R. would expect Mr. T. M. R. to meet him either that night (which he preferred) or in the morning. Mr. Coles said he was too much engaged in the public business at that time to see his friend, but would do it as soon as he could, and let Mr. Garnett know the result. Mr. Garnett returned with this statement to Mr. John Randolph, who was in a remote room of the Capitol, and then took his seat in the House. In a few minutes afterwards, Mr. Thomas Mann Randolph rose in his place, and said that he had been assured, by several of those who sat near him, that he had acted in what he had before said under a misapprehension of Mr. John Randolph's remarks, which none of them understood as having been intended for him; that under this misapprehension he had acted; it was the sole cause of his saying what he had said; and that he was then persuaded by the assurance of his friends of his mistake. He regretted very much what he had said, for he had no disposition to wound any gentleman's feelings who did not intend to wound his.

Mr. Garnett immediately went to Mr. John Randolph, and stated that Mr. T. M. R. had made such an apology in the House as Mr. Garnett conceived, and as every member said who mentioned the subject in his hearing (which several did) was proper for Mr. T. M. R. to make and for Mr. J. R. to receive.

Mr. Randolph then requested his friend to say to Mr. Coles that he received the apology of Mr. T. M. Randolph, and had no further commands for that gentleman, which Mr. Garnett did just as the House was breaking up; and thus the business terminated.

CHAPTER XXXII.

AARON BURR.

Misfortunes, 'tis said, come not alone; it proved so with Mr. Randolph on this occasion. In his retirement at Bizarre, after the stormy session just passed, and other occurrences of a domestic nature, his reflections could not have been of the most pleasant kind. However conscious of rectitude, the prospect before him must have been cheerless indeed. For four years he had been the popular leader of a triumphant party, who were successfully carrying into operation those great measures of reform that would bring back the Federal Government to the few simple and general subjects of legislation for which alone it was designed. Never had a young man risen so rapidly or so high in the public estimation. He was the idol of his party; his eloquence and his practical wisdom were extolled on every hand; and it seemed that there was no station or honor in the gift of the people that he was not destined to attain. But now the scene was changed. For having ventured to suggest a plan of action different from that which *seemed* to be favored by the Executive, he was denounced by his old friends, his motives calumniated, and he was charged with a design of pulling down the present administration. How bitter must have been his feelings, at the reflection that the highest stretch of patriotism, which could cause a sacrifice of all the bright prospects before him for the sake of doing his duty, should meet with such a reward. But it has always been so. In popular governments, the intolerant spirit of a triumphant majority will allow no deviation from that standard of orthodoxy which it has set up for itself. Freedom of opinion is professed, but you exercise it at the peril of being banished from the society of those who hold the reins and prescribe the course that ought to be pursued. There are so many interested in degrading a popular and leading man in a political party, that it is almost impossible for him ever to retrieve the first false step. It matters not how pure his motives, or how far it may be from his intention to separate from his party friends, yet there are always enough, from interested motives, to take advantage of the slightest deviation from the standard of the majority, to denounce him as a deserter, and to drive him into the opposition. Politicians, generally, are a heartless and selfish race of men. There are many honorable exceptions; but for the most part, their own aggrandizement is the end of their patriotism; and they always look with secret satisfaction on the disappointment or the fall of one whose superior talents overshadowed their own self-importance, or whose stern virtues and integrity stood in the way of the accomplishment of their selfish ends.

Mr. Randolph never deviated from those principles he professed, while in a minority; his party, in many instances, had departed from them; he undertook the ungracious task of holding up to view their own dereliction. Sovereign majorities, as well as sovereign princes, do not like to hear their own infallibility brought in question—especially will they not tolerate it in one who is a subject of their power. Mr. Randolph had no faith in the Cabinet, while he retained the utmost confidence in the Chief Magistrate. He knew that corruption had crept into the legislature, through the Post Office department and the Yazoo speculation, and that, as a body, they had surrendered their independence into the hands of the Executive. His great crime was that of maintaining the independence of the legislature, as a co-ordinate department of government. Let posterity judge how far he should be condemned for such an offence.

During the excited and sleepless hours of the past session, Mr. Randolph was assailed by his old hereditary disease, in its most aggravated form—he was prostrate on his bed for many weeks, racked with the most excruciating torture. With repeated accumulation of mental distress, and even of mental agony, caused by domestic occurrences, the diseases of the body seemed to keep pace with them, and to produce a degree of suffering such as no mortal man ever endured before. With heroic fortitude, he suppressed his feelings, and the world, while they condemned his outbursts of passion, never knew the real cause of his eccentricities. With a pride and a haughty reserve rarely equalled, he shut himself up from common observation, and was content to be the subject of misrepresentation and of malicious calumny, without condescending to explanation or reply. To a few only did he unbosom himself, and expose the wounds of body and of soul, which he carried, with increased aggravation, to the grave.

Hereafter, the reader will have an opportunity of reading his confessions, poured into the bosom of his most intimate friend, and to weep over the many sufferings he endured, in what he chose to call his "most unprosperous life."

But there was one occurrence, which took place in the month of March, that affected Mr. Randolph more than all things else. The reader is already aware of the great attachment he had formed, many years ago, to a young lady of remarkable beauty, virtues, and accomplishments—*one I loved more than my own soul, or the God that made it.* Many untoward events had prevented their union, and made it impossible—yet he vainly cherished the hope that their love, sublimated into a pure, Platonic affection, might last to the end of life—idle expectation, that no other human being could have indulged. There was no reason in the indulgence of such a wish; but love is blind, tyrannical, and has no reason. The lady thought proper to unite her fortunes with one in whose society she might hope to live a more happy life, than in that of her present most devoted but unfortunate lover. This event, which took place in the midst of the excited debates of Congress, and at a moment when his friends were deserting him on every hand, struck deep into the heart of Mr. Randolph—he never recovered from it—it had a visible influence on the whole of his after life. His love, now purified of all earthly desire, became a genuine worship—the image of the beloved object, mirrored in the distance, hovered over his path, like some angelic being, whose celestial smiles shed benignest influence on his heart, where all else had grown cold and desolate. Long years afterwards, when the body was locked in the fitful embraces of a feverish sleep, and the soul wandering in dreams, that once loved name has been heard to escape from his lips, in a tone that evinced how deeply the love of the being who bore it had been engraven on the inmost sanctuary of his heart. But why do we call up these things? Reader! there was a tragedy in the life of this man, more thrilling than romance. But this is a subject not for us to deal with; we promised not to touch it more; let it go down to the oblivion of the grave, and there sleep with those who, in life, endured its agonies. We ask pardon for having glanced at it here, and for the last time, because it is impossible to form a correct estimate of the man, without some knowledge of this occurrence, which constituted one of the most important events of his life. Let the skeptical look into his own heart, and see whether he is capable of elevating his affections above a mere sensual appetite. If not, then he is no fit judge of that man, whose exalted passion, rising above all earthly desire, knows no other bounds but the infinite longing of an immortal soul.

Let us now proceed with our narrative.

Notwithstanding the harsh and unfriendly manner in which he had been treated, Mr. Randolph returned to Washington in December, with every disposition to harmonize and co-operate with the republican party. His difference from them last session, was on a question of mere expediency—the propriety of which time alone could prove. Unless they intended to abandon, in the conduct of affairs, all the principles they professed while in a minority, it was impossible for him to co-operate with any other body of men. However much he might be irritated in his feelings towards certain individuals, he did not allow that circumstance so far to influence his judgment as to cause him to vote for or against a measure merely to be in opposition to them. Accordingly we find him, on most occasions, working in harmony with the friends of the administration; and there seems to have been a good feeling restored between him and some of the leading members. It is true, there was no important question on which there was likely to be a diversity of sentiment. The non-importation law, by the terms of its enactment, was not to go into operation till the last of November; and now that the time had arrived, it was proposed, on the part of its friends, to postpone it to a still later period. It was alleged that the British commissioners desired not a repeal, but a postponement merely, while negotiations were pending between the two countries. Of course Mr. Randolph readily united with them in this measure; and it is not surprising that he took occasion to intimate that, in his judgment, time had proved the impolicy and inefficiency of the original enactment. But the only question of any importance to which their attention was called, during the last session of the *ninth* Congress, was the conspiracy of Aaron Burr. After his bitter disappointments, both on the national theatre and in New-York, his adopted State—after the sudden and irretrievable fall of this ambitious man, and when the cold eye of neglect had chilled, like a frost, the last spark of patriotism in the breast of this legalized murderer, he had gone into the great Mississippi Valley, in search of some adventure adequate to his genius and his ambition. Here, indeed, was a vast field for enterprise—abundant material for any undertaking that might require perseverance, privation, and heroic daring—there was also a little discontent in the popular mind, in some parts of the West, which might have inspired a less sanguine man than Aaron Burr with hopes of tampering with their patriotism.

Soon rumors came that this man was planning and organizing some vast expedition, the precise object of which was the subject only of conjecture. Whether it was his design to make war on the Spanish province of Mexico, or whether, in co-operation with Spain, he was aiding her in the long cherished scheme of separating the western country from the United States, none could tell; but all agreed that the genius and the resources of the chief director of the enterprise were adequate to any desperate adventure, whether of foreign aggression or domestic treason.

The Executive was soon apprised of the state of things, and were endeavoring to get all the information they could in regard to the matter. But the newspapers were so full of rumors and statements, implicating the Spanish Government as the prime mover of this conspiracy, that Mr. Randolph, after having waited five or six weeks for official intelligence, at length moved a resolution to call on the President for information. We give his speech entire on this occasion, as it shows his views of the Spanish question twelve months after his separation from the administration on that subject.

"In the President's Message," said Mr. Randolph, "at the commencement of the session, he announced to us as follows:

"'Having received information, that in another part of the United States a great number of private individuals were combining together, arming and organizing themselves, contrary to law, to carry on a military expedition against the territories of Spain, I thought it necessary, by proclamation, as well as by special orders, to take measures for preventing and suppressing this enterprise, for seizing the vessels, arms, and other means provided for it, and for arresting and bringing to justice its authors and abettors.'

"So long," said Mr. Randolph, "as the illegal movements of these persons were supposed to be directed against a foreign nation, although the interest of the United States, and their honor too, required that prompt and decisive measures should be taken for suppressing their designs, yet I believe there is no gentleman in this House but will agree with me in the opinion that the United States, and this House in particular, could not feel so deep and lively an interest against a conspiracy of that kind as against one for the subversion of the Union, and perhaps of the liberties of those who compose it. I have waited with anxious solicitude for some information in relation to this subject, that might be depended upon—for some official information. I contented myself for a long time with the belief, inasmuch as no information had been given to the House, that there were imperious reasons connected with the public welfare which forbade a disclosure; but the aspect which affairs have taken on the Mississippi is such, that I can no longer reconcile it to my sense of duty, as the independent representative of an independent people, to rest satisfied in that state of supineness and apathy in which the House has been satisfied to remain for the six or seven weeks past. Sir, from the information I have been able to collect—and it is such that I am obliged to place great if not implicit reliance on it—it does appear to me, that if the government of Spain is in any wise connected in these measures, it is concerned not as the defendant, but as the plaintiff—as the aggressing party, and not as the party on whom the aggression is made. So long as I was induced to believe, that by withholding correct information from the Legislature the substantial interests of the nation would be more essentially subserved than by laying it before them, so long, though not without reluctance, I acquiesced in its being withheld. But from the hostile appearances on the Mississippi, it seems to me that the state of things is such as requires the most prompt and efficacious measures for securing the Union. The bubble is said to have burst, and there no longer remains any reason why the information in the possession of the Executive ought to be withheld. But to guard against all possible objection, I have endeavored so to frame the motion as to do away with any objection arising from this consideration. It does appear—from the newspapers it is true, but under a much higher sanction than is generally attached to information received through such a channel—it does appear in evidence, under the sanction of an examination before the legislature of Kentucky, that ever since the peace of 1783, Spain has incessantly labored to detach the western people from the Union; that subsequently to the peace of San Lorenzo she has carried on intrigues, and in the most faithless manner withheld acceding to its stipulations, in order to excite a spirit in the western country subversive of the Union; that she subsequently made a proposition of the most flagitious kind to several leading characters in Kentucky, and as I believe elsewhere. It seems, indeed, that she has never lost sight of this object; and I believe she never will lose sight of it so long as she shall find materials to work upon, or a shadow of hope that she will succeed. It appears to me that she has found those materials; that they are of the most dangerous nature; that they are now in operation; and that, perhaps, at this moment, while I am addressing you, at least for a time, the fate of the Western country may have been decided.

"Sir, this subject offers strong arguments, in addition to the numerous reasons offered at the present session of Congress, to justify the policy avowed by certain gentlemen during the last session, so highly condemned; and if I am correctly informed, the other branch of the Legislature are now acting on that policy so condemned and despised.

"We have had a bill before us authorizing the President to accept volunteers. A member of the committee with whom this bill originated, and with whom I have the pleasure of concurring, intimately connected and domesticated with the Secretary of War, did make a proposition before that committee, substantially the same with that rejected the last session—to augment the military forces to meet the pressing exigencies of the times; and which I presume must have had the sanction of that officer. Is there a man in this House who at this day doubts, that if the Government—I mean the Executive and Legislature—had taken a manly and decisive attitude towards Spain, and instead of pen, ink, and paper, had given men and arms—is there a man who disbelieves that not only Spain would have been overawed, but that those domestic traitors also would have been intimidated and overawed, whose plans threaten to be so dangerous? Would any man have dreamed of descending the Mississippi at the head of an unprincipled banditti, if New Orleans had been fortified, and strong fortifications erected in its neighborhood? What did we then hear? Money! dollars and cents! Is there not now every reason to believe, especially when we consider the superintendence under which the expenses are incurred, that the saving of the campaign on the Sabine, and the saving of the costly measures taken by the commander-in-chief on his own responsibility, would have been equal to the expense of raising and maintaining for one year the additional forces proposed at the last session to be raised. There can be no doubt, but that on the principle of economy, without taking into view the effect on the Union, the United States would have been gainers. A spectator, not in the habit of reading our public prints, or of conversing with individuals out of doors, but who should draw his ideas of the situation of the country from the proceedings of this House during the present session, would be led to infer that there never existed in any nation a greater degree of peace, tranquillity, or union, at home or abroad, than in the United States at this time; and yet, what is the fact? That the United States are not only threatened with external war, but with conspiracies and treasons, the more alarming from their not being defined. And yet we sit, and adjourn; adjourn, and sit; take things as schoolboys, do as we are bid, and ask no questions. I cannot reconcile this line of conduct to my ideas of the duty of a member on this floor. Yes, the youngest member of the federal family has been found to be the first to ward off the impending danger, while the eldest members are sleeping, snoring, and dozing over their liberties at home.

Under this view of the subject, I beg leave to offer the following resolution:

"Resolved—That the President of the United States be and he is hereby requested to lay before this House any information in possession of the Executive, except such as he may deem the public welfare to require not to be disclosed, touching any illegal combination of private individuals against the peace and safety of the Union, or any military expedition planned by such individuals against the territories of any power in amity with the United States; together with the measures which the Executive has pursued and *proposes to take* for suppressing or defeating the same."

The resolution was carried by a large majority. As more authentic news came of the designs and actual movements of the conspirators, the country became still more alarmed; every one of discernment saw the danger of this enterprise; they knew the combustible materials that artful intriguer had to work upon, and could readily perceive how he might take advantage of the unfriendly relations existing between the United States and Spain, and by the secret aid, if not the open co-operation of that discontented power, effect a dismemberment of the Union.

The Senate, in their alarm, went so far as to suspend the "Habeas Corpus Act," which is never resorted to except in extreme cases of danger to the peace and integrity of the country. This act of suspension was arrested in the House. Mr. Randolph was most active and efficient in his opposition: he denounced it as unnecessary, oppressive, and tyrannical. Most fortunately it was rejected by the House, and can never be set up as a precedent.

Aaron Burr, it is well known, was arrested in Alabama, and brought to trial in Virginia, on the ground that he had levied his forces and commenced his treasonable acts within the borders of that State. The trial took place in the city of Richmond, in the month of May, 1807; it excited a great deal of interest, and brought together many of the most distinguished men of the Union. John Randolph was foreman of the grand jury that brought in a true bill against Aaron Burr of high treason against his country. It is not our purpose to go into the details of this trial, or the incidents of the conspiracy: they belong to the general historian, and must form an interesting and important chapter in the history of those critical and eventful times.

During his sojourn in Richmond on this occasion, Mr. Randolph formed many new and valuable acquaintances. Mr. Wirt was at this time collecting materials for his Life of Patrick Henry. He was conversing one day on that subject in a company of gentlemen, when Mr. Tazewell, who was present, said to him: "Mr. Wirt, you should, by all means, see John Randolph on that subject; he knows more of Patrick Henry than any other man now living." Mr. Wirt confessed that he was not personally acquainted with that gentleman. The difficulty was, how to bring them together; for Tazewell said it would not do to make a formal introduction, and say, "This is Mr. Wirt, sir, who is desirous of obtaining from you some materials for his Life of Henry. In that case Randolph would not open his lips. However," said he, "I will contrive a meeting." In a few days Mr. Wirt was invited to Tazewell's room, where he found Randolph and other gentlemen assembled. Very soon, in the course of conversation, as if by accident, the name of Patrick Henry was mentioned. Randolph immediately caught up the theme, and delighted the company with a graphic account of his personal appearance, his habits, and his eloquence. He frequently rose from his seat, and repeated passages from the speeches, and imitated the peculiar style and fervid manner of the renowned orator. Wirt was so much pleased, that when he retired he wrote a note to Mr. Randolph, thanking him for the rich treat he had given him, and begging that he would put down in writing the substance of what he had said. Randolph now saw the trick that was played upon him. He immediately went to his friend Tazewell, and chided him soundly for having made an exhibition of him in that way. Tazewell turned it off as a pleasant joke; nevertheless, the biographer of Patrick Henry never got from that quarter any additional materials for the subject of his memoir. It was on this occasion also that Mr. Randolph first made the acquaintance of Dr. John Brockenbrough, who from that time to the day of his death was the most intimate friend of his bosom—the friend to whom he daily unfolded without reserve or fear of exposure the inmost thoughts and feelings of his heart. The doctor was a member of the grand jury, and the acquaintance commenced in a way peculiar to John Randolph. "I did not seek his acquaintance," says the doctor, "because it had been impressed on my mind that he was a man of a wayward and irritable temper; but as he knew that I had been a school-fellow of his brothers, Richard and Theodoric (while he was in Bermuda for the benefit of his health), he very courteously made advances to me to converse about his brothers, to whom he had been much devoted, and ever afterwards I found him a steady and confiding friend. He frequently passed much of his time at my house, and was the most agreeable and interesting inmate you can imagine. No little personal attention was ever lost on him, and he rendered himself peculiarly a favorite with my wife by his conversation on belles-lettres, in which he was so well versed; and he read (in which he excelled) to her very many of the choice passages of Milton and Shakspeare. Mr. Randolph also had another remarkable quality, irritable and sensitive as he was; *when alone* with a friend he would not only bear with patience, but would invite a full expression of his friend's opinion on his conduct, or acts and sentiments, on any subject, either private or public."

CHAPTER XXXIII.

EMBARGO—THE ILIAD OF ALL OUR WOES.

By Jay's treaty of 1794, our difficulties with Great Britain, though not settled, were quieted for the time being; while in consequence of the same cause we were nearly involved in an open rupture with France.

The change of administration and the convention with France in 1800 restored a more friendly feeling between the two republics—and the purchase of Louisiana in 1803 was accomplished with more ease than Mr. Jefferson himself could have expected. Our commerce for the first four years of the new administration was exceedingly prosperous—and the management of our domestic affairs was conducted on strictly republican principles. Had peace continued in Europe during the remainder of his term, Mr. Jefferson's would have been a most brilliant and successful career. But after the rupture of the treaty of Amiens and the renewal of hostilities between the great belligerent powers, an unfavorable change took place in our foreign relations.

By a series of extraordinary victories, Great Britain had annihilated the combined fleets of France, Spain and Holland, and made herself undisputed mistress of the sea. The trade between these countries and their colonies, their navies being destroyed, was now for the first time opened to foreign bottoms. The United States were the only people that could avail themselves of this advantage. Their commercial marine in consequence was greatly enlarged, and commerce itself was more than ever expanded and prosperous.

But England soon perceived that so long as this kind of traffic was permitted she would derive no advantage from her naval victories. She commenced a series of measures to put an end to it.

Bonaparte, in the mean time, having elevated himself to the imperial throne of France, had conquered nearly all Europe, driven the Russian bear back into his polar regions, and was now seriously contemplating the destruction of England as the only barrier in the way of universal conquest. But sad experience had taught him that the only way in which he could reach that sea-girt empire was through her manufactures and commerce. His restrictive system on the continent was designed to sap and undermine these two sources of English wealth and power. In their gigantic efforts to destroy each other, these great belligerents paid no respect to neutral rights or to the laws of nations—might became right, and Robin Hood's law of the strongest was the only available rule. Whatever could affect the other injuriously was unhesitatingly adopted without regard to the effect it might have on the rights of neutral parties. They even resolved there should be no neutrals in the contest; and as the United States were the only independent power left, this warfare on their commerce was intended to force them into the controversy on the one side or the other.

The first act of hostility was commenced by Great Britain on the 16th May, 1806: the British government, by an order of the King in council, decreed that all the rivers and ports from Brest to the Elbe (being about a thousand miles of sea-coast) should be considered in a state of blockade. Where a port is actually blockaded by an adequate force, any vessel attempting to enter is liable to be captured by the besieging squadron, and to be condemned as lawful prize. But where no fleet was stationed on the prohibited coast, and the blockade merely consisted in a decree of the government, all vessels laden or sailing for the ports decreed to be in a state of siege, were liable to be captured and condemned wherever found. This was regarded as a gross violation of neutral rights; and on the 21st November, Bonaparte commenced his acts of retaliation. After charging England with disregarding the law of nations and the rights of neutrality, and with declaring places in a state of blockade before which she had not a ship, he declared all the British Isles in a state of blockade, and prohibited all trade and commerce with them. He provided also in the decree (Berlin decree) for the capture and condemnation of English produce and manufactures, and prohibited all neutral ships coming direct from England or the English colonies, or having been there, from entering the ports of France.

By this decree all commerce between England and the continent and between the United States and England was intended to be cut off. Any neutral vessel (and there were none but those belonging to citizens of the United States) sailing for England, or from an English port to the continent, was subject to capture and condemnation. The French minister, in consequence of a remonstrance on the part of the United States, gave it as his opinion, that the decree of blockade would be so qualified by the existing treaty as not to operate on American commerce. Not much respect, however, was paid to this opinion by French cruisers; and in September 1807 the decree was ordered to be fully enforced against all neutrals.

In the mean time a negotiation was going on between the commissioners of England and the United States. On the 30th of December, 1806, a treaty was signed settling amicably, if not satisfactorily, all the difficulties between the two nations. But Bonaparte's Berlin decree having come to their knowledge, the British commissioners, in a note delivered by order of the King, declared to the American commissioners, that if France should execute that decree, and the United States acquiesce in it, the British government would hold themselves discharged from the treaty and issue retaliatory orders against neutral commerce with France. Had the treaty been ratified on that condition, it would have pledged the United States to such a co-operation with Great Britain against France, as must have ended in hostilities with the one and alliance with the other. This was the object of England—but Mr. Jefferson was determined if possible to continue in his position of neutrality. The treaty was received before the adjournment of Congress, the 4th March, 1807; but he boldly suppressed it, and would not even submit it to the Senate for their consideration. He remembered too well the effect of Jay's treaty on the public mind to venture one himself. A total surrender of all her claims by Great Britain at that time would not have been acceptable, because it would have forced the United States into an alliance with England, contrary to the popular sentiment, which was decidedly in favor of the French cause. In times of peace that treaty would have been favorably received, but under existing circumstances, the President had no intention of suffering himself to be *treaty-foundered* as his predecessors had been. Mr. Monroe, the principal negotiator, was much offended at the rejection or rather unceremonious suppression of his treaty; he had hoped to gain much credit by this act of pacification.

In the mean time the affair of the Chesapeake took place, which greatly inflamed the public mind. A British squadron it seems was lying near the mouth of Hampton Roads, in Lynnhaven Bay; several sailors deserted and took refuge on board the American frigate Chesapeake, then in the port of Norfolk, fitting out for sea, the sailors were demanded, but were refused to be given up on the ground that they were American citizens. As the Chesapeake, on her destined voyage, passed out of the Capes, she was followed by a British vessel detached from the squadron for that purpose; so soon as the Chesapeake got out of neutral waters into the ocean, she was fired upon, her hull and rigging were much injured and several persons were killed; she was boarded, the sailors recaptured, and some of them were put to death. This gross outrage, though unauthorized and disavowed by the government, had an unhappy effect on the public mind in the United States. A spirit of revenge seized the people; and although England sent over a special minister to settle the difficulty, a slight punctilio in the forms and etiquette of diplomacy was seized upon as a pretext to prevent any advancements or explanations on the part of the British envoy.

Such was the situation of affairs, when, on the 11th of November, 1807, before the Berlin decree had been enforced against American vessels, and while the government had reason to hope it would not be enforced, Great Britain executed her threat intimated at the signing of the treaty. By an order in council (with a preamble, charging France with a want of respect to the laws of nations and rights of neutrality), it was decreed that all the ports and places of France and her allies, or any other country at war with his majesty, and all other ports and places in Europe from which, although not at war with his majesty, the British flag is excluded, and all ports and places in the colonies belonging to his majesty's enemies, shall from henceforth be subject to the same restrictions, in point of trade and navigation, (with certain exceptions,) as if the same were actually blockaded by his majesty's naval forces, in the most strict and vigorous manner.

By these acts of England and France, professing to be acts of retaliation, and not at all in a spirit of hostility to the United States, the neutral commerce of America was entirely destroyed. Not a vessel could sail to Europe or to England, to the vast colonial regions of North and South America, and the East and West Indies, without being subject to capture and condemnation. The trade of the whole world, in fact, was interdicted, and could not be carried on without the risk of forfeiture. Both belligerents, however, had distinctly intimated that if the United States would side with them, every advantage should be given to their commerce. But this is what they did not intend to do; they did not mean to surrender all the advantages they had hitherto enjoyed from their neutral position, if it could be avoided. To side with England was war with France—with France was war with England. Mr. Jefferson was not prepared for either alternative. What was to be done? Commerce, left thus exposed, must be ground into powder between the upper and nether millstone, and be scattered as chaff before the winds of heaven. The President advised a dignified retirement from the ocean, until the storm should have passed over. For the first time since our difficulties with foreign nations, he took the responsibility of advising a definite course of action. In a secret message to Congress, about the 19th of December, 1807, he recommended that an embargo should be laid on all American vessels. In a few days a bill to that effect was passed into a law: all American vessels were prohibited, under high penalties, from sailing to foreign ports, or from port to port within the United States, without license.

The measure of an embargo was at first advocated by Mr. Randolph. He introduced the resolution, in accordance with the President's message; but the bill which was finally adopted, originated in the Senate; it contained provisions that he could not approve, and he opposed it on its passage. This is given as an instance of Mr. Randolph's fickleness and want of object in his parliamentary course. The debates were conducted in secret—in fact, the bill was hurried through the forms of legislation, with scarcely any debate. We do not know, therefore, what was said on the occasion, and are left to infer the grounds of Mr. Randolph's opposition to the bill, from his general views on the subject of an embargo. He approved of such a step in the beginning, as a war measure. An embargo of sixty or ninety days, collecting and protecting all our resources, followed by a declaration of war, at the end of that period, against that one of the belligerents whose restrictive course manifested the strongest spirit of hostility, would have fulfilled Mr. Randolph's idea of such a measure. But such was not the intention of the friends of the administration, in passing the act now under consideration. It was designed as a measure to be permanent for an indefinite period. France and England were told that it was not conceived in a spirit of hostility to them, but was merely intended as a *municipal regulation*. The truth was, however, and they did not fail to perceive it, that the whole object of withdrawing our commerce from the ocean, was to operate on those two nations. It was intended to starve France and her dependencies, and to break England, unless they would abandon their absurd pretensions over the rights of neutral nations. But when this happy result would take place, it was impossible to tell. For a measure of this kind to come home to the bosom and the business of a great nation, must necessarily take a very long time. Indeed, it was reasonable to suppose that the desired object never could be accomplished in that way. The resources of England and of France were too great and too varied, to be seriously affected by a suspension of even the whole of American commerce. The event proved what, it would seem, a little forethought ought to have anticipated. After the embargo had been in operation for twelve months, those two nations were no nearer being forced into terms than they were at first; while their spirit of hostility was greatly exasperated.

But what effect did the measure have on affairs at home—on the character of our own people? Here, it was disastrous in the extreme. An embargo is the most heroic remedy that can be applied to state diseases. It must soon run its course, and kill or cure in a short time. It is like one holding his breath to rush through flame or mephitic gas: the suspension may be endured for a short time, but the lungs at length must be inflated, even at the hazard of suffocation. Commerce is the breath that fills the lungs of a nation, and a total suspension of it is like taking away vital air from the human system; convulsions or death must soon follow. By the embargo, the farmer, the merchant, the mechanic, the capitalist, the ship-owner, the sailor, and the day-laborer, found themselves suddenly arrested in their daily business. Crops were left to rot in the warehouses; ships in the docks; capital was compelled to seek new channels for investment, while labor was driven to every shift to keep from starvation.

Sailors, seeing the uncertain continuation of this state of things, flocked in great numbers to the British navy. That service which, in former years, they most dreaded, necessity now compelled them to seek with avidity. Smuggling was extensively carried on through the whole extent of our wide-spread borders; the revenue was greatly reduced; and the morals of the people were corrupted by the vast temptations held out to evade the laws. It is difficult to tell on what classes of the community this disastrous measure did not operate. On the planting and shipping interest, perhaps, it was most serious. On the one, it was more immediate, on the other, more permanent, in its evil consequences.

In cities and commercial regions, capital and labor are easily diverted from one employment to another. That which to-day is profitably engaged in commerce, may to-morrow, if an inducement offers, be as readily turned into successful manufactures. Not so with the labor and capital employed in agriculture; here the change must be slow. But with the capital and the *kind* of labor employed in the tobacco and cotton planting of the South, no change, to any perceptible degree, was possible. The Southern people, being wholly agricultural, could live a few years without the sale of their crops; but the Northern people, being mainly dependent on their labor and commerce, could not exist with an embargo of long duration. Hence we find a patient endurance of its evils on the part of the South, while a spirit of insurrection pervaded the people of the North. In this restless condition, much of their capital and labor were permanently directed to manufactures. The bounties offered by a total prohibition of foreign articles, stimulated this branch of business in a remarkable degree; and when the embargo, non-intercourse, and war ceased to operate as a bounty, they have had to be sustained by heavy duties imposed on foreign commerce, at the expense of the planting interest of the South, which is mainly dependent on a foreign market for the sale of its commodities. Every dollar taken from commerce, and invested in manufactures, was turning the current from a friendly into a hostile channel, to that kind of agriculture which was dependent on foreign trade for its prosperity. The immediate effect of the embargo was, to starve New England. Its more permanent consequence has been, to build it up at the expense of the planting interest of the South. New England has now two sources of wealth, in her manufactures and commerce; while the South have still the only one of planting tobacco and cotton on exhausted lands, and with a reduced market for the sale of her commodities.

It was impossible for Mr. Randolph to advocate such a measure. He could not foresee all the evils it might entail on his country; but his practical wisdom, aided by his deep interest in the welfare of his constituents, taught him that no good could come out of an embargo reduced to a system, and made a part of the municipal regulations of the Government. As the first step towards an immediate preparation for war, he could approve the act; but as a scheme destined to act on foreign countries, while it was wasting the resources of Government, and consuming the substance of the people at home, it met his decided disapprobation.

Twelve months had now rolled around, and all parties had become of his opinion. No impression abroad. Nothing but disaster at home. The legislature of Massachusetts pronounced it an unconstitutional act. They were not far from the truth. For a short period, and as a war measure, an embargo would be constitutional; but the embargo acts adopted from time to time by Congress, and persisted in for more than a year, were very far from being clearly constitutional. Massachusetts pronounced them not only unconstitutional, but unjust and oppressive.

In 1799, when Virginia interposed her State authority, and declared the alien and sedition laws unconstitutional, Massachusetts then said, that the Supreme Court was alone competent to pronounce on the constitutionality of a federal law. But she now saw the error and the evil consequences of such a doctrine. The Supreme Court had declared the embargo acts to be constitutional; while a sovereign State, crushed and ruined by the burdens they imposed, saw those enactments in a very different light. Was she to be silent, and bear the evils inflicted by those laws, merely because the courts had pronounced in their favor? By no means. She was one of the sovereign parties who had ordained the Constitution as a common government, endowing it with certain general powers for that purpose; and surely, from the very nature of things, she had a right to say whether this or that law transcended those delegated powers or not.

Whether Massachusetts strictly followed the doctrine of State rights, as laid down by Mason, Jefferson, and Madison, we pretend not to say; but we do say, that she had a right to interpose her authority, to pronounce the embargo laws unconstitutional, to show their injustice and oppression, and to demand their repeal by instructions to her own senators and representatives. Massachusetts did interpose; pronounced her repugnance to the law; and her will was respected.

Mr. Jefferson might have taken a very different course from the one pursued by him. He might have said, This disaffection is only found among the federalists; they despise State rights, and have only resorted to them on this occasion to abuse them; the people of Massachusetts are favorable to my administration, and to the obnoxious law; my popularity and influence are unbounded in other sections of the Union; by persevering a little longer, we shall accomplish all that was designed by the embargo; I will therefore disregard the clamors of these people, and persist in enforcing the law, even should it drive them to extremity. But Mr. Jefferson did not reason in this way. He saw that a sovereign State, through her regular legislative forms, had pronounced against the law; it was not for him to scrutinize the character and composition of that legislature; it was enough for him to know, that a State had solemnly declared the law unconstitutional, unjust, and oppressive. When, in addition, he was told by a distinguished statesman from Massachusetts, that a longer persistence might endanger the integrity of the Union, he unhesitatingly acquiesced in a repeal of the most important and favored measure of his administration.

What might have been the consequences if Massachusetts had been driven to extremities, we will not conjecture—we do not reason from extreme cases. All we have to say is, that so long as the States have the independence to maintain those rights guaranteed to them by the Constitution, and that so long as there is patriotism and virtue in the administration of the Federal Government, there will never be the necessity of driving the States into those extreme measures of secession or nullification.

CHAPTER XXXIV

GUNBOATS.

The question may be asked here, Why did Mr. Jefferson make so little preparation for a war which, sooner or later, seemed to be inevitable? To understand his policy, we must first know the political principles that governed his conduct. He came into power as the leader of the republican State-Rights party. During the first four years of his administration, he applied the few simple and abstemious doctrines of that party most successfully in the management of our domestic affairs. But now a new and untried scene was opened before him. Never were the embarrassments of any government in regard to foreign powers more intricate and perplexing; and, to increase his difficulties, he had to deal with the most powerful nations on earth, who, in their hostility to each other, paid no respect to the laws of nations or the rights of neutrality. The Constitution was ordained mainly for the purpose of regulating commerce, foreign and domestic, and establishing a common rule of action in our intercourse with other countries. While the States at home preserved their political existence, retained much of their original sovereignty, were distinct, variant, and even hostile in some of their domestic interests, to the world abroad they presented but one front. At home each pursued its own policy, developed its own internal resources, and was unconscious of the existence of a common government, save in the negative blessing that it bestowed upon them of peace with each other and with the world. They literally fulfilled the spirit of their national motto, *E pluribus unum*—at home many, abroad one. It is obvious that peace must be an essential element in the successful operation of such a complicated system of government. War of whatever kind, especially an aggressive war, whether by land or sea, must destroy its equilibrium, and precipitate all its movements on the common centre, which, by an intense over-action, must finally absorb all countervailing influences. Mr. Jefferson was thoroughly penetrated with the true spirit of our Constitution; so was John Randolph. These profound statesmen thought alike on that subject: they differed as to certain measures of policy, but not at all in their principles. They both sought the peace of the country, not only as the best condition for developing its resources, but as an essential means for preserving the purity of its institutions. Neither could look with complacency on a standing army or a large naval establishment. They did not even consider them as essential in the present emergency, more imminent, perhaps, than any that could possibly occur at a future period.

Negotiation having failed, and both belligerents still continuing to plunder our commerce, Mr. Jefferson recommended, as the only remedy, a total abandonment of the ocean. Mr. Randolph's advice was to arm the merchant marine, and let them go forth and defend *themselves in the* highways of a lawful commerce. As the means of home defence, Jefferson recommended the construction and equipment of gunboats, in numbers sufficient to protect the harbors and seaports from sudden invasion. Randolph advised to arm the militia, put a weapon in the hands of every yeoman of the land, and furnish the towns and seaports with a heavy train of artillery for their defence.

In all this we perceive but one object—a defence of the natal soil (*natale solum*) by the people themselves, and a total abstinence from all aggression. "Pour out your blood," said these wise statesmen to the people; "pour out your blood in defence of your borders; but shed not a drop beyond." Happy for the country could this advice have always been followed! As Randolph foresaw and predicted, we came out of the war with Great Britain without a constitution; mainly to his exertions in after years are we indebted for its restoration. The late war with Mexico has engendered a spirit of aggression and of conquest among the people, and has taught the ambitious, aspiring men of the country, that military fame achieved in an hour is worth more than the solid reputation of a statesman acquired by long years of labor and self-sacrifice. Where these things are to end it does not require much sagacity to foresee. Let the people take warning in time, and give heed to the counsel of their wisest statesmen; let them dismiss their army and their navy, relieve the country of those burthensome and dangerous accompaniments of a military government, and trust to negotiation, justice, and their own energies and resources for defence. What was visionary and impracticable in the warlike days of Jefferson, is now wholly reasonable and proper. What gunboats could not do, steam vessels can fully accomplish. For defence there is no need of a navy; for aggressive war, we trust the day may never come when it shall be called into requisition.

There was one subject on which Randolph and Jefferson differed so essentially that it would seem to indicate a more radical divergency of principles than we are willing to admit existed between them. They both sincerely labored to preserve a strict neutrality between the great belligerents of Europe; but when driven to extremity, and forced to choose between the one and the other, Jefferson would have selected France as a friend, whilst Randolph would have chosen England. In the days of John Adams these predilections would have marked their political characters as being essentially different on all the great principles of government. But Randolph contended that since that day circumstances had greatly altered. France was then a free republic, fighting for the liberties of Europe, while England was in coalition with the old monarchies to destroy them. France was now a military despotism, grasping at the empire of the world, while England was the only barrier in the way of universal conquest. To suffer old partialities and prejudices to influence their conduct in such a state of affairs, he thought, was the height of folly and madness. He had no greater friendship for England and her institutions than before; but she had become essential for his own protection, and he was willing to use her for that purpose. These views seem not only to be plausible, but just. A practical statesman, at that time, looking at events as they transpired around him, and gazing on the rapid strides of Napoleon towards universal conquest, would have coincided with Mr. Randolph—have exclaimed with him that it was poor consolation to reflect that we were to be the last to be devoured, and have taken refuge behind the floating batteries of England as the last retreat to the expiring liberties of the world. But Thomas Jefferson did not view the subject in this practical way: he was the profound philosopher that looked at political causes and consequences in their radical and essential relations to each other, and the bold pioneer that dared to sacrifice what seemed to be the present interest to the future and more permanent welfare of his country.

In his judgment the great causes that produced the marvellous events then daily transpiring on the theatre of Europe, had not changed; it was still the spirit of democracy contending against the old feudal aristocracy, which had so long oppressed and enslaved the nations. The crusade of Bonaparte, aside from his own personal ambition, had no other end but the overthrow of those rotten dynasties that sat like a leaden weight on the hearts of the people; and a revival of those old memories of privileges and franchises that lay buried and forgotten beneath the rubbish and worthless trivialities of a profligate court and a heartless monarchy.

To repress the numerous factions that were tearing her vitals within, and to beat back the myrmidons of power that assailed her from without, it was necessary that France should concentrate all her energies in the hands of a military despot. The times called for a dictator. But Napoleon himself was a phenomenon that must soon pass away; his long existence was incompatible with the just order of things; his downfall must be followed by a restoration of the Bourbons, or by a revival of the Republic, chastened and purified by the ordeal through which she had passed. Bonaparte saw to the root of the matter when he said, that in a few years Europe must be Republican or Cossack. Jefferson perceived and acted on this profound principle long before Bonaparte gave utterance to it. He knew well that England was the same now that she was in the days of the coalition; her allies were gone, because the arms of France and the insurrection of their own subjects had overturned their power; the *French evil* had spread over Europe, and her battle was still against that; the right of the people to pull down and to build up dynasties—the doctrine that governments belong to the people and not the people to governments, and that they can alter or abolish them at pleasure, were principles that she fought against and labored to repress and to destroy. Had she succeeded in overturning the power of Napoleon, she would have forced on the nations of Europe, by virtue of her cherished doctrine of legitimacy, the worst of all governments—a restoration of the old monarchies claiming to rule, not by the will of the people, but by the divine right of kings. It was not in the nature of Thomas Jefferson to aid in the remotest degree in the accomplishment of such an end. Besides all this, he knew there was no sympathy between the democracy of America and the aristocracy of England; the one was progressive, the other conservative;

the one readily embraced every measure that tended to elevate and to improve the masses of mankind, the other repressed every proposition that contemplated a change in the present order of things; the one held that government must spring from the will of the people, and is but an agent in the hands of their representatives for the good of the whole; the other that all wealth and power belong to the few, and government but an instrument to preserve and perpetuate their authority. Any coalition or union between elements so repugnant would have produced evil rather than good; it would have shed a malign influence on the one hand, while on the other the contact would have been regarded as a vile contamination. Jefferson was the embodiment of American democracy; the masses of the people felt that he gave form and expression to the great sentiments that lay confused and voiceless in their own bosoms, and they knew that he would be faithful in following the impulses of that mighty concentration of a people's will in his own person: hence his influence over the public mind—his almost despotic sway over the legislation of the country. In 1806, a subservient legislature, in obedience to his secret wishes, voted him money without restriction to negotiate with Spain and France, when his public messages declared that negotiation was at an end, and breathed the strongest spirit of resistance. In 1807 his commissioners, his favorite negotiator, Monroe, being one of them, had made a treaty with England, as favorable as could be expected at that time, but he put it in his pocket and refused to submit it to the consideration of that branch of the government which had a right and might have advised its ratification. When Great Britain sent a special envoy to make reparation for the unauthorized attack on the Chesapeake, he stood on an untenable point of etiquette, refused to receive or even to hear any propositions on that subject, and suffered the public mind to be inflamed by an unnecessary delay of adjustment. Before he had any official information of the orders in council, issued in retaliation to the Berlin decree, on the mere authority of newspaper reports, he sent a secret message to Congress advising an embargo: in silence and in haste his will was obeyed—a sudden pause was given to business—at his command the people stood still, and let fall from their hands the implements of trade and the means of their subsistence. This measure, whether so intended or not, coincided with the views of Napoleon: while it could affect

France but slightly, it formed an essential part of that great continental system that had for its object the subjugation of England by a destruction of her commerce and manufactures.

Bonaparte approved, and the indomitable Saxon spirit of England refused to yield: the dire recoil was most severely felt at home, but the patriotism of the people increased with the disasters inflicted upon them; and they continued to follow their bold leader with a fortitude and intrepidity that would have persevered to the bitter end, had he not said, enough! and acquiesced in the repeal of his favorite measure. Jefferson stood to the people of America as Napoleon to the people of France—he embodied the will of a free and enlightened republic, devoted to the arts of peace, and governed by laws and a written constitution; Napoleon was the dread symbol of a wild democracy, sprung from the bosom of a volcano, chaotic in all its fiery elements, and armed with firebrands to burn up the dross and stubble of the worn-out and rotten monarchies that surrounded it; both were invincible, so long as they continued to stand in the focus, and to reflect the mighty energies that were concentrated in their own person.

We say, then, that the policy of Jefferson, viewed by a practical statesman, would seem to be unwise. It inflicted many evils on the country at the time, and entailed a lasting injury on the planting interests of the South: but it saved the principles of democracy; and it saved the country, if not from an actual participation in the Congress of Vienna, it saved them from a humiliating acquiescence in the holy alliance of despots, confederated under a solemn oath to smother and extinguish every sentiment of liberty that might dare to breathe its existence in the bosoms of their oppressed and degraded subjects.

CHAPTER XXXV.

JAMES MADISON—PRESIDENTIAL ELECTION.

Mr. Randolph was opposed to the elevation of James Madison to the presidency. His objections extended back to an early period in the political history of that gentleman. As we have said, the country is indebted to the efforts of Mr. Madison for their present Constitution. His great labors and untiring zeal, both in the Federal convention that framed it, and the Virginia convention that ratified it, overcame every obstacle, and finally presented to the people a form of government to strengthen and consolidate their union. But the happy blending of national and federal features in the constitution, whereby the States have preserved their independence, and much of their sovereignty, was not the conception of Mr. Madison. He thought the States ought not to be entirely obliterated; but until the plan of George Mason was developed, he did not understand how their existence could be made compatible with a common central government, operating alike on all the people. He did not cordially acquiesce in the States-rights doctrine ingrafted on the Constitution. In all the debates in both conventions, he is generally found opposed to the views of Mr. Mason. And it was charged against him, that in the essays which he wrote, in conjunction with Jay and Hamilton, with the view of recommending the Constitution to the people, he advocated, with as much earnestness as those avowed centralists, a strong consolidated government. When party excitement grew very violent, in the times of the whisky insurrection, and of Jay's treaty, when Randolph was driven, in disgrace, from the Cabinet, and Monroe recalled, under sentiments of strong displeasure, Mr. Madison was charged with having abandoned his post on the floor of Congress, and seeking ease and personal safety in retirement. In the Virginia legislature it was said he opposed the general ticket system, which was adopted with the view of casting the whole vote of the State in favor of Mr. Jefferson, at the approaching election, and without which he would have been defeated. But the weightiest charge of all was that preferred by John Randolph, on the floor of Congress. The reader is already familiar with that subject. Randolph declared that the Secretary of State, in a conversation with him, expressed his willingness to buy peace with Spain, by paying tribute to France; and he averred that, on the expression of such pusillanimous sentiments, his confidence, which at no time was very great, had entirely vanished. Mr. Madison, it was also said, was a mere closet philosopher—an able logician, but a weak and timid statesman. The times required a man of nerve and energy. James Monroe was held up by his friends, as combining, more than any other man, all the qualities needed for the present exigency. A number of the republican members of Congress met together in caucus, and nominated Mr. Madison for the presidency. John Randolph and some sixteen or seventeen others, denounced this nomination, and protested against the right of members of Congress to make it. They said that such a plan had been resorted to on a former occasion, in order to concentrate the votes of the republican party on one candidate, to prevent their defeat by the federalists; but there was no necessity for that concert of action now; the federalists, as a party, had been annihilated, had no intention of bringing out a candidate; and that whoever was elected must be a republican. They contended, therefore, that each should have a fair field, and that no advantage should be given to either by a resort to party machinery. Shortly after this, Mr. Monroe was nominated by a convention in Virginia, called together from the different counties of the State. Thus we see two candidates from the same state, for the highest office within the gift of the people; both professed the same political principles, each had high claims to the confidence and support of their country, and each was put forward and sustained by a fraction of the same party. We may well imagine the heart-burnings and the angry feelings excited by such a contest. The ablest men in the State employed their talents in writing for the newspapers. Their essays, for the most part, were elaborate, well written, and not unfrequently filled with wit, ridicule, irony, and the bitterest sarcasm, and too frequently did they descend to the most direct and pointed personalities. Mr. Madison was the candidate of the administration—Monroe of the *Tirtium Quids*, as they were called. John Randolph was the master-spirit of this third party. He of course came in for his full share of abuse. Even ridicule and doggerel rhyme were resorted to as the means of bringing his name into disrepute.

"Thou art a pretty little speaker, John—
Though some there are who think you've spoke too long;
And even call, sweet sir, your tongue a bell,
That ding-dong, dong-ding, tolls away!
Yet mind not what such 'ragamuffins' say,
Roar still 'gainst 'back-stairs influence,' I pray,
And lash 'the pages of the water-closet' well;
To 'dust and ashes' pray thee grind 'em,
Though I'm told 'twould puzzle you to find 'em.

"But John, like water, thou must find thy 'level,'
Those horn-book politicians are the devil,
Some how or other they've so pleased the nation;
For spite of 'cobweb theories' and 'sharks,'
Russels, Garnetts, Clays and Clarks,
'Strait-jackets,' 'water gruel,' and 'depletion,'
Yes, yes, in spite of all those *curious things*,
The name of each with glory around us rings,
Whilst *thou* of even patriotism doubted,
Art on all hands detested—laughed at—'scouted,'
Nay, many think (though this perhaps is scandal,)
That soon you'll nothing be but plain Jack R——dal."

Many a volley was aimed at his head, and many a valiant pen was wielded in his defence. He sometimes descended into the lists himself, and under a borrowed name hurled his polished and effective shafts against the exposed and vulnerable points of his adversaries. Many of the most distingushed men of the State were on his side of the question; indeed, it may be said that most of the young men of talents and independence of character were his admirers and followers. But it soon became manifest that Mr. Monroe would get no support out of the State of Virginia, and that the contest would be between Mr. Madison and DeWitt Clinton, of New-York. Many of the best friends of Mr. Monroe were unwilling to contribute to the election of Clinton, by a loss of the State of Virginia to his opponent; they therefore determined, however reluctantly, to cast their votes for Mr. Madison; so that when the election came on, the vote for Monroe was very thin. It would seem that the Tirtium Quids, with all their genius, eloquence, and fine writing, had made no impression on the people. We can well conceive how this exposure of their weakness operated on the nerves of those politicians who love always to be found on the side of the majority. One by one they began to recant their heresies, and to fall into the ranks of the administration. Mr. Monroe became a candidate for the legislature in the county of Albemarle: he was interrogated on the subject, and professed himself friendly to the new dynasty; was elected; appointed Governor of the State; and in due time was placed by Mr. Madison in his Cabinet.

Very soon Randolph was left with only a few personal and devoted friends to stand by him. Those who valued consistency more than office, and who regarded it as an act of dishonor to abandon a friend in his hour of need, still adhered to him; but the majority of politicians, who look only to the loaves and fishes, had no hesitation in making their escape from what they conceived to be a falling house. This "ratting," as he called it, Mr. Randolph never forgot nor forgave. His pride was cut to the quick; his disgust was unbounded; and to the events of this period may be traced much of that bitterness of feeling which he manifested towards certain individuals in after life. Never did he suffer an occasion to pass that he did not make them feel, by some cutting allusion, his deep indignation. This seemed to the world a wanton indulgence of a vile, cruel, and sarcastic temper: but the parties themselves understood and keenly felt the meaning of his allusions; and well did they repay his disgust and contempt, by a most cordial hatred.

"Why have you not gone to Philadelphia?" says one of his flatterers, writing to him about this time—"every one there whose attention could confer either pleasure or honor was prepared for your reception. The learning, the genius, and the eloquence of the city, with all its train of social manners, wit, beauty, gayety and innocence, were prepared to spread for you a rich and varied feast of enjoyment. You have ceased to be the head of a great triumphant party, but, rely upon it, you are at the head of the taste, feeling and honor of the nation."

Yet this man in a few years glided into the ranks of the administration—became the secret reviler of one on whom he had bestowed the grossest adulation: and finally supported all the Federal measures of Monroe and John Quincy Adams; bank, tariff, internal improvements, and whatever else that tended to produce a strong, magnificent, corrupt, and consolidated government. It is not surprising that a man of Mr. Randolph's temper, exasperated as it had been by so many instances of the same kind, could not look with complacency on such characters; but he visited as a crime on the head of the offender that which he should have forgiven as a weakness of our common nature. He understood mankind too well not to have known the certain consequences of defeat; the abdicating Emperor at Fontainebleau, when abandoned by all those whom he had made marshals and princes, might have told him that misfortune is like a nipping frost, that scatters the leaves and the blossoms, and leaves bare the naked limbs to battle alone with the rude blasts of winter.

The following extract taken from an unpublished essay, dated August 31, 1808, will throw much light on the excited and angry nature of the controversy carried on at that time between the followers of John Randolph and the adherents of Mr. Madison:

"I addressed you formerly with a view to the approaching presidential election; but before I could recover from the repulse which I met in my first attempt to approach the people, it was already too late. Every man had already chosen his part in that drama—many were already in imagination tricked out in the robes of office in which they were to assist at the installation of Mr. Madison; and, so far as it could depend upon the votes of Virginia, that election was already decided. The partisans of government have ceased to bestow their attention upon this subject, and have already turned it to another. I mean the election of a representative from the counties of Cumberland, &c. The stormy rage of the presidential contest has been no sooner hushed, than both the Argus and the Enquirer have, at once, turned their batteries against the gentleman who at present represents that district. Writers, scarcely worthy to be noticed, and whom it would be a disgrace to answer, have hastened to engage in the meritorious service of removing the only eye that watches over the administration. Looking forward to the election of Mr. Madison, they no doubt anticipate much from this attempting to destroy the man, before whom, in spite of all the pomp of office, he would be compelled to feel the intrinsic littleness of his character. Unworthy as their childish arguments and groundless assertions are of the poor respect of refutation and contradiction, they at least remind us of the proverbial truth, 'that straws show the course of the wind;' and if I mistake them not, it is not the only occasion on which they have displayed the properties of the weathercock. Though their arguments prove nothing, their attempts at argument prove much. They show the real offence of Mr. R., they show the real causes of the clamor which is raised against him. It is the usual fate of fools and knaves that the weapons which they pretend to wield, recoil upon their own heads. These men have endeavored to detract from the merit of Mr. R., but they have exposed their own weakness; they have evinced the irreconcileable malignity of themselves and their party towards him, at the same time that they have stated objections, which, if true and well founded, as they are false and groundless, would be utterly inadequate to the production of such an effect; and they compel us to believe that there is some other secret cause or motive for their antipathy to that gentleman, which is not revealed, only because it will not bear the light. Mr. R's constituents have been much at a loss to know wherefore the whole force of the government has been exerted to provide them a representative, some worthy associate of John Love and John Dawson. They feel indeed the importance of his past services, and they see in them some evidence of abilities not to be despised. They perceive also that he differs from the administration on some points. They are even told by the newspapers that he is opposed to them on all, but at the same time they are assured, that he stands alone in this opposition, without a party, even without personal friends, and that there is more to pity in his infatuation than to dread from this hostility. Why then all this struggle, this ceaseless anxiety? and (to use a quotation of your own Mr. Ritchie,) this 'ocean into tempest wrought to drown a fly?' Is the spirit of federalism then extinct; is that monster no more, that nothing remains but to turn the whole force of the administration to the destruction of such an insect, as they would represent Mr. Randolph? This surely is not the case. The federal representation of Connecticut yet remains entire. Its banners are yet displayed, and those who yesterday deserted, are, to-day, returning to them. The mighty State of Massachusetts, which of late the administration so proudly numbered among their supporters, has already repented of her conversion; while the Vermontese are newly baptized to the federal faith in the blood of their countrymen. Perhaps indeed they balance all this with the conversion of Mr. J. Q. Adams, and by the same political arithmetic, which teaches them that the downfall of Mr. Randolph is of more importance than the defeat of the federalists, they think the acquisition of this gentleman an ample compensation for the loss of two entire States. No doubt indeed they augur well from it, no doubt they regard it as an all-sufficient evidence of Mr. Adams's conviction of the stability of their power. Ten years ago they would have told you that this gentleman knew, as well as any one, who kept the key of the exchequer, and it would be strange indeed, if, when his father held it so long, he had not found out the value of the coin. They perhaps remember too, that about that time he was talked of as the contemplated successor to the crown of these realms, and they possibly regard his accession to their party as an implied relinquishment of his title, in favor of the hopeful progeny of our modern Livia. I would warn them, however, not to build too much upon that. They should rather infer from the example of Spain, that the minority of the imperial nephew of his majesty, the emperor and king, may be terminated by an invitation to Bayonne.

"But it cannot be that the administration, and the friends of the administration, think that there is less to be feared from the federal party than there was three years ago. How then does it happen that the necessity of putting down this great and growing evil is forgotten in the struggle to remove that gentleman from the confidence of his constituents? They tell us indeed, themselves, that the republican cause has nothing to fear from Mr. R., and they say true, sir. They know that the republican cause has nothing to fear from him; but they feel at the same time, that the pretended supporters of that cause have every thing to fear from him. They see in him the only man on the floor of Congress who has the sagacity to detect and the spirit to expose their unconstitutional practices and their nefarious designs, and they wish his ruin, for the same reason that rogues wish the absence of the sun. How else can their conduct be explained? At a time when the shattered forces of the federalists are again assembling, when they are even enjoying a partial triumph, the Government are seen endeavoring to drive from their ranks the most distinguished and formidable adversary to that cause. No, sir; they love not the light, because their deeds are evil. And do those who urge this clamor against Mr. R. suppose that the people are blind to the real cause of it, that they form no judgment of the motives and characters of the men who seek his ruin, by the means they use for that purpose? No; they know that dirty tools are used for dirty work, and that he who employs them in that way cannot have clean hands. What can they think when they see his private letters betrayed, and his unguarded moments of gayety and conviviality watched and exposed? Shall they be told that these are private occurrences? No, sir. Mr. G. will not do even an act of treachery for nothing.

Indeed, some of the partisans of Mr. Madison have not scrupled to declare, that they consider his election as of little more importance than the defeat of Mr. R. Can the people be at a loss to understand wherefore? As long as the views of Mr. Madison are constitutional, and his conduct honorable, he can have nothing to fear from Mr. R. In questions of mere policy, the weight of Executive patronage will always preponderate, and, in questions of right, always powerful, becomes invincible when supported by the name and authority of a President. It is not until he transcends the limits of the Constitution that any opposition can be formidable. If such be their projected course—if the system of standing armies and navies, of treason bills and habeas corpus acts, of unauthorized expenditures, and splendid impunity to favored traitors and felons, with the practice of buying peace, and giving to the President the powers of Congress—are still to be persisted in, let them beware of Mr. R. Already has he declaimed against these practices, and he has not been heard; but they know that the slumbers of the people are not to last for ever, and they look forward with the apprehensions of a sinner, trembling in the midst of his guilt, to the day when the vengeance of a deluded nation shall be roused; and at the sound of his voice, as at that of the last trump, they shall call upon the mountains to cover them. I have no doubt that those who made this avowal have somewhat transcended their orders. Their instinctive sagacity leads them to the game which their master is in pursuit of; but in the eagerness of their zeal, they have flushed it too soon. They are at this moment trembling in the expectation of being corrected for the blunder; but they are not so true spaniels as I take them to be, if they will not consent to have their ears pulled for the mistake, provided they be fed for their activity."

CHAPTER XXXVI.

WAR WITH ENGLAND.

The great event of Mr. Madison's administration was the war with England. For a long time, the grounds of complaint against that Government were, the carrying trade and the impressment of seamen. Since 1806, another and more serious difficulty, if possible, had been thrown in the way of an amicable arrangement between the two countries. By the Berlin decree and its supplements, France interdicted all trade between the United States and Great Britain and her dependencies. By her orders in council, professing to be in retaliation of the Berlin decree, Great Britain interdicted all trade between the United States and France, and her allies and their dependencies, which embraced nearly all Europe and the civilized world. These edicts did not affect the carrying trade merely, which was of very doubtful justice, but they destroyed all commerce whatever.

By the British orders in council, American citizens were not allowed to carry the products of their own country, in their own ships, to a country hostile to England, and to bring back, in exchange, the commodities of that country, without first paying tribute in a British port, and obtaining license for that purpose. This extraordinary assumption of power was acknowledged to be contrary to the law of nations and the rights of neutrality; but it was justified on the ground of necessity. *Lex talionis* was the only plea. To bring about a sense of justice in the great belligerents, and a repeal of their unwarrantable edicts, the embargo law was enacted; but that proved to be a two-edged sword, more deeply wounding our own sides than those of the parties it was designed to effect. It was repealed, and a non-importation act, as to England and France, substituted in its place. This proving ineffectual, also, the olive branch was at length held out, with these words: "That if Great Britain or France (Act of May 1, 1810,) should cease to violate the neutral commerce of the United States, which fact the President should declare by proclamation, and the other should not, within three months thereafter, revoke or modify its edicts in like manner, that then certain sections in a former act, interdicting the commercial intercourse between the United States and Great Britain and France, and their dependencies, should, from and after the expiration of three months from the date of the proclamation, be revived, and have full force against the former, its colonies, and dependencies, and against all articles the growth, produce, or manufacture of the same." France acceded to this proposition. On the 5th of August, 1810, the minister of foreign affairs addressed a note to the minister plenipotentiary of the United States at Paris, informing him that the decrees of Berlin and Milan were revoked—the revocation to take effect on the first of November following; that the measure had been taken by his Government, in confidence that the British Government would revoke its orders, and renounce its new principles of blockade, or that the United States would cause their rights to be respected. The means by which the United States should cause their right to be respected, in case Great Britain should not revoke her edicts, it was understood, consisted merely in the enforcement of the non-importation act against that nation.

Great Britain declined to revoke her edicts; insisted that those of France had not been revoked, and complained that the United States had done injustice, by carring into effect the non-importation act against her.

Great Britain contended that, in the French decrees, it was expressly avowed, that the principles on which they were founded, and the provisions contained in them, were wholly new, unprecedented, and in direct contradiction to all ideas of justice, and the principles and usages of civilized nations. The French Government did not pretend to say that any one of the regulations contained in those decrees was a regulation which France had ever been in the previous practice of. They were, consequently, to be considered, and were indeed allowed by France herself to be, all of them, parts of a new system of warfare, unauthorized by the established law of nations. It was in this light in which France herself had placed her decrees, that Great Britain was obliged to consider them.

The submission of neutrals to any regulation made by France, authorized by the law of nations, and practised in former wars, would never be complained of by Great Britain; but the regulations of the Berlin and Milan decrees did, and were declared to violate the laws of nations and the rights of neutrals, for the purpose of attacking, through them, the resources of Great Britain. The ruler of France had drawn no distinction between any of them, nor had he declared the cessation of any one of them.

Not until the French decrees, therefore, it was contended by the British minister, shall be effectually repealed, and thereby neutral commerce be restored to the situation in which it stood previously to their promulgation, can his royal highness conceive himself justified, consistently with what he owes to the safety and honor of Great

Britain, in foregoing the just measures of retaliation which his majesty, in his defence, was necessitated to adopt against them.

The Berlin and Milan decrees prohibited every thing that was the manufacture or product of Great Britain from being imported to the Continent, under any pretence whatever, whether owned by British subjects, or owned and transported by neutrals. This latter part of the decrees was in violation of the rights of neutrality. They also, at the same time, prohibited all trade, on the part of neutrals, with the British dominions. This portion was now repealed, so far as it affected the United States. They were allowed to trade with Great Britain and her dependencies, but were not permitted to carry to the Continent any goods that were the manufacture or produce of Great Britain, though they might have been purchased, and were actually owned by American citizens. Great Britain insisted that she could not repeal her orders in council, so long as the United States suffered this infraction of their rights of neutrality. On the other hand, it was contended that Great Britain had pledged herself to repeal the orders in council whenever the decrees were revoked. The decrees, it was said, were now revoked as it regarded the United States; but Britain, in violation of her pledge, persisted in refusing to repeal her orders. The whole question, then, was narrowed down to this: Had the Berlin and Milan decrees been revoked, in the sense it was understood by the parties, at the time of the pledge? Great Britain said they had not. The United States said they had been revoked, according to the understanding.

In this attitude matters stood, when Congress, on the 4th of November, 1811, was called together by proclamation of the President. "At the close of the last session of Congress," says the message, "it was hoped that the successive confirmations of the extinction of the French decrees, so far as they violated our neutral commerce, would have induced the government of Great Britain to repeal its orders in council, and thereby authorize the removal of the existing obstructions to her commerce with the United States. Instead of this reasonable step towards satisfaction and friendship between the two nations, the orders were, at a moment when least to have been expected, put into more rigorous execution; and it was communicated, through the British envoy just arrived, that whilst the revocation of the edicts of France, as officially made known to the British Government, was denied to have taken place, it was an indispensable condition of the repeal of the British orders that commerce should be restored to a footing that would admit the manufactures and productions of Great Britain, when owned by neutrals, into markets shut against them by her enemy—the United States being given to understand that, in the mean time, a continuation of the non-importation act would lead to measures of retaliation. * * * * * *

"With the evidence of hostile inflexibility, in trampling on our rights, which no independent nation can reliquish, Congress will feel the duty of putting the United States into an armor and an attitude demanded by the crisis, and corresponding with the national spirit and expectations."

The subject was referred to a committee, who, in a report, reviewed the grounds of complaint, and concluded with offering a series of resolutions, the object of which was, to put the United States immediately "into an armor and attitude demanded by the crisis." The friends of the administration admitted that they urged the resolutions as an immediate preparation for war. That war was inevitable, and would be declared so soon as the nation was put into a posture of defence. It was also said in debate that one of the objects, and a necessary result of the war, would be the conquest of Canada.

On the 10th day of December, Mr. Randolph made one of his most powerful and eloquent speeches in opposition to these war measures. As the speech is to be found in most of the collections of American eloquence that have been published from time to time, we must content ourselves with an extract here and there, barely sufficient to explain in his own words the grounds of opposition.

"It is a question," said Mr. Randolph, "as it has been presented to the House, of *peace* or *war*. In that light it has been regarded; in no other light can I consider it, after declarations made by members of the Committee of Foreign Relations. Without intending any disrespect to the chair, I must be permitted to say, that if the decision yesterday was correct, 'that it was not in order to advance any arguments against the resolution, drawn from topics before other committees of the House,' the whole debate—nay, the report itself on which we are acting—is disorderly, since the increase of the military force is a subject at this time in agitation by the select committee raised on that branch of the President's message. But it is impossible that the discussion of a question, broad as the wide ocean, of our foreign concerns, involving every consideration of interest, of right, of happiness, and of safety at home; touching in every point all that is dear to freemen—'their lives, their fortunes, and their sacred honor;' can be tied down by the narrow rules of technical routine. The Committee of Foreign Relations has indeed decided that the subject of arming the militia (which I pressed upon them as indispensable to the public safety) does not come within the scope of their authority. On what ground, I have been, and still am, unable to see. They have felt themselves authorized (when the subject was before another committee) to recommend the raising of standing armies, with a view (as has been declared) of immediate war—a war not of defence, but of conquest, of aggrandizement, of ambition—a war foreign to the interests of this country, to the interests of humanity itself.

"I know not how gentlemen calling themselves republicans can advocate such a war. What was their doctrine in 1798–9, when the command of the army, that highest of all possible trusts in any government, be the form what it may, was reposed in the bosom of the Father of his country! the sanctuary of a nation's love!—the only hope that never came in vain? When other worthies of the revolution, Hamilton, Pinckney, and the younger Washington, men of tried patriotism, of approved conduct and valor, of untarnished honor, held subordinate command under him? Republicans were then unwilling to trust a standing army even to his hands, who had given proof that he was above all human temptation. Where now is the revolutionary hero to whom you are about to confide this sacred trust? To whom will you confide the charge of leading the flower of your youth to the heights of Abraham? Will you find him in the person of an acquitted felon? What! *Then* you were unwilling to vote an army, when such men as have been named held high command! When Washington himself was at the head, did you *then* show such reluctance, feel such scruple? And are you now nothing loth, fearless of every consequence? Will you say that your provocations were less then than now, when your direct commerce was interdicted, your ambassadors hooted with derision from the French court, tribute demanded, actual war waged upon you? Those who opposed the army then were indeed denounced as the partisans of France, as the same men—some of them at least—are now held up as the advocates of England; those firm and undeviating republicans, who then dared, and now dare, to cling to the ark of the Constitution, to defend it even at the expense of their fame, rather than surrender themselves to the wild projects of mad ambition. There is a fatality, sir, attending plenitude of power. Soon or late some mania seizes upon its possessors; they fall from the dizzy height, through the giddiness of their own heads. Like a vast estate, heaped up by the labor and industry of one man, which seldom survives the third generation. Power gained by patient assiduity, by a faithful and regular discharge of its attendant duties, soon gets above its own origin. Intoxicated with their own greatness, the federal party fell. Will not the same causes produce the same effects now as then? Sir, you may raise this army, you may build up this vast structure of patronage, this mighty apparatus of favoritism; but 'lay not the flattering unction to your souls,' you will never live to enjoy the succession: you sign your political death warrant. * * * *

"This war of conquest, a war for the acquisition of territory and subjects, is to be a new commentary on the doctrine that republics are destitute of ambition; they are addicted to peace, wedded to the happiness and safety of the great body of their people. But it seems this is to be a holiday campaign; there is to be no expense of blood or treasure on our part; Canada is to conquer herself; she is to be subdued by the principles of fraternity. The people of that country are first to be seduced from their allegiance, and converted into traitors, as preparatory to the making them good citizens. Although I must acknowledge that some of our flaming patriots were thus manufactured, I do not think the process would hold good with a whole community. It is a dangerous experiment. We are to succeed in the French mode—by the system of fraternization. All is French! But how dreadfully it might be retorted on the southern and western slaveholding States. I detest this subornation of treason. No: if we must have them, let them fall by the valor of our arms; by fair, legitimate conquest; not become the victims of treacherous seduction.

"I am not surprised at the war-spirit which is manifesting itself in gentlemen from the South. In the year 1805–6, in a struggle for the carrying trade of belligerent colonial produce, this country was most unwisely brought into collision with the great powers of Europe.

By a series of most impolitic and ruinous measures, utterly incomprehensible to every rational, sober-minded man, the Southern planters, by their own votes, succeeded in knocking down the price of cotton to seven cents, and of tobacco (a few choice crops excepted) to nothing, and in raising the price of blankets (of which a few would not be amiss in a Canadian campaign), coarse woollens, and every article of first necessity, three or four hundred per cent. And now that by our own acts we have brought ourselves into this unprecedented condition, we must get out of it in any way but by an acknowledgment of our own want of wisdom and forecast. But is war the true remedy? Who will profit by it? Speculators; a few lucky merchants, who draw prizes in the lottery; commissaries and contractors. Who must suffer by it? The people. It is their blood, their taxes, that must flow to support it.

"But gentlemen avowed that they would not go to war for the carrying trade; that is, for any other but the direct export and import trade—that which carries our native products abroad, and brings back the return cargo; and yet they stickle for our commercial rights, and will go to war for them! I wish to know, in point of principle, what difference gentlemen can point out between the abandonment of this or of that maritime right? Do gentlemen assume the lofty port and tone of chivalrous redressers of maritime wrongs, and declare their readiness to surrender every other maritime right, provided they may remain unmolested in the exercise of the humble privilege of carrying their own produce abroad, and bringing back a return cargo? Do you make this declaration to the enemy at the outset? Do you state the minimum with which you will be contented, and put it in her power to close with your proposals at her option? give her the basis of a treaty ruinous and disgraceful beyond example and expression? and this too after having turned up your noses in disdain at the treaties of Mr. Jay and Mr. Monroe? Will you say to England, '*End the war when you please; give us the direct trade in our own produce, we are content?*' But what will the merchants of Salem, and Boston, and New York, and Philadelphia, and Baltimore—the men of Marblehead and Cape Cod, say to this? Will they join in a war professing to have for its object what they would consider, and justly too, as the sacrifice of their maritime rights, yet affecting to be a war for the *protection of commerce?*

"I am gratified to find gentlemen acknowledging the demoralizing and destructive consequences of the non-importation law; confessing the truth of all that its opponents foretold when enacted; and will you plunge yourselves in war, because you have passed a foolish and ruinous law, and are ashamed to repeal it? 'But our good friend, the French Emperor, stands in the way of its repeal,' and, as we cannot go too far in making sacrifices to him, who has given such demonstration of his *love for the Americans*, we must, in point of fact, become parties to this war. 'Who can be so cruel as to refuse him this favor?' My imagination shrinks from the miseries of such connection. I call upon the House to reflect whether they are not about to abandon all reclamation for the unparalleled outrages, 'insults and injuries' of the French Government; to give up our claim for plundered millions, and ask what reparation or atonement we can expect to obtain in hours of future dalliance, after we shall have made a tender of our persons to this great deflowerer of the virginity of republics. We have, by our own wise (I will not say *wise-acre*) measures, so increased the trade of Montreal and Quebec, that at last we begin to cast a wistful eye at Canada. Having done so much towards its improvement, by the exercise of our 'restrictive energies,' we begin to think the laborer is worthy of his hire, and to put in claim for our portion. Suppose it ours, are we any nearer our point? As his minister said to the King of Epirus, 'May we not as well take our bottle of wine before as after this exploit?' Go! march to Canada! Leave the broad bosom of the Chesapeake, and her hundred tributary rivers, the whole line of sea-coast, from Machias to St. Mary's, unprotected: you have taken Quebec—have you *conquered England?* Will you seek for the deep foundations of her power in the frozen deserts of Labrador?

'Her march is on the mountain wave,
Her home is on the deep!'

Will you call upon her to leave your ports and harbors untouched, only just till you can return from Canada to defend them? The coast is to be left defenceless, whilst men of the interior are revelling in conquest and spoil. But grant for a moment, for mere argument's sake, that in Canada you touched the sinews of her strength, instead of removing a clog upon her resources—an incumbrance, but one, which, from a spirit of honor, she will vigorously defend. In what situation would you then place some of the best men of the nation? As Chatham and Burke, and the whole band of her patriots prayed for her defeat in 1776, so must some of the truest friends of the country deprecate the success of our arms against the only power that holds in check the arch enemy of mankind.

"Our people will not submit to be taxed for this war of conquest and dominion. The government of the United States was not calculated to wage *offensive foreign war;* it was instituted for the common defence and general welfare; and whosoever will embark it in a war of offence, will put it to a test which it is by no means calculated to endure. Make it out that Great Britain did instigate the Indians on a late occasion, and I am ready for battle, but not for dominion. I am unwilling, however, under present circumstances, to take Canada at the risk of the Constitution; to embark in a common cause with France, and be dragged at the wheels of the car of some Burr or Bonaparte. For a gentleman from Tennessee, or Genesee, or lake Champlain, there may be some prospect of advantage. Their hemp would bear a great price by the exclusion of foreign supply. In that, too, the great importers were deeply interested. The upper country on the Hudson and the lakes, would be enriched by the supplies for the troops, which they alone could furnish. They would have the exclusive market; to say nothing of the increased preponderance from the acquisition of Canada, and that section of the Union, which the southern and western States had already felt so severely in the apportionment bill."

Mr. Randolph dwelt on the danger arising from the black population. He said he would touch this subject as tenderly as possible; it was with reluctance that he touched it at all; but in cases of great emergency the state physician must not be deterred by a sickly, hysterical humanity, from probing the wound of his patient; he must not be withheld by a fastidious and mistaken humanity from representing his true situation to his friends, or even to the sick man himself, where the occasion called for it. "What, sir, is the situation of the slaveholding States? During the war of the Revolution, so fixed were their habits of subordination, that while the whole country was overrun by the enemy, who invited them to désert, no fear was ever entertained of an insurrection of the slaves. During a war of seven years, with our country in possession of the enemy, no such danger was ever apprehended. But should we therefore be unobservant spectators of the progress of society within the last twenty years? of the silent but powerful change wrought by time and chance upon its composition and temper? When the fountains of the great deep of abomination were broken up, even the poor slaves escaped not the general deluge. The French revolution polluted even them. Nay, there were not wanting men in that House—witness their legislative *Legendre*, the butcher who once held a seat there—to preach upon that floor, these imprescriptable rights to a crowded audience of blacks in the galleries; teaching them that they are equal to their masters; in other words, advising them to cut their throats. Similar doctrines are disseminated by pedlars from New England, and elsewhere, throughout the Southern country; and masters have been found so infatuated, as by their lives and conversation, by a general contempt of order, morality and religion, unthinkingly to cherish those seeds of self-destruction to them and their families. What is the consequence? Within the last ten years, repeated alarms of insurrection among the slaves; some of them awful indeed. From the spreading of this infernal doctrine, the whole Southern country has been thrown into a state of insecurity. Men dead to the operation of moral causes, have taken away from the poor slave his habits of loyalty and obedience to his master, which lightened his servitude by a double operation—beguiling his own cares, and disarming his master's suspicions and severity; and now, like true empirics in politics, you are called upon to trust to the mere physical strength of the fetter which holds him in bondage. You have deprived him of all moral restraint; you have tempted him to eat of the tree of knowledge, just enough to perfect him in wickedness; you have opened his eyes to his nakedness; you have armed his nature against the hand that has fed, that has clothed him, that has cherished him in sickness; that hand which, before he became a pupil of your school, he had been accustomed to press with respectful affection. You have done all this, and then, show him the gibbet and the wheel, as incentives to a sullen, repugnant obedience. God forbid, sir, that the southern States should ever see an enemy on their shores, with these infernal principles of French fraternity in the van. While talking of taking Canada, some of us are shuddering for our own safety at home. I speak from facts when I say, that the night-bell never tolls for fire in Richmond, that the mother does not hug the infant more closely to her bosom. I have been a witness of some of the alarms in the capital of Virginia."

Mr. Randolph then proceeded to notice the unjust and illiberal imputation of *British attachments*, against certain characters in this country; sometimes insinuated in the House, but openly avowed out of it. "Against whom are these charges brought? Against men who in the war of the Revolution were in the councils of the nation, or fighting the battles of your country. And *by whom* are they made? By *runaways*, chiefly *from the British dominions*, since the breaking out of the French troubles. It is insufferable! It cannot be borne! It must, and ought, with severity, to be put down in this House, and out of it, to meet the *lie direct*. We have no fellow-feeling for the suffering and oppressed Spaniards! Yet even *them* we do not reprobate. Strange! that we should have no objection to any other people or government, civilized or savage, in the whole world. The great autocrat of all the Russias receives the homage of our high consideration; the Dey of Algiers, and his divan of pirates, are very civil, good sort of people, with whom we find no difficulty in maintaining the relations of peace and amity; 'Turks, Jews, and Infidels;' *Melimelli*, or the *Little Turtle;* barbarians and savages, of every clime and color, are welcome to our arms; with chiefs of banditti, negro or mulatto, we can *treat* and can *trade*—name, however, but England, and all our antipathies are up in arms against her. Against whom? Against those whose blood runs in our own veins; in common with whom we can claim Shakspeare, and Newton, and Chatham for our countrymen; whose form of government is the freest on earth, our own only excepted; from whom every valuable principle of our own institutions has been borrowed—representation, jury trial, voting the supplies, writs of habeas corpus—our whole civil and criminal jurisprudence; against our *fellow-protestants*, identified in blood, in language, in religion with ourselves. In what school did the worthies of our land, the Washingtons, Henrys, Hancocks, Franklins, Rutleges, of America, learn those principles of civil liberty which were so nobly asserted by their wisdom and valor? And American resistance to British usurpation had not been more warmly cherished by these great men and their compatriots; not more by Washington,

Hancock, and Henry, than by Chatham, and his illustrious associates in the British Parliament. It ought to be remembered, too, that the *heart* of the *English people* was with us. It was a selfish and corrupt ministry, and their servile tools, to whom *we* were not more opposed than they were. I trust that none such may ever exist among us; for *tools* will never be wanted to subserve the purposes, however ruinous or wicked, of kings and ministers of state.

"But the outrages and injuries of England. Bred up in the principles of the Revolution, I can never palliate, much less defend them. I well remember flying with my mother, and her new-born child, from Arnold and Philips; and they had been driven by Tarleton, and other British pandours, from pillar to post, while her husband was fighting the battles of his country. The impression is indelible on my memory; and yet (like my worthy old neighbor, who added seven buckshot to every cartridge at the battle of Guilford, and drew a fine sight at his man) I must be content to be called a tory by a patriot of the last importation. Let us not get rid of one evil, supposing it possible, at the expense of a greater. Suppose France in possession of the British naval power—and to her the trident must pass should England be unable to wield it—what would be your condition? What would be the situation of your seaports and their seafaring inhabitants? Ask Hamburg, Lubec—ask *Savannah?* What! sir, when their privateers are pent up in our harbors by the British bull-dogs; when they receive at our hands every rite of hospitality, from which their enemy is excluded; when they capture within our waters, interdicted to British armed ships, American vessels; when such is their deportment toward you, under such circumstances, what could you expect if they were the uncontrolled lords of the ocean? Had those privateers at Savannah borne British commissions, or had your shipments of cotton, tobacco, ashes, and what not, to London and Liverpool been confiscated, and the proceeds poured into the English exchequer, my life upon it! you would never have listened to any miserable wire-drawn distinctions between 'orders and decrees affecting our neutral rights,' and 'municipal decrees,' confiscating in mass your whole property. You would have had instant war! The whole land would have blazed out in war.

"And shall republicans become the instruments of him who has effaced the title of Attila to the 'SCOURGE OF GOD!' Yet, even

Attila, in the falling fortunes of civilization, had, no doubt, his advocates, his tools, his minions, his parasites, in the very countries that he overran—sons of that soil whereon his horse had trod, where grass could never after grow. If perfectly fresh," Mr. Randolph said, "instead of being as I am—my memory clouded, my intellect stupefied, my strength and spirits exhausted—I could not give utterance to that strong detestation which I feel toward (above all other works of the creation) such characters as Zingis, Tamerlane, Kouli Khan, or Bonaparte. My instincts involuntarily revolt at their bare idea—malefactors of the human race, who ground down man to a mere machine of their impious and bloody ambition. Yet, under all the accumulated wrongs, and insults, and robberies of the last of these chieftains, are we not, in point of fact, about to become a party to his views, a partner in his wars?

"I beseech the House, before they run their heads against this post, Quebec, to count the cost. My word for it, Virginia planters will not be taxed to support such a war; a war which must aggravate their present distresses; in which they have not the remotest interest. Where is the Montgomery, or even the Arnold, or the Burr, who is to march to the Point Levi?

"I call upon those professing to be republicans, to make good the promises held out by their republican predecessors when they came into power; promises, which for years afterwards, they honestly, faithfully fulfilled. We vaunted of paying off the national debt, of retrenching useless establishments; and yet have now become as infatuated with standing armies, loans, taxes, navies and war, as ever were the Essex junto. What republicanism is this?"

Mr. Randolph resolutely and earnestly combated every measure that had a tendency to widen the breach between the United States and Great Britain, and to precipitate them into a war.

On the 1st of April, 1812, the President sent in a secret message, recommending an immediate embargo. The Committee of Foreign Relations, in anticipation of the message, had a bill already prepared: it was read the first and second time, reported to the Committee of the Whole, referred back to the House, and immediately put on its passage. Some member wished to know whether it was to be considered as a peace measure, or a precursor to war.

Mr. Grundy, a member of the committee, replied that he understood it as a war measure; and it is meant, said he, that it shall lead directly to it.

Mr. Clay (the Speaker) warmly expressed his satisfaction and full approbation of the message, and the proposition before the House.

Mr. Randolph then rose: "I am so impressed," said he, "with the importance of the subject and the solemnity of the occasion, that I cannot be silent. Sir, we are now in conclave; the eyes of the surrounding world are not upon us: we are shut up here from the light of heaven, but the eyes of God are upon us. He knows the spirit of our minds. Shall we deliberate upon this subject with the spirit of sobriety and candor, or with that spirit which has too often characterized our discussions upon occasions like the present? We ought to realize that we are in the presence of that God who knows our thoughts and motives, and to whom we must hereafter render an account for the deeds done in the body. I hope, sir, the spirit of party, and every improper passion, will be exorcised, that our hearts may be as pure and clean as fall to the lot of human nature.

"I am confident in the declaration, Mr. Chairman, that this is not a measure of the Executive; but that it is engendered by an extensive excitement upon the Executive— * * * *

"I will appeal to the sobriety and reflection of the House, and ask, what *new* cause of war for the last twelve months? What *new* cause of embargo within that period? The affair of the Chesapeake is settled.—No new principles of blockade interpolated into the laws of nations. I suppose every man of candor and sober reflection will ask why we did not go to war twelve months ago? Or will it be said we ought to make up, by our promptness now, for our slowness then? Or will it be said, that if the wheat for which we have received two dollars a bushel had been rotting in our barns, we should have been happier and richer. What would the planter say, if you were to ask him which he would prefer,—the honorable, chivalrous course advocated by the Speaker, with the consequences which must attend it, the sheriff at his back, and the excise collector pressing him? He would laugh in your face. It is not generally wise to dive into futurity; but it is wise to profit by experience, although it may be unpleasant. I feel much concerned to have the bill on the table for one hour."

But he was not allowed that privilege. The bill was immediately hurried through the forms of legislation, and became a law in a short time after the President's message that recommended it had been read.

On the 29th of May, 1812, having learned that a proposition would certainly be made in a few days to declare war, he rose and stated that he had a motion to make. He then commenced a speech, involving generally the present state of our relations with France and Great Britain. After he had spoken for some time, a question of order was raised, and it was decided by the Speaker that the gentleman ought, previous to debating so much at large, to submit his motion to the House.

"After some desultory debate, and decisions on points of order, Mr. Randolph submitted the following proposition: "*That under present circumstances, it is inexpedient to resort to a war with Great Britain.*"

The question being taken, that the House do now proceed to the consideration of the said resolution, it was by a large majority decided in the negative. By this most unparliamentary proceeding, as he thought, the subject was taken from before the House, and Mr. Randolph was deprived of an opportunity, if not denied the right, of addressing them on the momentous questions involved in his resolution. Next day he addressed the following letter to his constituents:

To the Freeholders of Charlotte, Prince Edward, Buckingham, and Cumberland.

Fellow-Citizens,—I dedicate to you the following fragment. That it appears in its present mutilated shape, is to be ascribed to the successful usurpation which has reduced the freedom of speech in one branch of the American Congress to an empty name. It is now established, *for the first time, and in the person of your representative*, that the House may and will refuse to hear a member in his place, or even to receive a motion from him, upon the most momentous subject that can be presented for legislative decision. A similar motion was brought forward by the republican minority in the year 1798, before these modern inventions for stifling the freedom of debate were discovered. It was discussed as a matter of *right*, until it was abandoned by the mover, in consequence of additional information (the correspondence of our envoy at Paris) laid before Congress by the President. In "the reign of terror," the father of the sedition law had not the hardihood to proscribe liberty of speech, much less the right of free debate on the floor of Congress. This invasion of the public liberties was reserved for self-styled republicans, who hold your understandings in such contempt, as to flatter themselves that you will overlook their every outrage upon the great first principles of free government, in consideration of their professions of tender regard for the privileges of the people. It is for you to decide whether they have undervalued your intelligence and spirit, or whether they have formed a just estimate of your character. You do not require to be told that the violation of the rights of him whom you have deputed to represent you is an invasion of the rights of every man of you, of every individual in society. If this abuse be suffered to pass unredressed—and the people alone are competent to apply the remedy—we must bid adieu to a free form of government for ever.

Having learned from various sources that a declaration of war would be attempted on Monday next, *with closed doors*, I deemed it my duty to endeavor, by an exercise of my constitutional functions, to arrest this heaviest of all calamities, and avert it from our happy country. I accordingly made the effort of which I now give you the result, and of the success of which you will have already been informed before these pages can reach you. I pretend only to give you the substance of my unfinished argument. The glowing words, the language of the heart, have passed away with the occasion that called them forth. They are no longer under my control. My design is simply to submit to you the views which have induced me to consider a war with England, under existing circumstances, as comporting neither with the *interest* nor the *honor* of the American people; but as an idolatrous sacrifice of both, on the altar of *French rapacity, perfidy and ambition.*

France has for years past offered us terms of undefined commercial arrangement, as the price of a war with England, which hitherto we have not wanted firmness and virtue to reject. That price is now to be paid. We are tired of holding out; and, following the example of continental Europe, entangled in the artifices, or awed by the power of the destroyer of mankind, we are prepared to become instrumental to his projects of universal dominion. *Before these pages meet your eye, the last republic of the earth will have enlisted under the banners of the tyrant and become a party to his cause.* The blood of the American freemen must flow to cement his power, to aid in stifling the last struggles of afflicted and persecuted man, to deliver up into his hands the patriots of Spain and Portugal, to establish his empire over the ocean and over the land that gave our fathers birth—to forge our own chains! And yet, my friends, we are told, as we were told in the days of Mr. Adams, "*the finger of heaven points to war.*" Yes, the finger of heaven *does* point to war! It points to war, as it points to the mansions of eternal misery and torture—as a flaming beacon warning us of that vortex which we may not approach but with certain destruction. It points to desolated Europe, and warns us of the chastisement of those nations who have offended against the justice, and almost beyond the mercy, of heaven. It announces the wrath to come upon those who, ungrateful for the bounty of Providence, not satisfied with the peace, liberty, security and plenty at home, fly, as it were, into the face of the Most High, and tempt his forbearance.

To you, *in this place*, I can speak with freedom; and it becomes me to do so; nor shall I be deterred by the cavils and the sneers of those who hold as "foolishness" all that savors not of worldly wisdom, from expressing fully and freely those sentiments which it has pleased God, in his mercy, to engrave on my heart.

These are no ordinary times; the state of the world is unexampled; the war of the present day is not like that of our revolution, or any which preceded it, at least in modern times. It is a war against the liberties and the happiness of mankind; it is a war in which the whole human race are the victims, to gratify the pride and lust of power of a single individual. I beseech you, put it to your own bosoms, how far it becomes you as freemen, as Christians, to give your aid and sanction to this impious and bloody war against your brethren of the human family. To such among you, if any such there be, who are insensible to motives not more dignified and manly than they are intrinsically wise, I would make a different appeal. I adjure you by the regard you have for your own safety and property, for the liberty and inheritance of your children—by all that you hold dear and sacred—to interpose your constitutional powers to save your country and yourselves from the calamity, the issue of which it is not given to human foresight to divine.

Ask yourselves if you are willing to become the virtual allies of Bonaparte? Are you willing, for the sake of annexing Canada to the Northern States, to submit to that overgrowing system of taxation which sends the European laborer supperless to bed, to maintain, by the sweat of your brow, armies at whose hands you are to receive a future master? Suppose Canada ours; is there any one among you who would ever be, in any respect, the better for it?—the richer, the freer, the happier, the more secure? And is it for a boon like this that you would join in the warfare against the liberties of man in the other hemisphere, and put your own in jeopardy? Or is it for the *nominal* privilege of a licensed trade with France that you would abandon your lucrative commerce with Great Britain, Spain and Portugal, and their Asiatic, African, and American dependencies; in a word, with every region of those vast continents?—that commerce which gives vent to your tobacco, grain, flour, cotton; in short, to all your native products, which are denied a market in France? There are not wanting men so weak as to suppose that their approbation of warlike measures is a proof of personal gallantry, and that opposition to them indicates a want of that spirit which becomes a friend of his country; as if it required more courage and patriotism to join in the acclamation of the day, than steadily to oppose one's self to the mad infatuation to which every people and all governments have, at some time or other, given way. Let the history of Phocion, of Agis, and of the De Witts, answer this question.

My friends, do you expect to find those who are now loudest in the clamor for war, foremost in the ranks of battle? Or, is the honor of this nation indissolubly connected with the political reputation of a few individuals, who tell you *they* have gone too far to recede, and that you must pay, with *your ruin*, the price of their *consistency?*

My friends, I have discharged my duty towards you, lamely and inadequately, I know, but to the best of my poor ability. The destiny of the American people is in their own hands. The net is spread for their destruction. You are enveloped in the toils of French duplicity, and if—which may Heaven in its mercy forbid—you and your posterity are to become hewers of wood and drawers of water to the modern Pharoah, it shall not be for the want of my best exertions to rescue you from the cruel and abject bondage. This sin, at least, shall not rest upon my soul.

John Randolph of Roanoke.

May 30th, 1812.

CHAPTER XXXVII.

CLAY—CALHOUN.

On the 18th of June, 1812, an act was approved by the President declaring that a state of war existed between the United States and Great Britain. It forms no part of the plan of this biography to enter into the details of the war. From them the student of history can derive but little information as to the causes of the growth, development and decay of nations. But there is an inquiry that might properly be made here, immediately bearing on this great subject, and deeply affecting the public conduct of John Randolph at the same time: *might not this war have been avoided?* might not the nation have saved the blood and treasure wasted in its prosecution, and escaped the evil consequences, both moral and political, that followed in its train? John Randolph declared that it might have been done; his whole opposition was based on the conviction that there was no need for such an extreme measure. "We can escape this conflict, said he, with honor—it is our duty to wait." No new cause of war had arisen—there would have been as much reason for the step in the June preceding as there was at the time of the declaration. The reader is already aware of the grounds of complaint against Great Britain; he must be satisfied also that there was at least some color of reason for the course which she declared she was compelled to pursue towards neutrals, in order to save her own existence in the general wreck of European nations.

As to the impressment of seamen, she only claimed the right to search for British subjects on board of American merchant vessels; yet it was one, arising from the common origin of the two nations, most difficult to be enforced, liable to be abused, and was greatly abused by proud and insolent naval officers. But because there was right and reason on both sides, this was not between rational people a subject of war, but of adjustment and compromise, and in truth it was adjusted to the satisfaction of Mr. Monroe and Mr. Pinckney in the treaty of December, 1806; but the President, as we know, put that treaty in his pocket, and refused to submit it to the consideration of the Senate.

As to the denial of our right to the *carrying trade*, and the question of *constructive blockade*, which had been so much discussed, and were charged as interpolations by Great Britain into the law of nations, they were now swallowed up by the orders in council. The reader is informed of the exact posture of that question on the 4th of November, 1811, when Congress was first assembled. It was narrowed down to this: Britain declared, that, notwithstanding the revocation of the French decrees so far as they affected the United States, she could not repeal her orders until the United States should procure a further modification so as to allow goods of British origin owned by American citizens to be carried to France and other parts of the continent. As the matter stood they were only restored to half their rights as a neutral power. By the law of nations, enemy's goods not contraband of war, purchased and owned by neutrals, are lawful subjects of trade; but there lay the rub; in the exercise or non-exercise of this right was involved the commercial jealousy and rivalry of the two nations. The United States did not want a restoration of their rights, because if British goods under cover of the American flag could be carried to the continent, it would at once open a vast and profitable outlet to the manufactures and other products of England, now locked up in their warehouses, and would cut off that monopoly enjoyed by the citizens of the United States in consequence of the prohibition laid on all articles of English origin. It was not then a question of principle, but one of pure commercial rivalry.

England urged on the United States that she should demand a restoration of all her rights as a neutral nation; the United States replied that they had been restored as far as they required, and insisted that England should comply with her pledges, and proceed *pari passu* with France in the repeal of her orders in council. The true motives for the persistence of both in their demands, were very perceptible, but by neither were avowed. Here then was the whole question, and on this issue the Congress of the United States resolved to go to war.

But in the position assumed by the British ministry, which was certainly plausible, if not just, they were not sustained by the nation. The clamors of the commercial and manufacturing interests were heard in Parliament and by the Royal cabinet. There was a powerful and influential party, with Canning at their head that demanded a repeal of the orders in council; the ministry were dissolved, and a commission given by the prince regent to one of the opposition party to form a cabinet friendly to American interests. Owing to the discordant elements of the opposition itself, and not to any difficulty on this question, the new organization did not take place at that time, but these circumstances manifested the temper of the nation, and showed plainly that the obnoxious measures of government must soon be condemned and repealed. These facts were known to the Congress of the United States before the declaration of war, and they must have convinced any reasonable and candid mind that a favorable change in the posture of affairs was to be expected at no distant period. And in fact on the 23d day of June, just five days after the declaration of war, it was ordered and declared by the prince regent, in council, "that the order in council, bearing date the 7th of January, 1807, and the order in council bearing date the 26th of April, 1809, be revoked, so far as may regard American vessels and their cargoes, being American property, from the first day of August next."

The embargo that was laid preparatory to war, commenced the 4th of April, and was to last ninety days—until the 4th of July. No one expected war to be declared before that period. Mr. Madison, it was well known, wished the embargo to be extended to four months; that is, to the 4th of August. A motion was actually made in the House to this effect, but was rejected. He said, that if at the end of four months no favorable news came from abroad, he would then be ready to recommend a declaration of war. By the 4th of August, news came of the repeal of the orders in council! Had his inclinations then been followed, the nation might have been saved from all the disastrous consequences of the precipitate action of Congress.

Mr. Madison, indeed, was not favorable to the embargo—it was forced upon him. "I am confident in the declaration," said Mr. Randolph, in conclave, "that this is not a measure of the executive, but that it is engendered by an extensive excitement upon the executive." The relation of the two great departments of government had entirely changed from what it was in the days of Mr. Jefferson; then the commanding power of a great mind and a determined will gave direction to all the measures of the legislature, but now the master-spirits that controlled affairs were to be found on the floor of Congress. The Speaker of the House of Representatives, and the leading member of the Committee of Foreign Affairs, from their position, if they had talents, were most likely to exert a large influence over the proceedings of the House. The persons occupying those stations were Henry Clay and John C. Calhoun. They were both possessed of great minds, endowed with extraordinary powers of eloquence, were young, ardent, ambitious, and for the first time members of the popular branch of the national legislature. In the excited state of the country, a better field could not have been found for the display of their talents. The deep enthusiasm of their souls, the chief element of their greatness, enlivened by a brilliant imagination in the one, and tempered by large faculties of reason in the other, gave such a strength and boldness to their thoughts, that they imparted confidence to the timid, clearness to the obscure, and infused a portion of their own zeal into more phlegmatic natures,—none could escape the contagion of their influence.

A few months after the opening of Congress, Mr. Randolph, while speaking of these new lights of the administration, said to a friend, "They have entered this House with their eye on the Presidency, and mark my words, sir, we shall have war before the end of the session!" Aside from the aspiration of a noble mind to tread some brilliant and high career, we do not believe they had any selfish end in view. Cold and calculating natures only influence others by motives akin to their own. Neither calculation nor logic, but the sympathizing impulses of a great soul, can deeply move the masses of mankind. A magnanimous spirit, animated with the inspiring breath of a whole people, may go forth with the confidence of a Moses, feeling that the voice of the people is the voice of God. But not always are the acts even of a great nation the result of divine inspiration. Sometimes they are influenced from the opposite quarter of the spiritual world, and partake more of the demoniac than the godlike.

The mere abstract question of international law involved between Great Britain and the United States, if left to a court of admiralty and a jury composed of citizens of the world, might have been decided against them. But neither courts nor attorneys can decide the fate of empires.

The democracy of America, which constituted the great mass of the people of America, were thoroughly anti-British; a common origin and a common tongue served only as points of contrast. There was a deep-rooted antipathy between them and the proud, pampered aristocracy of England. Their sympathies were all on the side of France and her struggles for liberty; even Bonaparte came in for a share of their regard. His boldness, his humble origin, his brilliant success, shed such a halo of glory around his brow as to obscure the darker features of his tyrannical nature. Then there were the old memories of Bunker's Hill, Monmouth, La Fayette, Rochambeau, and Yorktown—these household themes were familiar to every domestic fireside. Add the long catalogue of modern grievances—the plunder of our commerce, the capture of our seamen, the insults to our national flag, the insolence, and proud, contemptuous bearing of British officers even in our own ports—this is too much! we will not endure it! We will fight rather than suffer their aristocratic insolence any longer—"Free trade and sailors' rights! God and Liberty!" We will fight for these, come what will of it! We will teach these insulting English better manners, or blow them to the devil!

Such was the universal sentiment throughout the vast regions of the south and west. Their newspapers and their popular orators (who was not an orator in those excited times?) proclaimed *Free trade and sailors' rights!* Without a sailor or a ship on the sea, the fiery multitude echoed back, *Free trade and sailors' rights!* This comprehensive phrase served the same turn now, that *millions for defence, not a cent for tribute*, had served on a former occasion. A deep sense of indignation and wrong, vaguely shadowed forth in that expression "*free trade and sailors' rights*," pervaded the whole country. It was vain to argue with people in such a temper; he who had the folly to attempt it would imagine that he could arrest the bellowing thunder storm on the point of a bodkin. Henry Clay and John C. Calhoun were the representatives of these excited elements on the floor of Congress; it was in their power to temper these impetuous energies, and to have served as conductors to the surcharged electric fires that threatened momentary explosion; but they were too full themselves of the same fiery impulses to repress them in others; they boldly marched forward; and knowing and feeling that the people were pressing close behind them, plunged the nation headlong into a ruinous war—we do not mean ruinous in a military sense—no one ever doubted that our people, sooner or later, would be triumphant in every conflict, by land and by sea. The energies and the courage of a free people are irrepressible and unconquerable—we mean disastrous in the sense predicted by John Randolph; disastrous to the Constitution and to the principles of the people.

Two of the avowed objects of this war were, the conquest of Canada, and the plunder of the high seas; ends that fostered a spirit of aggression and of retaliation unbecoming the character of our country or of its peaceful institutions. We say nothing of the disturbance of that balance of power between the States and the Federal Government so necessary for their just and harmonious action, which was the necessary consequence of the enormous patronage and excessive energy of the executive in the time of a foreign war. Exhausted of its resources by a long series of restrictive measures, the nation commenced hostilities with borrowed money; a large national debt was accumulated; a depreciated, ruinous, demoralizing paper currency deluged the whole land, and a hot-bed system of domestic manufactures were stimulated into existence, at the expense of agriculture and commerce, which were the natural sources of wealth and prosperity to a new, wide-spread, and sparsely populated country.

The proclamation of peace found the people burdened with a national debt, ruined by a depreciated currency, corrupted, as far as they could be corrupted, by all the demoralizing influences which for years had been working on their integrity; and incumbered with innumerable domestic manufactures, which, like Jonah's gourd, had sprung up in a night, and could not bear the rude shocks of foreign competition produced by returning commerce.

Those who brought on and sustained the war were necessarily expected to find a remedy for the evils that followed in its train. The same master-spirits who conducted the war, controlled the course of legislation for years after the restoration of peace. They recommended a National Bank as the agent for managing and liquidating the national debt, and as the means of restoring and regulating the currency; they advocated the imposition of heavy duties on the importation of foreign goods, as the means of producing a revenue to pay the national debt, and also as a protection to those infant manufactures, which, since the death of their nurses and foster-mother, non-intercourse, embargo, and war, would be left entirely exposed to the crushing weight of maturer rivals; and as these enormous duties were likely soon to furnish means to pay off the national debt and to take away the pretext for imposing them, a convenient sinking fund was found in a system of internal improvements by the Federal Government. These were the remedies furnished by the advocates of the war to cure the evils it had produced. And how do we find them? just such as the federalists would have recommended—gross violations of the Constitution, that nothing but the most imperious necessity could tolerate, are established into precedents and made part of a regular system of legislation—vile excrescences, that like a cancer had eaten into the heart of the body politic, and defaced the fair features of the Constitution, are hailed as the beautiful outgrowth of her vital functions.

By some righteous retribution of Providence both these great men—for truly great they were—have been punished for their sins in precipitating a war that might have been retarded, and perhaps honorably avoided, and for violating the Constitution to find a remedy for its evils. If Randolph's supposition be true, they both failed of their end. The reason is very plain—they ceased to embody the sentiment and to reflect the will of the great body of the democracy, when they began to undermine the Constitution to find a remedy for evils they had inflicted on the country, and became the advocates of special interests, monopolies, and a moneyed aristocracy. Mr. Clay, with a zeal and perseverance worthy of a better cause, labored all his days to force his miscalled American System as a permanent institution on the country: but the people were against him, and not one of his measures can now be found on the statute book.

Mr. Calhoun, when too late, saw and acknowledged the error of his ways, and in a desperate effort to retrieve his own section of the country from the evil consequences of his own measures, well nigh involved the whole in civil war and ruin.

But, for the time being, they rode triumphantly on the full tide of popularity, while Randolph, who foresaw and warned them of the consequences of their rash measures, was driven into retirement. All the powers of two administrations and the political presses in their employment, the government at Washington, and the government at home in his native State, were employed to crush and destroy him. John W. Eppes, the most distinguished and experienced leader of the administration party, was induced to make his residence in the county of Buckingham, that Randolph might have the most able and formidable opposition the country could afford. These two men, who had been friends and companions in their youth, and rival leaders on the floor of Congress, met for the first time, in 1811, as candidates for the suffrages of the same people. But the long services of their old servant were triumphant on this occasion. Again they met, in the spring of 1813; times had changed; the country was involved in war, and all its resources were pledged to a successful issue; redoubled efforts must now be made to drive him from the councils of the nation, who had opposed its measures, and foreboded nothing but evil as their consequence. Never was a political canvass conducted with more animation. In Buckingham, Mr. Randolph was threatened with personal violence if he attempted to address the people. Some of the older and more prudent persons advised him to retire, and not appear in public. "You know very little of me," said he, "or you would not give such advice." He was a man incapable of fear. Soon proclamation was made that Mr. Randolph would address the people. A dense throng gathered around; he mounted the hustings; on the outskirts there hung a lowering and sullen crowd that evidently meditated insult or violence on the first opportunity; he commenced: "I understand that I am to be insulted to-day if I attempt to address the people—that a mob is prepared to lay their rude hands upon me and drag me from these hustings, for daring to exercise the rights of a freeman." Then fixing his keen eye on the malcontents, and stretching out and slowly waving his long fore-finger towards them, he continued: "My Bible teaches me that the fear of God is the beginning of wisdom, but that the fear of man is the consummation of folly." He then turned to the people, and went on with his discourse. No one dared to disturb him—his spell was upon them—like the Ancient Mariner, "he held them with his glittering eye," and made them listen against their will to the story of their country's wrongs, and to feel that deep wounds had been inflicted in the sides of her constitution by those that now sought his political destruction, if not his life.

Mr. Randolph made extraordinary exertions during this canvass; he felt that something more than his own success or his own reputation were staked on the issue, and never was he more powerful, more commanding, more overwhelming in his eloquence.

In his favorite county of Prince Edward, where the people loved him like a brother, he surpassed even himself. A young man, who was a student in a neighboring college, declares that he stood on his feet for three hours unconscious of the flight of time—that he never heard such burning words fall from the lips of man, and was borne along on the tide of his impassioned eloquence like a feather on the bosom of a cataract. When he had ceased—when his voice was no longer heard, and his form had disappeared in the throng, no one moved—the people stood still as though they had been shocked by a stroke of lightning—their fixed eyes and pallid cheeks resembled marble statues, or petrified Roman citizens in the forum of Pompeii or Herculaneum.

But it was all in vain; the overwhelming pressure from without was more than even Charlotte District could withstand; and their favorite son was compelled to retire for a short time, while the storm of war was passing over the land, and to seek repose in the shades of Roanoke. How magnanimously he bore this defeat shall be made known in the following chapters.

END OF VOL. I.

HISTORICAL

AND

MISCELLANEOUS QUESTIONS.

BY RICHMALL MANGNALL.

First American, from the Eighty-fourth London Edition. With large Additions Embracing the Elements of Mythology, Astronomy, Architecture, Heraldry, &c. Adapted for Schools in the United States

BY MRS. JULIA LAWRENCE.

Illustrated with numerous Engravings. One Volume, 12mo. $1.

CONTENTS.

A Short View of Scripture History, from the Creation to the Return of the Jews—Questions from the Early Ages to the time of Julius Cæsar—Miscellaneous Questions in Grecian History—Miscellaneous Questions in General History, chiefly Ancient—Questions containing a Sketch of the most remarkable Events from the Christian Era to the close of the Eighteenth Century—Miscellaneous Questions in Roman History—Questions in English History, from the Invasion of Cæsar to the Reformation—Continuation of Questions in English History, from the Reformation to the Present Time—Abstract of Early British History—Abstract of English Reigns from the Conquest—Abstract of the Scottish Reigns—Abstract of the French Reigns, from Pharamond to Philip I—Continuation of the French Reigns, from Louis VI to Louis Phillippe—Questions Relating to the History of America, from its Discovery to the Present Time—Abstract of Roman Kings and most distinguished Heroes—Abstract of the most celebrated Grecians—Of Heathen Mythology in general—Abstract of Heathen Mythology—The Elements of Astronomy—Explation of a few Astronomical Terms—List of Constellations—Questions on Common Subjects—Questions on Architecture—Questions on Heraldry—Explanations of such Latin Words and Phrases as are seldom Englished—Questions on the History of the Middle Ages.

"This is an admirable work to aid both teachers and parents in instructing children and youth, and there is no work of the kind that we have seen that is so well calculated "to awaken a spirit of laudable curiosity in young minds," and to satisfy that curiosity when awakened."

HISTORY OF ENGLAND,

From the Invasion of Julius Cæsar to the Reign of Queen Victoria.

BY MRS. MARKHAM.

A new Edition, with Questions, adapted for Schools in the United States.

BY ELIZA ROBBINS,

Author of "American Popular Lessons," "Poetry for Schools," &c.

One Volume, 12mo. Price 75 cents.

There is nothing more needed in our schools than good histories; not the dry compends in present use, but elementary works that shall suggest the moral uses of history, and the providence of God, manifest in the affairs of men.

Mr. Markham's history was used by that model for all teachers, the late Dr. Arnold, master of the great English school at Rugby, and agrees in its character with his enlightened and pious views of teaching history. It is now several years since I adapted this history to the form and price acceptable in the schools in the United States. I have recently revised it, and trust that it may be extensively serviceable in education.

The principal alterations from the original are a new and more convenient division of paragraphs, and entire omission of the conversations annexed to the chapters. In the place of these I have affixed questions to every page that may at once facilitate the work of the teacher and the pupil. The rational and moral features of this book first commended it to me, and I have used it successfully with my own scholars.—*Extract from the American Editor's Preface.*

THE

FIRST HISTORY OF ROME,

WITH QUESTIONS.

BY E. M. SEWELL,

Author of Amy Herbert, &c., &c. One volume, 16mo. 50 cts.

Extract from Editor's Preface.

"History is the narrative of real events in the order and circumstances in which they occurred; and of all histories, that of Rome comprises a series of events more interesting and instructive to youthful readers than any other that has ever been written.

"Of the manner in which Mrs. Sewell has executed this work, we can scarcely speak in terms of approbation too strong. Drawing her materials from the best—that is to say, the most reliable—sources, she has incorporated them in a narrative at once unostentatious, perspicuous, and graphic; manifestly aiming throughout to be clearly understood by those for whom she wrote, and to impress deeply and permanently on their minds what she wrote; and in both of these aims we think she has been eminently successful."

Norfolk Academy, Norfolk, Va.

I must thank you for a copy of "Miss Sewell's Roman History." Classical teachers have long needed just such a work: for it is admitted by all how essential to a proper comprehension of the classics is a knowledge of collateral history. Yet most pupils are construing authors before reaching an age to put into their hands the elaborate works we have heretofore had upon Ancient History. Miss Sewell, while she gives the most important facts, has clothed them in a style at once pleasing and comprehensible to the most youthful mind.

R. B. TSCHUDI,
Prof. of Anc't Languages.

THE

MYTHOLOGY OF ANCIENT GREECE AND ITALY,

FOR THE USE OF SCHOOLS.

BY THOMAS KEIGHTLEY.

One vol. 16mo. 42 cts.

"This is a volume well adapted to the purpose for which it was prepared. It presents, in a very compendious and convenient form, every thing relating to the subject, of importance to the young student."

GENERAL

HISTORY OF CIVILIZATION IN EUROPE,

FROM THE FALL OF THE ROMAN EMPIRE TO THE FRENCH REVOLUTION.

BY M. GUIZOT.

Eighth American, from the second English edition, with occasional Notes, by C. S. HENRY, D.D

One volume, 12mo. 75 cts.

"M. Guizot, in his instructive lectures, has given us an epitome of modern history, distinguished by all the merit which, in another department, renders Blackstone a subject of such peculiar and unbounded praise. A work closely condensed, including nothing useless, omitting nothing essential; written with grace, and conceived and arranged with consummate ability."—*Boston Traveller.*

☞ *This work is used in Harvard University, Union College, University of Pennsylvania, New-York University, &c. &c.*

ENGLISH SYNONYMES,

CLASSIFIED AND EXPLAINED,

WITH

PRACTICAL EXERCISES.

DESIGNED FOR SCHOOLS AND PRIVATE TUITION.

BY G. F. GRAHAM,

Author of 'English, or the Art of Composition,' &c.

WITH AN INTRODUCTION AND ILLUSTRATIVE AUTHORITIES,

BY HENRY REED, LL. D.,

Prof. of English Literature in the University of Penn.

One neat Vol. 12mo. $1.

CONTENTS.—SECTION I. Generic and Specific Synonymes. II. Active and Passive Synonymes. III. Synonymes of Intensity. IV. Positive and Negative Synonymes. V. Miscellaneous Synonymes. Index to Synonymes. General Index.

Extract from American Introduction.

"This treatise is republished and edited with the hope that it will be found useful as a text book in the study of our own language. As a subject of instruction, the study of the English tongue does not receive that amount of systematic attention which is due to it, whether it be combined or no with the study of the Greek and Latin. In the usual courses of education, it has no larger scope than the study of some rhetorical principles and practice, and of grammatical rules, which, for the most part, are not adequate to the composite character and varied idiom of English speech. This is far from being enough to give the needful knowledge of what is the living language, both of our English literature and of the multiform intercourse—oral and written—of our daily lives. The language deserves better care and more sedulous culture; it needs much more to preserve its purity, and to guide the progress of its life. The young, instead of having only such familiarity with their native speech as practice without method or theory gives, should be so taught and trained as to acquire a habit of using words—whether with the voice or the pen—fitly and truly, intelligently and conscientiously."

"For such training, this book, it is believed, will prove serviceable. The '*Practical Exercises*,' attached to the explanations of the words, are conveniently prepared for the routine of instruction. The value of a course of this kind, regularly and carefully completed, will be more than the amount of information gained respecting the words that are explained. It will tend to produce a thoughtful and accurate use of language, and thus may be acquired, almost unconsciously, that which is not only a critical but a moral habit of mind—the habit of giving utterance to truth in simple, clear and precise terms—of telling one's thoughts and feelings in words that express nothing more and nothing less. It is thus that we may learn how to escape the evils of vagueness, obscurity and perplexity—the manifold mischiefs of words used thoughtlessly and at random, or words used in ignorance and confusion.

"In preparing this edition, it seemed to me that the value and literary interest of the book might be increased by the introduction of a series of illustrative authorities. It is in the addition of these authorities, contained within brackets under each title, and also of a general index to facilitate reference, that this edition differs from the original edition, which in other respects is exactly reprinted. I have confined my choice of authorities to poetical quotations, chiefly because it is in poetry that language is found in its highest purity and perfection. The selections have been made from three of the English poets—each a great authority, and each belonging to a different period, so that in this way some historical illustration of the language is given at the same time. The quotations from Shakspeare (born A. D. 1564, died 1616) may be considered as illustrating the use of the words at the close of the 16th and beginning of the 17th century; those from Milton (born 1608, died 1674) the succeeding half century, or middle of the 17th century; and those from Wordsworth (born 1770) the contemporary use in the 19th century.

English.

A DICTIONARY OF THE ENGLISH LANGUAGE,

CONTAINING THE PRONUNCIATION, ETYMOLOGY, AND EXPLANATION OF ALL WORDS AUTHORIZED BY EMINENT WRITERS;

To which are added, a Vocabulary of the Roots of English Words, and an Accented List of Greek, Latin, and Scripture Proper Names

BY ALEXANDER REID, A. M.,

Rector of the Circus School, Edinburgh.

With a Critical Preface, by HENRY REED, Professor of English Literature in the University o Pennsylvania, and an Appendix, showing the Pronunciation of nearly 3000 of the most important Geographical Names. One volume, 12mo. of nearly 600 pages, bound in Leather. Price $1.

Among the wants of our time was a good dictionary of our own language, especially adapted for academies and schools. The books which have long been in use were of little value to the junior students, being too concise in the definitions, and immethodical in the arrangement Reid's English Dictionary was compiled expressly to develop the precise analogies and various properties of the authorized words in general use, by the standard authors and orators who use our vernacular tongue.

Exclusive of the large number of proper names which are appended, this Dictionary includes four especial improvements—and when their essential value to the student is considered, the sterling character of the work as a hand-book of our language will be instantly perceived.

The primitive word is distinguished by a larger type; and when there are any derivatives from it, they follow in alphabetical order, and the part of speech is appended, thus furnishing a complete classification of all the connected analogous words of the same species.

With this facility to comprehend accurately the determinate meaning of the English word, is conjoined a rich illustration for the linguist. The derivation of all the primitive words is distinctly given, and the phrases of the languages whence they are deduced, whether composite or simple; so that the student of foreign languages, both ancient and modern, by a reference to any word, can ascertain the source whence it has been adopted into our own form of speech. This is a great acquisition to the person who is anxious to use words in their utmost clearness of meaning.

To these advantages is subjoined a Vocabulary of the Roots of English Words, which is of peculiar value to the collegian. The fifty pages which it includes, furnish the linguist with a wide-spread field of research, equally amusing and instructive. There is also added an Accented List, to the number of fifteen thousand, of Greek, Latin, and Scripture Proper Names.

RECOMMENDATIONS.

REID'S Dictionary of the English Language is an admirable book for the use of schools. Its plans combine a greater number of desirable conditions for such a work, than any with which I am acquainted: and it seems to me to be executed in general with great judgment, fidelity, and accuracy.

C. S. HENRY,

Professor of Philosophy, History, and Belles Lettres, in the University of the City of New-York.

Reid's Dictionary of the English Language is compiled upon sound principles, and with judgment and accuracy. It has the merit, too, of combining much more than is usually looked for in Dictionaries of small size, and will, I believe, be found excellent as a convenient manual, for general use and reference, and also for various purposes of education.

HENRY REED,

Professor of English Literature in the University of Pennsylvania.

After a careful examination, I am convinced that Reid's English Dictionary has strong claims upon the attention of teachers generally. It is of convenient size, beautifully executed, and seems well adapted to the use of scholars, from the common school to the university.

D. H. CHASE,

Principal of Preparatory School.

MIDDLETOWN, Ct.

After a thorough examination of "Reid's English Dictionary," I may safely say that I consider it superior to any of the School Dictionaries with which I am acquainted. Its accurate and concise definitions, and a vocabulary of the roots of English words, drawn from an author of such authority as Bosworth, are not among the least of its excellencies.

M. M. PARKS,

Chaplain and Professor of Ethics, U. S. Military Academy, West Point.

English.

A MANUAL

OF

GRECIAN AND ROMAN ANTIQUITIES.

BY DR. E. F. BOJESEN,

Professor of the Greek Language and Literature in the University of Soro.

Translated from the German.

EDITED, WITH NOTES AND A COMPLETE SERIES OF QUESTIONS, BY THE

REV. THOMAS K. ARNOLD, M. A.

REVISED WITH ADDITIONS AND CORRECTIONS.

One neat volume, 12mo. Price $1.

The present Manual of Greek and Roman Antiquities is far superior to any thing on the same topics as yet offered to the American public. A principal Review of Germany says:—"Small as the compass of it is, we may confidently affirm that it is a great improvement on all preceding works of the kind. We no longer meet with the wretched old method, in which subjects essentially distinct are herded together, and connected subjects disconnected, but have a simple, systematic arrangement, by which the reader easily receives a clear representation of Roman life. We no longer stumble against countless errors in detail, which though long ago assailed and extirpated by Niebuhr and others, have found their last place of refuge in our Manuals. The recent investigations of philologists and jurists have been extensively, but carefully and circumspectly used. The conciseness and precision which the author has every where prescribed to himself, prevents the superficial observer from perceiving the essential superiority of the book to its predecessors, but whoever subjects it to a careful examination will discover this on every page."

The Editor says:—"I fully believe that the pupil will receive from these little works a correct and tolerably complete picture of Grecian and Roman life; what I may call the POLITICAL portions—the account of the national constitutions and their effects—appear to me to be of great value; and the very moderate extent of each volume admits of its being thoroughly mastered—of its being GOT UP and RETAINED."

"A work long needed in our schools and colleges. The manuals of Rennet, Adam, Potter, and Robinson, with the more recent and valuable translation of Eschenburg, were entirely too voluminous. Here is neither too much, nor too little. The arrangement is admirable—every subject is treated of in its proper place. We have the general Geography, a succinct historical view of the general subject; the chirography, history, laws, manners, customs, and religion of *each* State, as well as the points of union for all, beautifully arranged. We regard the work as the very best adjunct to classical study for youth that we have seen, and sincerely hope that teachers may be brought to regard it in the same light. The whole is copiously digested into appropriate questions."—*S. Lit. Gazette.*

From Professor Lincoln, of Brown University.

"I found on my table after a short absence from home, your edition of Bojesen's Greek and Roman Antiquities. Pray accept my acknowledgments for it. I am agreeably surprised to find on examining it, that within so very narrow a compass for so comprehensive a subject, the book contains so much valuable matter; and, indeed, so far as I see, omits noticing no topics essential. It will be a very useful book in Schools and Colleges, and it is far superior to any thing that I know of the same kind. Besides being cheap and accessible to all students, it has the great merit of discussing its topics in a consecutive and connected manner."

Extract of a letter from Professor Tyler, of Amherst College.

"I have never found time till lately to look over Bojesen's Antiquities, of which you were kind enough to send me a copy. I think it an excellent book; learned, accurate, concise, and perspicuous; well adapted for use in the Academy or the College, and comprehending in a small compass, more that is valuable on the subject than many extended treatises."

English.

HAND BOOK

OF

MEDIÆVAL GEOGRAPHY AND HISTORY.

BY

WILHELM PUTZ,

PRINCIPAL TUTOR IN THE GYMNASIUM OF DUREN.

Translated from the German by

REV. R. B. PAUL, M. A.,

Vicar of St. Augustine's, Bristol, and late Fellow of Exeter College, Oxford.

1 volume, 12mo. 75 cts.

HEADS OF CONTENTS.

I. Germany before the Migrations.
II. The Migrations.

THE MIDDLE AGES.

FIRST PERIOD.—From the Dissolution of the Western Empire to the Accession of the Carlovingians and Abbasides.

SECOND PERIOD.—From the Accession of the Carlovingians and Abbasides to the first Crusade.

THIRD PERIOD.—Age of the Crusades.

FOURTH PERIOD.—From the Termination of the Crusades to the Discovery of America.

"The characteristics of this volume are: precision, condensation, and luminous arrangement. It is precisely what it pretends to be—a manual, a sure and conscientious guide for the student through the crooks and tangles of Mediæval history. * * * * All the great principles of this extensive Period are carefully laid down, and the most important facts skilfully grouped around them. There is no period of History for which it is more difficult to prepare a work like this, and none for which it is so much needed. The leading facts are well established, but they are scattered over an immense space; the principles are ascertained, but their development was slow, unequal, and interrupted. There is a general breaking up of a great body, and a parcelling of it out among small tribes, concerning whom we have only a few general data, and are left to analogy and conjecture for the details. Then come successive attempts at organization, each more or less independent, and all very imperfect. At last, modern Europe begins slowly to emerge from the chaos, but still under forms which the most diligent historian cannot always comprehend. To reduce such materials to a clear and definite form is a task of no small difficulty, and in which partial success deserves great praise. It is not too much to say that it has never been so well done within a compass so easily mastered, as in the little volume which is now offered to the public."—*Extract from American Preface.*

"This translation of a foreign school-book embraces a succinct and well arranged body of facts concerning European and Asiatic history and geography during the middle ages. It is furnished with printed questions, and it seems to be well adapted to its purpose, in all respects. The mediæval period is one of the most interesting in the annals of the world, and a knowledge of its great men, and of its progress in arts, arms, government and religion, is particularly important, since this period is the basis of our own social polity."—*Commercial Advertiser.*

"This is an immense amount of research condensed into a moderately sized volume, in a way which no one has patience to do but a German scholar. The beauty of the work is its luminous arrangement. It is a guide to the student amidst the intricacy of Mediæval History, the most difficult period of the world to understand, when the Roman Empire was breaking up and parcelling out into smaller kingdoms, and every thing was in a transition state. It was a period of chaos from which modern Europe was at length to arise.

The author has briefly taken up the principal political and social influences which were acting on society, and shown their bearing from the time previous to the migrations of the Northern nations, down through the middle ages to the sixteenth century. The notes on the crusades are particularly valuable, and the range of observation embraces not only Europe but the East. To the student it will be a most valuable Hand-book, saving him a world of trouble in hunting up authorities and facts."—*Rev. Dr. Kip, in Albany State Register.*

MANUAL

OF

ANCIENT GEOGRAPHY AND HISTORY.

BY WILHELM PÜTZ,

PRINCIPAL TUTOR IN THE GYMNASIUM OF DUREN

Translated from the German.

EDITED BY THE REV. THOMAS K. ARNOLD, M. A.,

AUTHOR OF A SERIES OF "GREEK AND LATIN TEXT-BOOKS."

One volume, 12mo. $1.

"At no period has History presented such strong claims upon the attention of the learned, as at the present day; and to no people were its lessons of such value as to those of the United States. With no past of our own to revert to, the great masses of our better educated are tempted to overlook a science, which comprehends all others in its grasp. To prepare a text-book, which shall present a full, clear, and accurate view of the ancient world, its geography, its political, civil, social, religious state, must be the result only of vast industry and learning. Our examination of the present volume leads us to believe, that as a text-book on Ancient History, for Colleges and Academies, it is the best compend yet published. It bears marks in its methodical arrangement, and condensation of materials, of the untiring patience of German scholarship; and in its progress through the English and American press, has been adapted for acceptable use in our best institutions. A noticeable feature of the book, is its pretty complete list of 'sources of information' upon the nations which it describes. This will be an invaluable aid to the student in his future course of reading."

"Wilhelm Pütz, the author of this 'Manual of Ancient Geography and History,' is Principal Tutor (*Oberleher*) in the Gymnasium of Duren, Germany. His book exhibits the advantages of the German method of treating History, in its arrangement, its classification, and its rigid analysis. The Manual is what it purports to be, 'a clear and definite outline of the history of the principal nations of antiquity,' into which is incorporated a concise geography of each country. The work is a text-book; to be *studied*, and not merely *read*. It is to form the groundwork of subsequent historical investigation,—the materials of which are pointed out, at the proper places, in the Manual, in careful references to the works which treat of the subject directly under consideration. The list of references (especially as regards earlier works) is quite complete,—thus supplying that desideratum in Ancient History and Geography, which has been supplied so fully by Dr. J. C. I. Gieseler in Ecclesiastical History.

"The nations whose history is considered in the Manual, are: in *Asia*, the Israelites, the Indians, the Babylonians, the Assyrians, the Medes, the Persians, the Phœnicians, the States of Asia Minor; in *Africa*, the Ethiopians, the Egyptians, the Carthaginians; in *Europe*, the Greeks, the Macedonians, the Kingdoms which arose out of the Macedonian Monarchy, the Romans. The order in which the history of each is treated, is admirable. To the whole are appended a 'Chronological Table,' and a well-prepared series of 'Questions.' The pronunciation of proper names is indicated,—an excellent feature. The accents are given with remarkable correctness. The typographical execution of the American edition is most excellent."—*S. W. Baptist Chronicle.*

"Like every thing which proceeds from the editorship of that eminent Instructor, T. K. Arnold, this Manual appears to be well suited to the design with which it was prepared, and will, undoubtedly, secure for itself a place among the text-books of schools and academies thoughout the country. It presents an outline of the history of the ancient nations, from the earliest ages to the fall of the Western Empire in the sixth century, the events being arranged in the order of an accurate chronology, and explained by accompanying treatises on the geography of the several countries in which they transpired. The chief feature of this work, and this is a very important one, is, that it sets forth ancient history and ancient geography in their connection with each other.

"It was originally prepared by Wilhelm Pütz, an eminent German scholar, and translated and edited in England by Rev. T. K. Arnold, and is now revised and introduced to the American public in a well written preface, by Mr. George W. Greene, Teacher of Modern Languages in Brown University."—*Prov. Journal.*

English.

COURSE OF MATHEMATICAL WORKS,

BY GEORGE R. PERKINS, A. M.,

Professor of Mathematics and Principal of the State Normal School

I. PRIMARY ARITHMETIC. Price 21 cts.

A want, with young pupils, of rapidity and accuracy in performing operations upon written numbers; an imperfect knowledge of Numeration; inadequate conceptions of the nature and relations of Fractions, and a lack of familiarity with the principles of Decimals, have induced the author to prepare the PRIMARY ARITHMETIC.

The first part is devoted to MENTAL EXERCISES and the second to *Exercises on the Slate and Blackboard.*

While the minds of young pupils are disciplined by mental exercises (if not wearisomely prolonged), they fail, in general, in trusting to "head-work" for their calculations; and in resorting to written operations to solve their difficulties, are often slow and inaccurate from a want of early familiarity with such processes: these considerations have induced the Author to devote part of his book to *primary written exercises.*

It has been received with more popularity than any Arithmetic heretofore issued.

II. ELEMENTARY ARITHMETIC. Price 42 cts.

Has recently been carefully revised and enlarged. It will be found concise, yet lucid. It reaches the radical relations of numbers, and presents fundamental principles in analysis and examples. It leaves nothing obscure, yet it does not embarrass by multiplied processes, nor enfeeble by minute details.

In this work *all of the examples or problems are strictly practical,* made up as they are in a great measure of important statistics and valuable facts in history and philosophy, which are thus unconsciously learned in acquiring a knowledge of the Arithmetic.

Fractions are placed immediately after Division; Federal Money is treated as and with Decimal Fractions; Proportion is placed before Fellowship, Alligation, and such rules as require its application in their solution. Every rule is marked with verity and simplicity. The answers to all of the examples are given.

The work will be found to be an improvement on most, if not all, previous elementary Arithmetics in the treatment of Fractions, Denominate Numbers, Rule of Three, Interest, Equation of Payments, Extraction of Roots, and many other subjects.

Wherever this work is presented, the publishers have heard but one opinion in regard to its merits, and that most favorable.

III. HIGHER ARITHMETIC. Price 84 cts.

The present edition has been revised, many subjects rewritten, and much new matter added; and contains an APPENDIX of about 60 pages, in which the philosophy of the more difficult operations and interesting properties of numbers are fully discussed. The work is what its name purports, a *Higher* Arithmetic, and will be found to contain many entirely new principles which have never before appeared in any Arithmetic. It has received the strongest recommendations from hundreds of the best teachers the country affords.

IV. ELEMENTS OF ALGEBRA. Price 84 cts.

This work is an introduction to the Author's "Treatise on Algebra," and is designed especially for the use of Common Schools, and universally pronounced "admirably adapted to the purpose."

V. TREATISE ON ALGEBRA. Price $1 50.

This work contains the higher parts of Algebra usually taught in Colleges; a new method of cubic and higher equations as well as the THEOREM OF STURM, by which we may at once determine the number of real roots of any Algebraic Equation, with much more ease than by previously discovered method.

In the present *revised edition,* one entire chapter on the subject of CONTINUED FRACTIONS has been added.

VI. ELEMENTS OF GEOMETRY, WITH PRACTICAL APPLICATIONS. $1.

The author has added throughout the entire Work, PRACTICAL APPLICATIONS, which, in the estimation of Teachers, is an important consideration.

An eminent Professor of Mathematics, in speaking of this work, says: "We have adopted it, because it follows more closely the best model of pure geometrical reasoning, which ever has been, and perhaps ever will be exhibited; and because the Author has *condensed* some of the important principles of the great master of Geometricians, and more especially has shown that his *theorems* are not mere *theory,* by many *practical applications:* a quality in a text-book of this science no less uncommon than it is important."

DR. ARNOLD'S WORKS.

I.

THE HISTORY OF ROME,

From the Earliest Period. Reprinted entire from the last English edition. Two vols., 8vo. $5 00.

II.

HISTORY OF THE LATER ROMAN COMMONWEALTH.

Two vols. of the English edition reprinted entire in 1 vol., 8vo. $2 50.

"The History of Rome will remain, to the latest age of the world, the most attractive, the most useful, and the most elevating subject of human contemplation. It must ever form the basis of a liberal and enlightened education, and present the most important subject to the contemplation of the statesman. It is remarkable, that until the appearance of Dr. Arnold's volumes, no history, (except Niebuhr's, whose style is often obscure) of this wonderful people existed, commensurate either to their dignity, their importance, or their intimate connection with modern institutions. In the preparation and composition of the history, Dr. Arnold expended many long years, and bent to it the whole force of his great energies. It is a work to which the whole culture of the man, from boyhood, contributed—most carefully and deeply meditated, pursued with all the ardor of a labor of love, and relinquished only with life. Of the conscientious accuracy, industry, and power of mind, which the work evinces—its clearness, dignity, and vigor of composition—it would be needless to speak. It is eminently calculated to delight and instruct both the student and the miscellaneous reader."—*Boston Courier.*

III.

LECTURES ON MODERN HISTORY.

Delivered in Lent Term, 1842, with the Inaugural Lecture delivered in 1841. Edited, with a Preface and Notes, by Henry Reed, M. A., Prof. of English Literature in the University of Pa. 12mo. $1 25.

"The Lectures are *eight* in number, and furnish the best possible introduction to a philosophical study of modern history. Prof. Reed has added greatly to the worth and interest of the volume, by appending to each lecture such extracts from Dr. Arnold's other writings as would more fully illustrate its prominent points. The notes and appendix which he has thus furnished are exceedingly valuable."—*Courier and Enquirer.*

IV.

RUGBY SCHOOL SERMONS.

Sermons preached in the Chapel of Rugby School, with an Address before Confirmation. One volume, 16mo. 50 cts.

"There are thirty Sermons in this neat little volume, which we cordially recommend to parents and others, for the use of the young, as a guide and incentive to deep earnestness in matters of religious belief and conduct; as a book which will interest all by its sincerity, and especially those who have become acquainted with Dr. A. through his Life and Letters, recently published by the Appletons."—*Evening Post.*

V.

MISCELLANEOUS WORKS.

With nine additional Essays, not included in the English collection. One volume, 8vo. $2 00.

"This volume includes disquisitions on the 'Church and State,' in its existing British combinations—on Scriptural and Secular History—and on Education, with various other subjects of Political Economy. It will be a suitable counterpart to the 'Life and Correspondence of Dr. Arnold,' and scholars who have been so deeply interested in that impressive biography will be gratified to ascertain the deliberate judgment of the Author, upon the numerous important themes which his 'Miscellaneous Works' so richly and clearly announce."

VI.

THE LIFE AND CORRESPONDENCE OF THOMAS ARNOLD, D. D.

By Arthur P. Stanley, A. M. 2d American from the fifth London edition. One handsome 8vo. volume. $2 00.

"This work should be in the hands of every one who lives and thinks for his race and for his religion; not so much as a guide for action, as affording a stimulant to intellectual and moral reflection.'—*Prot. Churchman.*

HISTORICAL AND BIOGRAPHICAL WORKS.

ARNOLD, (Dr.) Early History of Rome. 2 vols. 8vo. - - - $5 00
ARNOLD, (Dr.) History of the Later Roman Commonwealth. 8vo. - - - - - - - 2 50
ARNOLD, (Dr.) Lectures on Modern History, edited by Professor Reed. 12mo. - - - 1 25
ARNOLD, (Dr.) Life and Correspondence, by the Rev. A. P. Stanley. 2d ed. 8vo. - - 2 00
BURNETT'S History of the North-western Territory. 8vo. - - 2 50
CARLYLE'S Life of Schiller. A new edition. 12mo. - - - 75
COIT'S History of Puritanism. 12mo. - - - - - 1 00
EVELYN'S Life of Mrs. Godolphin, edited by Bishop of Oxford. 12mo - - - - - 50
FROST, (Professor) History of the United States Navy. Plates. 12mo. 1 00
FROST, (Professor) History of the United States Army. Plates. 12mo. - - - - - 1 00
FROST, (Professor) History of the Indians of North America. Plates. 12mo. - - - - - 1 00
FROST, (Professor) History of the Colonies of America. 12mo. Illustrated - - - - - - 1 00
FROST, (Professor) Life of Gen. Zachary Taylor. 12mo. Illustrated. - - - - - - 1 25
GUIZOT'S History of Civilization in Europe, edited by Professor Henry. 12mo - - - 1 00
GUIZOT'S Complete History of Civilization, translated by Hazlett. 4 vols. - - - 3 50
GUIZOT'S History of the English Revolution, 1640. 12mo. - 1 25
GAYARRE'S Romance of the History of Louisiana. 12mo. - - 1 00
HULL, (General) Military and Civil Life. 8vo. - - - - 2 00
KING, (Colonel) History of the Argentine Republic. 12mo. - 75
KOHLRAUSCH'S Complete History of Germany. 8vo. - - 1 50
MAHON'S (Lord) History of England, edited by Professor Reed. 2 vols., 8vo. - - - - 5 00
MICHELET'S History of France from the Earliest Period. 2 vols. 5 50
MICHELET'S History of the Roman Republic. 12mo. - - 90
MICHELET'S History of the People. 12mo. - - - 63
MICHELET'S Life of Martin Luther. 12mo. - - - - $0 7[illegible]
NAPOLEON, Life of, from the French of Laurent De L'Ardeche. 2 vols. 8vo. 500 cuts - - 4 00
O'CALLAGHAN'S Early History of New York. 2 vols. 8vo. - 5 00
ROWAN'S History of the French Revolution. 18mo. 2 vols. in 1 63
SEWELL'S Child's History of Rome. 18mo. - - - - - 50
SOUTHEY'S Life of Oliver Cromwell. 18mo. - - - - - 38
SPRAGUE'S History of the Florida War. Map and Plates. 8vo. 2 50
STEVEN'S History of Georgia. vol. 1 - - - - - - 2 50
TAYLOR'S Natural History of Society in the Barbarous and Civilized State. 2 vols. 12mo. - 2 25
TAYLOR'S Manual of Ancient and Modern History. Edited by Professor Henry. 8vo. - - 2 50
TAYLOR'S Ancient History—Separate - - - - - - - 1 25
TAYLOR'S Modern History—Separate - - - - - - 1 50
Used as a Text-book in several Colleges.
TWISS. History of the Oregon Territory. 12mo. - - - - 75

LAW BOOKS.

ANTHON'S Law Student ; or, Guides to the Study of the Law in its Principles.
HOLCOMBE'S Digest of the Decisions of the Supreme Court of the U. S., from its Commencement to the present time. Large 8vo., law sheep - - - - 6 00
HOLCOMBE'S Supreme Court Leading Cases on Commercial Law. 8vo., law sheep - 4 00
HOLCOMBE'S Law of Debtor and Creditor in the United States and Canada. 8vo. - - - - 3 50
SMITH'S Compendium of Mercantile Law. With Large American Additions, by Holcombe and Gholson. 8vo., law sheep - 4 00
These volumes are highly commended by Justices Taney and Woodbury, Daniel Webster, Rufus Choate, and Chancellor Kent, &c.
WARREN'S Popular and Practical Introduction to Law Studies. With American additions, by Thomas W. Clerke. 8vo., law sheep - - - - - - 3 50

www.ingramcontent.com/pod-product-compliance
Lightning Source LLC
LaVergne TN
LVHW020213110826
845151LV00003B/699

* 9 7 8 1 4 2 5 5 3 3 9 7 7 *